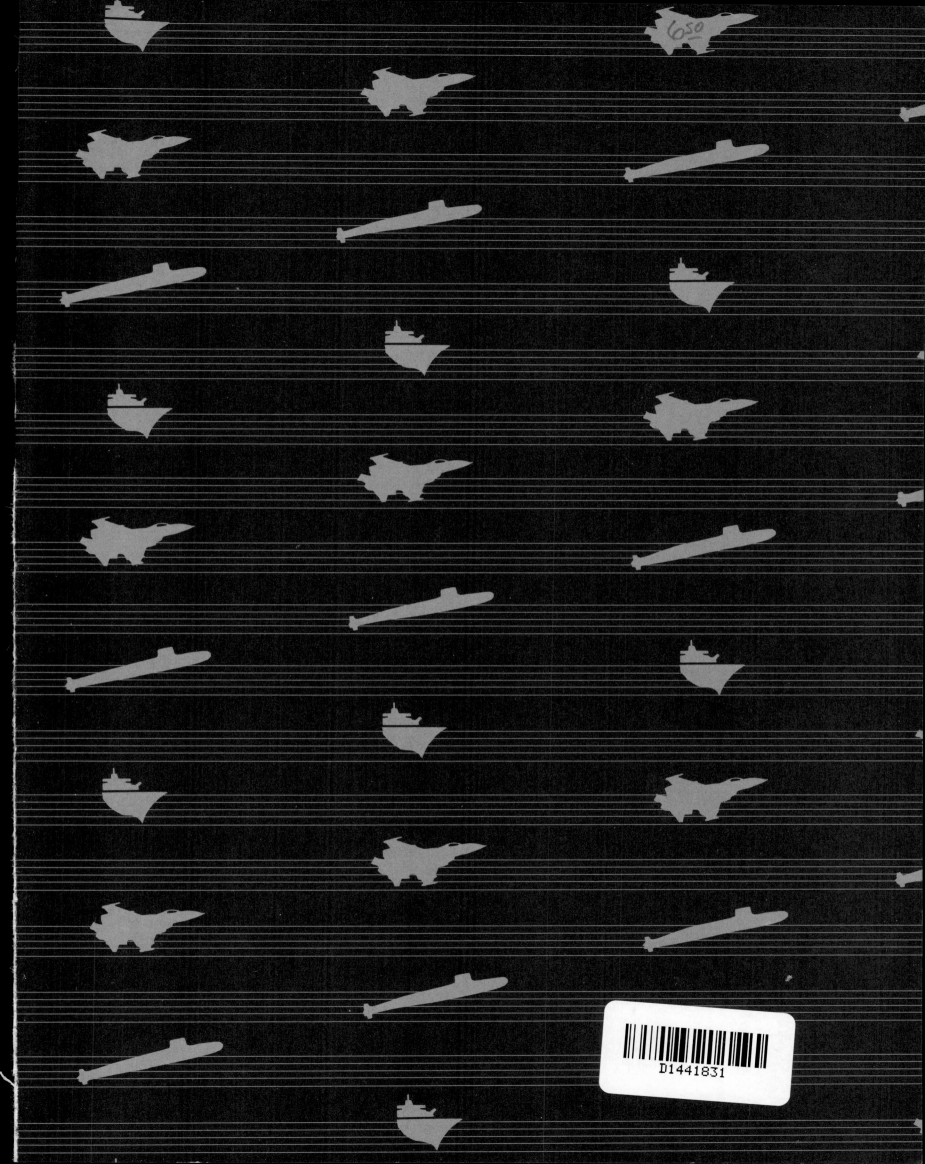

650

D1441831

THE COMPLETE BOOK OF

U.S.
NAVAL POWER

PUBLICATIONS INTERNATIONAL, LTD.

Louis Weber, C.E.O.
Publications International, Ltd.
7373 North Cicero Avenue
Lincolnwood, IL 60646

Printed in Hungary

8 7 6 5 4 3 2 1

ISBN: 0-88176-958-4
Library of Congress Catalog Number: 90-63316

Front cover, main image: *The* Constellation, *a nuclear-power aircraft carrier of the* Kitty Hawk *class.* **Front cover, upper left:** *The frigate* Lockwood *fires an ASROC antisubmarine rocket.* **Front cover, upper right:** *The number two turret on the battleship* Iowa *fires a salvo from its 16-inch guns.*

CONTENTS

A CONCISE HISTORY OF THE UNITED STATES NAVY

Invasion by foreign armies has been a rare occurrence in United States history. During the War of 1812, British armies landed on the Gulf Coast and near Washington, D.C.; one of these armies was defeated at the Battle of New Orleans, while the other burned the nation's capitol before withdrawing from American soil. The fact that this country has not been subjected to further invasions is undoubtedly due in large measure to the existence and efforts of the United States Navy.

Comprising hundreds of ships, thousands of aircraft, and tens of thousands of men and women, today's United States Navy is a mighty force capable of striking anywhere in the world, on land, on sea, and in the air. The power the Navy wields in the form of nuclear and conventional weapons is truly vast—so vast, that stories about the Navy's humble origins may sound almost too fantastic to believe. Yet such indeed was the case.

REVOLUTIONARY BEGINNINGS

The United States Navy was founded by the Continental Congress on October 13, 1775—only five months after the American Revolution began at the battles of Lexington and Concord. On that date, Congress approved plans for the purchase of two ships, the *Andrew Doria* and the *Cabot*. Thus ended a lengthy and often acrimonious debate among the Congressional delegates over the question of whether a navy was either desirable or necessary.

The *Andrew Doria* and the *Cabot* were charged with the task of intercepting British transport ships carrying supplies and troops from England to Canada. On June 3, 1775, the Royal Navy schooner *Margaretta* became an American ship when it was captured by Maine sailors off Machias. On the same day the government of Rhode Island commissioned two ships, which were subsequently used by sea captain-turned-privateer Abraham Whipple to capture the British vessel *Gaspee*. And although Congress did not know it at the time, General George Washington had already commissioned the schooner *Hannah* on his own authority as Commander in Chief of the Continental Army.

During the next two years, General Washington would commission seven more vessels. Known as "George Washington's Navy," this tiny force was used to seize British supply ships for the cargoes they carried. In November 1775, one of his ships captured the British brig *Nancy*, which was packed with powder, shot, muskets, and a 13-inch mortar—all valuable stores that were put to good use by the Continental Army.

To prosecute the war at sea in a truly vigorous fashion, however, more ships were needed. In December 1775,

George Washington reviews the ships of the Continental Navy at the close of the Revolutionary War.

An early victory at sea: The Surprise, *flying the "Don't Tread on Me" flag, captures the HMS* Harwich Packet *in 1778.*

Congress authorized the building of 13 frigates, which would add to a number of ships already acquired through leasing or outright purchase. In February 1776, eight ships under the command of Captain Esek Hopkins sallied forth from the Delaware estuary to attack British warships in the vicinity of Chesapeake Bay. Daunted by a combination of bad weather and the poor seamanship of his crews, Hopkins opted instead for a raid on the British-held Bahamas. In the Navy's first amphibious action, 200 marines and 50 sailors captured a British fort on what is now Nassau. Unfortunately, this victory was offset by a smallpox epidemic that ravaged the fleet on the way home, and by the failure of Hopkins' ships to capture a lone British frigate encountered in Long Island Sound. Shortly after this incident, Hopkins was relieved of his command.

One of Hopkins' subordinates, John Paul Jones, was destined to enjoy considerably more success as a naval commander. In 1778 Jones sailed the *Ranger* into British territorial waters, where he made a daring, if ineffectual, raid on the town of Whitehaven on England's northwest coast. On September 23, 1779, Jones commanded the *Bonhomme Richard* to a stunning victory over the more heavily gunned British frigate *Serapis*. Theirs was a fierce engagement fought mostly at close quarters, with the two ships laid alongside each other. At one point in the struggle, the British captain somehow became convinced that his vessel had gained the upper hand. Shouting above the din of battle, he asked Jones if the American was striking his colors—a gesture that indicated surrender. Jones' reply—"I have not yet begun to fight"—won him lasting renown in the annals of naval warfare.

Small-scale engagements like the one between the *Bonhomme Richard* and the *Serapis* were typical of the American naval effort. Large fleet actions were rare, and for good reason: the Americans simply did not have the monetary resources to equip such a force. Nor did it have the human resources. Experienced captains like John Paul Jones were in short supply; so were trained crews. And even the experienced captains usually lacked the kind of fleet command skills required to challenge British mastery of the seas. Although the Americans did deploy fleets—most famously on Lake Champlain—their naval war was fought for the most part by commerce-raiding privateers acting alone or in small flotillas. Consequently, the job of besting the vaunted British Navy fell to the French. On September 5, 1781, a French fleet did just that when it defeated a British squadron in the waters off the Virginia Capes. The British ships had been sent to relieve the besieged army of Lord Cornwallis on nearby Yorktown Peninsula; when they failed to complete their mission, Cornwallis was forced to surrender, thus bringing the Revolutionary War to an end. This French naval triumph proved more decisive to the success of the American Revolution than any victory achieved by the Continental Navy.

Above: John Paul Jones. *Right:* Jones was commanding the Ranger when it received the first salute given to the Stars and Stripes by a foreign warship, the French Robuste. The date was February 14, 1778.

OF PIRATES AND THE QUASI-WAR

The end of the Revolutionary War brought with it an end to the Continental Navy, which was voted out of existence by Congress. Except for a few armed sloops belonging to the Treasury Department's Revenue Service, the United States was virtually without a navy for the next ten years. Congress was finally brought to its collective senses by deteriorating relationships with the government that ruled France after the revolution of 1789, and by the increasingly brazen behavior of pirates operating from ports on North Africa's Barbary Coast. The latter had been making a nuisance of themselves by seizing American merchant vessels and their crews and holding them for ransom—a practice that prompted Congress to authorize the building of eight frigates in 1794.

When a treaty was signed with the Dey of Algiers—the paramount Barbary pirate chieftain—Congress immediately suspended construction on all but three of these ships. But

even as the pirate threat receded, the threat of hostilities with France was steadily increasing. By 1796 that threat was realized when the United States and France drifted into a state of open, but undeclared, naval war. In the first nine months of what is known as the "Quasi-War," France seized 316 American vessels. Congress responded, somewhat reluctantly, by passing the Navy Act on July 1, 1797. This is the date always cited when mention is made of the birth of the United States Navy.

The undeclared Quasi-War between the United States and France continued for the next two-and-a-half years. In that time, the U.S. Navy directed the bulk of its efforts toward preventing French privateers and naval vessels from capturing American merchantmen. The war ended when Napoleon Bonaparte, upon assuming power in France, obtained a negotiated settlement to the war so that he could devote his energies to European concerns.

The war with France having ended, Congress once again attempted to disband the Navy. The folly of this

attempt was exposed by none other than the Barbary pirates, who were up to their usual depredations against American merchant shipping and citizens. On May 10, 1801, these depredations reached a climax when the pirate government of Tripoli declared war on the United States. Without knowing about the declaration of war, President Thomas Jefferson had already dispatched a Navy squadron to the Mediterranean; when he learned of the Tripolitan action, he sent another squadron to the region in 1802. The ensuing conflict dragged on until 1805, when a small army comprised of U.S. Marines and mercenaries marched 600 miles across the Libyan desert to seize the pirate port of Derna. Shortly thereafter the Tripolitans signed a peace treaty with the United States, after which American warships were slowly withdrawn from the region.

*Below: U.S. sailors storm a Barbary pirate gunboat in Tripoli harbor. **Right:** Captured by Barbary pirates, the Philadelphia was set ablaze by an American raiding party seeking to deny its use to the enemy.*

IMPRESSMENT AND ANOTHER WAR WITH THE BRITISH

No sooner had the problems in the Mediterranean been settled, than America became embroiled in a new conflict with Great Britain. War with France had caused the British to become increasingly less tolerant of America's commercial success, which had been achieved largely through friendly—and profitable—trade relations with Napoleon's regime. The result was an escalating number of incidents involving British warships and American merchant and naval vessels.

Such incidents often culminated in the British boarding of American ships, ostensibly to search for deserters from the Royal Navy. Sometimes deserters were found; more often than not, however, American sailors were seized (or "impressed") for service aboard the offending British vessel. In June 1807 the unprepared American frigate *Chesapeake* was accosted by the British warship *Leopard*; after the encounter had run its course, 18 Americans were wounded, three were

dead, and three more had been impressed into British service. In response, an outraged American citizenry clamored for war. Instead of war, however, the Jefferson administration demanded that Britain recognize the rights of neutral ships on the high seas. When Britain ignored Jefferson's demand, the President declared a unilateral embargo on all trade with France, Great Britain, and their respective allies. The result was disaster for American commerce, and a drastic rise in smuggling. In 1809, the embargo was modified to the Non-Intercourse Act, which restored trade with all nations except France and Britain, and which allowed the Secretary of State to reopen trade with either of those two nations if they agreed to stop harassing American shipping.

The Non-Intercourse Act proved to be as ineffective as the embargo. Despite American protests, the Royal Navy continued to impress American seamen aboard British ships. By 1812, some 10,000 Americans had lost their freedom in this manner. The United States finally decided to put an end to this outrageous state of affairs on

Images of the War of 1812. **Above, left:** *The USS* Wasp *engages the HMS* Reindeer, 1814. **Above, right:** *The USS* Constitution *versus the HMS* Java, 1812. **Below, right:** *The Battle of Lake Erie, 1813.*

June 18, 1812, when it formally declared war on Britain.

Although its ships were vastly outnumbered by the Royal Navy, the U.S. Navy performed well in the "War of 1812." In 1812 alone, the *Constitution* defeated and captured the Royal Navy's *Guerriere*, and sank the *Java;* the American sloop *Wasp* defeated the British brig *Frolic;* and the *United States* defeated and captured the British frigate *Macedonian.* In September of 1813, a flotilla under the command of Oliver Hazard Perry defeated a British force on Lake Erie; in September of the following year, an American flotilla scored another impressive victory over British warships in a key battle on Lake Champlain.

But the Americans enjoyed fewer successes as the war progressed. The problem was, the British had too many ships. The U.S. Navy simply could not cope with them all. The U.S. Navy had

sought to compensate for its lack of warships by using many small coastal gunboats in a seagoing role. But these vessels proved inadequate to the task of halting Britain's attacks on American commercial shipping. Neither could they prevent a British amphibious landing force from burning Washington, D.C., and a flotilla from bombarding Baltimore. The U.S. Navy was also unable to prevent a second British army from landing just outside of New Orleans in December of 1814—although American ships did use their guns to bombard the enemy force as it advanced on the city.

The inconclusive War of 1812 officially ended on December 24, 1815, with the signing of the Treaty of Ghent. But news of the treaty did not reach the United States in time to prevent the fighting of the Battle of New Orleans on January 8, 1815. Slow communications also caused the war at sea to continue well into June, when the American sloop *Peacock* defeated and captured the British brig *Nautilus* in the distant waters of the Sunda Strait between Java and Sumatra.

NEW FRONTIERS, NEW TECHNOLOGIES

In the War of 1812, the United States learned that a strong navy was essential to both economic and territorial well being. As the nation was to discover, this was a lesson that had peacetime applications as well. A large merchant fleet required a sizeable navy to protect it. Yet the necessary expansion of American naval power in the years following the War of 1812 was limited by a number of factors, including economic depression, and the demands imposed on the nation's consciousness—not to mention its treasury—by the development of the western frontier. Preoccupied by these concerns, Congress often canceled or delayed new naval ship construction, and deactivated larger and more expensive ships in favor of smaller vessels.

Nevertheless, the Navy remained quite active during this period. In 1815, two American naval squadrons were dispatched to the Mediterranean to deal yet again with their old nemesis, the Barbary pirates. In the Caribbean and Gulf Coast region, pirates occupied the attention of the Navy's Caribbean Squadron for over a decade before they were eliminated as a threat to merchant shipping. On the opposite side of the world, the Pacific

Squadron worked to safeguard American interests from South America to Southeast Asia.

Not all of America's far-flung naval squadrons performed their duties with equal zeal. The African Squadron was a case in point. Established in 1820, this force was assigned the task of enforcing the 1807 law prohibiting the importation of slaves into the United States. It did so without much enthusiasm, or success, until 1842, when the United States and Britain signed an antislavery accord. Even after that date, the pro-slavery sentiments of the Southern states caused the African squadron to remain chronically undermanned. American ships accordingly captured only two percent of the number of slave ships that were captured by the Royal Navy in one five-year period.

In contrast, the Mexican War (1846–48) proved to be a showcase for American naval power. Not coincidentally, this was a war that the South supported wholeheartedly, mainly because the acquisition of vast Mexican territories represented equally vast opportunities for the expansion of slavery. On the West Coast, Marines and sailors from the

The Caribbean Squadron's Kearsage, Constitution, *and* Macedonian *illustrate a navy transitioning from sail to steam.*

Pacific Squadron occupied Monterey and San Francisco, and landed at several points along the West Coast. In the Gulf of Mexico, the Home Squadron first blockaded the Mexican coast; then, in 1847, it put ashore 8,600 troops just south of Vera Cruz in what was at the time the largest amphibious operation in modern military history.

During the 1850s, the settling of California and the Oregon territory led to the expansion of American trade into the Pacific basin. Soon, all mercantile eyes in that region were focused on Japan, a little-known and less understood island kingdom that had remained closed to almost all foreign commerce for the past 200 years. After failing in two previous attempts to open the trade door with Japan through diplomatic means, the U.S. government ordered a flotilla of four warships under the command of Commodore Matthew C. Perry to kick the door down, as it were, by cruising straight into Tokyo harbor. This Perry did, on July 8th, 1853. His bold action was eventually rewarded by a treaty that provided for the opening of two Japanese ports to American ships and the granting of most-favored nation status to the United States.

Two of the ships that Perry took into Tokyo harbor were steam-driven vessels with massive paddlewheels on each side. As such, they represented an advancement in propulsion technology that was destined to eliminate sails on all U.S. warships by the end of the century. The shift from sail to steam began in 1837 with the commissioning of the *Fulton* into Navy service. The success of this vessel convinced Congress of the practicality of steam propulsion, and in 1839 two more steam driven men-of-war were authorized. In 1842, the *Missouri* and the *Mississippi*, both wooden side-wheel frigates, were completed and commissioned; in 1843 the iron-hulled steamship *Michigan* was commissioned to serve on the Great Lakes.

A U.S. naval battery, relocated ashore, bombards enemy fortifications at Vera Cruz in the final weeks of March, 1847, during the Mexican-American War.

The use of steam-driven paddlewheels mounted on a ship's side required that the engines be mounted above the waterline, where they were vulnerable to enemy gunfire. The space required for the large paddle wheels also reduced the area available for mounting guns. Ship designers responded to this challenge by inventing the underwater, stern-mounted screw, or "propeller." The Navy's first screw-driven ship was the sloop *Princeton*, which was launched in 1844. The engine on the *Princeton* was located beneath the waterline and used blowers to force air into its

furnace. It also burned anthracite, or "hard" coal, which generated more power and reduced the amount of smoke put out by earlier steamships burning bituminous, or "soft" coal.

Weapons were changing, too. Rifled cannons firing conical shells with explosive tips were beginning to replace cannonball-firing weapons. Early shell-firing guns were often dangerously unstable weapons prone to exploding their shells in the breech; they also lacked the range and accuracy of the solid shot cannons. But improvements in technologies related to metallurgy, barrel-casting

techniques, rifling, gunpowder, and fuses had combined to make the shell gun as safe to those who fired it as it was deadly to those at whom it was aimed. Sadly, the American Civil War would demonstrate the deadliness of these weapons against the very countrymen they were supposed to defend.

Below: The Michigan. ***Top, right:*** *Upon becoming the first warship to cross the Atlantic under steam, the* Missouri *was destroyed by a fire in Gibraltar harbor on August 26, 1843.* ***Bottom, right:*** *The* Fulton.

NAVAL GUNS

In the latter half of the 18th century, naval vessels were armed with a variety of smoothbore cannon, each developed for a specific task. Guns firing round balls up to 32 pounds formed the main armament of the most powerful warships, followed by guns firing balls weighing 24, 16, 12, eight, six, and even four pounds. The four-through-eight-pound guns had barrels of varying lengths. Longer barrels allowed for the burning of more powder, which produced greater shot acceleration, which thereby increased the range of the shot.

The ability of one ship to smash another with the sheer weight of its shot was the major victory determinant in ship-to-ship duels. Quite naturally, then, a frigate carrying 48 24-pounder guns was expected to prevail over a frigate carrying only 32 24-pounders because the former could unleash a broadside that would send 576 pounds of metal into its foe, whereas the latter's broadside contained a mere 384 pounds of metal.

Warships were categorized in the U.S. Navy by "rate" before 1810. A first rate ship carried 100 or more guns; second rate between 84 and 100; third rate between 70 and 84; fourth rate 50 to 70; fifth rate 32 to 50; and sixth rate, up to 32 guns. During the American Revolution and the War of 1812, the 32- and 48-gun frigates were the most common large warships in the U.S. Navy. Their standard armament was the 24-pounder cannon which had a range of one mile when firing solid shot. Like all other naval cannons, the 24-pounder also fired grape shot (numerous small caliber balls) against

personnel, and bar, or chain, shot to slash rigging and sails. Bar, or chain, shot consisted of two projectiles fastened together with a chain or sliding bar that whirled as it flew toward its target.

In 1779 the Scottish firm of Carron and Company invented the carronade, a short barreled cannon of comparatively light weight. The carronade used a heavy ball but a small powder charge. The heavy ball was propelled at low velocity over a short distance but when it struck, it did far more damage than a smaller ball traveling at a higher speed. The carronade was widely adopted and had a big influence on naval tactics, especially in the British Navy. Fighting ships armed with carronades closed faster with enemy ships in order to fire heavy broadsides. But its short range was soon shown to be a detriment. During the Battle of Lake Erie in 1812, the American fleet was armed with cannons and the British fleet primarily with carronades. While sailing out of range of the Royal Navy's carronades, the American ships shot the British ships to pieces.

From roughly the beginning of the 16th to the middle of the 18th centuries, naval guns changed little in form and type, although there were steady improvements in construction, metallurgy, ammunition, and gunpowder. The development of iron-hulled naval vessels and steam propulsion—which did away with the sails and rigging that had constituted the most vulnerable part of a warship—required the development of more powerful guns as well. At first, guns were merely made in larger calibers—sometimes too large to

withstand the pressures that built up in the breech during discharge. In 1844 a poorly forged 12-inch wrought-iron cannon on the war sloop Princeton exploded during a demonstration, killing five people, including the secretaries of state and the Navy.

In the mid-1850s the technique of manufacturing powerful guns from wrought iron was perfected in Britain by William Armstrong. At the same time, a German weapons engineer named Friedrich Krupp perfected his method of casting gun barrels from steel. Both men then developed breech-loading mechanisms. In the United States, naval gun development was led by a naval officer, J.A. Dahlgren, who continued to make improvements on the cast iron, smoothbore design. T.J. Rodman perfected casting methods that allowed the construction of guns with 20-inch bores.

The traditional methods for absorbing cannon recoil involved the use of ropes and pulleys fastened to the ship's bulwarks. This method made it difficult to train (aim) a gun to one side or the other, a problem that was only partially solved by the use of wheeled gun carriages set on half-circle tracks. The track system was replaced by

steam-powered turntables, which were in turn supplanted by rotating turrets. The practicality of the turret was demonstrated by the Monitor during its famous battle with the Virginia in 1862. In the 1870s, steam power was replaced by the more reliable hydraulic power to move turrets. The principles of hydraulics also found applications in mechanisms used for gun reloading and recoil absorption.

Gunpowder was also the focus of a great deal of experimentation. By the middle of the 18th century the development of gunpowder, or black powder, had reached its peak. In 1886, French scientists produced a smokeless powder with a base of nitrated cellulose (gun cotton) which not only developed more energy than black powder, but far less smoke. In 1890 the British began to use a smokeless powder called cordite, which was made from nitroglycerin. By the turn of the century, the U.S. Navy had also switched to nitrocellulose smokeless powder.

In the mid-1800s breech-loading rifled cannons began

The crew of a smoothbore Dahlgren gun drills aboard the USS Mendota in 1864.

to replace smoothbore muzzle loading guns in navies and armies with the wherewithal to do so. But while the breech-loaders were more accurate and powerful than their predecessors, their effective range was limited by the naked-eye sighting techniques of their gunners. Then, in 1892, Navy Lieutenant Bradley A. Fiske invented a telescopic sight for artillery pieces that allowed guns to be aimed at targets from ten to 20 miles distant. In 1906, periscopic gun sights improved accuracy even more. Mounted in a ship's superstructure, the periscopic sights allowed aiming to be done remotely while extending range even farther.

The director system did more than anything else to move naval gunfire from the category of art to science. First developed in the Imperial German Navy, the director system aimed and fired guns electrically in salvos according to commands received from a gunnery director. The director, usually situated on a control platform high on the ship's foremast, used an optical sighting system that measured range and calculated the elevation of the guns from prepared tables, then fired the guns only when the ship was on an even keel. By the end of World War I, the U.S. Navy had even included various dyes in their powder formulations to produce different colored explosions so that shots from a particular gun could be detected and the aim corrected.

In World War II the emergence of aircraft as offensive weapons created a need for antiaircraft guns on warships. In the early years of the war, however, the antiaircraft capability of most Allied ships was grossly inadequate. In December 1941, for

example, the British battleship *Prince of Wales* and battlecruiser *Repluse* were lost off Malaya in part because they lacked fighter protection, but also because they lacked an antiaircraft armament sufficient to deal with the Japanese bombers that sent them to the bottom. The loss of these two powerful warships galvanized navies everywhere to mount more antiaircraft guns on their surface vessels. By 1945, the *Iowa*-class battleships were armed with up to 140 20 millimeter and 40mm antiaircraft guns. In addition, the Navy armed many of its ships with three- and five-inch guns that fired shells fitted with proximity fuses, which detonated when they came within a preset distance of an aircraft.

During World War II the most powerful guns in the U.S. Navy were 16-inch rifles mounted on battleships. These guns were mounted three to a turret, with two tur-

rets forward and one aft. The 16-inch rifles had a range of up to 23 miles, depending on whether or not the heavier high-explosive or the lighter armor-piercing rounds were being fired. A heavy cruiser's main armament usually consisted of three eight-inch rifles in three turrets, two forward and one aft. Light cruisers were armed with six-inch or five-inch main batteries, and destroyers were armed with five-inch or four-inch guns.

Secondary battleship and cruiser armament generally consisted of five-inch rifles mounted in single or twin turrets. Similar guns and turrets were used in destroyers and frigates. They could be used for high-angle antiaircraft fire or for dealing with surface craft.

With the development of the guided missile after 1945, naval guns declined in importance. While most Navy warships still mount guns, the

The 16-inch guns of the battleship New Jersey.

two *Iowa*-class battleships are the only vessels armed with guns larger than five-inches. The five-inch guns, as well as the three-inch guns that are mounted on a number of Navy ships, have a limited antiaircraft capability, but are used primarily for antisurface warfare. Many Navy ships (e.g., the *Oliver Hazard Perry*-class frigates and PHM *Pegasus*-class patrol boats) mount the Italian-made OTO Melara 76mm quick-firing gun, which is excellent for use as both an antiaircraft and antisurface weapon. A majority of Navy combatant ships are also armed with the 20mm multi-barrel Phalanx gun system, which can fire as many as three thousand rounds per minute to form a defense against approaching enemy missiles.

THE CIVIL WAR

When the American Civil War started in April 1861, all U.S. military personnel were forced to decide whether to fight for the Union or the Confederacy. As was the case with the Army—and, for that matter, the nation itself—naval personnel usually went over to the same side their home states had joined. In this respect the Navy fared better than the Army. Before the war ended, only one quarter of all commissioned naval officers joined the Confederacy, whereas nearly half the commissioned Army officers did so.

The Federal Navy was called upon to blockade the South almost immediately after the outbreak of war. Since the South had to import almost all of its arms and machinery, the blockade was a sound strategy. But the implementation of that strategy was complicated by nearly 3,500 miles of Confederate coastline. In the war's

first month the Navy could muster only 42 warships to guard that seemingly endless shore, and many of those vessels were stationed in foreign ports. Making matters worse, the Navy had lost roughly half of its bases to the Confederacy.

Notwithstanding these problems, the Navy pressed forward with the blockade, which was known as the Anaconda Plan—named, rather optimistically, after the giant South American snake that killed its prey by squeezing it to death. While the Anaconda Plan was applied to the Confederate seacoast, the Navy also intended to seize control of the Mississippi River and other major inland waterways within the Confederacy.

As ill-equipped as the Federal Navy was for this task, it still had the Confederate Navy at a distinct disadvantage. For all practical purposes, in 1861 the idea of a Confederate Navy was just that: an

idea. Although the South was in possession of many excellent deep water ports (including the facilities at the Norfolk Navy Yard in Virginia), it had almost no ships to speak of. Confederate leaders quickly realized that this was a situation that had to change, and soon. Without ships to penetrate the Federal blockade, the South's foreign trade—which pretty much consisted of trading cotton for arms and munitions—would be shut down, and the war would be lost.

To avoid this fate, the Confederacy sent abroad agents empowered with the money and the authority to either purchase vessels or have them built in foreign ship yards. The ships so acquired were usually quite fast, and were used primarily as blockade runners or commerce raiders. To counter the Confederacy's efforts, the

A Confederate "David," a type of torpedo boat used by the South with little success to break the Federal blockade.

Federal Navy subjected virtually every ship it encountered on the high seas to a thorough search. If the captain of the Federal vessel determined that the cargo of the searched ship was contraband—that it was destined for the South—the cargo was confiscated on the spot. The owners of foreign ships that had lost their cargoes in such a fashion could file suit in a Federal court to get them back—a frustratingly lengthy, and not always successful, process. Not surprisingly, nations engaged in what they regarded as perfectly legal, and therefore inviolable, trade with the South deeply resented the Union's blockade. This was especially true of Britain, which almost entered the war on the Confederacy's side in retaliation for the Navy's high-handed tactics.

The Confederate Navy could have used Britain's help. In the event, it had to fend for itself. In this it showed considerable ingenuity, as evidenced by the modification of a ship known as the *Virginia*. Formerly named the *Merrimac*, this steam-driven ironclad featured an armored deckhouse with walls that were slanted and greased to deflect enemy projectiles; it also had a powerful armament consisting of six

nine-inch Dahlgren smoothbore cannons and two 6.4-inch rifles mounted in the sides, and one seven-inch rifle mounted in the bow and the stern. Being virtually invulnerable to even the heaviest-caliber cannon fire, it was admirably suited to the task for which it had been specifically designed, the sinking of blockading Federal warships.

To counter the threat posed by the *Virginia*, the Union hastily built an ironclad of its own: the *Monitor*. This was a curious-looking craft that resembled, according to one contemporary observer, a "cheesebox on a raft." Armored with eight inches of iron plate and mounting a pair of 11-inch Dalgren guns in a revolving turret, it was a formidable vessel indeed. But only time would tell whether it was a match for the *Virginia*.

That time came in the spring of 1862. On March 7, the Confederate ironclad emerged from its lair on the Elizabeth River to engage a Federal blockading fleet in the waters off Hampton Roads, Virginia. Before retiring from the scene at nightfall, the *Virginia* had sunk the Federal sloop *Cumberland* and set fire to the frigate *Congress*. On March 8 the *Virginia*

The encounter between the Monitor *and the* Virginia, *March 8, 1862.*

ventured out once again to wreck havoc on the Federal fleet, only to find its way blocked by the *Monitor*. The battle that followed lasted for the better part of four hours, with the two ironclads pounding each other with salvo after salvo from their big guns. However, despite countless hits scored by Confederate and Federal gunners alike, the protective armor plating of the two vessels kept damage to an inconsequential minimum. Finally, both ships broke off this indecisive combat, which has gone down in history as the first battle ever fought between armored steamship vessels.

Although the duel between the *Monitor* and the *Virginia* grabbed headlines, it is arguable as to whether it had any bearing on the outcome of the war. Of true strategic importance was the struggle waged by Federal vessels and their accompanying armies to gain control of the Mississippi River and its tributaries. Collectively known as the "Brown Water Navy," these ships were commanded by Flag Officer Andrew H. Foote, who in turn took his orders from General Ulysses S. Grant. The pride of Foote's fleet were seven flat-bottom stern-wheeler gunboats called "Pook's Turtles" after their designer, Samuel Pook. In February 1862, Pook's Turtles steamed south out of Cairo, Illinois, on a mission to eliminate three Confederate forts situated on the Mississippi, Tennessee, and Cumberland rivers, respectively. In April, two of the gunboats—the *Carondelet* and *Pittsburg*—participated in a successful Federal attempt to capture the Confederate fort on Island No. 10 in the Mississippi River. The Brown Water Navy also played a vital role in the Federal victory at the Battle of Shiloh, and in the capture of Memphis, Tennessee.

Further south, the West Gulf Squadron under the command of Flag Officer David Glasgow Farragut captured New Orleans on April 24, 1862. A strong proponent of combined land/sea operations, Farragut and his ships would contribute a great deal to the Federal capture of Vicksburg on July 4, 1863. Farragut's most famous battle, however, occurred at Mobile Bay, Alabama, on August 5, 1864. It was there that he allegedly uttered the command, "Damn the torpedoes, full speed ahead!" when his ships balked at entering a suspected Confederate mine field.

Due in large part to the efforts of Federal Navy commanders like Farragut, it became increasingly evident to Confederate leaders that the only satisfactory outcome to the

war lay in a negotiated peace. Many Southerners thought such a peace could be attained by prolonging the war until the Union lost the will to fight it. This was a desperate measure that called for equally desperate tactics. Few would argue that the use of the submarine *Hunley* was the most desperate tactic of them all.

Invented by Horace Hunley, the vessel that bore his name was shaped like a cigar and powered by 18 men turning a handcrank that drove a stern-mounted screw propeller. The

Below: The Battle of New Orleans, April 24, 1862. **Below, inset:** Admiral David G. Farragut, Federal victor at New Orleans. **Top, right:** The Baron de Kalb, a "Brown Water Navy" gunboat. **Bottom, right:** The doomed Hunley.

The USS Kearsage (left) engages the Confederate commerce raider Alabama off the coast of France.

navigator stood in a narrow casemate that rose above the hull and shouted steering directions to a pilot who sat in the craft's nose. A "torpedo" (which was really more like a modern mine) was attached to the vessel's bow by a spar. The Hunley was quite literally a murderous craft that killed over 20 crewmen (including Hunley himself) by drowning or suffocation during a series of disastrous underwater trials. Raised up and provided with a replacement crew, the Hunley was used as a surface craft to attack the Federal sloop Housatonic on February 17, 1864, in Charleston Harbor. The Hunley detonated its torpedo by deliberately ramming the weapon into the side of the Housatonic, which promptly sank. Unfortunately, as the Federal ship settled to the bottom, the Hunley was dragged down with it, and its entire crew perished.

Far more successful than this ill-starred foray into submarine warfare was the Confederacy's use of the aforementioned commerce raiders. By the war's end, raiders flying the Confederate flag had destroyed or captured over 200 Federal merchant ships carrying more than 25 million dollars worth of cargo. The most famous (or notorious, depending on one's point of view) of the Confederate commerce raiders was the armed cruiser Alabama. Commanded by the brilliant Captain Raphael Semmes, the Alabama roamed the world's oceans from August 1862 to June 1864, capturing some 65 Federal vessels and their cargoes. On June 19, 1864, the Alabama was finally brought to bay off the coast of Cherbourg by the Federal steam sloop Kearsage, which sank the Confederate warship after an hour-long fight.

By the time the Alabama met its fate, the Federal blockade held the Confederacy in a tight grip. Nevertheless, the Union's chronic shortage of warships allowed Southern vessels to slip through the Federal cordon on a regular basis. The South's long, uneven coastline offered a host of islands, coves, and inlets that were ideal for conducting blockade-running operations. But such locales by their very nature limited the influx of supplies. To keep the South properly stocked for war, real ports were needed. And as time went on, the number of ports in Southern hands dwindled steadily as they fell, one by one, to the advancing Federal armies. By the first week of 1865 the last major port capable of supporting blockade runners was Wilmington, North Carolina. On January 13, 1865, this avenue was closed when a combined force of Federal sailors, marines, and army troops captured Fort Fisher, which covered the approaches to Wilmington. The Anaconda had completely encircled its prey.

The capture of Fort Fisher was the Navy's last major campaign of the Civil War. When the Civil War came to an end in April, the Navy could justly take pride in the contribution it had made to the Union's victory. The Navy's blockade by sea, as well as its role in the closing of the Mississippi River system, had served to weaken the South for the knockout blows that the Federal armies on land ultimately delivered.

FROM STAGNATION TO EMPIRE

In the years following the end of the Civil War, Congress drastically reduced the Navy's size from a wartime high of 700 ships to 48 ships in 1880. Funding was also cut, leaving the Navy with the money to do little else than send out exploratory missions to the Arctic and Antarctic, and mount weak patrols along the Pacific and Atlantic trade routes. A brief conflict in Korea in 1871 marked the only break in this otherwise peaceful era. It was a time of technological stagnation for the Navy, which clung to the use of sailing ships even as the navies of other nations were abandoning such vessels in favor of steam-driven warships. The rationale for using sailing ships was grounded in the fact that the United States did not have foreign holdings to serve as coaling stations. Beyond that, however, the elderly admirals who ran the Navy disliked steamships for purely emotional reasons. Their antipathy to the new steam technologies was often carried to what now seem absurd lengths. For example, the fast cruiser *Wampanoag*—which had used superheated steam to obtain a top speed of 17.7 knots in 1868—was stripped of two of its boilers by a traditionalist-minded Naval Review Board that feared what this vessel portended for the future of their cherished sailing ships. *Wampanoag* rotted at her moorings for years afterward, a monument to short-sightedness in the Navy's upper ranks.

The Navy's fortunes reached a nadir around 1878. By then there were only 6,000 men in the entire service. Funding was so limited that, to save a few dollars, the Navy had its Model 1851 percussion Colt pistols converted to fire cartridges, rather than going to the expense of purchasing new cartridge-firing revolvers. Even the Navy's time-honored role of defending the national coastline was left pretty much to the Army, which built massive fixed artillery batteries for that purpose.

A turnaround in this sorry state of affairs came in the late 1880s. In those years clear-thinking naval officers and a few congressmen began to stump for a Navy that could protect American merchant ships on the high seas or

The battleship Texas *(left) and the armored cruiser* Olympia *were among the first of the U.S. Navy's modern steel-hulled warships.*

PROPULSION

The United States Navy was the first navy in the world to commission a steam-powered vessel, the *Fulton*, in 1815. The *Fulton* was destroyed by an explosion in 1829, and not until 1837 was a new Navy steamship commissioned, also named the *Fulton*. By then, France had 23 steam-powered warships in service and Great Britain had 21.

Two more Navy "tea kettles," as the steamships were nicknamed, were authorized in 1839. The next year, the first U.S. Navy iron-hulled steamer, the *Michigan*, was laid down. Despite the advances these ships represented, however, steam power was considered to be auxiliary to sails for the next 50 years.

During the American Civil War, the navies of both the Confederacy and the Union built the first all steam-powered, iron warships. The Union Navy also perfected the tactical use of a steam-powered river navy during the struggle for the inland waterways of the Confederacy.

In 1908, the monitor *Cheyenne* became the first U.S. Navy ship to convert from coal-burning to oil engines. Oil-fueled engines used less fuel per unit of energy and were cleaner burning. The following year, the destroyer *Smith* had its ponderous reciprocating engines replaced by steam turbines.

Boilers were built to withstand higher and higher pressures until by World War II, boilers that could contain 600 pounds of steam per square inch (psi) were standard. Postwar vessels had engines with boilers capable of withstanding 1,200 psi. Such ships could make and maintain 20 knots for days on end if necessary. The conventionally powered super carriers of the *Kitty Hawk* class, the cruisers of the *Belknap* and *Leahy* classes, and all postwar steam-powered destroyers and frigates were equipped with the 1,200-psi boilers.

In the postwar period as well, two new methods of propulsion extended the Navy's range, speed, and payload. One was the nuclear reactor, which heated water to create steam to drive a turbine. Not only did nuclear power make the first true submarines possible, it also provided the Navy with warships that had cruising distances limited only by the necessity to replenish food and other consumables.

The other, and in some ways, more revolutionary method of propulsion, was the adoption of the gas turbine engine for shipboard power. Used at first only for generating auxiliary or boost power, gas turbines now power vessels of every description from cruisers to patrol boats to hovercraft.

The Wampanoag, *an 1868-vintage cruiser with an innovative steam propulsion system.*

fight a war if need be. In 1883, Congress took a step toward building such a Navy by funding the construction of four new steel ships. This "ABCD Squadron," as it was nicknamed, included the 3,000-ton protected cruisers *Atlantic* and *Boston*, the 4,500-ton protected cruiser *Chicago*, and the 1,500-ton dispatch vessel *Dolphin*. All four ships were built with full steam power plants, double hulls, and watertight compartments. In a bow to tradition, they were also fitted with masts and sails. In 1885, two additional 4,000-ton protected cruisers were built: these were the *Charleston* and the *Newark*. In 1886, Congress authorized the building of the second-class battleships *Texas* and *Maine*. The latter two ships were initially famous for having been built entirely of American-made steel on American-made machinery.

In 1884, Congress also authorized the establishment of the Naval War College. The second president of the Naval War College was Alfred Thayer Mahan, author of an 1890 book titled *The Influence of Sea Power Upon History, 1660–1783*. This bestseller was destined to change forever the way military strategists thought about sea power. In it, Mahan set forth the idea that Britain had built a world empire because it had no land frontiers that needed protecting. Britain's frontier was the sea, which *did* need to be protected, and which therefore necessitated the creation of a powerful navy. That same Navy, Mahan pointed out, was also used to secure trade rights with other nations, seize distant territories for colonial exploitation, safeguard commercial shipping, maintain hegemony over vast and far-flung regions—and only rarely fight wars. There was a lesson in all this for the United States, which, Mahan argued, was essentially an island nation like Britain; as such it could, like Britain, derive immense political and economic benefits from having a large navy. Mahan's book proved to be the bible of American imperialists. It was also highly

Top: *The ABCD Squadron's* Chicago.
Right: *Alfred Thayer Mahan, brilliant architect of modern naval strategy.*

regarded by Germany's Kaiser Wilhelm II, who ordered that copies of Mahan's book be kept on every warship in the German fleet.

As the 19th century drew to a close, the competition among the European powers to secure overseas markets and colonies in what is now referred to as the "Third World" produced buildups in military might—and corresponding increases in international tensions. Worried by this trend, Congress saw to it that the early 1890s was a period of rejuvenation for the Navy. The Naval Act of 1890 provided funding for three 10,288-ton battleships, the *Indiana*, *Massachusetts*, and *Oregon*. Each vessel was armed with four 13-inch, eight 8-inch, and four 6-inch guns;

each was also protected by up to 18 inches of steel armor. Two years later, this *Indiana* class of battleships was enhanced by the building of the *Iowa*, and in the remaining years of the 19th century, the fleet was enlarged by the addition of five more battleships. By the late 1800s the Navy's growing strength had earned it a fifth-place ranking among the world's navies.

In 1898 the nation tested the Navy's strength in a war with the mordant Spanish Empire. The road to war began in Cuba, which was just then in the throes of a revolution against Spanish rule. On February 15, 1898, the battleship *Maine* was destroyed by an explosion while it lay at anchor in Havana Harbor. Although the cause of

Above: *The battleship* Maine *blows up in Havana Harbor, an incident that sparked war between the United States and Spain.* **Opposite:** *Commodore Dewey's Asiatic Squadron engages the moored ships of the Spanish fleet in the Battle of Manila Bay.*

the blast was never definitely ascertained, a jingoistic American press lost no time in blaming Spain. This had the desired effect of stirring up war fever among the American public, which was sympathetic to the Cuban revolutionary cause. Harkening to the mood of their respective constituencies, spurred by their own imperialist ambitions, Congress and President William McKinley joined forces to declare war on Spain on April 19, 1898.

Because Spain was thought to have an excellent navy, many Americans expected a long war. But Alfred Thayer Mahan, now a retired admiral, thought otherwise. In predicting a war lasting three months, Mahan pointed out that command of the Atlantic Ocean and the Caribbean Sea was the key to victory. In these arenas, Mahan observed, the United States held the advantage with three first-line battleships, one second-line battleship, two armored cruisers, and numerous smaller ships. Moreover, the crews on these ships were well-trained and highly motivated to perform the tasks assigned them.

Mahan's confidence in the Navy was shared by the Assistant Secretary of

the Navy, Theodore Roosevelt. That the Navy was ready to fight a war on such short notice was due largely to the efforts of this dynamic man. As early as February 25, Roosevelt had sent a telegram to Commodore George Dewey, the commander of the Asiatic Squadron, instructing him to be prepared to move against the Spanish fleet in the Philippines. Thus, when war came, Dewey's flotilla (which was then at Hong Kong) was able to move quickly. It did so on April 27, 1898, steaming from a neutral anchorage just up the coast from Hong Kong, bound for Manila Bay some 600 miles distant.

The Asiatic Squadron arrived at its destination at dawn on May 1, 1898.

Proceeding eastward into Manila Bay, the American ships were fired on by Spanish ships and shore batteries at Cavite naval station just south of Manila. At 5:41 a.m. Dewey ordered his ships to return fire. For the next hour and a half Dewey's ships steamed back and forth in front of the Cavite anchorage, pounding the Spanish fleet with every gun they could bring to bear. The Americans broke for breakfast at 7:30 a.m., then returned to finish the job at 11:00 a.m. By noon nearly every Spanish vessel was either sunk or burning out of control. It was the most complete victory ever achieved by the U.S. Navy—until the Battle of Santiago, Cuba, just two months later.

31

The Battle of Santiago occurred on July 3, 1898. On that day the Spanish fleet, which had been languishing for several weeks in Santiago Harbor, tried to break through a blockading American squadron that included the battleships *Oregon*, *Massachusetts*, *Indiana*, *Iowa*, and *Texas*, as well as the cruisers *Brooklyn* and *New York*. In a three-hour running battle, the powerful American squadron utterly smashed the Spanish force, which lost all of its ships and sustained 474 casualties. Yet if this was a tremendous victory for the Navy, it was also one that was rather ineptly achieved. Throughout the battle the Americans had maneuvered their ships in an uncoordinated fashion, and their gunnery had been atrocious. Of the over 8,000 shells the Americans had fired, only 120 had hit their targets. That the Spanish were even more inept in their battle conduct was a lucky stroke for the Americans. It was also cause for concern. Commenting later upon the battle, the sage Alfred Thayer Mahan opined that the U.S. Navy would never again encounter an enemy as weak as the Spanish Navy. Implicit in his words was a warning: The Navy would have to improve if it were to carry out its duties in a conflict with a competent foe.

Five weeks after the Santiago sea battle, the city of Santiago was captured by American troops. The Spanish-American War came to end on August 12, 1898, leaving Cuba independent and the United States in possession of Puerto Rico, Guam, and the Philippines. In addition to the latter three territories, the United States annexed Hawaii, Wake Island, and Samoa, ostensibly as coaling stations. Thus did America acquire almost as an afterthought an overseas empire that extended from the Atlantic Ocean to the South China Sea.

Big guns firing relentlessly, two U.S. battleships (center and right) pursue the fleeing Spanish fleet along the coast of Cuba during the Battle of Santiago. Spain lost all six ships it committed to the battle, which led shortly thereafter to the end of nearly 400 years of Spanish rule in the New World.

THE NAVY ACQUIRES BIG-GUN BATTLESHIPS AND LEARNS TO FLY

The Navy's sometimes inadequate performance during the Spanish-American War had given naval planners much to think about. Out of this thinking came the realization that the Navy needed to reorganize its forces. This was done in 1902. In that year the Atlantic and Pacific fleets were established with eight and three battleships respectively, while the South Atlantic and European Squadrons were abolished and merged into the Atlantic Fleet. The Asiatic Squadron remained in existence, although it was neglected and allowed to deteriorate until, by the mid-1930s, it consisted of little more than a handful of gunboats on China's Yangtze River.

Reorganization was followed by a construction program, begun in 1907, that would increase the Navy's battleship force to 20 vessels. Pay and living conditions were improved, and training schools were opened for the purpose of instructing sailors in the many special tasks required for operating modern warships. Perhaps more importantly from the lowly sailor's standpoint, the traditional meals of "hardtack and salt pork" were banished from the Navy's mess, to be replaced by a healthier, more satisfying diet.

Perhaps the most significant building program undertaken on the Navy's behalf in this era involved, not ships, but a canal—namely, the Panama Canal. The idea of a canal extending across the Central American isthmus to connect the Atlantic and Pacific oceans had been around for centuries; one only had to look at a map of the region to grasp the possibilities that such a waterway offered. But it took a war between the United States and Spain to turn the idea of a canal into a reality. During the Spanish-American War the battleship *Oregon*, dispatched from the West Coast to join the American squadron at Santiago, could only do so after completing a 6,000-mile journey that took it down around Cape Horn and back up through the South Atlantic to the Caribbean. Although the journey was made in

record time, the whole episode proved to the Navy that a Central American canal was essential to the defense of the United States. The sword-rattling presence of German Navy vessels at Samoa in 1889, at Manila Bay in 1898, and again in Venezuela 1902, served to reinforce this certainty.

To obtain the rights to build and use a canal across the Panamanian isthmus, President Theodore Roosevelt was forced to deal with Columbia, which owned the region that is now the nation of Panama. When negotiations stalled, the President resorted to his famous "big stick" method of settling international disputes. In this instance Roosevelt's big stick was the cruiser *Nashville*, which was used to assist a successful Panamanian uprising against Columbian rule. Out of gratitude for the role the *Nashville* played in helping it to gain independence, the new nation of Panama granted the United States the canal right-of-way it sought. In due course, the canal was built, with the first ship passing through its locks in August 1914.

Coming as it did on the heels of two convincing naval victories in the Spanish-American War, the incident involving the *Nashville* was an emphatic demonstration of America's willingness and capability to use sea power in the furtherance of its geopolitical aims. Among those who took note of this fact were the Japanese, who were busy creating a powerful navy of their own. During the Russo-Japanese War in 1905, this navy astounded the world by annihilating a Russian fleet at the Battle of Tsushima. Although the United States and Japan had been on friendly terms since Commodore Matthew Perry sailed into Tokyo Bay in 1855, the Battle of Tsushima ensured that henceforth the two nations would have to regard themselves more as rivals than friends. In short order this rivalry took a

Below: The Panama Canal under construction. Opposite, top: Theodore Roosevelt, campaigning for the presidency in 1904. Opposite, bottom: The Great White Fleet passes through the straits of Magellan.

definite turn for the worse when President Roosevelt negotiated a settlement to the Russo-Japanese War that seemed to favor the Russians. Angered by this development, the Japanese were further outraged by America's efforts to curb Japanese immigration through the passage of racially discriminatory legislation.

Although at this juncture there existed only a remote possibility of war between the United States and Japan, the threat of such a conflict could not be ignored. To impress the Japanese, as well as any other potential enemies, that the U.S. Navy was a force to be reckoned with, President Roosevelt ordered the American battle fleet off on a round-the-world cruise in 1907. As much a publicity stunt as it was a display of military prowess, the 14-month cruise of the "Great White Fleet"—so-named because its ships had been painted white—also served to reveal the strengths and weaknesses of the Navy's at-sea command and control techniques. Interestingly enough, the

Great White Fleet received a warm welcome in every country it visited—even in Japan, where the reception accorded the American vessels and their crews was genuinely enthusiastic.

While the Great White Fleet represented the epitome of naval power, the submarine represented its future—although few individuals in or out of the Navy realized this at the time. John P. Holland was one of the few. In 1900 a submarine that Holland built and named after himself became the first such vessel to be purchased by the Navy. The *Holland* and other early submarines were cramped, dirty, and dangerous to operate; small wonder, then, that their crews only half-humorously dubbed them "pigboats." At first the unreliable performance of submarines made them suspect in the minds of Navy planners, who often held them in the same contempt that sailing ship proponents once reserved for steam-driven warships. With the invention of

Right: *John Holland stands in the conning tower of the* Holland, *the Navy's first submarine.* **Below:** *The* Holland *in Long Island Sound, 1899.*

the gyrocompass in 1908, however, prolonged underwater operations became possible—and the submarine accordingly became a vessel to be taken seriously.

The submarine owed its existence as a practical ship of war to the self-propelled torpedo, a weapon that first made its appearance around 1864. The self-propelled torpedo also gave rise to the torpedo boat, which naturally led to the torpedo boat destroyer. The Navy's first torpedo boat destroyer—or simply "destroyer"—was the *Bainbridge*, commissioned in 1902. A diminutive vessel that displaced a mere 420 tons, the *Bainbridge* could travel at speeds approaching 30 knots, and was armed with torpedoes and three-inch guns.

In contrast to the little *Bainbridge*, the Navy launched the battleships *Michigan* and *South Carolina* in 1909. These powerful ships were modeled

after the Royal Navy's HMS *Dreadnought*, which was launched in 1906. The first of the "all big-gun" battleships, the *Dreadnought* mounted ten 12-inch rifles in five turrets located forward, aft, and amidships. This arrangement was a significant departure from previous battleship designs, which were characterized by an armament consisting of four large guns mounted in two turrets, and several smaller guns mounted in the hull and on the decks. The *Dreadnought*'s ability to concentrate the fire of ten 12-inch rifles on a single target made all other battleship designs obsolete. Like the *Dreadnought*, the new American battleships carried an all big gun armament—eight 12-inch guns mounted in four turrets, two forward and two aft. In an improvement over the *Dreadnought*, however, the forward and after turrets on the *Michigan* and

the *Indiana* were "stepped": that is, the rear turret in each two-turret grouping was raised above the turret in front of it to give all guns a clear field of fire.

The post-Spanish American War years saw the Navy adopt numerous other technological and procedural innovations. This it usually did, however, only after overcoming the tenacious resistance of hide-bound traditionalists. So set in their ways were many of the older admirals that it sometimes took a direct order from the president himself to make changes happen. Angered and dismayed by the wretched display of gunnery at the Battle of Santiago, President Roosevelt demanded (and

continued on page 40

The South Carolina, *launched in 1909, was one of the Navy's first all big-gun battleships. Note the stepped turrets, fore and aft.*

TORPEDOES

The earliest torpedoes were actually bombs mounted on the end of spars projecting from the bows of small boats. They were detonated either by a fuse burning inside a leather tube or, when the technology became available, by an electrical spark. During the American Civil War, such a torpedo on the Confederate submarine *Hunley* was used to sink the Federal frigate *Housatonic*.

In 1866 an Englishman named Robert Whitehead developed the first practical self-propelled torpedo that could operate entirely under water. The Whitehead torpedo was powered by compressed air at about eight miles per hour; it was 11 feet long and was armed with a charge that carried 19 pounds of gun cotton. In 1868 the Austrian Navy became the first to purchase Whitehead's invention. The Austrian naval torpedo carried a warhead with up to 60 pounds of gun cotton. Numerous other countries adopted similar torpedoes.

The United States Navy preferred the Howell torpedo, an inertia-driven device that used a heavy flywheel rather than compressed air to power its propeller. Although the Howell torpedo lacked the speed and range of the Whitehead torpedo, it was nevertheless an extremely stable and accurate weapon.

In 1903, the E.W. Bliss Company of New York purchased the patents to the Whitehead torpedo, which it began to market in an improved version the following year. The United States Navy obtained the manufacturing rights, and in 1908 the Naval Torpedo Station at Newport, Rhode Island, was established.

In the 1890s the torpedo gave rise to a new class of war vessel, the torpedo boat. These were small, high-speed motor boats armed with one or two launching tubes from which torpedoes were ejected by small explosive charges or compressed air. The torpedo boat was supposed to dart within range (usually around 2,000 yards or less) of larger warships and launch their torpedoes.

The torpedo boat spawned the torpedo destroyer, a purpose-built craft designed to hunt down and sink torpedo boats. By the beginning of World War I in 1914, the torpedo destroyer had grown to around 1,000 tons and 315 feet in length. By now full-fledged warships, destroyers mounted fairly powerful batteries of four- to six-inch guns, but their deadliest weapons against larger warships were torpedoes. These the destroyers fired from four or more swivel tubes mounted on their decks. Even large cruisers and battleships were armed with torpedoes. All U.S. destroyers, but no cruisers or battleships, were armed with torpedoes in World War II.

During World War I, torpedoes attracted the most attention as submarine weapons. In particular, German U-boats used torpedoes to deadly effect against Allied shipping in the North and South Atlantic oceans.

Torpedoes were also used to arm aircraft specially designed for that purpose. By the beginning of World War II, the torpedo bomber was a feature of most naval air arms. Generally, pilots executed a torpedo attack by throttling down to about 100 miles per hour and descending in a shallow dive to 50 or 75 feet above the water before releasing their weapons. In the hard laboratory of combat, however, naval aviators quickly discovered this tactic to be tantamount to suicide. At the 1942 Battle of Midway, for example, all 15 planes from one U.S. torpedo plane squadron (Torpedo 8, off the carrier *Hornet*) were shot down while attacking the Japanese fleet. All but one of the American airmen who participated in the attack were killed. Improvements in aircraft, torpedoes, and release mechanisms were

Technicians work on a Mark 48 ADCAP torpedo.

eventually made, and by the end of the war torpedoes were being dropped with great accuracy, and improved chances of air crew survival, from 2,000 feet at 400 miles per hour.

While the torpedo bomber passed out of favor following World War II, aerial-borne torpedoes did not. The postwar aerial torpedoes were antisubmarine rather than antiship weapons. They were carried by long-range submarine-hunting aircraft like the Lockheed P-2 Neptune and P-3 Orion, and aboard submarine-hunting helicopters. Torpedoes were also fitted with more powerful engines, some electrically driven, others using monopropellant fuels that do not require a separate fuel and oxidizer system. The torpedoes were also equipped with sonar seekers, both passive and active.

Today, the U.S. Navy has standardized on two types of torpedoes. The first is the Mark 46, a light torpedo with a 98-pound warhead that is carried by aircraft and surface ships for antisubmarine warfare activities. The Mark 46 weighs 568 pounds and its range, while classified, is estimated to be no more than ten miles. The Mark 46 carries an active and passive sonar for hunting its prey. It is also the weapons part of the CAPTOR (Encapsulated Torpedo) mine. The CAPTOR is placed on the seabed by a submarine, or dropped by a surface vessel or aircraft. It lies dormant until an enemy submarine comes within range of its sensors. When that happens, the CAPTOR launches the Mark 46, which uses its passive sonar to search for the submarine. If it does not acquire the submarine, it will then use its active sonar. Once locked in, the Mark 46 torpedo chases its quarry until it either strikes it or runs out of fuel.

The other torpedo in U.S. Naval service is the Mark 48 Advanced Capability (ADCAP) torpedo. These large torpedoes are 21 inches in diameter and are carried only by submarines. Like the smaller Mark 46, they also contain an active/passive sonar guidance system and will pursue their quarry. Their range is also classified, but is thought to be in excess of 20 miles. The Mark 48 warhead carries 650 pounds of high explosive and is powered by a Gould engine which uses a monopropellant to spin a piston, which is also called a "swashplate." During the initial phase of the Mark 48's run, it can be connected to the submarine by a thin trailing wire. The torpedo's passive sonar searches for an enemy submarine or surface vessel. Data is also relayed through the trailing wires to the submarine, where the latter's larger computers can process the signals for additional information. If the torpedo's passive sonar does not acquire the enemy vessel, then the active sonar is turned on. Once the enemy is locked in, the trailing wire is discarded and the torpedo operates independently.

A destroyer launches a Mark 46 torpedo over the side from a Mark 32 single tube. The Mark 32 tubes may also be grouped in twin or triple arrangements.

continued from page 37
got) the establishment of rigorous training programs to correct this problem. The media instigated another important change. In January 1908 the popular *McClure's Magazine* published an article blasting the inadequate armor protection on U.S. warships, and a turret design that served to promote rather than inhibit flash fires in the ships' powder magazines. The resulting public outcry stung the Navy into rectifying these problems on subsequent warship designs.

Certainly the most revolutionary step taken by the Navy in this period was the creation of an aviation force. Initial movements into this realm were marred by tragedy. In 1908 a Navy lieutenant named George Sweet volunteered to participate in a test flight that Orville Wright was conducting for a group of Navy and Army officers. But an army lieutenant went up in Sweet's place—only to die moments later in a crash that left Wright seriously injured. Despite this accident, Sweet filed a favorable report on Wright's aircraft. Two years later on November 12, 1910, a civilian pilot, Eugene Ely, flew a Curtiss biplane off a ramp erected on the cruiser *Birmingham*, which was anchored off Hampton Roads, Virginia. Ely landed on a nearby beach a few minutes later, thus completing the first ship-to-shore flight in aviation history. In January 1911, Ely made a similar trip in reverse when he took off from the shore of San Francisco Bay and landed a Curtiss biplane on a wooden platform built above the stern of the cruiser *Pennsylvania*. He then flew the aircraft back to shore. Several years would pass before the first American aircraft carrier put to sea, but by these two flights Ely had demonstrated the practicality of such vessels.

Demonstrations like those provided by Ely induced Congress to set aside $25,000 for the purchase of the first Navy aircraft. In due course a naval aviation unit came into being, with Lieutenant Theodore G. Ellyson earning the distinction of becoming the Navy's first aviator. By 1913, Ellyson and men like him had proven in fleet exercises that they and their aircraft could perform a valuable service in the reconnaissance and surveillance role.

In 1914, naval aviation went to war for the first time when Curtis AB-3 flying boats flown from the battleship *Mississippi* were used to search for mines in Vera Cruz harbor and to scout for Army units on shore.

Below: Eugene Ely takes off from the Pennsylvania. *Right:* Theodore Ellyson, the Navy's first pilot.

WORLD WAR I

American troops were withdrawn from Vera Cruz in August, 1914. That same month, Europe was plunged headlong into the cataclysm of World War I. Although neither the government nor the people of the United States wanted anything to do with the war, the U.S. Navy continued to grow as if it intended otherwise. Before the end of 1914 the *New Mexico*-class battleships were authorized, and the battleship *Nevada* was launched, thus becoming the first oil-powered battleship to enter U.S. Navy service.

World War I at sea initially went well for the British, who used their fine navy to institute an effective blockade against Germany and its allies. Germany countered this tactic with the use of submarines, or "U-boats." A desperate struggle for mastery of the Atlantic ensued—a struggle in which the Germans steadily gained the upper hand. German submarines

subsequently sank so many cargo-ladened ships bound from the United States to the British Isles that Britain found itself facing critical food shortages by the spring of 1917.

Even so, the submarines proved to be a mixed blessing for Germany. While the U-boats enjoyed considerable success in interdicting the flow of supplies to Britain, they also outraged the American public with their indiscriminate attacks on neutral shipping. The fact that a large proportion of that shipping flew the American flag only served to deepen this sense of outrage. What it all boiled down to was a question of sovereignty—long a sensitive issue for Americans. Since the War of 1812 and before, the principle of free trade and travel on the high seas was one that Americans had shown a willingness to uphold, through force of arms if necessary. The Germans either failed to understand this fact or, if they did, chose to ignore it. In the event,

repeated warnings from the United States government over the use of unrestricted submarine warfare went unheeded in Germany. On May 7, 1915, a German U-boat sank the British passenger liner *Lusitania* off the Irish coast. Of the 1,198 men, women, and children killed when the British ship went down, 128 were Americans. In America, public outrage reached new heights. Germany apologized for the incident, paid an indemnity, and ordered its submarine captains to avoid attacking large ocean liners. But to no avail. Formerly neutral in their sentiments, Americans now began to view Germany as a potential enemy.

The sinking of the *Lusitania* spurred the United States to begin a dramatic military buildup. "A navy second to

A remarkable photograph of a German U-boat halting an American freighter on the high seas, c. 1915.

none" became the rallying cry in Congress, which in 1916 authorized the building of four new battleships, as well as scores of lesser vessels. Another step forward in modernizing the Navy was taken in 1917 when Congress created the Chief of Naval Operations (CNO) post, which would direct the Navy's efforts as it prepared for war.

In February 1917, Germany resumed unrestricted submarine warfare. The German High Command knew full well that submarine attacks on neutral shipping would likely bring the United States into the war, but it was gambling that Germany could achieve victory before American troops arrived in France in any significant numbers. By April 6, 1917, enough American lives had been lost to German submarine attacks to compel President Woodrow Wilson to ask Congress for a declaration of war. Congress complied with the President's request, thus entering America in the so-called "war to end all wars." The Navy reacted quickly. On May 4, Destroyer Division 8 was dispatched to Ireland, from where it would patrol Atlantic sea lanes leading from America to the British Isles.

The American Navy's arrival in Ireland was timely, since German submarines were now sinking British merchant vessels faster than they could be replaced. In May, Britain's food supplies fell to less than three weeks reserve. Despite this grim situation, however, the Royal Navy had not been convoying merchant shipping in the North Sea and the Atlantic. British naval leaders believed that convoys would fail as a protective measure due to the inability of undisciplined merchant ships to steam in a tight formation. The British much preferred to hunt the U-boats down before the Germans could attack merchant vessels. It fell to U.S. Navy leaders to persuade the British to adopt the convoy system. Two test convoys were assembled in May at Halifax, Canada, and Gibraltar, and both sailed to England with only one

The U.S. Navy's Destroyer Division 8 arrives at Queenstown (now Cobh), Ireland, May 4, 1917.

ship lost to U-boat attack. The Royal Navy, now convinced, instituted regular convoying procedures.

Although eight U.S. battleships were stationed in British waters to counter the threat of German surface warships, the twin tasks of providing convoy protection and hunting submarines comprised the U.S. Navy's primary duties during World War I. The more specific job of ferrying American troops to the European continent went to the Navy's Cruiser and Transport Force. By the war's end this force had transported two million U.S. troops to France and Great Britain without a single loss in ships or men.

To perform such duties, the Navy grew to an unprecedented size—from a prewar strength of 67,000 men and women, to over half a million by 1918. The naval air arm also expanded, from 282 pilots and maintenance personnel operating just 54 aircraft in 1916, to 37,400 pilots and maintenance personnel operating 2,107 aircraft (mostly of French or British manufacture) in late 1918. The Marines had also formed an aviation unit that grew to a total of 1,462 officers and enlisted men. Navy and Marine airmen flew bombing missions against German and Austrian submarine pens on the Belgian and Adriatic coasts and provided an air guard for convoys in the Atlantic, the North Sea, and the English Channel.

Below: The British troop transport Lapland *displays a camouflage scheme intended to confuse German U-boats.*
Right: *This poster urging Americans to buy war bonds shows the gun crew of a U.S. destroyer in action.*

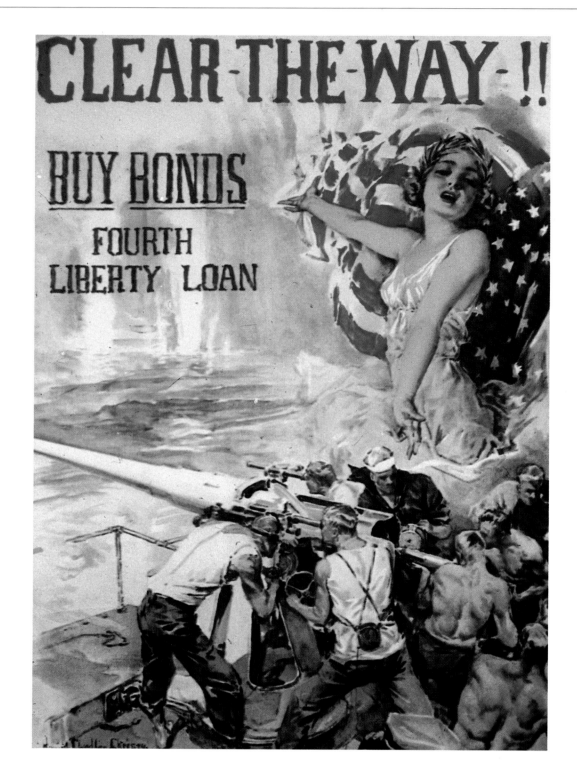

BETWEEN WORLD WARS

World War I ended with an armistice on November 11, 1918. The guns in Europe had scarcely fallen silent when President Wilson urged Congress to continue the wartime naval buildup that was intended to produce a navy that was "second to none." This, despite American hopes that the war would result in the kind of lasting peace that the war to end all wars was supposed to guarantee. Wilson was evidently not convinced that such a peace was attainable—at least not without a strong navy. The President's urgings in this regard were based in part on his concerns over Japanese ambitions in the Pacific. Riding the crest of its own naval expansion wave, Japan had seized German colonies and possessions in China, Manchuria, and the Pacific. Thus, the Japanese had gotten ownership of three Pacific island chains—the Marshalls, the Marianas, and Gilberts—that lay astride or in close proximity to U.S. trade routes and lines of communication to Hawaii and the Philippines. But Japan wasn't Wilson's only concern. The President was also leery of Britain. There was no getting around the fact that America was now Britain's chief commercial rival. History had shown that Britain did not suffer such rivals gladly, and Wilson wanted the Navy to be prepared for any trouble that might arise between America and its former ally.

By and large, Congress ignored Wilson's concerns—rightfully so in Britain's case, but erroneously so with regard to Japan. Like the American public, Congress was in an isolationist mood. It was also in the mood for disarmament. After refusing to approve U.S. admission to the League of Nations—a pet project of Wilson's—Congress set about the task of reducing the size of the Navy. In 1922, the United States, Britain, Japan, France, and Italy agreed on a naval disarmament formula that limited the number of warships that each nation could maintain. Under the terms of this Washington Naval Treaty, Britain would be allowed to retain 22 battleships and battle cruisers, while the U.S. and Japan could retain 18 and ten of these ships, respectively.

The effect of the Washington Naval Treaty was to establish Japan as the most powerful Navy in the Western Pacific. The situation worsened when the United States and Great Britain agreed not to further fortify their naval bases west of Pearl Harbor in the Hawaiian Islands, including those in Singapore and the Philippines. Japan, in turn, pledged not to build or fortify any naval bases outside the home islands—a pledge it did not keep.

By the middle 1920s U.S. Navy manpower had fallen to about 100,000 men, while restricted annual budgets had severely limited the Navy's ability to keep its ships maintained and at sea. In the meantime, the Japanese Navy was steadily growing in size and strength. In angry response to the 1924 passage of the Johnson Act (which ended Japanese immigration to the United States), Japan laid down 12 new heavy cruisers armed with eight-inch guns. But in the United States, an attempt in 1927 to fund seven new *Northhampton*-class cruisers was quashed by President Coolidge, who canceled all but two of the vessels. In 1930, the Navy suffered a further setback with the 1936 signing of the London Naval Treaty, which extended

the moratorium on battleships. Against this background of disarmament, the Japanese military intervened in Manchuria in 1931. What many historians have since regarded as the first shots of the Second World War were fired in this distant Asian realm.

During this period air power became a dominant theme in progressive Navy circles. In 1919 Navy aviators demonstrated the potential of air power by attempting to fly across the Atlantic Ocean in three Curtiss flying boats. Taking off from the naval air station at Rockaway Beach, New York, the flying boats were to proceed on a course that would take them to Lisbon, making stops in between in Newfoundland and the Azores Islands. Only one of the flying boats, the NC-4, actually completed the journey, but the mission was nevertheless counted as an important success for naval aviation. In 1926, another laurel was added to the standard of Navy aviation when Lieutenant Commander Richard

The 1920s and '30s saw many advances in aviation technology, such as the enclosed cockpits and retractable landing gear on these TBD-1 Devastator torpedo bombers.

Byrd and Floyd Bennet, a civilian pilot, crossed the North Pole in a Fokker Trimotor. In 1929, Byrd performed a similar feat over the South Pole, this time flying a Ford Trimotor named *Floyd Bennet*.

Another big boost to naval aviation was provided, oddly enough, by the army. In July 1921, Army aircraft commanded by Brigadier General Billy Mitchell bombed and sank a condemned German battleship off the Virginia Capes, thus demonstrating

that attack from the air was a viable tactic against warships. One year later, the converted collier *Langley* became the first aircraft carrier to enter Navy service.

In 1927 the carrier *Langley* was joined by the *Lexington* and *Saratoga*, which were saved from the scrap heap by their conversion from battle cruisers to aircraft carriers. That same year Congress authorized the *Ranger*, which was to be the Navy's first purpose-built aircraft carrier. Proof

that carrier-borne aircraft could be used in an offensive role was supplied in 1929 when dive bombers from the *Saratoga* staged a successful mock-attack on the Panama Canal. In 1932, aircraft from the *Lexington* and the *Saratoga* staged another mock-attack on the naval base at Pearl Harbor. The lessons to be learned from these attacks were heeded not only by American naval officers, but by members of the Japanese Navy as well. And the Japanese proved

Opposite, top: The Langley, *the Navy's first aircraft carrier. Opposite, bottom: The Navy's first purpose-built aircraft carrier was the* Ranger. *Above: The* USS Macon *over Manhattan, c. 1933. Right: The* Lexington *steams past Diamond Head, Hawaii, in 1933.*

especially apt pupils, as they would demonstrate nine years later during their own attack on Pearl Harbor.

In addition to aircraft, the Navy experimented with blimps and rigid airships, or dirigibles, during the interwar years. The Navy acquired one dirigible, the renamed *Los Angeles*, from Germany, and built three airships—the *Shenandoah*, *Akron*, and *Macon*. The large rigid airships were uniquely beautiful craft, but as events

were to prove, they were terribly unsafe. The *Shenandoah* crashed in 1925, and the *Akron* crashed in 1933, killing 72 crewmen as well as the Chief of the Bureau of Naval Aeronautics, Rear Admiral William A. Moffett. The *Macon* crashed in February 1925, killing two men. After the *Macon*'s crash, no more rigid airships were built and the *Los Angeles* was retired from service. The Navy had more success with blimps, which were used during World War II for antisubmarine patrol off America's east coast.

Like the Navy's aviation arm, the Marine Corps was also undergoing a period of experimentation. This involved the development of equipment and tactics for waging amphibious warfare, a role perfectly in keeping with the hard-charging, rough-and-ready image the Marines had fashioned for themselves.

With the onset of the Great Depression in the early 1930s, Navy development lagged as the financially strapped nation instituted massive cuts in military spending. This trend was somewhat ameliorated, however, with the 1932 election of Franklin D. Roosevelt to the presidency. A former Secretary of the Navy and cousin of Theodore Roosevelt, Franklin Roosevelt gave the Navy a monetary shot in the arm by including naval warship construction in the National Industrial Recovery Act. Ultimately, the Recovery Act provided funding for the construction of some 32 warships (including the carriers *Yorktown* and *Enterprise*), as well as 1,000 naval aircraft.

The construction of new aircraft coincided with the development of aviation-related technologies. Supercharged engines were developed that enabled aircraft to fly higher than was previously thought possible. New radios did away with the telegraph key, and vastly improved in-flight communications. And in the late 1930s

retractable landing gear, folding wings, and canopy-enclosed cockpits became a standard feature of carrier-borne aircraft, even as streamlined monoplanes replaced the venerable but obsolete biplane design.

Coming close on the heels of the National Industrial Recovery Act, the 1933 Vinson-Trammel Act authorized a total of 102 new ships as part of an effort to maintain naval parity with Japan. Such parity was not easy to come by. After serving notice in 1934 that they would no longer abide by the terms of the Washington and London naval treaties, the Japanese embarked on a huge naval construction program. In 1937 the Japanese laid down the 68,000-ton *Yamato* and *Musashi*, which were to be the largest battleships ever built. That same year, the United States laid down the 35,000-ton battleships *North Carolina* and *Washington*. Also in 1937, relations with Japan were strained to the breaking point when Japanese aircraft bombed and strafed the U.S. Navy gunboat *Panay* on the Yangtze River in China. A quick and sincere apology from Japan defused the resultant crisis in relations with the United States, which in any event was not prepared to go to war with the Japanese over this incident.

In Europe, meanwhile, tensions were mounting as a rearmed Germany became increasingly hostile toward those nations unfortunate enough to share a border with the Nazi state. Then, on September 1, 1939, Germany invaded Poland, thus provoking a declaration of war from Britain and France. World War II had begun in Europe.

Opposite: *President Franklin D. Roosevelt signs the Vinson-Trammel Act.* **Below:** *The* Panay *sinks in the Yangtze River following a 1937 attack by Japanese bombers.*

WORLD WAR II

Germany's conquest of Poland was accomplished in less than a month. A six-month lull in the European land war ensued, to be followed in the spring of 1940 with German invasions of Norway, Denmark, the Low Countries, and France. In quick succession one European nation after another fell to the German Army. By July 1940, Great Britain stood alone against what appeared to be the irresistible tide of German conquest.

The possibility that Britain might be conquered by Germany was cause for much concern in the United States. In particular, U.S. naval strategists were fearful that the German Navy would absorb His Majesty's warships in the event of Britain's collapse. This was a nightmarish prospect for the U.S. Navy, which was already hard-pressed to cope with rising Japanese naval strength in the Pacific. But help was on the way. Even as German troops were overrunning Western Europe, Congress was appropriating funds for a "two-ocean" navy that would be enlarged by the construction of 257 ships—among them, a new class of fast battleships, and 27 aircraft carriers.

The United States also sought to improve its strategic position in the Atlantic by providing material assistance to Britain. Such aid was forthcoming in September of 1940 when President Roosevelt, acting in response to an urgent plea by British Prime Minister Winston Churchill, sent 50 World War I-vintage four-stack destroyers to Britain in exchange for 99-year leases on British bases extending from Canada to the Caribbean. The following March, Congress took another step on Britain's behalf by passing the Lend-Lease Act. This law made available credit for the purchase of arms by nations whose security President Roosevelt deemed vital to the defense of the United States.

So far, America had managed to stay out of the war, if not wholly apart from it. As was the case in World War I, however, the nation was drawn ever closer to the conflict by the threat of German U-boats. In mid-1941 the U.S. Navy responded to this threat by

escorting convoys from the eastern seaboard of the United States to Iceland—where Royal Navy warships provided escort the rest of the way to Britain. The Germans reciprocated in kind. Instead of operating singly, the U-boats began attacking convoys in "wolf packs" that would eventually number as many as 20 submarines, all directed by radio from U-boat headquarters in Kernevel, France (and later in Paris). Such attacks are remembered today as the most harrowing aspect of what came to be known as the Battle of the Atlantic. Being officially neutral, American warships had orders not to attack U-boats and German surface warships unless fired upon. Despite similar strictures on German U-boats, however, incidents did occur. In a two-month period, from September to October of 1941, U-boats attacked three American destroyers. Of the three, the *Greer* escaped unharmed, the *Kearney* was damaged, and the *Reuben James* was sunk. When the *Reuben James* went down, only 45 members of its 160-man crew survived. In light of the fact that America was not supposed to be at war, these were significant losses. But they soon paled next to the disaster the Japanese visited upon the Pacific Fleet in Pearl Harbor.

The attack on Pearl Harbor came at the end of several months of

diplomatic wrangling and economic skirmishing between the United States and Japan. The bone of contention in all this was China, where Japan had been conducting a brutal but inconclusive war of conquest since 1937. By the end of the decade the war in China had seriously depleted Japanese economic resources, prompting the Japanese military to contemplate the conquest of the oil and mineral-rich regions of Southeast Asia and the Dutch East Indies. The Japanese took their first step in this direction by occupying French Indo-China in July 1941. In retaliation President Roosevelt imposed an embargo on the export of oil and steel to Japan. This in turn decided Japan on a course of action centered on the capture of the Dutch East Indies. To achieve that goal, the Japanese would first have to eliminate the British and American navies in the Pacific. That meant attacking the installation at Pearl Harbor, where America's Pacific Fleet was based.

The Japanese made their move on the morning of December 7, 1941. Some 360 aircraft from six carriers swept in from the north over Oahu Island, catching the unprepared Americans at Pearl Harbor completely by surprise. At the conclusion of the attack, over 2,000 American soldiers and sailors were dead, nearly 2,000 more were wounded, some 265 U.S.

aircraft had been destroyed, and eight battleships had been sunk or badly damaged. But the Japanese had missed the real prize: the U.S. aircraft carriers, which were at sea.

Pearl Harbor was still a shambles when, three days later, Germany declared war against the United States. This act nicely coincided with the "Europe First" strategy that had recently been formulated by U.S. and British military leaders. Europe First gave priority to winning the war against Germany—a task that was, to say the least, easier said than done. As if to mock Allied aspirations, German U-boats were soon sinking ships along America's eastern seaboard, often within sight of land. When the Navy responded with an intensified antisubmarine warfare effort in this

Opposite, above: A German U-boat in the Atlantic. Top: The West Virginia *and the* Tennessee *burn after the Japanese attack at Pearl Harbor. Right: Sailors at the Ford Island Naval Air Station are stunned by the explosion of the battleship* Arizona *at Pearl Harbor.*

A careless word...

...A NEEDLESS SINKING

rocket-propelled depth charges, and improved sonar and radar. With the aid of these devices, plus a great deal of courage on the part of the men operating them, Allied ships and aircraft sank 41 U-boats in the mid-Atlantic in May 1943. Dismayed, Admiral Karl Dönitz, the chief of the German submarine force, shifted the focus of U-boat activities to the South Atlantic. The change in locale brought them little success and much failure as, one after the other, the U-boats were set upon and sunk by U.S. Navy "hunter-killer" groups consisting of escort carriers, destroyers, and frigates. Wolfpacks continued to operate until very late in the war, but with ever diminishing returns. It was Dönitz's hope that a new U-boat type then under construction, the Type XXIII, would reverse this trend. The Type XXIIIs were fitted with snorkels, a periscopelike device that allowed the submarine to recharge its batteries while submerged; and, they could move faster underwater than on the surface. But only a few of these vessels made it to sea before Germany surrendered in May 1945.

Naval action in the Atlantic was not exclusively a submarine-versus-warship affair. In Arctic waters, convoys bound for the Russian ports of Murmansk and Archangel often had to run a gauntlet of surface raiders and aircraft as well as U-boats. Long hours of daylight during the summer increased the likelihood of such attacks, while rough seas and freezing conditions made winter crossings and combat an almost unendurable agony.

In the Mediterranean theater the threat of German and Italian surface warships had been largely neutralized by the Royal Navy by the time the Americans arrived on the scene. Nor were U-boats much of a factor. The U.S. Navy was thus able to devote much of its energies to providing direct support for Allied amphibious operations in North Africa, Sicily, and along the Italian coast.

The Pacific was a different story. The conflict in that ocean had very quickly shaped up into a war in which navies would play a decisive role. In the first months of the war the battleship-bereft U.S. Navy did what it

area, the U-boats shifted their activities to the Caribbean and the Gulf of Mexico. There, in May of 1942, U-boats sank 41 ships totaling 220,000 tons. Chased out of these balmy waters by the U.S. Navy, the U-boats returned to their old haunts in the mid-Atlantic, operating in a 600-mile-wide zone (dubbed the "Black Pit") that lay beyond the reach of Allied land-based aircraft. The U-boat wolf packs sank an average of 500,000 tons every month from August to December 1942, and, after a winter lull, 563,000 tons in March 1943.

But March 1943 marked the high point of the U-boat offensive. The

Allies fought back with B-24 Liberator bombers equipped with depth charges. These aircraft were capable of providing convoys with air cover to the Black Pit and beyond. The advent of small Allied escort carriers carrying about 20 aircraft were even more effective in providing air cover for the convoys. The U-boats were further stymied by Allied warships fitted with high-frequency direction finders (HF/DF), nicknamed "huff duff," which located wolf packs by homing on German radio signals. The Allied ships were also equipped with new forward-firing "hedgehog"

could to strike back at the Japanese. Aircraft from the carrier *Enterprise* raided Japanese bases in the Gilbert and Marshall islands, while the *Lexington* sent its aircraft against the Wake and Marcus islands. Farther west, the Asiatic Fleet withdrew from the Philippines and moved south to the Dutch East Indies, there to join a combined American-British-Dutch-Australian (ABDA) fleet. Formed to contest the Japanese invasion of the Dutch East Indies, the ABDA fleet fought hard in several engagements but was ultimately destroyed in the Battle of the Java Sea in February 1942. In April, 16 Army B-25 bombers commanded by Lieutenant Colonel

James H. Doolittle flew off the deck of the carrier *Hornet* to raid Tokyo and its environs. Little damage was done by Doolittle's raiders, but the attack did manage to raise American morale—which was certainly in need of a boost in those dark early months of the Pacific war.

In the first week of May the Navy achieved more substantial results in the Coral Sea. Having broken the Japanese code, the Americans were able to position two aircraft carriers (*Yorktown* and *Lexington*) in the path of a Japanese invasion fleet that was headed for Port Morseby in New Guinea. The subsequent battle was a duel of aircraft carriers—or, more

*Opposite: An American freighter falls prey to U-boat attack in this propaganda poster. **Above:** The* Lexington, *sinking during the Battle of the Coral Sea.* **Inset:** *Doolittle's raiders on the* Hornet.

precisely, of carrier aircraft. As such, it was the first sea battle in history in which the warships of the two contending fleets never fired a shot at each other. Instead of slugging it out with big guns, the American and Japanese fleets did their fighting with fighters, dive bombers, and torpedo planes. The Americans were hardest hit, losing the big carrier *Lexington* in exchange for the small Japanese carrier *Shoho*. But the Japanese southward thrust had been halted; and for that reason, naval historians rightly regard the Battle of the Coral Sea as an American strategic victory.

Their aims in the South Pacific frustrated, the Japanese turned their attention to Midway Island. A remote outpost in the central Pacific, Midway was to serve as the locus for a battle of annihilation against the U.S. Pacific Fleet. That done, the Japanese intended to invade the Hawaiian Islands and thereby eject U.S. military power from the Pacific. To achieve these objectives, the Japanese assembled a powerful fleet consisting of four big aircraft carriers, one small carrier, nine battleships, a host of cruisers and destroyers, and 12 transports carrying 5,000 assault troops. The size of this force was a clear indication that the Japanese had planned well for the upcoming battle. Unfortunately for the success of their endeavor, they had not planned in secrecy. Thanks once again to American decoding efforts, the U.S. Navy knew what the Japanese had in mind. The Navy prepared itself accordingly. Three aircraft carriers— the *Enterprise*, *Yorktown*, and *Hornet*—were dispatched toward Midway to ambush the enemy fleet.

Fought on June 3–6, 1942, the Battle of Midway started badly for the Americans. At Midway Island an entire Marine fighter squadron was all but shot out of the sky, and Midway-based bombers failed to score a single hit on the Japanese fleet. The crisis point of the battle came on the second day, which witnessed the slaughter of American torpedo bombers, followed by an American dive bomber attack that sank no less than three of the big Japanese carriers. The fourth big Japanese carrier was sunk later in the day, while the *Yorktown* was damaged. Two days later American carrier aircraft sank the cruiser *Mogami*, and a Japanese submarine sank the crippled *Yorktown*. These final losses were irrelevant to the outcome of the battle. By then, it was quite evident that the Americans had achieved a victory of

SBD Dauntless *dive bombers attack a Japanese cruiser in this artist's rendering of the Battle of Midway.*

astounding proportions, one destined to alter the entire course of the war. The shattered Japanese fleet acknowledged this fact by withdrawing on a westerly heading, moving in the direction that the Pacific war would follow from that day forward.

Midway had been a defensive battle. Two months later the Americans went over to the offensive in the Southwest Pacific and the Solomon Islands. On August 7, Marines from the First Marine Division stormed ashore on the Japanese-held islands of Guadalcanal and Tulagi in the Solomons. On the night of August 9, a Japanese cruiser task force retaliated, sinking four American cruisers and one Australian cruiser at the Battle of Savo Island (just off Guadalcanal). It was the first of many naval battles to be fought in this area, which became the graveyard of so many sunken ships that it was nicknamed "Ironbottom Sound." The Japanese Navy demonstrated superior fighting ability in these clashes, but the U.S. Navy prevailed through raw courage, fierce determination, and not a little skill of its own. Army troops replaced the Marines on Guadalcanal in December and by February 9, 1943, the last Japanese troops had been withdrawn from the island.

On the other side of the world, the Allies were contemplating an invasion of the European Continent. Many Allied leaders and officials wanted to open a second front in Europe at the earliest possible date. This seemed urgently necessary to relieve the pressure on the Soviet Union, which was just then locked in a life-or-death struggle with Germany. But the military strength of Hitler's "Fortress Europe" was as yet too great for the Allies to challenge successfully. This the Allies discovered during their abortive raid on the French coastal town of Dieppe. Staged on August 19, 1942, by a combined force of British and Canadian troops, the Dieppe raid was undertaken to test German preparedness for the kind of seaborne invasion a second front offensive would entail. The result was a bloody fiasco for the Allies, who lost over 3,000 men before the raid was finally called off at the end of the day.

It wasn't until the summer of 1944 that sufficient forces and equipment

could be marshalled to mount an assault on the Continent. On June 6, 1944, the largest invasion fleet ever assembled landed some 200,000 American, British, Canadian, and French troops on the Normandy beaches. The troop transports were guarded by a massive armada of warships, including the battleships *Texas*, *Arkansas*, and *Nevada*. Nearly 800 warships bombarded German coastal fortifications. The battleships pounded away with their big guns at distant roads, junctions, and other communications points, thus inhibiting the flow of German reinforcements to the beachhead. Cruisers mounted a steady bombardment on inland artillery positions, while destroyers worked so close to shore that their gunners were able to pick out targets with the naked eye. The only major ship lost in the invasion was the U.S. destroyer *Corry*, which was sunk by a German mine off Utah Beach.

Well before the Allied landings in Normandy, the Americans were

Above: A pair of F6F Hellcats, the Navy's premier carrier-based fighters during World War II. **Left:** A portion of the Allied armada that assaulted Normandy on D-Day.

advancing steadily across the Pacific, leapfrogging from one island to the next as they moved ever closer to Japan itself. Navy and Marine forces took Tarawa in November 1943, Kwajalein in January 1944, and Eniwetok in February 1944. On June 15 the Marines landed on Saipan in the Marianas. Four days later the Japanese contested the landing with a fleet that included nine aircraft carriers and five battleships. The resulting Battle of the Philippine Sea (also known as "The Great Marianas Turkey Shoot") ended in a virtual slaughter for the inexperienced but brave Japanese pilots who assaulted the American fleet. In all, the Japanese lost 373 of 473 aircraft to American fighters and antiaircraft fire, plus two aircraft carriers to submarine attack. The next day, in a daring raid at sunset, American pilots sank a third Japanese carrier, damaged a fourth,

American submarine blockade was even more restrictive than the German submarine net thrown around Britain in 1941. An island nation that had to import most of its raw materials (including 100 percent of its oil), Japan was extremely vulnerable to submarine warfare. Yet the Japanese Navy did not devote much effort to antisubmarine activities. Nor did it do much to protect Japanese merchant shipping, even when the latter was organized into convoys. As a result, U.S. submarines operated with increasing effectiveness as the war went on. At war's end, nearly five million tons of Japanese merchant shipping and 276 warships had been lost to American submarines. For their part, the Americans had lost fewer than 50 submarines to Japanese antisubmarine warfare forces.

On October 20, 1944, American forces under the command of General Douglas MacArthur landed on the Philippine island of Leyte, prompting the Japanese to assemble the remnants of their fleet for a counter-strike. American code-breakers were aware of the Japanese plans, but could not pinpoint the precise location or approach route of the enemy naval forces—which were steaming for the Philippines in four separate groups, from four different bases. On October 25, Admiral William Halsey's Third Fleet turned back Admiral Jisiburo Ozawa's Northern Force at the Battle of Cape Engano. At the Battle of the Surigao Strait on October 24–25, Admiral Thomas Kinkaid's Seventh Fleet defeated the Japanese Southern Force under the command of Admiral Shoji Nishimura. The following day off Samar, Carrier Escort Group Taffy 3, which consisted of six small escort carriers and seven destroyers and destroyer escorts, engaged Admiral Takeo Kurita's Center Force—a powerful squadron that had five battleships, including the enormous *Yamato* and the *Musashi*. Center Force sank two of the American escort carriers, but failed to break through to the American beachhead on Leyte. The Battle of Leyte Gulf, as this series of engagements was called, was the largest sea battle in history. When it was over, the Japanese Navy was finished as a major fighting force,

having lost a catastrophic total of four aircraft carriers, three battleships, nine cruisers, and ten destroyers.

After Leyte Gulf, the primary threat to the U.S. Navy came from kamikaze aircraft. The kamikaze, or "divine wind," were suicide aircraft that took their name from a massive typhoon that had saved Japan from a Mongol invasion centuries earlier. They were flown mainly by young, inexperienced, but unquestionably brave pilots, who deliberately crashed their bomb-laden aircraft into American warships. The Japanese flung swarms of kamikazes at the U.S. fleet during the battle for Okinawa, which lasted from April through June of 1945. Due to the efforts of the suicide bombers, 34 American ships were sunk and 368 were damaged, while some 4,900 sailors were killed and another 4,800 were wounded. Yet the kamikazes' accomplishments were of little military value. For all their sacrifices, they had sunk no ship larger than a destroyer, and they had not halted the American offensive.

The last voyage of the mighty battleship *Yamato* was also a kamikaze mission. Sent to Okinawa with only enough fuel for a one-way voyage, the *Yamato* was spotted in the East China Sea and sunk by American aircraft, losing 2,488 crewmen when it went down.

After Okinawa, the Navy and the Marines prepared with great trepidation for the invasion of Japan itself. Then, on August 6, an American B-29 bomber dropped an atomic bomb on the Japanese city of Hiroshima. On August 9, another B-29 dropped a second atomic bomb on Nagasaki. Convinced by the devastation wrought by these two bombs that further resistance was useless, the Japanese capitulated. On September 2, 1945, the ritual of surrender was enacted in Tokyo Bay on board the battleship *Missouri*, which flew the same flag that had flown over the Capitol in Washington D.C. on the day Pearl Harbor was attacked.

and sank two fleet oilers. In the wake of that climactic battle, two more islands in the Marianas—Guam and Tinian—were taken in July.

While American surface forces were fighting in the mid-Pacific, American submarines were carrying the war literally to the shores of Japan. The

Left: This photograph of Task Force 38, taken in December 1944, provides a graphic image of U.S. naval power in the Pacific during the final year of the war.

ANOTHER PEACE, ANOTHER WAR

The end of World War II presented the U.S. military with a new adversary: the Soviet Union. The threat the Soviet Union posed to a Europe devastated by six years of war was not lost on President Harry S Truman, who was instrumental in forming the Truman Doctrine to "support the cause of freedom wherever it was threatened." In 1946, Truman showed that he meant business by sending American advisers to Greece to help put down a communist insurgency, and by dispatching American warships to both Greece and Turkey as a warning to the Soviet Union against further encroachments in that sphere. Further evidence of Truman's determination to contain the Soviet Union was provided in 1948, when U.S. Navy warships

called on Italian ports to discourage an armed takeover of the government by Italian communists; and again in 1949, when Navy and Air Force transports were used to airlift supplies into West Berlin during the Soviet blockade of that city.

The major test of American resolve to defend other nations against communist aggression came in Korea. Long a part of the Japanese empire, Korea regained its independence in 1945. The country was almost immediately split at the 38th parallel, with the northern half acquiring a Soviet-installed communist government, and the south acquiring a nominally democratic government that was backed by the United States. In an effort to force the union of the two Koreas, the North Korean Army attacked across the 38th parallel on June 25, 1950.

The North Korean invasion caught the U.S. Navy—and indeed, the entire American military establishment—in an unprepared state. As usual after any war in which America was involved, victory in World War II had been followed by a rush to demobilize. Having grown from 325,000 men and women in 1940 to 3,400,000 million men and women by August 1945, the Navy subsequently declined to 500,000 in 1946, and to 412,000 in 1950. The nearly 10,000 ships that had been under construction when the war ended were canceled immediately, another 2,000 ships were placed in mothballs, and almost 3,000 were declared surplus and sold for scrap, or sold or given to foreign governments.

In the halls of Congress and the Pentagon alike, it was believed by many that the imposition of drastic force reductions was appropriate

for the Navy. Impressed by the effectiveness of the strategic bombing campaigns over Germany and Japan, the men who held this view reasoned that aircraft carriers had been rendered obsolete by long-range bombers carrying nuclear bombs. Of course, this view was not shared by many high-ranking Navy officers and Navy proponents, who argued that the large aircraft carrier was still vital to the nation's defense. The National Security Act of 1947 aimed to resolve the controversy. Under the provisions of this act, the Air Force became independent of the Army, the Navy retained its air arm, and the Marine Corps remained a service separate from the Army. Additionally, the secretaries of the Army and Navy were removed from their cabinet positions and made subordinate to the Secretary of Defense.

But this did not end controversy in the military establishment. When Secretary of Defense Louis Johnson—who favored the B-36 program—canceled construction of the 60,000-ton aircraft carrier *United States* in April 1949, he provoked an uproar in Navy circles that has come to be known as the "Admirals' Revolt." The admirals involved in this bitter dispute pointed out that the B-36 was essentially useless for any kind of conflict except an all-out, all-annihilating nuclear exchange between the super powers. In the event, the *United States* was not built and the Air Force got the B-36, but the Navy's position focused American public opinion on the need to maintain a strong Navy that was capable of fighting limited conventional wars.

The Korean War was a textbook example of a conventional war in the nuclear age. It also provided ample opportunity for the Navy to demonstrate its worth in such wars. The Navy got involved in the conflict shortly after the United Nations Security Council (minus an absent Soviet Union) voted on June 27, 1950, to provide military assistance to South Korea. Even so, it was almost too late in arriving on the scene. Advancing swiftly, North Korean forces soon had a United Nations (UN) army (which consisted largely of American and South Korean troops) hemmed in around the port city of Pusan on the southeast coast. During this period naval aircraft from *Essex*-class

Opposite: *A jubilant President Harry S Truman reviews the U.S. fleet shortly after the surrender of Japan.* **Below:** *View of the UN landings at Inchon, Korea.*

carriers like the *Valley Forge* struck hard and often at North Korean supply lines and troop concentrations. Warships from the United States and Great Britain were also used to shell North Korean positions along the coast. In September, 1950, the U.S. Navy assembled a task force that landed the First Marine Division at Inchon, a port city on Korea's west coast near Seoul. At the same time, U.S. Army forces broke out of the Pusan perimeter. The North Korean Army was caught between the two forces and crushed.

The war now turned into a rout, with UN forces driving the shattered remnants of the North Korean army back across the 38th parallel to the Yalu River on the Chinese border. The only setback to the UN advance occurred at Wonsan on the northeast coast, where a second amphibious landing was held up for eight days while the Navy labored to clear some 3,000 mines from the harbor. Then, on November 25, Chinese forces entered the war in vast numbers. Once again, the UN army was forced to retreat. On Christmas Eve, 1950, 105,000 American and Korean troops, and 91,000 Korean civilians were evacuated through the port of Hungnam. By the following summer the front line stretched across the Korean peninsula just north of the 38th parallel, where it would remain with only minor fluctuations until a negotiated settlement ended the war in June 1953.

A huge explosion rips through the harbor installations of Hungnam, Korea, as the USS Begor *receives the last elements of the UN army to be evacuated through that port on December 25, 1950. The UN forces had just completed a harrowing, month-long fighting withdrawal from the border between China and North Korea, where it came perilously close to being annihilated by a Chinese army attacking in overwhelming numbers.*

CONTROVERSY AND COLD WAR

During the Korean War the Navy proved that it still had an important role to play in the modern era. As a result the Navy was now made the beneficiary of funding that, by 1955, would result in the simultaneous construction of six new supercarriers. Pro-Navy sentiment in the defense establishment would also produce the *Nautilus*, which began sea trials in January of 1955, as the world's first nuclear-powered submarine. Nearly three years later on December 2, 1957, construction began on the *Long Beach*, the Navy's first nuclear-powered surface warship, and the first U.S. warship to be armed solely with guided missiles. The *Long Beach* was followed by the aircraft carrier *Enterprise*, an 89,600-ton nuclear-powered vessel with a flight deck 300 yards long and an aircraft complement of 100.

The first nuclear-powered submarines to enter service after the *Nautilus* were armed with torpedoes. Soon, however, they were armed with the 500-mile-range Regulus cruise missile, which could only be fired from a surfaced position. In July 1960, the first Polaris missile was launched from the nuclear-powered submarine *George Washington* while the latter was submerged off the coast of Florida. Polaris-armed nuclear submarines quickly became the third

leg of the nation's nuclear defense triad, which includes the Air Force's manned bombers and intercontinental ballistic missiles. Today's ballistic missile submarines carry Poseidon or Trident missiles, which are direct descendants of the Polaris.

The development of submarine-launched ballistic missiles was both a symptom and a cause of Cold War tensions. In 1958 these tensions were heightened another notch when an army revolt in Iraq brought down that nation's pro-western government. Aware that the Iraqi revolutionaries were funded and supported by Egypt and the USSR, the government of Lebanon requested help from the United States, while the Jordanians did likewise from Great Britain. In July, 1958, U.S. Marines from the Sixth Fleet were landed in Lebanon and British troops were air- and sealifted into Jordan, thus forestalling the outbreak of revolt in either country.

One month later the Cold War focus shifted to the Far East. On August 23, the communist-ruled People's Republic of China began bombarding the island of Quemoy, which was held by Nationalist Chinese forces from Taiwan. In response to this new threat, the U.S. Seventh Fleet moved into the area to help resupply the Nationalist garrison, and to serve notice to the Red Chinese that the United States would not stand idly by were Quemoy to be invaded.

A Navy patrol plane flies past a Soviet freighter during the Cuban missile crisis.

In October 1962 the breaking point in superpower relations was almost reached when Cuban dictator Fidel Castro allowed the Soviet Union to establish medium-range ballistic missile sites on Cuban soil. When the Soviets ignored an American demand to remove the missiles, President John F. Kennedy clamped a naval blockade on the Caribbean nation. Both the Soviet Union and the United States placed their armed forces on standby alert, and for a few brief days at the end of October the world teetered on the brink of nuclear war. The crisis ended when Soviet Premier Nikita Khrushchev agreed to remove the missiles in exchange for a U.S. promise not to invade Cuba.

The Navy's role in these three incidents served to justify all the expenditures made on the Navy's behalf. In each case, Navy task forces had shown how American power could be projected abroad to protect friendly nations while thwarting the designs of nations and political factions hostile to the United States. And in each case, the situation had been resolved without any shots being fired. But the Navy would not be so fortunate once it became embroiled in the ongoing hostilities between North and South Vietnam.

FROM THE WAR IN VIETNAM TO COMMUNISM'S COLLAPSE

On August 2, 1964, North Vietnamese torpedo boats attacked the U.S. destroyer *Maddox* while the American vessel was on an intelligence gathering mission in the Gulf of Tonkin. Two days later, North Vietnamese torpedo boats again attacked the *Maddox*, and the destroyer *Turner Joy* as well. President Lyndon Johnson asked Congress for a joint resolution to use whatever force was necessary to protect American lives. Congress granted his request, thus opening the door for a full-scale military involvement in the war between North and South Vietnam.

The naval phase of the Vietnam War was the largest combat operation undertaken by the United States Navy since World War II. At one point, four carriers belonging to Task Force 77 were on Yankee Station in the Gulf of Tonkin. The battleship *New Jersey* was taken out of mothballs and used as a shore bombardment platform. Task Force 115 patrolled the coastal waters for junks and other small craft smuggling arms to the Viet Cong, while flotillas of riverine warfare boats (Task Forces 116 and 117) performed the same duties in the Mekong and Rung Sat river deltas.

From 1965 through 1968, Navy fighters and attack aircraft ranged over North Vietnam, striking at military and communications targets in an effort designed to halt the flow of supplies and soldiers into the South, and to persuade North Vietnam to end the war. The bombing campaign inflicted considerable damage on the North, but it was not nearly as effective as it might have been. The inhibiting factors were policy decisions made in Washington. The politically sensitive nature of many prime military targets caused Washington to declare them off-limits to American aircraft. For instance, North Vietnam's key port of Haiphong was for many years rendered immune to attack by American fears that the bombing of foreign merchant ships (particularly those belonging to the Soviet Union and China) would spark an international incident. These fears were finally set aside on May 8, 1972, when American aircraft mined Haiphong harbor in an action intended to force the North Vietnamese to the bargaining table.

In the early stages of the Vietnam War, aerial combat claimed one American aircraft for every four North Vietnamese aircraft shot down. This was an unacceptable kill ratio for the Navy and the Air Force, which were accustomed to kill ratios of ten-to-one and more in the Korean War and the final year of World War II. After studying the problem, the Navy concluded that the kill ratio was due to several factors, among them an over-reliance on air-to-air missiles, unrealistic rules of engagement, lack of training hours, and poorly developed aerial combat maneuvering skills. More simply put, Navy pilots were not adept at dogfighting. In 1969 the Navy sought to remedy this situation by establishing its Post-Graduate Course in Fighter Weapons, Tactics and Doctrine (PCFWTD)—otherwise known as Top Gun. The classroom for Top Gun was

The *Maddox, target of an attack by North Vietnamese torpedo boats on August 2, 1964.*

Navy fighter squadron VF-121, based at Miramar Naval Air Station, California. Top Gun was a smashing success that eventually helped American aircrews achieve a 13:1 kill ratio in the Vietnam War.

The completion of America's withdrawal from Vietnam in 1973 signaled the beginning of a painful period of adjustment for every U.S. military service branch. The Navy found itself in the difficult position of having to decommission hundreds of obsolete World War II-era ships even as it was left without the funds to construct new vessels. And, like the nation itself, the Navy was beset by racial turmoil as blacks and other minorities entered the service in increasing numbers—only to find that their lack of technology-oriented skills effectively barred them from all but the most menial jobs.

Unfortunately, even as the U.S. was experiencing problems of a varied sort the Soviet Navy was growing steadily in size and capability. To meet this and other challenges posed by a general buildup in Soviet military might, the U.S. armed forces underwent a restructuring process that began during the administration of President Jimmy Carter and continued on through the Reagan administration. One result of restructuring was a more professional Navy that set educational

requirements for new enlistees while instituting intensive training programs at all levels. Construction of new ships was also begun, reflecting a concomitant increase (during the Reagan administration) in naval funding and expenditures. The stated goal of the Reagan administration was a 600-ship navy, which Navy planners had established as the minimum number of ships required to fulfill America's defense commitments.

A navy of this size will not come to pass, however—at least not in the foreseeable future. The 600-ship navy was probably doomed by Mikhail Gorbachev's rise to power in the Soviet Union in 1984. As one of the "new Soviet men" who had no personal ties to the World War II-generation that had ruled the Soviet Union for decades, Gorbachev was able to set in motion sweeping changes in areas affecting the social, economic, and political organization of the Soviet Union. The collateral effect of these changes, which have yet to play themselves out, was to bring the Cold War to an end. Quite suddenly, it seemed, Soviet expansionism became a thing of the past, the victim of an impoverished economy and the demise of communism as a credible ideology. And just as suddenly, the related disintegration of the Warsaw Pact as a

A U.S. Navy air cushion boat patrols the Mekong River delta during the Vietnam War.

military bloc, coupled with the economic realities facing the United States as well as the Soviet Union, have forced yet more changes in military thinking and structures in both nations.

What has emerged from all this is the clear realization that the chief military danger to both superpowers lies not in a war with each other, but in the unrestrained acts of certain heavily militarized nations, particularly in the Middle East and Southwest Asia. The proliferation of nuclear and chemical weapons among such nations is cause for grave concern. The world may have already been given a grim foretaste of wars to come during the Iran-Iraq conflict, which saw both nations resort to the use of poison gas. Preventing the further use of these weapons may well become an important foreign policy objective of the United States, if not the Soviet Union as well. If so, a major instrument of that foreign policy will certainly be the U.S. Navy, which may present well into the next century the best available means of dissuading aggressive nations from the use of their so-called "terror weapons."

MINES

Mines and torpedoes share a common heritage—so common, that mines were called torpedoes for many years. Modern mines were first used by the Russians against the invading British and French fleets during the Crimean War (1854–1856). The first use of the modern mine by the U.S. Navy occurred during the American Civil War. Large charges of explosives were moored in harbors and river channels below the water's surface and detonated electrically from a land-based command post. Admiral David Farragut was referring to the mines—then called torpedoes—when, at the Battle of Mobile Bay, he uttered the famous battle cry, "Damn the torpedoes, full steam ahead."

The percussion mine came into general use at the turn of the century. This type of mine was also moored by a long anchor chain to the sea bottom so that it floated just below the surface. If a passing ship struck the mine, a percussion cap exploded and detonated the explosive charge.

During World War I, naval mines became a major weapon. The most common type of mine was the percussion mine; however, acoustic, magnetic, and pressure mines were also used. These mines lay quiescent until a ship passed within range of their sensors, then detonated. The Imperial German Navy laid over 43,000 mines around the British Isles. British losses to mines included 44 warships, 586 merchant ships, and Britain's leading general, Lord Kitchener (who was killed when the ship on which he was a passenger struck a mine and sank). The Royal Navy laid 126,000 mines, which sank 102 German warships and sub-

marines. The United States laid 56,000 mines in a barrier across the North Sea in an effort to hedge in German submarines.

Mines were also used extensively during World War II. Using ships, aircraft, and submarines, the United States laid 21,000 mines around the Japanese home islands. A total of 484 Japanese ships were sunk and another 500 damaged by these weapons. Included in these totals were two battleships, two aircraft carriers, eight cruisers, and seven submarines.

In the years following World War II, mines and minelaying techniques occupied a position of some importance in naval weapons development. In 1972, mines became a political weapon when President Richard M. Nixon ordered Haiphong Harbor mined to force the North Vietnamese to seriously negotiate an end to the Vietnam War. Since the end of the Vietnam War, mines have declined in importance, and few new mines have been procured since 1987.

Today, the vast majority of mines are laid by aircraft—carrier-based A-6Es, A-7Es, S-3A/Bs, and the land-based P-3 Orions. All American sub-

marines except for the *Los Angeles*-class vessels have been configured to carry and launch mines. But submarine minelaying is inefficient. Due to the weight and size of the naval mines, torpedoes and missiles must be left behind. This means that the submarine has to return to base to pick up a load of mines, then return again to rearm with torpedoes and missiles.

The principal submarine-laid mines in use today by the U.S. Navy are the Submarine Launched Mobile Mine (SLMM) Mark 67 and the CAPTOR (Encapsulated Torpedo) mine. The SLMM Mark 67 is designed for use in shallow waters containing surface and submarine port facilities. When the mine's multiple detectors (magnetic, acoustic, passive sonar, pressure) senors detect a ship moving toward it, it initiates a firing mechanism that propels the mine toward the target. The CAPTOR, which can also be laid by aircraft, contains a Mark 46 homing torpedo in a canister and operates in a similar manner. But its principle drawback is its limited warhead weight of 96 pounds of high explosive, which is thought to be of questionable effectiveness

against the newer classes of Soviet double- and titanium-hulled submarines.

The U.S. Navy has large numbers of Quickstrike mines—some sources suggest more than 80,000 units. This family of mines includes the Mark 65, which has a 2,390-pound aerial bomb in a special casing; the Mark 63, which has a 2,000-pound aerial bomb; and the Mark 62, which has a 500-pound aerial bomb. All are intended for use in shallow water. They are usually carried by Navy A-6E and A-7E carrier-based aircraft.

Another series of mines made from aircraft bombs are the Destructor Mark 41, Mark 40, and Mark 36 mines. These mines were used during the Vietnam War. Two additional mines in the Navy's inventory include: the Mark 57, which is armed with 340 pounds of explosive and is contained in a fiberglass case; and the Mark 56, which is armed with 360 pounds of explosive and was designed to be used against fast, deep-diving submarines. The Mark 57 is deployed by submarines, while the Mark 56 is deployed by aircraft.

Technicians assemble Quickstrike mines for the U.S. Navy.

TODAY'S NAVY

The mission of today's Navy is threefold: to prevent war, to control the seas in areas of interest to the U.S., and to project American power overseas whenever and wherever it is required to do so.

The military forces of the United States are governed under a dual command structure. The individual services—Army, Navy, Air Force, and Marine Corps—are responsible for training their own forces. Operational or combat command is exercised through a system of specified and unified commands.

To understand how this system works, one must start at the top—which is to say, the White House. As specified in the Constitution, the President of the United States is the Commander in Chief (CinC) of all American armed forces. Under the Defense Act of 1946, as amended in 1949, the Secretary of Defense is responsible for the overall operation of the military services, and reports directly to the President. To assist him, a secretary for each service is responsible for the overall management of that service. The secretaries report directly to the Secretary of Defense. The President and the Secretary of Defense, as well as their designated alternates, make up the National Command Authority (NCA), from which all military units receive their orders.

The Joint Chiefs of Staff are comprised of the senior four star officers of the United States Navy, Army, Air Force, and Marine Corps. In 1986, the Joint Chiefs ceased to function in a purely advisory role in order to exercise actual command of the various unified and specified commands of the military forces.

It is the specified and unified commands that control and direct the armed forces. A specified command comprises elements from one service only, whereas a unified command comprises elements from two or more services (e.g., the Army, Air Force, and the Navy). There are three specified commands: the Strategic Air Command, the Military Airlift Command, and the Forces Command. The unified commands include the

Atlantic, European, Central, Southern, Pacific, Space, Special Operations, and Unified Transportation commands. The commander in chief of a unified command is usually, but not always, selected from the service with the largest representation of personnel in the area.

As mentioned earlier, the individual services are responsible for training

and preparedness. In addition, the Navy also has an administrative command which is responsible for logistics, maintenance, personnel, procurement, and research and development. The Chief of Naval Operations (CNO) manages his responsibilities through a series of "offices" (see Table I).

The commanders of the Atlantic and Pacific fleets report to the CNO

through the administrative side of the chain of command and are responsible for the training and readiness of the forces under their commands. Moreover, the two fleet commanders also have operational duties and responsibilities as the CinCs of their respective unified commands.

Each of the fleet commanders also has four subordinate officers:

Commander, Naval Air Force (which includes aircraft carriers as well as aircraft); Commander, Surface Force; Commander, Submarine Force; and Commander, Fleet Marine Force. They are responsible for logistics and personnel support.

The naval components of the Atlantic and Pacific Unified Commands are the Atlantic and Pacific fleets, respectively

A U.S. carrier battle group in the Mediterranean. In the foreground (left to right) are the guided-missile cruiser Ticonderoga, *the stores ship* White Plains, *and the aircraft carrier* John F. Kennedy; *the frigate* Knox *brings up the rear.*

(see Table II). Atlantic Fleet operations are carried out under the direction of the Second Fleet, which presently has about 314 ships, including submarines. Traditionally known as the "Home Fleet," the Second Fleet can trace its origins to the formation of the Home Squadron in the early 1840s. The Second Fleet is charged with the defense of the entire Atlantic Ocean, and is headquartered in Norfolk, Virginia.

The Pacific Fleet can trace its origins to the Pacific Squadron, which was organized in the late 1820s. Pacific Fleet operations are carried out under the direction of the Third Fleet in the eastern Pacific, and the Seventh Fleet in the western Pacific. The Third and Seventh Fleets together comprise about 247 ships, including submarines. The Third Fleet supplies ships and personnel to the Seventh Fleet in the Western Pacific and in the Indian Ocean, and is also responsible for all antisubmarine activities in the eastern Pacific between America's West Coast and Hawaii. As more Soviet forces were deployed to the Pacific in the 1980s, the Third Fleet's aircraft carrier battle force component was also increased. The headquarters of the Third Fleet is at Pearl Harbor.

The Seventh fleet, which has its headquarters at Yokosuka, Japan, oversees the Pacific from the Kamchatka Peninsula to the Persian Gulf—an area that includes the Indian Ocean. Because there are only 14 operational aircraft carriers in the Navy, carrier battle groups from the Atlantic Fleet often deploy to the Seventh Fleet.

The Sixth Fleet operates in the Mediterranean both as a U.S. naval force and as a component of NATO South Command in the European Unified Command. (The intermediate command between the Sixth Fleet and European Unified Command—which is headed by an Air Force or Army General—is U.S. Naval Forces, Europe.) The volatile nature of Middle East politics, the relative frequency of war and terrorism, and the existence of tensions fostered by Arab-Israeli enmity have all combined to make the Mediterranean an area of major concern for the United States. Sixth Fleet Navy pilots have engaged in combat four times within the past decade and, until fairly recently, confrontations with Soviet ships occurred with enough regularity to fray the nerves of all involved.

In addition to the numbered fleets, task forces, task groups, task units, and task elements can be formed for specific activities. Task forces and the like are composed of combat and support ships drawn from the fleets, and/or from other naval units.

Tragic proof of the volatility of Middle Eastern politics: the frigate Stark *burns after being struck by an Exocet air-to-ground missile, launched by an Iraqi warplane.*

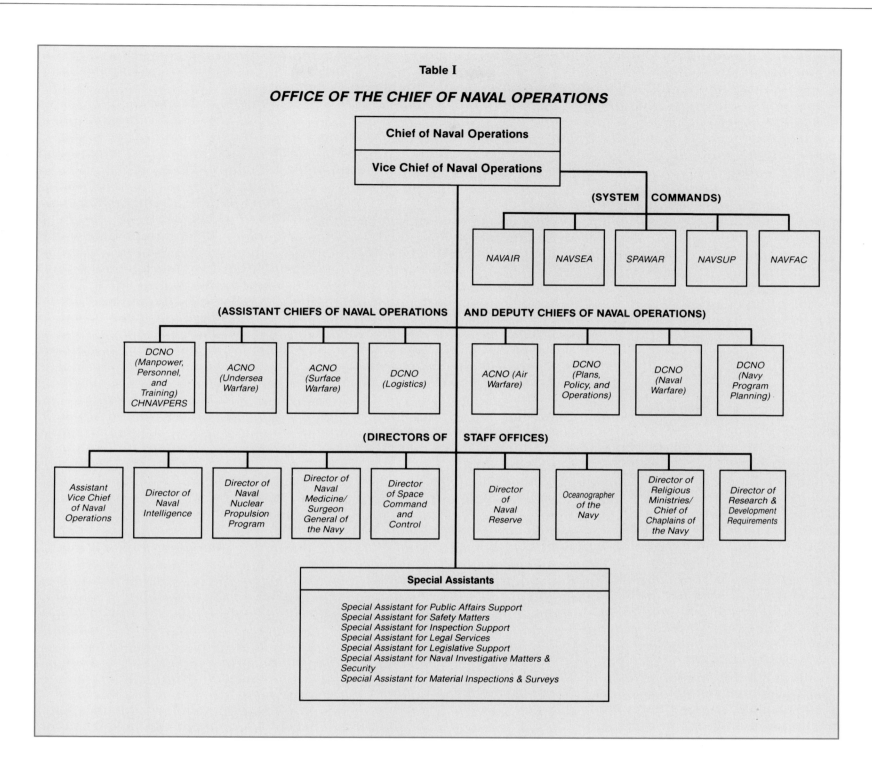

Table I

OFFICE OF THE CHIEF OF NAVAL OPERATIONS

Chief of Naval Operations

Vice Chief of Naval Operations

(SYSTEM COMMANDS)

NAVAIR | NAVSEA | SPAWAR | NAVSUP | NAVFAC

(ASSISTANT CHIEFS OF NAVAL OPERATIONS   AND DEPUTY CHIEFS OF NAVAL OPERATIONS)

DCNO (Manpower, Personnel, and Training) CHNAVPERS

ACNO (Undersea Warfare)

ACNO (Surface Warfare)

DCNO (Logistics)

ACNO (Air Warfare)

DCNO (Plans, Policy, and Operations)

DCNO (Naval Warfare)

DCNO (Navy Program Planning)

(DIRECTORS OF   STAFF OFFICES)

Assistant Vice Chief of Naval Operations

Director of Naval Intelligence

Director of Naval Nuclear Propulsion Program

Director of Naval Medicine/ Surgeon General of the Navy

Director of Space Command and Control

Director of Naval Reserve

Oceanographer of the Navy

Director of Religious Ministries/ Chief of Chaplains of the Navy

Director of Research & Development Requirements

Special Assistants

Special Assistant for Public Affairs Support
Special Assistant for Safety Matters
Special Assistant for Inspection Support
Special Assistant for Legal Services
Special Assistant for Legislative Support
Special Assistant for Naval Investigative Matters & Security
Special Assistant for Material Inspections & Surveys

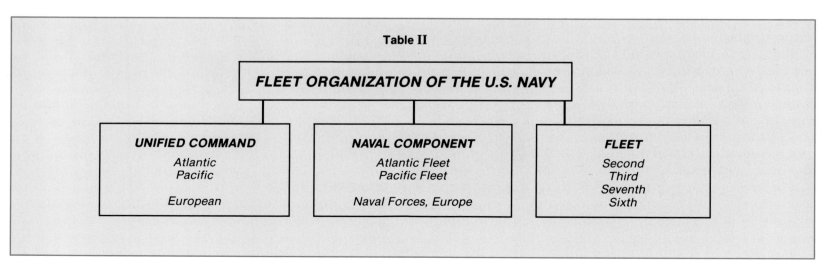

Table II

FLEET ORGANIZATION OF THE U.S. NAVY

UNIFIED COMMAND	NAVAL COMPONENT	FLEET
Atlantic	Atlantic Fleet	Second
Pacific	Pacific Fleet	Third
		Seventh
European	Naval Forces, Europe	Sixth

THE MARINE CORPS

Created by the Continental Congress in 1775, the United States Marine Corps (USMC) is the largest amphibious military force in the world, with over 190,000 men and women of all ranks. The Marine Corps is a military service located within the Department of the Navy. It comprises two major commands, the Fleet Marine Force, Atlantic, and the Fleet Marine Force, Pacific, both of which belong to the Atlantic and Pacific fleets, respectively.

The Marine Corps includes three infantry divisions plus one in reserve, three air wings plus one in reserve, and three service support groups, plus several small units in reserve. A Marine Corps division numbers 16,000 men and women, making it the largest divisional formation in the world. A division is organized into three infantry regiments and one artillery regiment, plus combat and support battalions. For combat, Marine units are organized into Marine Air/Ground Task Forces (MAGTF), the components of which vary depending on the nature of the mission assigned. All MAGTF organizations are combined arms units, and always include infantry, aviation, support, and naval elements. Three levels of MAGTFs can be formed: a Marine Expeditionary Unit (MEU) containing 2,350 Marines and 110 Navy personnel; a Marine Expeditionary Brigade (MEB) containing 14,000 Marines and 550 Navy personnel; and a Marine Expeditionary Force (MEF) containing 48,000 Marines and 2,600 Navy personnel. A MEF can include an entire aircraft wing, a Marine infantry division, and one Force Service Support Group.

Today, the Marine Corps maintain battalion-sized landing teams aboard ships in the western Pacific and Mediterranean. Landing teams afloat are also maintained at various times in the Caribbean and the Indian Ocean, depending on the level of political tension in those areas.

While an AH-1T SeaCobra gunship hovers protectively overhead, Marines disembark from AAV7A1 amphibian assault vehicles.

MILITARY SEALIFT COMMAND

The Military Sealift Command (MSC) operates and contracts ocean shipping to move material for all the armed forces; in addition, it operates a variety of replenishment ships, research ships, and special support ships for the Navy.

The Military Sealift Command cannot now, nor in the foreseeable future, provide enough ships to transport the vast amount of supplies and equipment that would be needed to sustain U.S. forces involved in a large-scale conventional war.

However, with the easing of East/West tensions in the early 1990s, a large-scale conventional war seems an unlikely prospect. The MSC may therefore be able to perform its duties with far fewer ships than were formerly required.

The MSC operates most of its ships under charter to private companies. The crews are civilian. Under contract to the MSC are the ships of the Naval Fleet Auxiliary Force (NFAF), the Near Term Prepositioning Squadron (NTPS), all Maritime Prepositioning Squadrons (MPS), all Fast Sealift Ships (FSS), the Ready Reserve Force (RRF), and various Special Mission Support Ships.

The MSC grew out of the Naval Ocean Transport Service (NOTS) and the oceangoing ships of the Army's Transportation Corps. All ships in the MSC have a T- prefix added to their hull numbers.

The PFC. James Anderson, Jr., *a maritime prepositioning ship, is one of the scores of noncombatant ships operated by the Military Sealift Command.*

NAVAL AVIATION

The United States Navy maintains an air force of some 5,500 fixed wing aircraft and helicopters, making it fourth in size behind the U.S. Air Force and the Soviet and Chinese air forces. Navy units (both active and reserve) operate about 4,200 of these aircraft, while the remaining 1,300 are operated by active and reserve Marine Corps units. At least 390 of the Navy's aircraft belong to the Naval Air Reserve, and 230 of the Marine's aircraft belong to the Marine Air Reserve.

As with units in the "sailing" Navy, all naval aviation units belong to an administrative as well as an operational unit. The administrative side is under the Assistant Chief of Naval Operations for Air Warfare (OP-05), who overseas the Naval Air Force, Atlantic Fleet, and the Naval Air Force, Pacific Fleet. Each Naval Air Force has a number of air wings.

The purpose of naval aviation is to operate aircraft in support of naval operations. Marine Corps pilots are also carrier-qualified and have their place in the rotation for carrier duty. The "notional," or typical, carrier air wing has about 86 fixed wing and rotary aircraft.

In recent years a notional carrier air wing comprised the following: two fighter squadrons (VF) with 12 F-14 Tomcats each; two light-attack squadrons (VA) with 12 A-7E Corsairs each, or two strike-fighter (VFA) squadrons with 12 F/A-18 Hornets each; one medium-attack squadron (VA) with ten A-6E Intruders and four KA-6D tankers; one electronic warfare squadron (VAQ) with four EA-6B Prowlers; one airborne early warning squadron (VAW) with four E-2C Hawkeyes; one antisubmarine warfare squadron (VS) with ten S-3A Vikings; and one antisubmarine helicopter squadron (HS) with six SH-3H Sea Kings.

The composition of the notional carrier air wing is currently undergoing changes. The A-7E Corsairs are being replaced by more versatile F/A-18 Hornets; fighter, strike-fighter, and attack squadrons are being reduced from 12 to ten aircraft to allow for more A-6Es; and the KA-6D tanker is being phased out. Moreover, the electronic warfare and airborne early warning squadrons will each receive one additional aircraft to increase their respective compliments to five. By the mid-1990s, then, it is expected that carrier air wings will comprise the following: two fighter squadrons (VF) with ten F-14 Tomcats each; two strike-fighter (VFA) squadrons with ten F/A-18 Hornets each; two attack squadrons (VA) with ten A-6E Intruders each; one electronic warfare squadron (VAQ) with five EA-6B Prowlers; one airborne early warning squadron with five E-2C Hawkeyes; one antisubmarine warfare squadron (VS) with ten S-3A/B Vikings; and one helicopter antisubmarine warfare squadron with six SH-3H Sea Kings or SH-60F Seahawks.

The Navy also maintains five patrol wings (PatWings) for coastal and antisubmarine patrol duties. PatWings 5 and 11 patrol the Atlantic and Mediterranean regions, while PatWings 10, 2, and 1 are assigned to the Pacific. Each Patrol Wing is composed of two or more of the 24 Patrol Squadrons (VP) currently active.

The Navy operates 18 different types of squadrons. They are:

- Air Test and Evaluation Squadrons (VX). These are specially developed squadrons that evaluate new weapons systems for Navy and Marine Corps aircraft.
- Antarctic Development Squadron (VXE). There is only one Antarctic Squadron: VXE-6 Puckered Penguins, based at Point Mugu, California. It provides logistics support for the Antarctic Programs of the National Science Foundation.
- Antisubmarine Squadrons (VS). The Navy's 12 antisubmarine fixed wing squadrons fly ten S-3A or B Vikings, and are assigned to all aircraft carriers except the *Midway*.
- Attack Squadrons (VA). There are currently 39 attack squadrons flying A-7E Crusaders, A-6E Intruders, or F/A-18 Hornets.
- Airborne Early Warning Squadrons (VAW). There are currently 16 such squadrons, all flying the E-2C Hawkeye. Four Hawkeyes per squadron are currently distributed to each of the 14 carrier air wings.
- Fleet Composite Squadrons (VC). The Navy maintains five Fleet Composite Squadrons, which are responsible for a range of services including Dissimilar Air Combat Training (DACT), aerial photography, transport, and airborne radar calibration.
- Fighter Squadrons (VF). There are currently 29 active-duty fighter squadrons in the U.S. Navy. Of these, 24 squadrons are in carrier air wings, while the remaining five are training squadrons. All Navy VF fighter squadrons fly the F-14 Tomcat.
- Fleet Air Reconnaissance Squadrons (VQ). There are four Navy reconnaissance squadrons. VQ-1 and VQ-2 fly the EA-3B Skywarrior, the ES-3A Viking, and the EP-3 Orion; VQ-3 and VQ-4 fly the EC-130 Hercules in the TACAMO (Take Charge and Move Out) communications relay role. The Boeing E-6A Hermes is replacing all EC-130 aircraft in the TACAMO role.
- Fleet Logistics Support (VR/VRC). There are five squadrons performing logistics support duties. They are equipped with the C-2A Greyhound and the C-130 Hercules. They are used to carry passengers and high priority freight.
- Helicopter Antisubmarine Squadrons (HS). The Navy's 13 antisubmarine helicopter squadrons fly either the SH-3H Sea King, or its successor, the SH-60F Seahawk.
- Helicopter Combat Search and Rescue and Special Warfare Support Squadrons (HCS). These two squadrons will fly the HH-60H Seahawk helicopter, and provide support to riverine squadrons in war.
- Helicopter Combat Support Squadrons (HC). These helicopter squadrons are used for search-and-rescue (SAR) operations and for Vertical Replenishment (VERTREP) of ships at sea. They fly the SH-3 Sea King and the CH-53E Super Stallion helicopters. One squadron also flies the UH-1 Huey.
- Helicopter Mine Countermeasures Squadrons (HM). Three HM squadrons fly the RH-53D Sea Stallion and the CH-53E Super Stallion helicopters. Their task is to

clear enemy mines from coastal, harbor, and river waterways.

- Helicopter Training Squadrons (HT). Two helicopter training squadrons train all Navy, Marine Corps, Coast Guard, and foreign student pilots. All learn to fly the fixed wing T-28 or T-34 before training on the TH-57 SeaRanger helicopter.
- Light Helicopter Antisubmarine Squadrons (HSL). There are 18 such squadrons, called "LAMPS" (Light Airborne Multi-Purpose System) squadrons. They fly the SH-2F or G Seasprite, or the SH-60B Seahawk helicopters. The helicopters are

based aboard cruisers, destroyers, and frigates in detachments drawn from each squadron.

- Oceanographic Development Squadron (VXN). One Oceanographic Development Squadron, VXN-8, is based at Patuxent Naval Air Station in Maryland. It conducts oceanographic research for the Navy and various civilian government agencies.
- Patrol Squadrons (VP). The Navy's 24 patrol squadrons each operate nine P-3C Orion aircraft. Two of the 24 patrol squadrons function in a transition-training role.

- Training Squadrons (VT). The Navy currently maintains 18 squadrons to train aircrews for fixed wing Navy and Marine Corps aircraft. These squadrons are also used to train Coast Guard and some foreign aircrews. They fly the T-34 Mentor, T-2C Buckeye, T-44 King Air, and T-47A Citation aircraft.

These F/A-18 Hornets represent the Navy's newest and most advanced aircraft. They can perform in the air-superiority fighter and tactical strike-fighter roles.

NAVAL AIR RESERVE

The Navy operates two carrier air wings manned by reservists. Each reserve air wing has 16 squadrons and operates a total of 390 aircraft.

The Navy's air reserve includes four fighter squadrons flying the F-14A Tomcat, four attack/fighter squadrons with F/A-18 Hornets replacing the A-7E Corsairs, two tactical electronic countermeasures squadrons equipped with EA-6A Prowlers, and two airborne early warning squadrons with E-2C Hawkeyes. The Navy also has two composite squadrons equipped with variants of the A-4 Skyhawk for aerial combat maneuver training. Naval Air Reserve personnel man 13 patrol squadrons and ten fleet logistics support squadrons. Twelve Reserve helicopter squadrons supplement the Navy's active helicopter squadrons in the following roles: antisubmarine, combat support, combat search and rescue, special warfare support, and mine countermeasures.

MARINE CORPS AVIATION

Marine Corps fixed wing aircraft and helicopters are organized into three active Marine Air Wings (MAW), and one reserve wing. Marine Aircraft Groups (MAG) are the next rung down on the organizational ladder, and include two or more squadrons of various aircraft types. MAWs working in conjunction with a Marine division form a Marine Expeditionary Force (MEF). The MAGs normally work with a Marine Expeditionary Brigade (MEB), while a composite squadron works with a reinforced battalion to form a Marine Expeditionary Unit (MEU). Composite squadrons usually

The AV-8B Harrier is a VSTOL (vertical/short takeoff and landing) aircraft. It is used exclusively by the Marine Corps and, like the F/A-18 Hornet, it may be employed as either an air-superiority fighter or a tactical strike fighter.

include four CH-53 Sea Stallions or Super Stallions, 12 CH-46 Sea Knights, four AH-1 SuperCobras, and four UH-1 Hueys. All are deployed aboard an amphibious assault ship. AV-8B Harriers may also form part of the composite squadron, depending on the mission.

The Marine Corps presently has 34 fixed wing and 36 helicopter active-duty squadrons, and 16 fixed wing and eight helicopter reserve squadrons. It also has a variety of training and administrative aircraft assigned to the seven Marine Corps air stations. The most well-known Marine Corps helicopter squadron is HMX-1, which is responsible for providing helicopter transportation for the President of the United States.

The following provides a breakdown of Marine Corps squadron types:

- Attack Squadrons (VMA). The Marine Corps currently operates eight attack squadrons and one training squadron flying the AV-8B Harrier, which has replaced the A-4 Skyhawk and the AV-8A Harrier. There will be 20 Harriers in each squadron when they reach full strength in the mid-1990s. Starting in 1990, the six Marine attack squadrons flying the A-6E Intruder will replace their aircraft with two-seat F/A-18D Hornets. The F/A-18D will be flown in an attack/ reconnaissance role. The Marines anticipate standing down one A-6E squadron and standing up one F/A-18D squadron per year until the process is completed.
- Electronic Warfare Squadrons (VMAQ). The Marines have only one VMAQ squadron; it is composed of 15 EA-6A Prowlers. Detachments from this squadron are sent to other Marine Air Wings as required.
- Fighter/Attack Squadrons (VMFA). Twelve Marine Corps squadrons fly the F/A-18 Hornet in the fighter/ attack role. Each squadron has 12 aircraft, although the Marines plan to reduce this number to ten. Marine Corps fighter/attack squadrons may be assigned carrier duty when needed by the Navy.
- Heavy Helicopter Squadrons (HMT). The Marine Corps presently maintains twelve heavy helicopter

squadrons, each flying 16 CH-53D and E helicopters.

- Medium Helicopter Squadrons (HMM). Fifteen Marine Corps medium helicopter squadrons fly 12 CH-46 Sea Knight helicopters per squadron. Plans to replace the CH-46 and CH-53D with the MV-22 Osprey have been cancelled.
- Observation Squadron (VMO). The Marine Corps flies the OV-10 Bronco in the observation role. Two squadrons of 18 aircraft each are now in service.
- Photo-Reconnaissance Squadrons (VMFP). The Marine Corps' one photo-reconnaissance squadron formerly flew the reconnaissance version of the Phantom, the RF-4B Phantom. The squadron is transitioning to the F/A-18D photo-reconnaissance version.
- Refueling and Transport Squadrons (VMGR). Four Marine Corps refueling and transport squadrons (plus one training squadron) fly the KC-130F Hercules.
- Utility/Attack Squadrons (HML/A). These are composite utility and attack units flying a combination of 12 UH-1N Hueys and 12 AH-1T or AH-1W SeaCobras in the attack role. The Huey was the original U.S. gunship and the SeaCobra is a greatly enhanced version of that aircraft.

The 4th Marine Aircraft Wing is the reserve wing and is composed of four Marine Air Groups (MAG). These include 15 fixed wing and nine helicopter squadrons. The reserve air wing is organized in the same manner as the active MAWs, and flies approximately 230 aircraft. Until January 1990, VMFT-401 was the only U.S. military unit to fly the Israeli-designed and -built F-21 Kfir, which is used in Dissimilar Aerial Combat Training (DACT) to simulate enemy fighter tactics.

The Marines use the AH-1W SuperCobra gunship (foreground) to support their infantry. In the background is a troop-carrying UH-1 Huey.

THE NAVY OF TOMORROW

Throughout the decade of the 1980s, the Navy's stated goal was to achieve a force level of 600 ships. In the late 1980s, this goal was almost achieved when the force level reached some 580 ships. By 1990, however, the total number of ships had declined (see Table III). The numbers given in Table III are liable to change—in fact, *are* changing, almost on a weekly basis. The possibility of a 600-ship navy has been eliminated; however, the 1991 Defense Budget (which has yet to be finalized) does provide for the building of 78 new ships through fiscal 1994, and the modernization of two ships, one of them an aircraft carrier. These will join the 19 new ships and the four modernized ships that were approved in the 1990 Naval Budget. In the meantime, the battleships *Iowa* and *New Jersey* will be laid up in reserve before the end of 1992, while the battleships *Missouri* and *Wisconsin* will probably be withdrawn from service by 1995 at the latest. Scheduled to be retired from service by 1994 are eight attack submarines from the *Permit* and *Sturgeon* classes, 11 destroyers of the *Adams* and *Farragut* classes, the nuclear-powered cruisers *Bainbridge* and *Truxtun*, and 54 other ships of various types and classes.

The Navy was forced to cancel all new F-14D fighter construction and upgrade existing F-14As instead. The V-22 Osprey has been canceled in spite of congressional support, and so has the Sea Lance antisubmarine missile and the Phoenix missile.

The building program for the *Ohio* class of ballistic missile submarines will continue, but the number of vessels will be reduced from earlier projections. A total of 18 to 20 *Ohio* submarines armed with Trident missiles are scheduled to be built by 1997. By this time U.S. ballistic missile submarines may have roughly 70 percent of the 4,900 nuclear warheads that have been allotted to the United States and the Soviet Union by the as-yet unratified Strategic Arms Reduction Talks (START).

The current force of nuclear-powered attack submarines will decline from its present total of about

Table III	
COMBAT VESSELS OF THE U.S. NAVY IN ACTIVE SERVICE, 1990	
Strategic Missile Submarines	34
Attack Submarines	95
Special Operation Submarines	2
Submarine Support Ships	10
Aircraft Carriers	14
Battleships	4
Cruisers	43
Destroyers—Guided-Missile	26
Destroyers	31
Frigates—Guided-Missile	35
Frigates	39
Patrol Combatants	6
Amphibious Ships	61
Mine Warfare	5
Mobile Logistics	19
Support Force Ships	47
National Reserve Force	
Frigates—Guided-Missile	16
Frigates	10
Mine Warfare	18
Amphibious Ships	2
TOTAL	578

92 submarines to 86 submarines by 1993. Further reductions are sure to follow, especially in the new *Seawolf* class. If the planned construction of the new *Seawolf* class is not reduced, the year 2000 could find as many as 12 *Seawolf* submarines in Navy service, along with as many as 62 *Los Angeles*-class attack submarines. But this is unlikely, given the present projected cost of 1.2 billion dollars per new *Seawolf*-class submarine.

The aircraft carrier is the key to the size of the surface fleet in the 1990s. The Navy is determined to maintain 13 carrier task forces. Current Navy plans

call for the *Midway* to be retired after 1992, at roughly the same time the new *Nimitz*-class carriers *George Washington* and *John C. Stennis* (both of which are now under construction) enter service.

However many aircraft carriers the Navy maintains, they will all require escort vessels of the latest design. The construction of the new *Arleigh Burke* class of destroyers is therefore a Navy priority. Fifteen *Arleigh Burke* ships have been authorized, but cost overruns and construction delays have not endeared the program to Congress. By the year 2000, the Navy will have

Artist's rendering of the Seawolf, *nameship of the Navy's newest attack submarine class.*

only 70 escort vessels less than 30 years old, plus whatever number of *Arleigh Burke* ships are built by that date. If five *Arleigh Burke* ships are built per year, then the minimum number of cruisers and destroyers required to fill out 13 carrier task forces will be realized.

The 1990s will also see changes in Navy personnel. By the end of 1991, it is estimated that the number of people serving in the Navy will fall from 591,000 to 585,000. The loss of some 6,000 men and women is certain to cause problems. Ideally, the Navy attempts to rotate its personnel through three years of sea duty and three years of shore duty. But the chronic shortage of trained personnel in many shipboard specialties has sometimes changed the ratio to four years aboard ship and three years ashore. Since most ships spend approximately six months out of every 18 months in "forward deployment" (i.e., on overseas stations) many Navy officers and enlisted personnel have found themselves spending a disproportionate amount of time away from their families and loved ones.

The situation is complicated somewhat by Congress having

prohibited women from serving aboard combat ships or in combat specialties, the majority of which involve shipboard duty. As a result, women tend to fill proportionally more billets ashore, making it harder for the men to rotate ashore.

Nevertheless, morale is high in today's Navy. The all-volunteer concept for the American military has produced a highly trained, highly motivated naval force that stands in stark contrast to the conditions that prevailed in the aftermath of the Vietnam War. The downside to all this lies in the fact that reenlistment rates have declined from 59 percent in 1984 to 52 percent in 1987–88. A similar decline among naval officers has also been experienced, especially in certain highly skilled categories.

The Navy has 99 ratings, or job classifications. The 54,000 women currently serving in the Navy are allowed to serve in 85 of these without restrictions. In the future, it is likely that the restricted categories will be opened to women as the nation's declining birth rate reduces the number of young men who choose to enter Navy service.

Certainly, Navy planners will have their work cut out for them during the decade of the 1990s. But there is no doubt that the Navy will remain a fighting force capable of meeting the challenges of a rapidly changing world.

As this photograph indicates, women are employed in increasingly important roles in today's Navy. The pilot pictured here is not yet allowed to serve in combat aircraft—a restriction that many women, eager to take the same risks and assume the same responsibilities as men, would like to see dropped.

COMMUNICATIONS

By day, flags were the traditional means of communicating between vessels at sea; at night, shuttered lanterns were used. Being visual in nature, these two communications methods were limited in the distance a message could be sent and received, and in the speed a message transmission can actually be transmitted from one ship to another.

The telegraph was already in wide use when James Clerk Maxwell formulated the theory of electromagnetism in 1873. In 1886 Heinrich Hertzberg, guided by the theoretical model Maxwell had provided, invented the spark coil, which made wireless telegraphy possible. In the late 1890s and early 1900s Gugliemo Marconi improved upon the idea by developing radio systems that could transmit radio signals over long distances. In 1904 Sir John Fleming introduced the vacuum electron tube, which added voice to radio transmissions.

Shipboard applications were among the earliest uses of this new form of communication. By World War I the "wireless" transmission of messages by radio had become indispensable to naval communications. The use of the radio in turn spawned a whole new growth industry centered around the theory and practice of coding and decoding radio transmissions.

Radio technology improved through World War II and beyond. When the Soviet Union launched the Sputnik I satellite in October 1957, a whole new era in communications began. Extremely long-range radio transmission techniques and facilities are now used to transmit radio messages that can be received even by submerged submarines. Recently, the U.S. Department of Defense has completed the Global Satellite Positioning System, which enables naval vessels, aircraft, ground vehicles, or individual soldiers to determine their position anywhere on the planet within a few feet.

Below: The Navy's long-range communications station in Annapolis, Maryland. ***Right, top:*** Signaling with flags. ***Right, bottom:*** Navy signal flags.

SENSORS: SONAR AND RADAR

SONAR

Germany's use of submarines to blockade the British Isles during World War I spurred Britain, France, Italy, and the United States to develop a means to detect submerged U-boats. The British invented ASDIC, which stands for Anti-Submarine Detection Investigation Committee— an organization that existed in name only. ASDIC is the same thing as "sonar," which is a U.S. Navy term that stands for "sound navigation and ranging."

If the sonar system only listens to sounds, it is said to be "passive." "Active" sonar transmits sound waves through water. When the waves are reflected from a hard surface they are detected by the sonar receiver in much the same fashion that a microphone picks up sounds in the air. The sound waves are converted to electrical energy which is then measured to determine direction (bearing) and distance (range).

Passive sonar is preferred by submarines during submarine hunting operations because it does not give away one's presence to the enemy. An active sonar beam, like light or radar beams, is composed of energy that can be detected and backtracked to its source—and followed up with a torpedo or missile. Surface ships use active sonar because their screws and movement give away their position anyway.

The ability of sonar to detect enemy submarines and other vessels at great distances was made possible by the development of the array

sonar. Sonar arrays are a number of sonar receivers or transmitters tuned to send and receive the same sound frequencies. By increasing the number of receivers, the sensitivity of the system is also increased and thus the enemy can be detected at greater distances. To extend the sensitivity of passive receivers even further, sonar receiver arrays are towed behind surface ships or submarines, well away from the disturbance (interference) caused by the vessel itself.

Once the enemy is detected by a passive sonar receiv-er, the hunter crew may decide to use its active sonar to refine bearing and range for the purpose of directing its missiles or torpedoes. The newest forms of active sonar "squirt" out a very brief burst of energy. These bursts of sound are difficult for the enemy to detect and even harder to backtrack.

Sonar systems have been developed that allow submarines to operate under the Arctic ice. These systems aim a burst of sound vertically to measure the distance from the submarine to the jagged underside of the ice pack.

Above: Sonobuoys are loaded aboard an SH-60 Seahawk helicopter. *Opposite, top:* Inside the sonar dome in the bow of the attack submarine Narwhal. *Opposite, bottom:* The sonar compartment in the attack submarine Atlanta.

RADAR

Radio detection and ranging (RADAR) operates by transmitting electromagnetic waves at an object. When the electromagnetic waves are reflected from the object, they are detected by a receiver tuned to their frequency.

Radar was developed simultaneously in Germany, Britain, and the United States in the mid-1930s. But the first military application of radar occurred in Great Britain. By the start of World War II in 1939, Britain was completing an array of radar transmitting and detecting stations around the circumference of England, Wales, and Scotland that could detect approaching aircraft. By 1941, the British were even able to determine the altitude of approaching aircraft.

As with sonar, American interest in radar was intense during the war. The first millimeter wave radar units—radar transmitters working in the extremely short radio frequency ranges—had been developed and were being employed by antisubmarine warfare surface ships to detect surfaced submarines.

The U.S. Navy was probably the most enthusiastic user of radar. Its ships were large enough to carry the massive radar antennas of the time. The "eyes" radar provided served to extend a warship's reach far over the horizon.

Today, an exceedingly complex phased-array system of radars adorns the upper works of the Navy's *Ticonderoga*-class cruisers. Termed Aegis, the system couples long-range radars to powerful computers to detect, assess, and control the response to a threat from the air to the Navy's carrier- or battleship-led task forces.

Right: A look at the SPY 1A radar on the guided-missile cruiser Ticonderoga. *Opposite, top: Aegis missile system radar screens in the* Ticonderoga. *Opposite, bottom: A radar console in the combat information center of the aircraft carrier* Kittyhawk.

COMPUTERS

As with radar, the Navy was an early and enthusiastic user of computers. In World War II, the Navy initiated an extensive computer development program, of which one of the first products was a complete revision of all Navy gunnery tables—an exceptionally complex task requiring millions of repetitive calculations.

In the postwar years, the Navy continued to develop and fund the development of computers, and just as important, the programming of software to make them work. In the mid-1950s, Navy compu- ter programmers and planners developed critical path planning (CPP), which was used for tracking the development of costly and complex weapon systems.

The Navy was a leader in the development of VHSIC (very high-speed integrated circuitry), which has found applications in a host of military computer systems. Today, super computers are being used to develop new sonar and radar detecting methods, to enhance the effects of naval weapons, to develop protective systems against enemy weapons, and to evaluate weapons threats.

The computer operations engineering control board on a guided-missile cruiser.

NAVY ROCKETS, MISSILES, AND NUCLEAR BOMBS

The rocket is the oldest chemical propulsion engine known, and has long been used as a naval weapon. The British bombarded Fort McHenry near Baltimore with rockets, an incident described in the first verse of the "Star Spangled Banner." On August 23, 1814, American troops were routed by rockets at the Battle of Bladensburg, which opened the way for British troops to attack Washington, D.C.

A type of rocket developed by an Englishman named William Congreve was widely used during the Napoleonic wars, but its use declined as more conventional artillery was improved. William Hale, another Englishman, added fins to stabilize rockets and improve their accuracy, but

throughout most of the 19th century the naval rocket was used primarily as a lifesaving device to carry lifelines to stricken ships.

Interest in rocketry was revived shortly after the turn of the century when a Russian physicist named Konstantin E. Ziolkovsky wrote a treatise on the use of rockets for interplanetary travel. His paper stimulated a fresh look at the rocket as a propulsive mechanism, and as a weapon. In 1918, Dr. Robert Goddard of the Massachusetts Institute of Technology proposed a rocket-powered antitank weapon much like the bazooka of World War II. Dr. Goddard also developed the idea of using rockets equipped with instrumentation to explore the upper reaches of the atmosphere, and ultimately the moon and planets. The object of frequent ridicule in the media, Dr. God-

dard worked in relative obscurity until his death in 1945. But his groundwork provided the basis for all future advances in rocketry.

During World War II, the Germans worked on a number of rocket development projects. The best known of these was the A-4, or V-2, rocket. This forerunner of the intercontinental ballistic missile was a liquid-fueled rocket armed with 2,000 pounds of explosive and had a range of between 200 and 220 miles. It is fortunate for the Allied war effort that Hitler, so certain of ultimate victory after the fall of France, slowed the development of the V-2 by relegating it to a low-priority status. Even so, the V-2s that rained on Great Britain in 1944 caused considerable damage and loss of lives. Some historians have suggested that, had the Germans launched their V-2 as-

sault one or two months sooner than they actually did, the Allied invasion of Europe might have been delayed into 1945.

Germany also had several antiaircraft rocket development projects underway, all delayed by lack of priority and mismanagement. Some of these weapons were deployed, but not in enough numbers to significantly hamper the Allied bomber offensive against Germany.

During World War II, Dr. Robert Goddard worked for the U.S. Navy to develop, among other items, a rocket-assisted takeoff (RATO) for

A captured German V-2 rocket is fired from the flight deck of the carrier Midway. *This experiment, conducted in October 1947, proved that missiles could be accurately launched from a moving ship or submarine.*

aircraft. Other rocket weapons developed during World War II included the Hedgehog antisubmarine rocket and the bazooka antitank weapon. The 2.75-inch and five-inch aerial rockets were also developed for use by American and British aircraft.

The development of spin-stabilized rockets for bombarding enemy beach positions was given high priority by the U.S. Navy during World War II. Thousands of rockets were launched against Japanese fortified positions during the Pacific islands campaign. By the time of the 1945 invasion of Okinawa, these weapons had proven so effective that the Japanese had moved their defenses inland, beyond the reach of the rockets.

The U.S. Navy experimentation with cruise missiles like the Regulus series began after World War II. The proliferation of missile types and their promise led the Navy to divide them into four categories: "air-to-air" to equip fighter aircraft, "antiship" missiles for the destruction of surface vessels, "surface-to-air" for antiaircraft defense, and "strategic nuclear" missiles.

SUBMARINE-LAUNCHED BALLISTIC MISSILES

In the mid-1950s, the Navy considered basing the Jupiter intermediate-range ballistic missile aboard certain warships. But the prospect of smaller and lighter nuclear warheads plus the problems associated with maintaining liquid-fueled missiles aboard ship caused the Navy to rethink its plans. The solution lay in the solid-fueled Polaris submarine-launched ballistic missile (SLBM). In 1960

the Navy's first ballistic missile submarine, the *George Washington*, was armed with 16 Polaris A-1 missiles. Production of the Polaris missile continued through the 1960s, with upgrades coming in the form of the A-2 and A-3 variants. The A-1 and A-2 variants were armed with the W47 warhead, and the A-3 was armed with the W58 warhead.

In the late 1960s, multiple independently targeted reentry vehicles (MIRV) were developed to counter the threat of Soviet anti-ballistic missiles (ABM). The Navy's MIRV was designated the Mark 3 Reentry Vehicle, and

carried W68 40-kiloton nuclear warheads. Starting in March 1971, the Navy began replacing the Polaris missiles with the Poseidon SLBM carrying MIRVed warheads. By 1975, over 5,000 W68 warheads had been built. The Poseidon C-3 UGM-73 is the oldest submarine-launched

ballistic missile in service. It has a 2,800-mile range, carries up to 14 W68 MIRVed warheads, and is fitted in the *Lafayette*-class ballistic missile submarines.

Beginning in June 1968, production of an estimated 3,200 W76 100-kiloton nuclear warheads was begun for the Trident I (C-4) SLBM. The Trident C-4 UGM-96 SLBM is a 4,600-mile range, three stage SLBM that can carry up to eight Mark 4 reentry vehicles—all of which can be targeted independently. The C-4 is carried aboard the *Benjamin Franklin*-class submarines, as well as the first eight submarines of the *Ohio* class.

The Trident D-5 is a longer-range and more accurate SLBM than the C-4. The D-5 became operational in *Ohio*-class submarines in 1990, beginning with the *Tennessee*. This missile has a range of 6,900 miles and carries W87 475-kiloton nuclear warheads in eight independently targetable reentry vehicles.

The Trident I C-4 *(right) and the* Poseidon C-3 *are two of the Navy's submarine-launched ballistic missiles. Not shown here is the newer* Trident II D-5, *which is arming the later-model* Ohio-*class submarines.*

CRUISE MISSILES

The BGM-109 Tomahawk Land Attack Missile (TLAM) was developed for use by both surface vessels and submarines. The TLAM-N has a 200-kiloton nuclear warhead; the TLAM-C and TLAM-D have conventional warheads with high explosives and submunitions, respectively. All three TLAM variants have a range of nearly 1,400 miles. A second Tomahawk variation is the Tomahawk Antiship Missile (TASM), which is designed for use against surface ships. The TASM has a 1,000-pound conventional warhead and a range of 285 miles.

The TLAM uses an inertial guidance system with a unique pattern matching system that compares the features of the surface terrain passing beneath the missile to a map stored in its computer. The TASM doesn't have this system, which is unnecessary for over-the-water flight.

The TLAM and the TASM are fitted on the *Iowa*-class battleships, the cruisers of the *Virginia*, *Long Beach*, and *Ticonderoga* classes, and the destroyers of the *Arleigh Burke* and the *Spruance* classes. Some of these ships fire their Tomahawks from armored-box launchers that serve as storage and launch containers, but most fire the missiles from vertical launchers. Tomahawks can also be fired from 21-inch submarine torpedo tubes and, in the later *Los Angeles*-class attack submarines, from vertical launch tubes.

A Tomahawk cruise missile in flight. The Tomahawk comes in an antiship and a land-attack variant, and may be armed with conventional or nuclear warheads.

AIR-TO-AIR MISSILES

As aircraft flew faster and higher, it became necessary to develop weapons other than machine guns and cannons to allow one aircraft to engage another at distances beyond visual range. In the years following World War II, American efforts in this regard produced a series of rocket-powered missiles that contained on-board guidance systems. The most effective of these missiles was the AIM-9 Sidewinder series, which used an infrared (IR) seeker to guide the missile. Since the first IR seekers had a narrow field of view, the attacking pilot had to approach the enemy from behind to lock the IR sensor onto the target's hot jet engine exhaust. By the mid-1970s the AIM-9L Sidewinder had an IR seeker so sensitive it could lock onto an aircraft from any angle of approach; it is therefore said to have an "all-aspect" guidance system.

The AIM-54 Phoenix is a long-range air-to-air missile (up to 100 miles) developed for use on the F-14 Tomcat. The Phoenix is guided by a semiactive radar seeker during most of its flight, then by active terminal guidance as it approaches its target at speeds up to Mach 5. In the development wings is the Advanced Air-to-Air Missile (AAAM), which will replace the Phoenix in 1996.

The Advanced Medium-Range Air-to-Air Missile (AMRAAM) is under joint development by the Navy and Air Force. The AMRAAM-120A will be hardened against enemy electronic and other countermeasures and will have a range of 40 miles. This missile will replace the 30-mile range Sparrow III AIM-7, which uses a semiactive doppler radar homing system.

An F/A-18 Hornet fires an Aim 9 Sidewinder air-to-air missile.

ANTISHIP MISSILES

The world's navies were convinced of the effectiveness of the antiship missile in 1967 when two Egyptian patrol boats sank the Israeli destroyer *Eliat* with three Soviet-built Styx missiles. During the Falkland Islands War in 1982, French-built Exocet missiles fired from Argentinean aircraft sank the HMS *Sheffield* and the merchant ship *Atlantic Conveyor*. In 1986, two Exocets fired by an Iraqi plane heavily damaged the American frigate *Stark*.

Antiship missile technology has progressed past the Exocet, although this missile is still in use. The U.S. Navy's Harpoon 84A is a highly versatile antiship missile that can be launched from aircraft, surface ships, or submarines. This missile, which has a range of up to 80 miles, homes in on its target using an onboard radar guidance system. It was first used against Libyan patrol boats in the Gulf of Sidra in 1986.

The Maverick AGM-65 is an aircraft-launched antiship missile. It was derived from the Air Force's Maverick anti-tank missile. Maverick has a range of 14 miles and carries a 300-pound high-explosive warhead. Maverick homes in on a target that has been illuminated with a laser, which is mounted in the launching aircraft, another aircraft, or even a surface vessel.

The Penguin Mark 3 AGM-119 is an antiship missile developed by the Norwegian Navy. The U.S. Navy is using it to equip the SH 60B LAMPS (Light Airborne Multi-purpose System) III helicopter. The missile has a fire-and-forget guidance system—the target is acquired by the missile's guidance system after launch and it goes on its way, allowing the launching aircraft to turn its attention to another target. Penguin has a range in excess of 25 miles and is armed with a 265-pound high-explosive warhead.

A Harpoon antiship missile, photographed at the instant it strikes a decommissioned target ship.

SURFACE-TO-AIR MISSILES

The Sea Sparrow RIM-7 anti-aircraft missile is the Sparrow air-to-air missile (AAM) adopted for use aboard ships. The Sea Sparrow is most commonly fired from either an eight-tube Mark 25 Basic Point Defense Missile System (BPDMS) launcher or the eight-tube Mark 29 launcher. The Sea Sparrow has a radar homing system and a range of 11 miles.

The Standard RIM-66B replaced the earlier Talos, Terrier, and Tartar missiles. It has a range of 95 miles, can reach an altitude of 80,000 feet, and is equipped with improved electronic countermeasures gear. The program to develop a nuclear warhead for this missile was canceled in 1985. The SM-1 medium-range version of the Standard is no longer in production but remains in service. It is being replaced by the Standard RIM-66C, which is an extended-range version capable of reaching enemy aircraft out to 46 miles. The RIM-66C uses a semiactive radar homing system and carries a high-explosive warhead. The RIM-66C is used on Aegis-equipped air-defense ships.

The Terrier RIM-2 entered Navy service in 1962. It remains in service because it is the only surface-to-air missile in the Navy's inventory that can carry a nuclear warhead, the one-kiloton W45-1. The Terrier is carried by ten cruisers and ten destroyers, and is designed for use against large formations of attacking aircraft. The missile rides a radar beam that must illuminate the target throughout the missile's flight. This limits the missile to line-of-sight flight and invites counterattack with antiradiation missiles.

A pair of Standard extended-range missiles in Mark 10 launchers on the guided-missile cruiser Long Beach.

ASROC

The ASROC (Antisubmarine Rocket) is a ship-launched antisubmarine weapon. Previously, the short-range ASROC could carry the one-kiloton W44 nuclear warhead; now it only carries a conventional Mark 46 homing torpedo. ASROC is fired from either a box launcher or a vertical launch system to the area where an enemy submarine is suspected to be operating. The Mark 46 torpedo separates from the rocket over the area and is lowered by parachute. Once in the water, the torpedo's guidance system takes over and, using a combination of passive and active sonar, tracks the enemy submarine. ASROC has a range of slightly more than seven miles.

ANTI-RADAR MISSILES

The HARM (High-Speed, Anti-Radar Missile) AGM-88A is an air-to-ground missile that homes in on sources of radar energy and destroys them with a warhead armed with 145 pounds of high explosive. The HARM may be launched from the F/A-18, A-6E, A-7E, or EA-6B carrier-based aircraft, and is replacing the shorter range Shrike AGM-45. HARMs were used against Libyan radar sites in 1986.

The Sidearm AGM-122 is an antiradar missile based on the design of the obsolete Sidewinders that were placed in storage in the 1970s. These short-range weapons, which became operational in 1986, are used for attacking mobile and fixed ground-based anti-aircraft weapons using radar.

Main image: *The frigate* Lockwood *fires an ASROC.*
Inset: *An AGM-88A HARM anti-radar missile.*

MISCELLANEOUS MISSILES

The Stinger FIM-92 one-man portable antiaircraft missile is used by both the Marines and the Navy for aircraft defense. Stingers have been carried aboard many Navy ships since the threat of terrorist attacks developed in the mid-1980s. The Stinger uses an infrared homing guidance system and can attack an aircraft from any angle. The missile has a range of 3.5 miles.

The Tube-launched, Optically-tracked, Wire-guided antitank 1 missile (TOW) is used by the Marine Corps as a mobile ground-based anti-tank weapon and as an airborne antitank weapon when mounted on the AH-1T/W SeaCobra Helicopter. The TOW has a range of just under two miles and is armed with a shaped-charge warhead capable of penetrating the armor of most main battle tanks in service today.

NUCLEAR BOMBS

The Navy's nuclear bomb capability began with the B-43 ten-kiloton bomb in 1961; a few are still in service. The 20-kiloton B-57 (1963) nuclear device is used in aerial and depth-bomb configurations, and may be carried by antisubmarine warfare aircraft such as the S-3 Viking, the P-3 Orion, and even the SH-3 helicopter. The B-61 has a yield of 350 kilotons and entered service in 1968. The B-61 can be configured for different yields up to 500 kilotons. Nuclear bombs can be carried by the A-7E Corsair (one) and the A-6E Intruder (two). The F/A-18 Hornet may also be configured to carry nuclear bombs.

A Marine prepares to fire a Stinger surface-to-air missile from the deck of the mine countermeasures ship Inflict.

THE SURFACE FLEET

The United States Navy has four major components, the surface fleet, the submarine fleet, naval aviation, and the Marine Corps. Of these four, the surface fleet is not only the oldest component but the largest as well, comprising approximately 400 ships in the early 1990s.

The surface fleet is divided into two broad categories, combat ships and auxiliary ships. The combat fleet is further divided into those ships on active duty and those on reserve duty, and includes eleven ship types: aircraft carriers, battleships, cruisers, destroyers, frigates, command ships, amphibious ships, landing craft, assault amphibians, patrol craft, and mine countermeasures ships. The role of the combat fleet is implied in its name: engaging enemy forces in combat.

The auxiliary fleet provides the support ships needed to keep the combat fleet functioning. It includes numerous types of logistics and research vessels, which may or may not be on active duty, depending on the needs of the combat fleet.

The surface fleet is divided between two major commands, the Atlantic and the Pacific fleets. Both of these fleets are subdivided into smaller fleets; for example, the Sixth Fleet, which serves in the Mediterranean, is part of the Atlantic Fleet, and the Third and Seventh fleets are elements of the Pacific Fleet. Each of these fleets may then be further subdivided into smaller task forces like the Middle East Force.

Above: The Saipan (right), a Tarawa-class assault ship, steams in formation with support ships. These are the world's largest amphibious assault ships. **Below:** A silhouette of a typical warship showing the location of major armament and electronic systems.

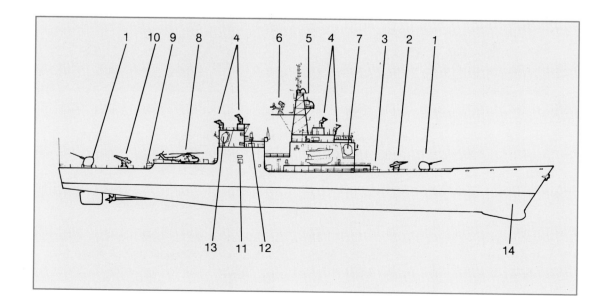

1. 3-inch or 5-inch gun
2. Mk 26 missile launcher system
3. Tomahawk missiles
4. Pulse-doppler tracking weapon
5. Fire control radar
6. Air search radar
7. Multifunction phased-array radar
8. LAMPS helicopter
9. Harpoon missiles
10. Mk 13 missile launcher
11. Torpedo hatch
12. Phalanx guns
13. AN/SPY-1A radar
14. AN/SQS-53A sonar

AIRCRAFT CARRIERS

The aircraft carriers of the United States Navy are the capital ships of the surface fleet. They are the largest and most powerful surface warships the world has ever known, with an offensive armament exceeded only by the Navy's ballistic missile submarines. When at sea, they lead heavily armed squadrons of fighting and support ships in units called battle groups. These battle groups serve to maintain the security of the United States and its allies, guarantee free travel along international waterways, project U.S. power to the world's trouble spots, and, when necessary, fight the nation's wars.

These mighty ships come in six distinct classes, of which two—*Enterprise* and *Nimitz*—are nuclear-powered. The carriers of the *Midway*, *Forrestal*, *Kitty Hawk*, and *Kennedy* classes are all powered by conventional means. In addition, one aircraft carrier of World War II-vintage, the *Lexington*, is operated as a pilot training ship.

The use of aircraft carriers was pioneered by the British and the Japanese, but it was the U.S. Navy that raised carrier warfare to a high art. Within the year following the attack on Pearl Harbor, American and Japanese carriers traded blows at the Battle of the Coral Sea, and American aircraft carriers at the 1942 Battle of Midway turned the tide of Japanese conquest. Following the Battle of Midway, aircraft carriers were used to spearhead America's Pacific counteroffensive, which ended with Japan's surrender in September 1945.

In the immediate postwar years aircraft carriers experienced a fall from military grace. This came about as a result of the belief that the long-ranged manned bomber had rendered aircraft carriers obsolete. Evidence to the contrary was supplied during the Korean War (1950–53), a conflict in

which the aircraft carrier once again played a pivotal role. Time and again during that war, carriers sent bomb-laden aircraft winging over South and North Korea to destroy enemy communications, logistics, armor, and troop transport facilities.

Even after the Korean War, however, there were still many who doubted the worth of aircraft carriers. Early in the

Kennedy administration (1963–65), these doubters fought a major political skirmish against the carrier admirals, who sought to retain the large aircraft carrier as the centerpiece of the surface fleet. A compromise was reached in the form of the *Kitty Hawk* ships, which were large but powered by conventional rather than nuclear means. Later, carrier operations off the

coast of Vietnam once again proved
the usefulness of the aircraft carrier.

As international tensions
heightened during the late 1970s and
early 1980s, the number of aircraft
carriers in operation was increased,
and three new ships of the *Nimitz*
class were ordered—the *Theodore
Roosevelt*, the *Abraham Lincoln*, and
the *George Washington*.

The *Kittyhawk, the lead carrier in its
class, has two fighter squadrons, two
strike fighter squadrons, one medium-
attack squadron, one electronic warfare
squadron, one antisubmarine warfare
squadron, and one helicopter squadron.*

Midway-Class (CV) Aircraft Carrier

The *Midway* class of aircraft carriers now consists of a single ship, the *Midway* (CV 41). This ship is the Navy's last active-duty aircraft carrier to be built during World War II. The design of the *Midway* and its sister ships was based on experience gained in the Coral Sea and Midway battles of 1942. Only three ships of this class were built: *Midway*, *Franklin D. Roosevelt* (CV 42), and *Coral Sea* (CV 43). None saw action during the war. Two other ships intended for this class were canceled. The *Roosevelt* was decommissioned after being replaced by the *Nimitz* in late 1977, and the *Coral Sea* was decommissioned in April 1990.

Having been taught by the Japanese to appreciate what bombs could do to its ships, the Navy outfitted the *Midway* carriers with armored flight decks. The *Midway* carriers were also heavily armed with batteries of five-inch, 40 millimeter, and 20mm weapons. Some 137 aircraft could be accommodated on their flight decks and in hangars below decks.

The *Midway* is 900 feet long at the waterline, displaces 67,000 tons, and has a flight deck that is 979 feet long. Considered huge by World War II standards, the *Midway* is actually smaller than all other U.S. aircraft carriers currently in service. Because of its size it cannot carry the F-14A Tomcat; however, it does carry 65 aircraft comprised of three F/A-18 Hornet fighter squadrons, two attack squadrons of A-6E Intruders, one tactical electronic warfare squadron of EA-6B Prowlers, one early airborne warning squadron of E-2C Hawkeyes, and one squadron of helicopter antisubmarine warfare SH-3H Sea Kings or SH-60 Seahawks. *Midway*'s carrier air wing is designated CVW-5.

Over the years the *Midway* has been extensively remodeled. An angled flight deck was added in the 1950s, and its open bow was closed in when a hurricane bow was added later in the yards. Its guns have all been removed and replaced by the 20mm Phalanx Close-In Weapons System (CIWS) Mark 15 multibarrel guns and two eight-cell Sea Sparrow missile launchers. The *Midway* is driven by four Westinghouse steam turbines that develop 212,000 horsepower. Power from 12 Babcock & Wilcox 600-psi boilers enables it to achieve a top speed of 32 knots (36.8 miles per hour).

The service record for the *Midway* includes an initial stint with the Sixth Fleet, after which it was sent to the Pacific in 1965. There, it took part in operations off the coast of Vietnam. *Midway* will continue to serve as a first-line carrier with the Pacific Fleet until at least the late 1990s.

MIDWAY-CLASS (CV) AIRCRAFT CARRIER

Operational (commissioned):	CV 41 USS *Midway* (September 1945)
Displacement:	67,000 tons
Dimensions:	
Length:	1,006 ft.
Width:	121 ft.
Draft:	36 ft.
Propulsion:	Four Westinghouse steam turbines, 212,000 hp Twelve Babcock & Wilcox 600-psi boilers
Speed:	32 knots (36.8 mph)
Armament:	Two 20mm Phalanx CIWS Mk 15 multibarrel guns Sea Sparrow SAMs fired from two Mk 25 octuple launchers
Fire control:	Two Mk 115 fire control systems
Aircraft:	F/A-18 Hornets, A-6E Intruders, EA-6B Prowlers, E-2C Hawkeyes, SH-3H Sea Kings or SH-60 Seahawks
Surveillance radar:	SPS-48C 3D search SPS-49 air search SPS-65 navigation
Sonar:	None
Crew:	
Navy:	2,826
Naval air wing:	1,860
Marines:	72

The *Midway was laid down in 1943 and commissioned at the close of World War II. Today, the Midway is based in Yosuka, Japan, as part of the Pacific Fleet.*

Forrestal-Class (CV) Aircraft Carriers

The *Forrestal*-class aircraft carriers were designed and built after World War II. They were the first of the so-called "super carriers." With a standard displacement of around 60,000 tons, they were even larger than the *Iowa*-class battleships of World War II.

This class came into service when the valuable contributions made by aircraft carriers in the Korean War managed to convince the Department of Defense that such ships still had an important role to play in modern warfare. Construction of the *Forrestal* class began in 1952. The *Forrestal* (CV 59) was laid down in July 1952, launched in December 1954, and commissioned in October 1955. The *Independence* (CV 62) was commissioned less than four years later, in January 1959.

The *Forrestal* carriers feature an angled flight deck, a British innovation that offers more usable space than the traditional straight flight deck. In addition to the angled deck, the *Forrestal* carriers also received four British-designed steam catapults capable of launching 80,000-pound aircraft—more than enough to handle the 73,000-pound F-14 Tomcat.

As aircraft size has increased, aircraft storage space on carriers has diminished. Thus the *Forrestal* carriers, which were designed to handle up to 100 World War II-type aircraft, generally have about 85 aircraft. However, they retain an enormous aviation fuel storage capacity of 750,000 gallons. The *Forrestal* and *Saratoga* have flight decks that are 20 feet shorter than the *Ranger* and *Independence*. Top speed on the four ships is about 33 knots (37.95 miles per hour). All are powered by four Westinghouse steam turbines that develop 260,000 horsepower in the *Forrestal*, and 280,000 horsepower in the *Saratoga* (CV 60), *Ranger* (CV 61), and *Independence*. All four ships are capable of steaming 12,000 nautical miles (13,800 miles) without refueling. All four ships carry an average complement of about 2,850 officers and men, plus an air wing crew of 3,400, plus 72 Marines.

Each carrier in this class generally has two fighter squadrons (VF) of F-14A Tomcat fighters; two or three attack squadrons (VA) of A-6E Intruders or A-7E Corsairs; one squadron of electronic warfare (VAQ) EA-6B Prowlers; one squadron of early warning (VAW) E-2C Hawkeyes; one squadron of antisubmarine warfare (VS) S-3A/B Vikings; and one squadron of helicopter antisubmarine warfare (HS) SH-3H Sea Kings or SH-60 Seahawks. *Independence* currently has two squadrons (VFA) of F/A-18 Hornets and no A-7E Corsairs, and *Ranger* has only two A-6E squadrons and no A-7E Corsairs. Carrier

FORRESTAL-CLASS (CV) AIRCRAFT CARRIERS

Operational (commissioned):	CV 59 USS *Forrestal* (October 1955) CV 60 USS *Saratoga* (April 1956) CV 61 USS *Ranger* (August 1957) CV 62 USS *Independence* (January 1959)
Displacement:	
CV 59–60:	59,650 tons
CV 61–62:	60,000 tons
Dimensions:	
Length:	
CV 59:	1,086 ft.
CV 60:	1,071 ft.
CV 61–62:	1,071 ft.
Width:	130 ft.
Draft:	37 ft.
Propulsion:	Four Westinghouse steam turbines, (260,000 hp in CV 59, 280,000 hp in CV 60, CV 61, and CV 62) Eight Babcock & Wilcox boilers (600 psi in CV 59; 1,200 psi in CV 60, CV 61, and CV 62)
Speed:	
CV 59:	33 knots (37.95 mph)
CV 60–62:	34 knots (39.1 mph)
Armament:	
All:	Three 20mm Phalanx CIWS Mk 15 multibarrel guns
CV 59–60:	Sea Sparrow SAMs fired from two Mk 29 octuple launchers
CV 61–62:	Sea Sparrow SAMs fired from three Mk 29 octuple launchers
Fire control:	Two Mk 91 fire control systems
Aircraft:	F-14A Tomcats, F/A-18 Hornets or A-7E Corsairs, A-6E Intruders, EA-6B Prowlers, E-2C Hawkeyes, S-3A/B Vikings, SH-3H Sea Kings or SH-60 Seahawks
Surveillance radar:	SPS-10 search SPS-48C 3D search SPS-49 air search
Sonar:	None
Crew:	
Navy:	
CV 59:	2,958
CV 60:	2,896
CV 61:	2,889
CV 62:	2,793
Naval air wing:	3,400
Marines:	72

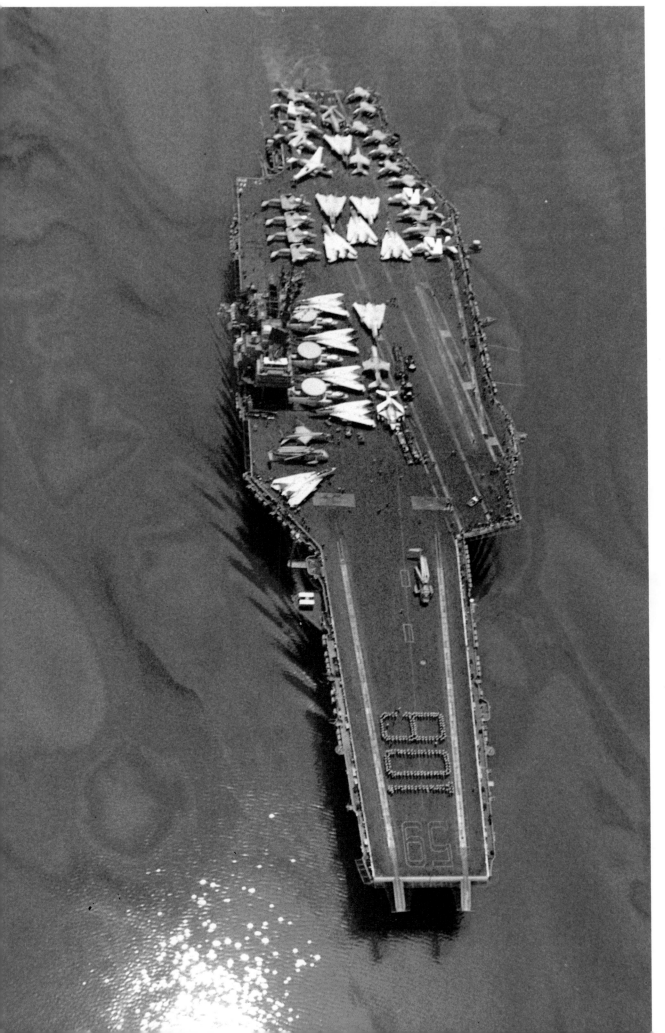

Air Wing-6 (CVW) currently serves aboard the *Forrestal*, CVW-17 aboard the *Saratoga*, CVW-2 aboard the *Ranger*, and CVW-10 aboard the *Independence*. All four carriers in this class have surface-search and air-search radars.

The *Forrestal* carriers have had a long and eventful service career. *Forrestal*, *Saratoga*, and *Independence* served in the Atlantic and Mediterranean until the mid-1960s. In late 1965, the *Independence* joined Task Force 77 in the Gulf of Tonkin and launched aircraft against targets in North and South Vietnam. The *Forrestal* was to have joined the task force in 1967, but its tour was cut short by a fire that caused 194 casualties and required seven months for repairs. *Saratoga* remained with the Atlantic Fleet. By 1975, all four *Forrestal*-class ships had been fitted with antisubmarine warfare (ASW) equipment and aircraft, and they were redesignated as multipurpose carriers (CV). Aircraft from *Saratoga* were engaged by Libyan fighters in 1986.

The *Forrestal*, *Saratoga*, and *Independence* have all undergone the Service Life Extension Program (SLEP), which is intended to add at least 15 years to their projected 30-year life spans. The *Forrestal* received its modifications between January 1983 and May 1985, the *Saratoga* between October 1980 and February 1983, and the *Independence* between April 1985 and August 1987.

The Forrestal *was one the first class of aircraft carriers to operate jet aircraft.*

107

Kitty Hawk-Class (CV) Aircraft Carriers

The *Kitty Hawk* aircraft carriers are the largest conventionally powered warships ever built. The class includes the *Kitty Hawk* (CV 63), *Constellation* (CV 64), *America* (CV 66), and *John F. Kennedy* (CV 67). This last carrier is considered a single-ship class, but is grouped with the other three *Kitty Hawk* carriers because of the similarities all four share in flight deck layout and propulsion systems.

Construction on the *Kitty Hawk* class began in the late 1950s. The *Kitty Hawk* was laid down at the New York Shipbuilding yards in Camden, New Jersey, in December 1957, launched in May 1960, and commissioned in April 1961. In 1987 it entered the Philadelphia Naval Shipyard to undergo a modernization process that will increase its service life from 30 to 45 years. Its entire service life has been spent with the Pacific Fleet.

Both the *Kitty Hawk* and the *Constellation*, which was commissioned in October 1961, incorporate several improvements over the *Forrestal* carriers. For instance, a larger flight deck was installed, and the port-side elevator was repositioned so that it can be used during flight operations. In addition, both the port-side elevator and the center deck elevator were redesigned to handle larger aircraft.

A funnel that is narrower than those found on its

predecessors is a distinguishing feature of the *America*, which was laid down in January 1961 and commissioned in January 1965. This ship also has a bow sonar dome. The SQS-23 search sonar was installed, then removed in 1981 when escort ships demonstrated that they could perform the sonar search function more efficiently.

The final carrier in this series, the *John F. Kennedy*, was originally not meant to be a *Kitty Hawk*-class ship. Instead, it was to be the first in a new class of nuclear-powered carriers. But due to a decision made by Secretary of Defense Robert S. McNamara, who was not convinced that the Navy needed another large nuclear carrier, it was laid down in 1964 as a conventionally powered ship. The *Kennedy* can be distinguished by its funnel, which is angled at about 40 degrees outboard to keep air currents produced by engine heat from interfering with flight operations.

Built as attack carriers (CVA), all four *Kitty Hawk* ships were modified to the multimission (CV) role between 1973 and 1975. The *Kitty Hawk* has completed Service Life Extension Program (SLEP) modifications; the *Constellation* is currently undergoing SLEP modifications, and the *America* and *Kennedy* are scheduled to follow suit in 1994 and 1996, respectively.

The carriers in this class are 990 feet long at the waterline and 130 feet wide. The flight decks of all four are nearly 1,050 feet long; flight deck width is 264 feet on the *Kennedy*, and 252 feet on the other three ships. *Kitty Hawk*, *Constellation*, and *America* displace 80,800 tons when fully loaded; the *Kennedy* displaces 80,940 tons. All are powered by four Westinghouse steam turbines that develop 280,000 horsepower and are driven by eight Foster Wheeler

1,200-psi boilers. Although top speeds are classified, these carriers are known to have attained over 30 knots (34.53 miles per hour).

Normal crew complement on the *Kitty Hawk* carriers ranges between 2,773 and 3,045 officers and men, plus an additional 2,500 air wing crew members. A Marine Corp detachment of 72 officers and enlisted men is responsible for security. The air wing operates about 85 aircraft, which are usually divided into two fighter

The aircraft carrier America *moves through the Suez Canal to the Red Sea and the Indian Ocean. The carrier has a range of 12,000 miles.*

KITTY HAWK-CLASS (CV) AIRCRAFT CARRIERS

Operational (commissioned):	CV 63 USS *Kitty Hawk* (April 1961)
	CV 64 USS *Constellation* (October 1961)
	CV 66 USS *America* (January 1965)
	CV 67 USS *John F. Kennedy* (September 1968)
Displacement:	
CV 63–64, 66:	80,800 tons
CV 67:	80,940 tons
Dimensions:	
Length:	
CV 63–64:	1,045 ft.
CV 66:	1,047 ft.
CV 67:	1,051 ft.
Width:	
CV 63–64, 66:	130 ft.
CV 67:	128.5 ft.
Draft:	37 ft.
Propulsion:	Four Westinghouse steam turbines, 280,000 hp
	Eight Foster Wheeler 1,200-psi boilers
Speed:	Classified
Armament:	Three 20mm Phalanx CIWS Mk 15 multibarrel guns
	Sea Sparrow SAMs fired from three Mk 29 octuple launchers
Fire control:	Three Mk 91 fire control systems
Aircraft:	F-14A Tomcats, F/A-18 Hornets or A-7E Corsairs, A-6E Intruders, EA-6B Prowlers, E-2C Hawkeyes, S-3A/B Vikings, SH-3H Sea Kings or SH-60 Seahawks
Surveillance radar:	SPS-10F/28B search
	SPS-48C 3D search
	SPS-49 air search
Sonar:	None
Crew:	
Navy:	
CV 63:	2,773
CV 64:	3,017
CV 66:	2,983
CV 67:	3,045
Naval air wing:	2,500
Marines:	72

squadrons (VF) of F-14A Tomcat fighters, and three attack squadrons (VA) of A-6E Intruders, A-7E Corsairs, or (VFA) of F/A-18 Hornets. The air wings also operate one electronic warfare squadron (VAQ) of EA-6B Prowlers, one squadron of early warning (VAW) E-2C Hawkeyes, one squadron of antisubmarine warfare (VS) S-3A/B Vikings, and one squadron of helicopter antisubmarine warfare (HS) SH-3H Sea Kings or SH-60 Seahawks. Carrier Wing-1 (CVW) serves aboard the *America*, CVW-3 serves aboard the *John F. Kennedy*, CVW-14 serves aboard the *Constellation*, and CVW-8 serves aboard the *Kitty Hawk*.

Defensive armament on *Kitty Hawk* carriers consists of three 20 millimeter Phalanx CIWS Mark 15 multibarrel guns, and three eight-cell Sea Sparrow missile launchers. The carriers also have surface search, air detection, and threat detection radars.

Enterprise-Class (CVN) Aircraft Carrier

When the *Enterprise* (CVN 65) launched its attack aircraft on a strike against North Vietnam in November 1965, it became history's first nuclear-powered ship in the world to engage in combat. Laid down in February 1958, it was also the first nuclear-powered aircraft carrier to be built.

The *Enterprise* represents a modification of both the *Forrestal* and *Kitty Hawk* classes of carrier design. The hull derives from the *Forrestal* class, and the two-deck launching arrangement (which includes two steam catapults and four deck edge elevators) derives from the *Kitty Hawk* ships. Unlike conventionally powered *Forrestal* carriers, however, the nuclear-powered *Enterprise* has no funnels aft of the island.

Commissioned in November 1961, the *Enterprise* was to have been joined by a second ship in its class, but the Eisenhower administration did not release the funds necessary for construction. At the time it entered service, the *Enterprise* was the largest ship ever built. It is 1,040 feet long at the waterline and 133 feet wide, and has a flight deck that is 1,101 feet long and 257 feet wide. Its top speed is classified, but it is known to make over 30 knots (34.53 miles per hour). Such speed is made possible by eight nuclear reactors, which power four steam turbines that

produce 280,000 horsepower. When the *Enterprise* was commissioned, it was estimated that its nuclear fuel would give it a cruising range of 200,000 miles. In fact, its first fuel cores were not replaced until it had surpassed the 207,000-mile mark.

The *Enterprise* was originally designated as an attack (CVAN) carrier. In 1964 it joined with the nuclear-powered missile cruiser *Long Beach* and the nuclear-powered frigate *Bainbridge* to form the world's first nuclear-powered task force. These ships traveled 37,522 miles around the world without refueling or replenishing, and they did so in 64 cruising days. In 1975 the *Enterprise* was converted into a multimission carrier (CVN).

The *Enterprise* is equipped with surface search, air detection, and threat detection radars. It is armed with the Phalanx Close-In Weapons System (CIWS) for air defense. A scheduled Terrier missile system was never installed, and it was not until a 1979 modernization that two Sea Sparrow missile launchers were installed (a third will be added in the mid-1990s). However, the use of nuclear power plants means that aviation fuel and other stores could be kept in space normally reserved for the fuel needed to power oil-fired boilers.

Enterprise normally carries a crew of 3,319 officers and men, plus an additional 2,625 air wing members and 72 Marines. The *Enterprise*'s air wing (CVW-11) contains the usual complement of two fighter squadrons (VF) of F-14A Tomcat fighters; three attack squadrons (VA), one of A-6E Intruders and two of F/A-18 Hornets; one squadron of electronic warfare (VAQ) EA-6B Prowlers; one squadron of early warning (VAW) E-2C Hawkeyes; one squadron of antisubmarine warfare (VS) S-3A/B Vikings, and one squadron of helicopter antisubmarine (HS) warfare SH-3H Sea Kings or SH-60 Seahawks.

ENTERPRISE-CLASS (CVN) AIRCRAFT CARRIER	
Operational (commissioned):	CVN 65 USS *Enterprise* (November 1961)
Displacement:	90,970 tons
Dimensions:	
Length:	1,101 ft.
Width:	133 ft.
Draft:	39 ft.
Propulsion:	Four steam turbines, 280,000 hp
	Eight Westinghouse A2W pressurized-water nuclear reactors
Speed:	Classified
Armament:	Three 20mm Phalanx CIWS Mk 15 multibarrel guns
	Sea Sparrow SAMs fired from two Mk 29 octuple launchers
Fire control:	Two Mk 91 fire control systems
Aircraft:	F-14A Tomcats, F/A-18 Hornets, A-6E Intruders, EA-6B Prowlers, E-2C Hawkeyes, S-3A/B Vikings, SH-3H Sea Kings or SH-60 Seahawks
Surveillance radar:	SPS-10F/28B search SPS-48C 3D search SPS-49 air search SPS-85 threat warning
Sonar:	None
Crew:	
Navy:	3,319
Naval air wing:	2,625
Marines:	72

CVN 65 is the Enterprise, *the world's first nuclear-powered aircraft carrier. Commissioned in November 1961, the* Enterprise *can cruise more than 200,000 miles between refuelings.*

Nimitz-Class (CVN) Aircraft Carriers

Designed in the 1950s to replace the *Midway*-class carriers, the carriers of the *Nimitz* class encountered many delays in their respective construction programs. Among the contributing factors in these delays were labor disputes and a shortage of skilled labor. The *Nimitz* (CVN 68) took seven years to build, finally entering service in May 1975. It was followed by the *Dwight D. Eisenhower* (CVN 69), which was commissioned in October 1977.

In the late 1970s budgetary constraints and the defense build-down philosophy of the Carter administration resulted in the cancellation of additional *Nimitz* carriers. Then came the 1979 Soviet invasion of Afghanistan—an action that spurred Congress to demand another ship in this class. In the event, two carriers were built: the *Carl Vinson* (CVN 70), commissioned in March 1982; and the *Theodore Roosevelt* (CVN 71), commissioned in October 1986. Four more *Nimitz* carriers were approved during the Reagan administration: the *Abraham Lincoln* (CVN 72), commissioned in February 1988; and the *George Washington* (CVN 73), the *John C. Stennis* (CVN 74), and the *United States* (CVN 75), all of which are building and scheduled for commissioning in the mid-to-late 1990s.

Four steam turbines developing 280,000 horsepower are needed to drive these immense ships, which displace 81,600 tons when fully loaded, provisioned, and armed. Power is supplied by two pressurized-water Westinghouse AW4 nuclear reactors with fuel cores estimated to have a life of 13 years or 800,000 to 1,000,000 miles. At the waterline, *Nimitz*

carriers are 1,040 feet long and 138 feet wide. Their flight decks are, on average, 1,089 feet long and 250 feet wide, and their hangar decks are 684 feet long, 108 feet wide, and 26.5 feet high. Because they use nuclear engines, they have no funnels—a point of identification—and all carrier island structures are boxy. The top speeds of these carriers are classified, but they are known to exceed 30 knots (34.53 miles per hour).

The 85 aircraft normally carried aboard Nimitz-class carriers are divided into two fighter squadrons (VF) of F-14A Tomcat fighters; three attack squadrons (VA) operating A-7E Corsairs or A-6E Intruders and F/A-18 Hornets; one electronic warfare squadron (VAQ) of EA-6B Prowlers; one squadron of early warning (VAW)) E-2C Hawkeyes; one squadron of antisubmarine warfare (VS) S-3A/B Vikings; and one squadron of helicopter antisubmarine warfare (HS) SH-3H Sea Kings or SH-60 Seahawks. Carrier Air Wing-8 (CVW) serves aboard the Roosevelt, CVW-7 aboard the Eisenhower, CVW-9 aboard the Nimitz, and CVW-15 aboard the Vinson. No CVWs have as yet been identified for the building Nimitz-class carriers. Standard crew complement ranges between 3,100 to 3,219 officers and men, plus an air wing complement of over 2,800, and 72 Marines.

Nimitz carriers launch their aircraft from two decks, one angled, one straight. Each deck has two steam catapults and is served by two elevators operating at the deck edges. Each carrier also has surface search, air detection, and threat detection radars, depending on the specific ship. Four 20 millimeter Phalanx Close-In Weapons System (CIWS) Mark 15 multibarrel guns provide close-in protection, while three eight-cell Sea Sparrow missile launchers provide longer-range protection. In the main, however, the Nimitz-class carriers depend on their escorts for air, surface, and submarine protection.

It is extremely doubtful whether or not warships as big or bigger than the Nimitz carriers will ever again be built by any nation, including the United States. The construction and maintenance expenses of such ships have simply become untenable. And their vulnerability has never been tested in a real shooting war—one in which extremely accurate cruise missiles might be launched at a carrier battle group in massive, and virtually unstoppable, numbers. Given the fact that many of these missiles would almost certainly be armed with nuclear warheads, it is reasonable to assume that the battle group's component ships—including the aircraft carriers themselves—would be severely damaged, or destroyed outright. In fairness it should be noted, however, that this is an arguable assumption, and one that has been convincingly disputed by carrier proponents who believe that the Nimitz ships are quite capable of defending themselves against missile attack.

The Carl Vinson *is one of the largest warships ever built. It is one of the Nimitz-class aircraft carriers, which stand as the bulwark of America's 14 surface task forces.*

NIMITZ-CLASS (CVN) AIRCRAFT CARRIERS

Operational (commissioned):	CVN 68 USS *Nimitz* (May 1975)
	CVN 69 USS *Dwight D. Eisenhower* (October 1977)
	CVN 70 USS *Carl Vinson* (March 1982)
	CVN 71 USS *Theodore Roosevelt* (October 1986)
	CVN 72 USS *Abraham Lincoln* (February 1988)
Building:	CVN 73 USS *George Washington*
	CVN 74 USS *John C. Stennis*
	CVN 75 USS *United States*
Displacement:	81,600 tons
Dimensions:	
Length:	1,089 ft.
Width:	134 ft.
Draft:	37 to 38.5 ft.
Propulsion:	Four steam turbines, 280,000 hp
	Two Westinghouse A4W pressurized-water nuclear reactors
Speed:	Classified
Armament:	
All:	Sea Sparrow SAMs fired from three Mk 29 octuple launchers
CVN 69–72:	Four 20mm Phalanx CIWS Mk 15 multibarrel guns
Fire control:	Three Mk 19 missile systems
Aircraft:	F-14A Tomcats, F/A-18 Hornets and A-8E Intruders or A-8E Intruders and A-7E Corsairs, EA-8B Prowlers, E-2C Hawkeyes, S-3A/B Vikings, SH-3H Sea Kings or SH-60 Seahawks
Surveillance radar:	SPS-49 air search
CVN 68–70:	SPS-10F/28B search
CVN 71–73:	SPS-228E
	SPS-64 threat detection
	SPS-65 threat detection
	SPS-67(V) surface search
Sonar:	None
Crew:	
Navy:	3,105 to 3,219
Naval air wing:	2,885
Marines:	72

BATTLESHIPS

In December 1942 Japanese land-based aircraft sank the British battleship HMS *Prince of Wales* off the coast of Malaya, thus signaling the end of an era in naval warfare. The loss of the *Prince of Wales*, in conjunction with the destruction of the U.S. battleship fleet at Pearl Harbor, heralded a new era in which the aircraft carrier—and the planes they carried—would dominate naval strategy and combat.

Yet if battleships no longer ruled the oceans, they would continue to reign supreme in the thoughts of many admirals for the balance of World War II. And these admirals would continue to take seriously the threat of battleships, and adjust their strategic thinking accordingly. For example, the danger posed to Allied shipping by the German battleship *Tirpitz*—which spent most of its active-duty career lurking in Norwegian fjords—was enough to tie up a significant portion of the British Home Fleet at its base in Scapa Flow, Scotland.

Completed in 1943–44, the *Iowa*-class battleships were the last ships of their kind to enter Navy service. The *Iowa*-class vessels had been on the drawing boards since 1938. They were designed to be fast, well-protected ships that did not attain these attributes at the expense of armament. The *Iowa* battleships were armed with nine 16-inch rifles in three massively armored turrets, as well as 20 five-inch rifles in smaller turrets. It was an armament designed for ship-to-ship duels, and aside from the Japanese battleships *Yamato* and *Musashi*, there was not a capital ship in the world that could be expected to stand up against it. Yet the real threat to battleships came not from surface ships, but from aircraft armed with bombs and torpedoes. For that reason the *Iowa* ships were also armed with scores of 40 millimeter and 20mm guns.

The *Iowa*-class battleships have never engaged another battleship, nor any other major surface ship—and it is

unlikely that they ever will. Having entered service late in World War II, the four ships of this class—*Iowa*, *Missouri*, *New Jersey*, and *Wisconsin*—were relegated almost exclusively to the antiaircraft and shore bombardment roles. In the years just after the war the *Iowa*, *New Jersey*, and *Wisconsin* were placed in the mothball fleet, and the construction of the *Illinois* and the *Kentucky* was canceled (the *Missouri* remained in commission until the mid-1950s). The three mothballed battleships were reactivated for use during the Korean War as shore bombardment ships. The *New Jersey* was reactivated a second time for a 120-day cruise in 1968–69, to serve in the Vietnam War.

In the 1980s the *Iowa*-class battleships were once again activated as part of an effort to compete with the ongoing Soviet military buildup. As part of the modifications that came with this reactivation, many of their five-inch guns were replaced by Harpoon and Tomahawk missile launchers. The remaining antiaircraft guns were replaced by four 20mm Phalanx multibarrel guns.

In effect, modern missile technology has given the battleships a new lease on life. While not as versatile as the large aircraft carriers, missile-armed *Iowa*-class battleships are still capable of playing an important role in American military strategy. Many naval experts also contend that the battleships' big guns could, in certain situations, prove more useful than missiles against enemy surface threats, and more efficient than aircraft for shore bombardment missions. Nevertheless, the cost required to maintain the battleships may have sealed their fate in the budget-conscious '90s. In the summer of 1990 Defense Secretary Dick Cheney proposed the retirement of all four battleships, possibly as early as 1995, citing personnel and budget cuts as the reason. A 1989 turret explosion on the *Iowa* that killed 47 crew members provided yet another reason for retirement. If Cheney's proposal is adopted, then the battleships may once again sail into the mists of history, this time forever.

The New Jersey's 16-inch guns unleash a powerful broadside.

Iowa-Class (BB) Battleships

No longer intended to engage opposing ships of their own kind, America's four *Iowa*-class battleships have been extensively modified. In their present configuration, they are intended to serve as gun- and missile-launching platforms in areas in which the threat of air and submarine attacks are judged to be "moderate." As such, they lead special surface action groups (SAG) to fill the gap between the larger and far more expensive carrier-led task forces on the one hand, and convoys shepherded by destroyers and frigates on the other. Reactivated in the early 1980s, they are the only battleships remaining in service with any of the world's navies.

In March 1983 the *New Jersey* became the second ship in the U.S. Navy to receive the Tomahawk missile. Along with the Harpoon antiship missile, Tomahawk land-attack and antiship missiles now constitute the main armament of *Iowa*-class battleships. Missile complements consist of 16 Harpoons in four Mark 141 quadruple-tube launchers and 32 Tomahawk cruise missiles in quadruple

The battleship Wisconsin *has 12 mighty 16-inch guns in three turrets. Each gun fires shells the size of small cars up to distances of 26 miles. Additional armament includes long-range cruise missiles and close-in weapons systems.*

armored-box launchers. The Harpoons have a range of 80 nautical miles (92 miles). The Tomahawk anti-ship cruise missiles have a range of 250 nautical miles (287.5 miles); the land-attack version has a range of 1,200 nautical miles (1,380 miles).

The installation of missiles has not come at the expense of traditional heavy guns, however. All *Iowa* ships still retain three 16-inch gun turrets protected by heavy armor. The guns are 66.6 feet long and fire a shell that is propelled by a cordite composition known in the Navy as "black powder." This explosive propellent is packed in 110-pound bags, which are loaded separately behind a shell, or warhead. Powder and warhead are stored in separate magazines. The guns can fire three types of 16-inch rounds: a high capacity (HC) projectile, which weighs 1,900 pounds and carries a high-explosive payload; a submunition round, which also weighs 1,900 pounds and carries antiarmor and anti-personnel mines or bomblets; and an armor-piercing (AP) round weighing 2,700 pounds. The HC projectiles have been fitted with a variety of fuses to achieve surface bursts as well as air bursts at varying levels, with one fuse producing an air burst at 20 feet over a target. Muzzle velocity of the AP round is 2,425 feet per second; that of the HC round is 2,690 feet per second.

The *Iowa*-class battleships also have six turrets housing a total of 12 five-inch guns. The turrets are situated along the ships' sides. The five-inch guns fire a shell at a muzzle velocity of 2,400 feet per second.

Augmenting these guns is a defensive armament of four 20 millimeter Phalanx Close-In Weapons System (CIWS) Mark 15 multibarrel guns. Inclusion of the Sea Sparrow point defense missile system for anti-air warfare defense was proposed but not instituted, because the missiles could not withstand the concussion when the 16-inch guns were fired.

Four General Electric turbines (Westinghouse in the *New Jersey*) produce a total of 212,000 horsepower providing a maximum top speed of 33 knots (37.95 miles per hour). The turbines are driven by eight Babcock & Wilcox boilers.

Each battleship leads a Surface Action Group (SAG) that can be composed of one *Ticonderoga*-class antiaircraft missile cruiser, one *Kidd*-class or *Arleigh Burke*-class guided-missile destroyer, one *Spruance*-class destroyer, three *Perry*-class guided-missile frigates, and one support ship. The *New Jersey* was active off the Lebanese coast in late 1983 and early 1984, firing its guns at shore targets. In 1987 the *Missouri* served as part of a multinational task force that was sent into the Persian Gulf to protect merchant shipping during the Iran-Iraq war.

IOWA-CLASS (BB) BATTLESHIPS

Operational (commissioned):	BB 61 USS *Iowa* (April 1984)
	BB 62 USS *New Jersey* (December 1982)
	BB 63 USS *Missouri* (May 1986)
	BB 64 USS *Wisconsin* (November 1988)
Displacement:	57,350 tons
Dimensions:	
Length:	887.25 ft.
Width:	108.2 ft.
Draft:	38 ft.
Propulsion:	
BB 61, 63–64:	Four General Electric steam turbines, 212,000 hp
BB 62:	Four Westinghouse steam turbines, 212,000 hp
All:	Eight Babcock & Wilcox 600-psi boilers
Speed:	33 knots (37.95 mph)
Armament:	Sixteen Harpoon (RGM-84A) SSM Mk 141 launchers (four quadruple mounts)
	Thirty-two Tomahawk land-attack and antiship cruise missiles fired from eight quadruple armored-box launchers
	Nine Mk 7 16-inch guns in triple mounts
	Twelve Mk 28 5-inch dual-purpose guns in twin mounts
	Four 20mm Phalanx CIWS Mk 15 multibarrel guns
Fire control:	SWG-2 Tomahawk weapon control system
	Four Mk 37 gun fire control systems
	Two Mk 38 gun directors with Mk 25 radar
	Mk 40 gun director with Mk 27 radar
Aircraft:	None
Surveillance radar:	
All:	SPS-49 air search
BB 61, 63–64:	SPS-67 surface search
BB 62:	SPS-10F search
Sonar:	None
Crew:	
Navy:	1,515
Marines:	40

CRUISERS

Cruisers have long been the naval mainstay of all great maritime powers. They were originally designed to act alone as powerfully armed ships or to lead squadrons of smaller warships. During World War II, U.S. cruisers became the "utility ships" of the Navy, a role that involved them in the majority of ship-to-ship battles with enemy ships. Four different types of cruisers evolved out of that conflict: large cruisers (CB) with 12-inch guns; heavy cruisers (CA) with main batteries of eight-inch guns; light cruisers (CL) with six-inch guns; and antiaircraft defense cruisers (CLAA) with five-inch guns.

None of the 80 U.S. cruisers that were built during World War II are in service. All have been replaced by modern designs in which missiles have been substituted for guns. The 33 cruisers now in service are divided into eight classes; nine of the 33 are nuclear-powered (CGN), and the rest are powered by conventional oil-fired boilers (CG). No so-called "gun ships" remain in commission: the only two remaining eight-inch gun cruisers are in the mothball fleet. Thirteen cruisers are equipped with five-inch guns, and ten cruisers have no guns at all except for Phalanx multibarrel guns.

Like the cruisers of yesteryear, these newer ships serve as antiaircraft escorts for task forces headed by aircraft carriers. All are fitted with antiaircraft missiles and Harpoon antiship missiles, and some are fitted with Tomahawk land-attack and antiship cruise missiles, and vertical launch missiles such as the ASROC (anti-submarine rocket). The cruiser force supports seven carrier battle groups containing two aircraft carriers each, and four battleship-led surface action groups.

Thirteen cruisers are now under construction. The high cost of nuclear power plants and related equipment, coupled with improvements in superpower relations, has made it unlikely that any more nuclear-powered cruisers will be built.

U.S. guided-missile cruisers head out to sea in close formation. Pictured here are (left to right), the Virginia, South Carolina, Arkansas, California, Mississippi, *and* Texas.

119

Long Beach-Class (CGN) Cruiser

The cruiser *Long Beach* (CGN 9) was the world's first nuclear-powered surface warship, and the first to be armed entirely with missiles rather than guns. Commissioned on September 9, 1961, it followed the world's first nuclear-powered ship, the submarine *Nautilus*, by seven years, and the first nuclear-powered surface ship, the Soviet icebreaker *Lenin*, by two years. The *Long Beach* was originally classified as a light guided-missile cruiser (CLGN) but was reclassified to a CGN even before it was laid down. Its original assigned number was CGN 160, but in July 1957 it was renumbered to CGN 9.

The *Long Beach* underwent a number of design changes both before and during construction. It was originally designed to be a 7,800-ton "frigate" equipped with guided missiles. Before it was laid down, however, its size and displacement had doubled, and it was placed in the cruiser class.

The ship's missile armament also underwent many changes before it was finalized. As planned, it was to fire the Regulus II surface-to-surface missile, which was an early cruise missile with a range of 1,000 nautical miles (1,150 miles). But the Regulus was never installed. Instead, the Polaris ballistic missile was to be put aboard in eight launch tubes fitted amidships. But this too was canceled. Until the completion of its modernization (1980–83), *Long Beach* had no long-range surface-to-surface missiles. During refit, it was equipped with the Tomahawk (BGM-109) cruise missile, both antiship and land-attack versions, which are fired from two quadruple Mark 141

The Long Beach *was the U.S. Navy's first nuclear-powered surface ship. Originally intended to be armed with Polaris ballistic missiles, it is now armed with Tomahawk cruise missiles carrying nuclear and conventional warheads. It is also equipped with a host of sophisticated satellite communications facilities.*

launchers located on the rear deck. Shorter-range antiship missile capability is supplied by eight Harpoon (RGM-84A) missiles fired from two quadruple Mark 141 launchers, which are mounted on the after superstructure. Antisubmarine warfare weaponry includes 20 antisubmarine rockets (ASROCs) fired from one Mark 16 eight-cell launcher.

In keeping with its role as an antisubmarine and antiaircraft escort ship, the Long Beach was also armed with Terrier (RIM-2) guided missiles in two twin launchers mounted forward, and Talos (RIM-8) missiles in a single launcher at the stern. The Terrier was a surface-to-air missile that had a solid-fuel motor and rode a radar beam to its target. It was later fitted with a homing warhead and could carry nuclear or nonnuclear warheads. The Talos was a surface-to-air missile with a solid-propellant rocket/ramjet engine that could also carry nuclear or nonnuclear warheads. This missile has been replaced by the far more capable and reliable Standard-Extended Range (RIM-67B), which has a range of 90 nautical miles (103.5 miles). In addition, two five-inch dual-purpose single-barrel guns were installed for use against low-flying, subsonic aircraft, and surface threats. Two 20 millimeter Phalanx multibarrel guns have also been installed on the aft superstructure for point defense against missile threats. Ships in this class are also armed with Mark 46 torpedoes fired from two 12.75-inch Mark 32 triple tubes.

The Long Beach ships were to have been fitted with the Aegis weapon system, but this was canceled in the late 1970s because of high costs and the possible effect on other cruiser construction underway or planned at that time. The Long Beach received the upgraded SPS-48C and SPS 49 radars instead.

Antennas for the paired SPG-55B missile guidance radars are mounted on the deckhouse forward of the bridge. The SPS-48C 3D air search and SPS-67 surface search radar antennae are mounted on the bridge superstructure. These radars replaced the earlier SPS-32 and SPS-33 phased-array antennas. All four radar antennas enhance the ship's futuristic superstructure, which resembles the carrier Enterprise's superstructure.

The Long Beach is capable of more than 30 knots (34.5 miles per hour). It is powered by two pressurized-water Westinghouse C1W nuclear reactors, which are similar to the Westinghouse A2W nuclear reactor in the carrier Enterprise. The reactors provide steam to four General Electric turbines, which produce a total of 80,000 horsepower driving two propeller shafts.

Upon entering service, the Long Beach proceeded to travel over 160,000 miles— much of it high-speed steaming—before its original fuel cores were changed. In a 1964 exercise undertaken to demonstrate the capability and range of nuclear-powered ships, the Long Beach, the aircraft carrier Enterprise (CVN 65), and the cruiser Bainbridge (CVN 25)—all nuclear-powered— sailed around the world without refueling. The Long Beach has been in service for nearly 30 years, and is scheduled to be decommissioned shortly.

LONG BEACH-CLASS (CGN) CRUISER

Operational (commissioned):	CGN 9 USS Long Beach (September 1961)
Displacement:	17,100 tons
Dimensions:	
Length:	721.3 ft.
Width:	73.3 ft.
Draft:	29 ft.
Propulsion:	Four General Electric steam turbines, 80,000 hp
	Two Westinghouse pressurized-water C1W nuclear reactors
Speed:	30+ knots (34.5 mph)
Armament:	One ASROC (RUR-5A) Mk 16 quadruple launcher
	Approximately 120 Standard-ER (RIM-67B) or Terrier SAMs fired from two Mk 10 twin launchers
	Eight Harpoon (RGM-84A) SSM Mk 141 launchers (two quadruple mounts)
	Eight Tomahawk land-attack and antiship cruise missiles fired from two Mk 141 quadruple armored-box launchers
	Two 20mm Phalanx CIWS Mk 15 multibarrel guns
	Mark 46 torpedoes, fired from two 12.75-inch Mk 32 triple tubes
	Two Mk 30 dual-purpose guns
Fire control:	SWG-2(V)5 Tomahawk fire control system
	Mk 14 weapon direction system
	Two Mk 56 gun fire control systems
	Mk 76 missile fire control system
	Mk 111 antisubmarine warfare fire control system
	Two SPG 49B radars
	Four SPG 55B radars
	Two SPG-55B radars
Aircraft:	None
Surveillance radar:	SPS-48C 3D search
	SPS-49 air search
	SPS-67 surface search
Sonar:	SQQ-23 PAIR keel mount
Crew:	985

Leahy-Class (CG) Guided-Missile Cruisers

Originally designed and built as "frigates" (DLG), the nine ships of the Leahy class are the smallest ships in the United States Navy to be classified as cruisers (CG). They received this classification in June 1975 during a Navy-wide revision of ship classifications. The task of the Leahy cruisers is to defend carrier battle groups against aircraft and missile threats.

The Leahy class is known for having introduced the new "mack" superstructure, a combination of mast and stack that was designed to lighten the superstructure. With less weight above the center of gravity, more capable radar installations could be added. In contrast to the later Belknap-class cruisers, which had anti-air warfare (AAW) missiles forward only, the Leahy ships are armed with AAW missile launchers on both the bow and the stern. Hence, they are referred to as "double-ended" ships.

Because these ships were always intended for the AAW role, they never had five-inch guns fitted for surface warfare, nor did they carry helicopters for antisubmarine warfare. They were, however, fitted with two three-inch antiaircraft guns amidships in twin mounts. These have since been removed to make space for Harpoon (RGM-

84A) missiles. *Leahy* ships also have a vertical replenishment (VERTREP) helicopter landing area on the stern that is capable of landing SH-2F Seasprites. They carry no maintenance facilities for helicopters.

Each ship is equipped with two Mark 10 twin launchers for the Standard-Extended Range (RIM-87B) surface-to-air missiles, which have a range of up to 90 nautical miles (103.5 miles). Point air-defense protection is provided by two 20 millimeter

The Harry E. Yarnell, *a* Leahy-*class cruiser, is armed with Harpoon and Standard missiles.*

Phalanx Close-In Weapons System Mark 15 multibarrel guns mounted on either side of the aft deckhouse. The eight Harpoon missiles are contained in two quadruple Mark 141 launchers amidships.

Leahy ships are also armed with ASROCs (anti-submarine rockets), which are fired from one Mark 16 launcher forward of the bridge. The ASROC is a rocket-propelled unit that carries the Mark 46 homing torpedo. The homing torpedo separates from the rocket carrier after entering the water. It then circles until its passive radar picks up an

enemy submarine. Accelerating to 40 knots (46 miles per hour) it homes in on the submarine, using active sonar for course corrections during the final stages of its run. *Leahy* ships also carry 12.75-inch Mark 46 torpedoes, which can be fired from two Mark 32 triple tubes located amidships on the rail near the aft end of the forward deckhouse.

Each *Leahy* cruiser is capable of making 32 knots (36.8 miles per hour). All of the ships in this class are 533 feet long and displace 8,200 tons. They are powered by two General Electric, De Laval, or Allis-Chalmers

steam turbines that develop 85,000 horsepower and drive two propeller shafts. Steam is supplied by four Babcock & Wilcox or four Foster Wheeler boilers.

The ships in this class were all commissioned between 1962 and 1964. Three of the nine *Leahy*-class cruisers are deployed to the Atlantic Fleet, and the rest went to the Pacific Fleet. The *Leahy*-class cruisers of the post-World War II Navy have seen combat action in places ranging from the Gulf of Tonkin to the Gulf of Sidra. The *Leahy* ships are nearing 30 years of service, and may be retired in the mid-1990s.

LEAHY-CLASS (CG) GUIDED-MISSILE CRUISERS

Operational (commissioned):	CG 16 USS *Leahy* (August 1962) CG 17 USS *Harry E. Yarnell* (February 1963) CG 18 USS *Worden* (August 1963) CG 19 USS *Dale* (November 1962) CG 20 USS *Richmond K. Turner* (June 1964) CG 21 USS *Gridley* (May 1963) CG 22 USS *England* (December 1962) CG 23 USS *Halsey* (July 1963) CG 24 USS *Reeves* (May 1964)
Displacement:	8,200 tons
Dimensions:	
Length:	533 ft.
Width:	55 ft.
Draft:	25 ft.
Propulsion:	
CG 16–18:	Two General Electric steam turbines, 85,000 hp
CG 19–22:	Two De Laval steam turbines, 85,000 hp
CG 23–24:	Two Allis-Chalmers steam turbines, 85,000 hp
CG 16–18:	Four Babcock & Wilcox 1,200-psi boilers
CG 19–24:	Four Foster Wheeler 1,200-psi boilers
Speed:	32 knots (36.8 mph)
Armament:	One ASROC (RUR-5A) Mk 16 octuple launcher Standard-ER (RIM-87B) SAMs fired from two Mk 10 twin launchers Eight Harpoon (RGM-84A) SSM Mk 141 launchers (two quadruple mounts) Two 20mm Phalanx CIWS Mk 15 multibarrel guns Mark 46 torpedoes fired from two 12.75-inch Mk 32 triple tubes
Fire control:	Mk 14 weapon direction system Mk 76 missile fire control system with SPG-53F radar Mk 114 antisubmarine warfare fire control system Four SPG 55B radars
Aircraft:	None
Surveillance radar:	SPS-1OF or 67 surface search SPS-49(V)3 air search SPS-48A 3D search
Sonar:	
All:	SQS-23 bow mount
CG 17:	SQQ-23B PAIR
Crew:	423

Bainbridge-Class and Truxtun-Class (CGN) Cruisers

Both *Bainbridge* (CGN 25) and *Truxtun* (CGN 35) were originally designated as nuclear-powered guided-missile destroyers (DLGN), but they were reclassified as nuclear cruisers (CGN) in June 1975. Although they are not in the same class, the ships will be described together, since they are both one-ship classes and because the *Truxtun* was a follow-on to the *Bainbridge*.

The *Bainbridge* and the *Truxtun* were the third and fourth nuclear-powered ships built for the United States Navy. The *Bainbridge* was laid down in May 1959, launched in April 1961, and commissioned in October 1962. The *Truxtun* was laid down in June 1963, launched in December 1964, and commissioned in May 1967. Both ships are powered by two pressurized-water General Electric D2G nuclear reactors that furnish steam to two 60,000 horsepower turbines. Top speed for both is 30 knots (34.5 miles per hour) or greater.

Antiaircraft armament in this class originally consisted of the Terrier (RIM-2) missile

BAINBRIDGE-CLASS AND TRUXTUN-CLASS (CGN) CRUISERS

Operational (commissioned):	CGN 25 USS *Bainbridge* (October 1962) CGN 35 USS *Truxtun* (May 1967)
Displacement:	
CGN 25:	8,580 tons
CGN 35:	8,800 tons
Dimensions:	
Length:	
CGN 25:	550 ft.
CGN 35:	564 ft.
Width:	58 ft.
Draft:	
CGN 25:	29 ft.
CGN 35:	31 ft.
Propulsion:	Two steam turbines, 60,000 hp Two General Electric pressurized-water D2G nuclear reactors
Speed:	30 knots (34.5 mph)
Armament:	
All:	Standard-ER SAMs fired from two Mk 10 twin launchers Eight Harpoon (RGM-84A) SSM Mk 141 launchers (two quadruple mounts) Two 20mm Phalanx CIWS Mk 15 multibarrel guns Mark 46 torpedoes fired from two 12.75-inch Mk 32 triple tubes
CGN 25:	One ASROC (RUR-5A) Mk 16 octuple launcher
Armament cont'd:	
CGN 35:	Mark 46 torpedoes fired from two 12.75-inch Mk 32 twin tubes One ASROC (RUR-5A) Mk 10 launcher One Mk 45 5-inch single-barrel gun
Fire control:	
All:	Mk 14 weapon direction system Mk 76 missile fire control system Two SPG 55B radars
CGN 25:	Mk 111 antisubmarine warfare fire control system
CGN 35:	Mk 68 gunfire control system Mk 114 antisubmarine warfare fire control system
Aircraft:	
CGN 25:	None
CGN 35:	One SH-2F Seasprite LAMPS I helicopter
Surveillance radar:	
CGN 25:	SPD-48C surface search SPS-49 air search SPS-67 surface search
CGN 35:	SPS-40D air search SPS-48C 3D search SPS-67 surface search
Sonar:	
CGN 25:	SQQ-23
CGN 35:	SQS-26BX
Crew:	
CG 25:	558
CG 35:	591

system. This has been replaced by the Standard-ER (extended range) surface-to-air missile (RIM-67B). The Standard-ER has a longer range—up to 90 nautical miles (103.5 miles)—and an inertial reference system and mid-course guidance correction capabilities. In contrast to the Terrier, which rides a radar beam the entire distance from ship to target, the Standard-ER requires radar illumination of the target only during the final phases of its flight.

In the 1970s the three-inch guns on these cruisers were replaced by 20 millimeter antiaircraft weapons. Between 1983 and 1985 the 20mm weapons were replaced with two 20mm Phalanx Close-In Weapons System Mark 15 multibarrel guns. The Phalanx guns were mounted on the aft deckhouse on the *Bainbridge*, and forward of the bridge on the *Truxtun*. The two cruisers are also equipped with ASROC weapons. *Bainbridge*'s ASROCs are housed in a single Mark 16 eight-cell launcher; *Truxtun*'s are housed in a Mark 10 magazine. Both ships are also equipped with eight Harpoon (RGM-84A) surface-to-surface missiles.

Neither the *Bainbridge* nor the *Truxtun* mount any heavy guns. However, the *Truxtun* mounts a five-inch dual-purpose Mark 42 gun on the foredeck. *Truxtun* has two 12.75-inch Mark 32 twin tubes that fire the Mark 46 torpedo over the side from the aft deckhouse. *Bainbridge* also carries 12.75-inch Mark 46 torpedoes, fired from two Mark 32 triple tubes located amidships.

The *Truxtun* has a helicopter hangar and flight deck in the aft deckhouse. The hangar is 40.3 by 18.75 feet and can accommodate a Kaman SH-2F Seasprite Light Airborne Multipurpose System I (LAMPS I) helicopter. The *Bainbridge* has a landing area on the stern.

Upon commissioning, the *Bainbridge* was assigned to the Pacific Fleet. It was transferred to the Atlantic Fleet in 1987 after undergoing modernization. *Truxtun* serves with the Pacific Fleet.

The Bainbridge *executes a sharp turn on the open sea.*

125

Belknap-Class (CG) Guided-Missile Cruisers

Above: The bridge of the Belknap. **Opposite:** The Wainwright underway. Although built in the 1960s, all Belknap-class ships have been upgraded to incorporate the latest armaments and technologies.

Designed as guided-missile frigates (DLG), the Belknap-class ships were reclassified as cruisers in the Navy's 1975 service-wide reclassification program. The tasks of the Belknap ships are to provide anti-air (AAW), antiship, and antisubmarine (ASW) screens for carrier battle groups. The first of nine ships in this class, the Belknap (CG 26), was laid down in February 1962, launched in July 1963, and commissioned in November 1964. The last, the Biddle (CG 34), was commissioned in January 1967. Four ships are attached to the Atlantic Fleet and five to the Pacific Fleet. The Belknap was heavily modified and became the flagship of the Sixth Fleet on July 7, 1986.

The Belknap-class ships have one Mark 10 twin launcher on the forward deck ahead of the bridge, and a five-inch dual-purpose Mark 42 gun mounted on the rear deck. The Mark 10 launcher was originally developed to launch the Terrier (RIM-2) surface-to-air missile. These missiles have been retained and supplemented by the Standard-Extended Range (RIM-67B) surface-to-air missiles, which have a longer range—up to 90 nautical miles (103.5 miles). The Mark 10 Modification 7 missile launcher used aboard the Belknap-class ships is magazine-fed. Each magazine holds 20 missiles in several rings, and each launcher is equipped with three rings for a total of 60 missiles.

Additional air protection is now provided by the single five-inch dual-purpose Mark 42 gun and by two 20 millimeter Phalanx Close-In Weapons System Mark 15 multibarrel guns. The Phalanx guns are located outboard of the after deckhouse. The Belknap cruisers also carry eight Harpoon (RGM-84A) antiship missiles, which are fired from Mark 141 quadruple-mount launchers. One Harpoon launcher is located on the starboard side opposite the port-side Phalanx, and the other is on the port side at the forward end of the aft deckhouse. The Harpoon missiles have replaced the two three-inch guns with which the ships were originally armed.

For antisubmarine operations the Belknap ships carry ASROC (RUR-5A) antisubmarine rockets, which carry Mark 44 or Mark 46 homing torpedoes. Six 12.75-inch Mark 46 torpedoes can also be fired from two Mark 32 triple tubes, which are located amidships along the rail between the forward and aft deckhouses. The torpedoes are fired over the side.

The Belknap ships also each carry one Kaman SH-2F Seasprite Light Airborne Multipurpose System I (LAMPS I) helicopter. This aircraft is housed in a hangar on the 01 deck of the superstructure. The Belknap carries an SH-3 Sea King helicopter, but has no hangar for this aircraft.

Top speed of the Belknap ships is 33 knots (37.9 miles per hour). They have an unrefueled range of 7,100 nautical miles (8,165 miles) at 20 knots (23 miles per hour). Power is supplied by two steam turbines that together develop 85,000 horsepower. Four boilers provide steam. General Electric turbines and Babcock & Wilcox boilers are used in CG 26 through 28, CG 32, and CG 34; De Laval turbines and Combustion Engineering boilers are used in the others.

BELKNAP-CLASS (CG) GUIDED-MISSILE CRUISERS

Operational (commissioned):	CG 26 USS *Belknap* (November 1964)	**Armament cont'd:**	Eight Harpoon (RGM-84A) SSM Mk 141 launchers (two quadruple mounts)
	CG 27 USS *Josephus Daniels* (May 1965)		One Mk 42 5-inch single-barrel gun
	CG 28 USS *Wainwright* (January 1966)		Two 20mm Phalanx CIWS Mk 15 multibarrel guns
	CG 29 USS *Jouett* (December 1966)		Mark 46 torpedoes fired from two 12.75-inch Mk 32 triple tubes
	CG 30 USS *Horne* (April 1967)	**Fire control:**	
	CG 31 USS *Sterett* (April 1967)	**All:**	Mk 14 weapon direction system
	CG 32 USS *William H. Standley* (July 1966)		Mk 68 gunfire control system with SPG-53F radar
	CG 33 USS *Fox* (May 1966)		Two SPG 55B radars
	CG 34 USS *Biddle* (January 1967)	**CG 26:**	Mk 116 antisubmarine warfare fire control system
Displacement:	7,930 tons	**CG 27–34:**	Mk 114 antisubmarine warfare fire control system
Dimensions:			
Length:	547 ft.	**Aircraft:**	
Width:	54.75 ft.	**CG 26:**	One SH-3 Sea King helicopter
Draft:		**CG 27–34:**	One SH-2F Seasprite LAMPS I helicopter
Over sonar dome:	38.75 ft.		
Over hull:	19.33 ft.	**Surveillance radar:**	
Propulsion:		**All:**	SPS-10 or SPS-67 surface search
CG 26–28, 32, 34:	Two General Electric steam turbines, 85,000 hp		SPS-48D 3D search
	Four Babcock & Wilcox 1,200-psi boilers	**CG 26–30:**	SPS-49 air search
CG 29–31, 33:	Two De Laval steam turbines, 85,000 hp	**CG 31–34:**	SPS-40 air search
	Four Combustion Engineering 1,200-psi boilers	**Sonar:**	
		CG 26:	SQS-53A
Speed:	33 knots (37.9 mph)	**CG 27:**	SQS-26AXR
Armament:	One ASROC (RUR-5A) Mk 10 twin launcher	**CG 28–34:**	SQS-26BX
	Standard-ER SAMs fired from one Mk 10 twin launcher	**Crew:**	
		CG 26 (flagship):	111
		CG 27–34:	477

California-Class (CGN) Guided-Missile Cruisers

Although funded in fiscal year 1967 and ordered in calendar year 1968, the two ships of the *California* class of cruisers were not built until the early 1970s. This delay was due to the efforts of Secretary of Defense Robert S. McNamara, who was opposed to nuclear-powered ships because of their excessive cost. Construction was allowed to begin only after McNamara had left his office. The *California* (CGN 36) was launched in September 1971, and commissioned in February 1974; the *South Carolina* was launched in July 1972, and commissioned in January 1975. The completed *California* ships were to be the first of several ships in their class. However, their high cost and minimal armament caused the cancellation of any further ships in favor of the less costly and more capable *Virginia*-class nuclear-powered cruisers.

While resembling the later *Virginia*-class cruisers, *California* ships are distinguished by the ASROC Mark 16 launcher, and by a five-inch Mark 45 dual-purpose gun mounted on the aft deckhouse rather than on the deck itself. *California*-class cruisers are slightly longer, but displace 770 fewer tons than the *Virginia* ships. Their two engines produce 60,000 horsepower, and top speed is more than 30 knots (34.5 miles per hour).

The two *California*-class ships have a helicopter landing area at the stern but no hangar or maintenance facilities. Both the *California* and the *South Carolina* were originally armed with Tartar guided missiles for air defense; however, the Tartar missiles have been replaced by more capable Standard-MR (RIM-66C) missiles, which are housed in two single Mark 13 launchers. Two 20 millimeter Phalanx Close-In Weapons System Mark 15 multibarrel guns are carried as well, one on either side, and forward of, the aft mast.

Antiship weapons are limited to eight Harpoon (RGM-84A) missiles, which are carried in two quadruple storage/launch canisters on Mark 141 launchers. The port launcher is mounted on the superstructure's 01 deck behind the aft five-inch Mark 45 gun. The starboard launcher is mounted amidships between the fore and aft deckhouses. Antisubmarine weaponry includes ASROC weapons, which are fired from a Mark 16 launcher located on the main deck just in front of the deckhouse but behind the forward five-inch dual-purpose Mark 45 gun. The *California* cruisers are also armed with 12.75-inch Mark 46 torpedoes, which are fired over the sides from two Mark 32 twin tubes.

Although both ships are scheduled for upgrades, neither is scheduled to receive the Tomahawk (BGM-109) missile system. Both cruisers carry all the appropriate radar, sonar, and fire control systems.

CALIFORNIA-CLASS (CGN) GUIDED-MISSILE CRUISERS	
Operational (commissioned):	CGN 36 USS *California* (February 1974) CGN 37 USS *South Carolina* (January 1975)
Displacement:	10,530 tons
Dimensions:	
Length:	596 ft.
Width:	61 ft.
Draft:	31.5 ft.
Propulsion:	Two steam turbines, 60,000 hp Two General Electric pressurized-water D2G nuclear reactors
Speed:	30+ knots (34.5+ mph)
Armament:	One ASROC (RUR-5A) Mk 16 octuple launcher Standard-MR (RIM-66C) SAMs fired from two Mk 13 launchers Eight Harpoon (RGM-84A) SSM Mk 141 launchers (two quadruple mounts) Two Mk 45 5-inch dual-purpose guns Two 20mm Phalanx CIWS Mk 15 multibarrel guns Mark 46 torpedoes fired from two 12.75-inch Mk 32 twin tubes
Fire control:	Mk 11 weapon direction system SPG 60 and SPQ-9A radar with Mk 86 gun fire control system Mk 74 fire control system Mk 114 antisubmarine warfare fire control system
Aircraft:	None
Surveillance radar:	Two SPG-10 surface search SPS-40B air search SPS-48C 3D search
Sonar:	SQS-28CX
Crew:	
CG 36:	603
CG 37:	595

The South Carolina *is fitted with the Mark 13 launcher, which holds up to 40 vertically stowed missiles.*

Virginia-Class (CGN) Guided-Missile Cruisers

In the years following the end of World War II, nuclear power promised to provide an inexpensive means of providing high-speed, long-endurance propulsion for U.S. naval ships. Over time, however, nuclear power plants have in fact proved to be the most costly means of propelling ships. The four Virginia ships are therefore probably the last class of nuclear-powered warships that will be built for the Navy.

The four Virginia ships were originally classed as frigates (DLGN), but in 1975 they were reclassified as cruisers to reflect their actual role and capability. Larger than the gas turbine-powered Ticonderoga-class cruisers, they were designed specifically to provide nuclear-powered escort for the nuclear-powered carriers. Numerous proposals have been made to build either additional Virginia-class cruisers or modified versions, but these proposals have been rejected in favor of building the gas turbine-powered Ticonderoga-class cruisers.

For antiaircraft operations, Virginia ships are equipped with solid-state, digital SPS-40B air search radar. The SPS-48A 3D search radar is used by CG 38 and CG 39. The improved SPS-48C was installed on CG 40 and CG 41, which have automatic detection and tracking capability. Virginia-class cruisers have the Mark 26 missile launcher, which can fire a variety of missiles, including the ASROC and the Standard SM-2 medium-range missile. Harpoon (RGM-84A) surface-to-surface missile launchers are located forward of the deckhouse. These weapons are directed by the Mark 116 ASW (antisubmarine warfare) fire control system, which has a digital interface with the SQS-53A active/passive sonar system. The digital interface allows the ASROC missile to be aimed and launched at a much faster rate than had been the case with the previous SQS-26 system.

Virginia-class ships are also armed with two Mark 45 five-inch dual-purpose guns (effective against surface

VIRGINIA-CLASS (CG) GUIDED-MISSILE CRUISERS

Operational (commissioned):	CGN 38 USS Virginia (September 1976)
	CGN 39 USS Texas (September 1977)
	CGN 40 USS Mississippi (August 1978)
	CGN 41 USS Arkansas (October 1980)
Displacement:	11,300 tons
Dimensions:	
Length:	585 ft.
Width:	63 ft.
Draft:	29.5 ft.
Propulsion:	Two steam turbines, 70,000 hp
	Two General Electric pressurized-water D2G nuclear reactors
Speed:	30+ knots (34.5+ mph)
Armament:	One ASROC (RUR-5A) Mk 26 octuple launcher
	Standard-MR SAMs fired from two Mk 26 launchers
	Eight Tomahawk land-attack and antiship cruise missiles fired from two Mk 143 quadruple launchers
	Eight Harpoon (RGM-84A) SSM Mk 141 launchers (two
Armament cont'd:	quadruple mounts)
	Two Mk 45 5-inch dual-purpose guns
	Two 20mm Phalanx CIWS Mk 15 multibarrel guns
Fire control:	Mk 13 weapon direction system
	SPG 60 and SPQ-9A radar with Mk 86 gun fire control system
	Mk 74 fire control system
	Mk 116 antisubmarine warfare fire control system
	SWG-2 Tomahawk fire control system
Aircraft:	One SH-2F Seasprite LAMPS I (being replaced with Tomahawk missile cells)
Surveillance radar:	
All:	SPS-55 surface search
CG 38–39:	SPS-40B air search
	SPS-48A 3D search
CG 40–41:	SPS-48C 3D search
Sonar:	SQS-53A
Crew:	
CG 38:	565
CG 39:	572
CG 40:	613
CG 41:	582

targets), and two 20mm
Phalanx Close-In Weapons
System Mark 15 multibarrel
guns.

   Virginia ships are now in
the process of being refitted
to carry two quadruple-mount
Mark 143 Tomahawk missile
launchers in the stern. The
Tomahawk launchers carry
eight Tomahawk (BGM-109)
antiship and/or land-attack
missiles. More capable than
the Harpoon missile, which
has a range of 80 nautical

miles (92 miles) and carries a
warhead containing 510
pounds of high explosive,
Tomahawks have a range of
more than 250 nautical miles
(287.5 miles) and carry 1,000
pounds of high explosive.
One SWG-2 Tomahawk fire
control system is being
installed along with the
missiles, which are occupying
space that was previously a
hangar for the Kaman SH-2F
Seasprite Light Airborne
Multipurpose System I

(LAMPS I) helicopter.
Problems with the hangar
elevator mechanism and
trouble with maintaining a
watertight seal on the elevator
doors led to the decision to
remove the hangar and
replace it with the Tomahawk
launchers.

   Top speed on the *Virginia*
ships is over 30 knots (34.5
miles per hour); standard
displacement is 11,300 tons.
Two General Electric
pressurized-water D2G

nuclear reactors power two
steam turbines that produce
70,000 horsepower. The
Virginia and the *Mississippi*
are in service with the
Atlantic Fleet; the *Texas* and
the *Arkansas* serve with the
Pacific Fleet.

Above: *An antisubmarine
warfare weapon explodes in
close proximity to the*
Arkansas, *which launched the
device.*

Ticonderoga-Class (CG) Guided-Missile Cruisers

The *Ticonderoga* class of cruisers is the largest cruiser class in the U.S. Navy, with 26 ships in service or under construction. Their task is to defend carrier battle groups against air, surface, and submarine threats. They were developed in response to the Soviet naval tactic of saturation missile attacks on a carrier task force, which uses missiles launched from aircraft, submarines, and surface ships in an attempt to overwhelm the task force's air defense. The *Ticonderoga*-class cruisers are well suited to counter this tactic. All ships in this class carry the Standard RIM 86C SM-2 surface-to-air medium-range missile, which is launched from two twin Mark 26 launchers and has a semiactive radar homing system and a high-explosive warhead. The Standard replaced the earlier Talos, Terrier, and Tartar missiles. All ships have eight Harpoon antiship missiles (RGM-84A) launched from the Mark 141 quadruple box launcher. *Ticonderoga* cruisers mount two 20 millimeter Phalanx Close-In Weapons System Mark 15 multibarrel guns and two five-inch Mark 45 guns. The five-inch guns can also be used against surface targets.

All *Ticonderoga* ships are equipped for the antisubmarine warfare (ASW) role as well. The first five *Ticonderoga*-class cruisers carry the ASROC (RUR-5A) missile. This weapon can be fitted with the Mark 46 torpedo, or with a nuclear depth charge. Later ships use the Vertical Launch ASROC with the Vertical Launch System (VLS), which also permits them to launch the Tomahawk (BGM-109) cruise missile. All are also equipped with two 12.75-inch Mark 32 triple tubes, which can launch the Mark 46 torpedo. The *Ticonderoga*-class cruisers carry either two SH-2F Light Airborne Multipurpose System I (LAMPS I) Seasprite helicopters or two SH-60B Seahawk LAMPS III helicopters.

Because conventional radars using rotating antennas are limited in their ability to track multiple incoming air threats, the *Ticonderoga* cruisers have been fitted with the Aegis radar and fire control system. The heart of the Aegis system is the SPY-1 radar, which consists in part of four fixed antennas operating in the F-band frequency, with each antenna containing 4,480 radiating elements arranged in an octagon 12.5 feet across. Two of the antennas are mounted on the deckhouse facing ahead and to starboard, while the other two are mounted on the after deckhouse facing astern and to port. Four UYK-7 digital computers control the radar

beams, which are projected in hundreds of pencil-thin streams. Less than a second after a target is detected by even one beam, the computer aims several more beams at it. The computer can then measure the heading, distance, and height of the target, initiate a tracking sequence, and, if necessary, provide command guidance to ship-launched missiles. The computer can accomplish the same task simultaneously for hundreds of targets. If the Standard missile is fired, the SPY-1 tracks both missile and target, and updates the missile's course continuously. Up to 20 missiles can be simultaneously directed to separate targets. The SPY-1 system can also detect enemy jamming and shift to open frequencies.

When first designed, the *Ticonderoga*-class ships were designated guided-missile destroyers (DDG). Because of their size and capabilities, they were upgraded to cruisers before construction began. They are based on the design of the *Spruance*-class destroyers but have larger deckhouses to accommodate the SPY-1 radar. *Ticonderoga* ships are powered by four General Electric LM2500 gas turbine engines (modified TF39 aircraft turbofan engines) that generate a total of 86,000 horsepower.

The *Ticonderoga* ships can also serve as task force flagships. To do so, they are equipped with sophisticated combat information centers that enable them to receive and integrate data from other ships and aircraft in a battle group.

132

In recent years armor plate has been added to the magazines and other critical areas on the *Ticonderoga* ships. These internal changes were prompted by the destruction of British ships by air-launched missiles during the Falkland Islands War in 1982. The *Ticonderoga* cruisers are expected to remain in service well into the next century. These cruisers are capable of being upgraded as more effective weapons and detection systems become available.

Top: *Crewmen intently study their radar screens in the combat information center of the* Yorktown. **Above:** *The* Vincennes *launches a missile. The* Ticonderoga-*class cruisers are designed to protect carrier battle groups from air attack, and can engage numerous air threats simultaneously.*

TICONDEROGA-CLASS (CG) GUIDED-MISSILE CRUISERS

Operational (commissioned):	CG 47 USS *Ticonderoga* (January 1983)	
	CG 48 USS *Yorktown* (July 1984)	
	CG 49 USS *Vincennes* (July 1985)	
	CG 50 USS *Valley Forge* (January 1986)	
	CG 51 USS *Thomas S. Gates* (August 1987)	
	CG 52 USS *Bunker Hill* (September 1986)	
	CG 53 USS *Mobile Bay* (February 1987)	
	CG 54 USS *Antietam* (June 1987)	
	CG 55 USS *Leyte Gulf* (September 1987)	
	CG 56 USS *San Jacinto* (January 1988)	
	CG 57 USS *Lake Champlain* (August 1988)	
	CG 59 USS *Princeton* (February 1989)	
	CG 62 USS *Chancellorsville* (November 1989)	
	CG 60 USS *Normandy* (December 1990)	
	CG 61 USS *Monterey* (June 1990)	
Building:	CG 63 USS *Cowpens*	
	CG 64 USS *Gettysburg*	
	CG 65 USS *Chosin*	
	CG 66 USS *Hue City*	
	CG 67 USS *Shiloh*	
	CG 68 USS *Anzio*	
	CG 69 USS *Vicksburg*	
	CG 70 USS *Lake Erie*	
	CG 71 USS *Cape St. George*	
	CG 72 USS *Vella Gulf*	
	CG 73 USS *Port Royal*	
Displacement:		
CG 47–48:	9,530 tons	
CG 49–50, 51:	9,400 tons	
CG 52–68:	9,500 tons	
Dimensions:		
Length:	565 feet	
Width:	55 feet	
Draft:	31.5 feet	
Propulsion:	Four General Electric LM2500 gas turbines,	

Propulsion cont'd:	86,000 hp
Speed:	30+ knots (34.5+ mph)
Armament:	
All:	Eight Harpoon (RGM-84A) SSM Mk 141 launchers (two quadruple mounts)
	Two Mk 45 5-inch guns
	Standard-MR SAMs fired from two MK 26 twin launchers
	Two 20mm Phalanx CIWS Mk 15 multibarrel guns
	Mark 46 torpedoes fired from two 12.75-inch Mk 32 triple tubes
CG 47–51:	One ASROC (RUR-5A) Mk 26 octuple launcher
CG 52–68:	Twenty Tomahawk land-attack and antiship cruise missiles fired from two Mk 41 Vertical Launch Systems
Aircraft:	
CG 47–48:	Two SH-2F Seasprite LAMPS I helicopters
CG 49–68:	Two SH-60B Seahawk LAMPS III helicopters
Fire control:	
All:	Mk 7 Aegis weapon system
	Mk 86 gun fire control system with SPQ-9A radar
	Mk 99 missile directors with SPG-62 radar
	Mk 116 antisubmarine warfare fire control system
CG 52–68:	SWG-3 Tomahawk fire control system
Surveillance radar:	
All:	SPS-49(V)6 air search
CG 47–48:	SPS-55 surface search
CG 47–58:	SPY 1A multifunction
CG 59–68:	SPY 1B multifunction
Sonar:	
CG 47–55:	SQS-53A
CG 54–68:	SQR-19 tactical towed array
CG 58–68:	SQS-53B
Crew:	364

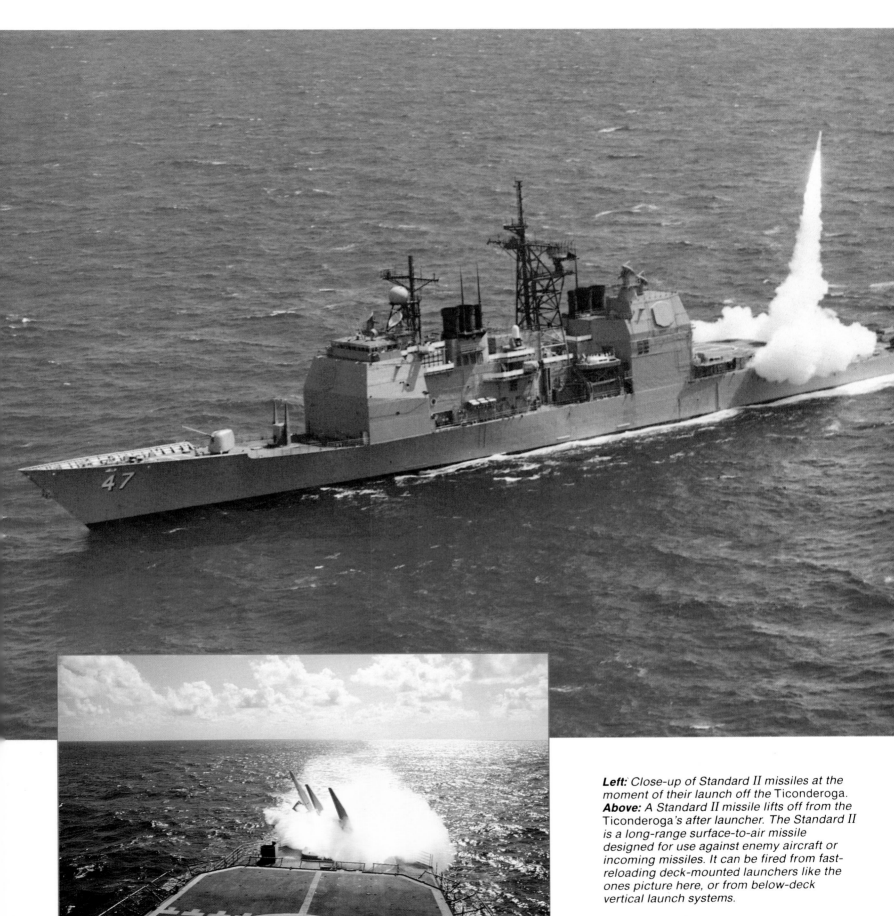

Left: Close-up of Standard II missiles at the moment of their launch off the Ticonderoga. **Above:** A Standard II missile lifts off from the Ticonderoga's after launcher. The Standard II is a long-range surface-to-air missile designed for use against enemy aircraft or incoming missiles. It can be fired from fast-reloading deck-mounted launchers like the ones picture here, or from below-deck vertical launch systems.

DESTROYERS

Destroyers saw their first major action during the Russo-Japanese War (1904–05). As originally conceived, they were to be torpedo carriers whose targets were armored cruisers and battleships.

World War I saw a steady decline in the use of destroyers as torpedo-firing warships against other warships. Among the Allies in particular, a new role for the destroyer emerged: that of convoy escort and antisubmarine ship. The success of destroyers in this role was due in large part to the development of the hydrophone. Essentially an underwater microphone, this device was used to listen for audible sound frequencies emitted by submarines.

The hydrophone led to the development of "searchlight" sonar in 1918. Sonar (which stands for sound navigation ranging) was originally known by its British name, ASDIC, which is an acronym for Anti-Submarine Detection Investigation Committee. The combination of the electronic amplifier and the piezoelectric transducer (which uses vibrating crystals to impart ultrasonic pressure waves into the water) made it possible for destroyers to make effective underwater distance measurement by sound.

During World War II, the destroyer expanded its antisubmarine warfare role, particularly as smaller frigates and corvettes took on more convoy duties. The U.S. destroyers were fast ships displacing between 1,020 and 2,400 tons. In addition to antisubmarine activities, they were used to support strike and amphibious forces, and provide anti-surface and antiaircraft defense for task forces. Since the end of World War II, however, the destroyer's weight and armament have changed, and so has the definition of a destroyer's roles.

Early in the postwar era the guided missile proved to be more accurate and more destructive to enemy aircraft than the gun, and it quickly replaced the gun as the destroyer's main weapon. Guided missiles were also developed for antisubmarine and antiship warfare, as well as for land-based targets. Today, a missile-armed destroyer can pack the punch of an entire World War II task force, even without the use of nuclear warheads.

The Navy currently has five destroyer classes containing a total of some 68 ships. Of these, 37 ships are classified as guided-missile destroyers, and are armed with surface-to-air missiles (SAM). While the remaining destroyers may also carry SAMs, their primary role is antisubmarine warfare. This is particularly true of the *Spruance*-class ships, which comprise the mainstay of the destroyer fleet. They are supplemented by the four ships of the *Kidd* class, which were designed and built for the Iranian Navy. When the Shah was deposed in 1979, they were acquired by the U.S. Navy. Over the next decade or so, both the *Spruance* and the *Kidd* ships will gradually be superseded by the new ships of the *Arleigh Burke* class. As the *Arleigh Burke* ships are commissioned, older ships will gradually be retired or reassigned.

The *Arleigh Burke* received its name from a famous World War II hero and Chief of Naval Operations from 1955–61. Admiral Burke is one of only three persons in this century to have had a U.S. Navy ship named for him while still living. Destroyers are traditionally named for deceased naval heroes and famous inventors—Dewey, Turner Joy, Fulton, Farragut, and so on.

Stern view of three Farragut-*class destroyers: from left to right, the* Coontz, King, *and* Farragut. *Although they appear dwarfed by the superstructures of the cruisers behind them, these destroyers possess tremendous antiaircraft capabilities that belie their relatively small size. The* Farragut *ships are the only destroyers to be retrofitted with deck-mounted Standard surface-to-air missiles.*

Charles F. Adams-Class (DDG) Guided-Missile Destroyers

Designed primarily to provide anti-air war defense (AAW) for aircraft carriers, the ships of the *Charles F. Adams* class were the most heavily armed ships of their type at the time of their construction (early to mid-1960s). The first eight ships in this class were designed as three-gun destroyers with five-inch guns, two of which were mounted forward, and one mounted aft. In 1966, the design and classification were changed and only two guns were mounted, one forward and the other aft. In place of the third gun, the new Tartar (RIM-24) missile system was installed.

The latter weapon is a small but highly capable missile that represents a significant improvement over the earlier, and more cumbersome, Terrier missile. The Tartar missile uses a semiactive guidance system that requires a much less sophisticated radar suite aboard the ship from which it is launched. It also uses a two-stage motor. The first stage launches the missile from its container and drives it to cruising speed; the second stage provides power for terminal maneuvers. The net effect of this two-stage motor arrangement was to reduce the size of both the missile and its launch facilities, thus permitting more missiles to be carried.

The *Charles F. Adams* ships use the Mark 11 or Mark 13

launchers for their Tartar missiles. The Mark 11 twin-rail missile launcher carries 42 reloads; the Mark 13 single-rail launcher carries 40 reloads. The launcher is mounted aft on the main deck above the magazine. The launchers can also accommodate the Harpoon (RGM-84) surface-to-surface missile. *Adams*-class ships do not carry the Phalanx point defense gun systems.

The ships in this class also have the 12.75-inch Mark 46 lightweight torpedo, which is launched from two Mark 32 triple tubes. Antisubmarine capabilities include the one eight-cell Mark 16 ASROC (RUR-5) launcher mounted amidships between the stacks. The ASROC is a propulsion unit attached to the Mark 46 lightweight torpedo that enables the ship to attack enemy submarines

up to a distance of six nautical miles (6.9 miles).

Top speed for these ships is nominally 31.5 knots (36.2 miles per hour), but in 1979, the *Strauss* set a speed record when it attained 35.2 knots (40.5 miles per hour). The *Charles F. Adams* ships are powered by four boilers built by either Babcock & Wilcox, Combustion Engineering, or Foster Wheeler. They provide steam to two turbines built by

CHARLES F. ADAMS-CLASS (DDG) GUIDED-MISSILE DESTROYERS

Operational (commissioned):	DDG 2 USS *Charles F. Adams* (September 1960)	**Dimensions cont'd:**	
	DDG 3 USS *John King* (February 1961)	Width:	47 ft.
		Draft:	22 ft.
	DDG 4 USS *Lawrence* (January 1962)	**Propulsion:**	
	DDG 5 USS *Claude Ricketts* (May 1962)	DDG 2–3, 7–8, 10–13, 15–22:	Two General Electric steam turbines, 70,000 hp
	DDG 6 USS *Barney* (August 1962)		
	DDG 7 USS *Henry B. Wilson* (December 1960)	DDG 4–6, 9, 14, 23–24:	Two Westinghouse steam turbines, 70,000 hp
	DDG 8 USS *Lynde McCormick* (June 1961)	DDG 2–3, 7, 10–13, 20–22:	Four Babcock & Wilcox 1,200-psi steam boilers
	DDG 9 USS *Towers* (June 1961)		
	DDG 10 USS *Sampson* (June 1961)	DDG 4, 6, 9, 14:	Four Foster Wheeler 1,200-psi steam boilers
	DDG 11 USS *Sellers* (October 1961)		
	DDG 12 USS *Robison* (December 1961)	DDG 15–19:	Four Combustion Engineering 1,200-psi steam boilers
	DDG 13 USS *Hoel* (June 1962)		
	DDG 14 USS *Buchanan* (February 1962)	Speed:	31.5 knots (36.2 mph)
	DDG 15 USS *Berkeley* (December 1962)	Armament:	Harpoon and either Tartar or Standard-MR SSM in Mk 11 twin-rail launcher or Mk 13 single-rail launcher
	DDG 16 USS *Joseph Strauss* (April 1963)		
	DDG 17 USS *Conyngham* (July 1963)		One ASROC (RUR-5A) Mk 16 octuple launcher
	DDG 18 USS *Semmes* (December 1962)		Two Mk 42 5-inch guns
	DDG 19 USS *Tatnall* (April 1963)		Mark 46 torpedoes fired from two 12.75-inch Mk 32 triple tubes
	DDG 20 USS *Goldsborough* (November 1963)		
	DDG 21 USS *Cochrane* (March 1964)	**Fire control:**	
		All:	Mk 4 or Mk 13 weapon director
	DDG 22 USS *Benjamin Stoddert* (September 1964)		Mk 68 gun fire control with SPG-53A radar or Mk 86 with SPG-60 and SPQ-9A radars
	DDG 23 USS *Richard E. Byrd* (March 1964)		Two Mk 74 missile fire controls
	DDG 24 USS *Waddel* (August 1964)	DDG 2–15:	Mk 111 ASW fire control
		DDG 16–24:	Mk 114 ASW fire control
		Aircraft:	None
		Surveillance radar:	SPS-10F or SPS-10D surface search
			SPS-4OB/D air search
			SPS-52 surface search
Displacement:	3,380 tons	Sonar:	SQS-23A or SQQ-23A PAIR
Dimensions:			
Length:	420 ft.	Crew:	360

either Westinghouse or General Electric. The turbines develop 70,000 horsepower.

In the early 1980s plans to modernize all ships in the class were rejected by Congress as being too costly. To date, only three *Charles F. Adams* ships—the *Tatnall*, *Goldsborough*, and *Benjamin Stoddert*—have been upgraded.

Opposite: *In total there are 23 Charles F. Adams guided-missile destroyers in service today, including the* Sampson *pictured here. Built in the 1960s, these destroyers are sorely in need of a variety of high-tech upgrades.*

Farragut-Class (DDG) Guided- Missile Destroyers

In addition to its bow-mounted five-inch gun, the Dahlgren (as well as other destroyers of its class) is armed with Harpoon antiship missiles.

140

In the 1950s and 1960s the Navy sought to redefine its role in naval warfare and consolidate its resources against the growing threat of enemy air and submarine attack. Changes brought on by this redefining process also led to many changes in the classification of the *Farragut* destroyers.

Designed in the early 1950s, the first three ships in the class were built originally as all-gun destroyers (DL 6 though 8). In November 1956, their classification was changed to frigates (DL). But by the time the first ship had been commissioned in December 1960, the three ships had been designated guided-missile frigates (DLG). As such, they were the Navy's first so-called anti-air war (AAW) ships. In June 1975, they were reclassified as guided-missile destroyers (DDG). This class is sometimes referred to as the *Coontz* class, because the *Coontz* (ex-DLG 9, now DDG 40) was the first in the class to be ordered as a guided-missile destroyer. Officially, the *Coontz* and the ships that came after it are considered *Farragut*-class ships.

Unlike the larger and later *Belknap* guided-missile cruisers, *Farragut* ships have flush deck hulls and latticework masts. All *Farragut*-class ships have a vertical replenishment (VERTREP) landing area for helicopters, but no hangar or maintenance facilities. They are powered by four Foster Wheeler or Babcock & Wilcox steam boilers, which provide power to two De Laval or Allis-Chalmers turbines. The propulsion system develops 80,000 horsepower and enables these ships to run at a top speed of 33 knots (37.95 miles per hour). However, their range is limited to only 4,500 nautical miles (5,175 miles) at 20 knots (23 miles per hour). As a consequence, all but the *Preble* were assigned to the Atlantic Fleet, where ship range is not as important as it is in the vast Pacific.

Two five-inch guns and two Mark 33 three-inch twin antiaircraft (AA) gun mounts comprised the original gun armament of the ten ships in this class. The three-inch guns have since been discarded. A Mark 16 eight-cell ASROC (RUR-5A) missile launcher is mounted on the afterdeck. In addition to this antisubmarine weapon, *Farragut* ships carry 12.75-inch Mark 46 torpedoes fired from two Mark 32 triple tubes. *Farragut* ships are also armed with eight Harpoon (RGM-84A) anti-surface ship missiles.

Because of weight and space limitations, the *Farragut* ships cannot be fitted with the 20 millimeter Phalanx Close-In Weapons System. However, these ships do carry the Mark 10 twin-arm launcher for the Terrier missile, and the Standard-Extended Range (RIM-67B) surface-to-air missile, which has a range of 90 nautical miles (103.5 miles).

FARRAGUT-CLASS (DDG) GUIDED-MISSILE DESTROYERS

Operational (commissioned):	DDG 37 USS *Farragut* (December 1960) DDG 38 USS *Luce* (May 1961) DDG 39 USS *MacDonough* (November 1961) DDG 40 USS *Coontz* (July 1960) DDG 41 USS *King* (November 1960) DDG 42 USS *Mahan* (August 1960) DDG 43 USS *Dahlgren* (April 1961) DDG 44 USS *William V. Pratt* (November 1961) DDG 45 USS *Dewey* (December 1959) DDG 46 USS *Preble* (May 1960)	**Propulsion cont'd: DDG 40–46:**	psi steam boilers Four Babcock & Wilcox 1,200-psi steam boilers
		Speed:	33 knots (37.95 mph)
		Armament: All:	Standard-ER SAMs and/or Terrier SAMs, fired from one Mk 10 twin launcher Eight Harpoon (RGM-84A) SSM Mk 141 launchers (two quadruple mounts) One ASROC (RUR-5A) Mk 16 octuple launcher One Mk 42 5-inch dual-purpose gun Mark 46 torpedoes fired from two 12.75-inch Mk 32 triple tubes
Displacement:	4,700 tons		
Dimensions:			
Length:	512.5 ft.	**Fire control:**	Mk 11 weapon director Mk 68 gun fire control Two Mk 76 missile fire control Mk 111 ASW fire control system
Width:	52.5 ft.		
Draft:	25 ft.		
Propulsion:			
DDG 37–39, 45–46:	Two De Laval steam turbines, 80,000 hp	**Aircraft:**	None
DDG 40–44:	Two Allis-Chalmers steam turbines, 80,000 hp	**Surveillance radar:**	SPS-10B/C surface search SPS-48 3D search SPS-53 surface search
DDG 37–39:	Four Foster Wheeler 1,200-psi steam boilers	**Sonar:**	SLQ-23 PAIR
		Crew:	400

Spruance-Class (DD) Destroyers

Designed in the 1970s, the 31 Spruance-class destroyers were built in modular fashion as weapon platforms on which new weapons and electronic devices could easily be installed. They were twice as large, twice as heavy, and twice as capable as the World War II era destroyers they were replacing—primarily the Sumner (DD 692) and the Gearing (DD 710) classes. The basic design was a highly successful one, and has served as the basis for the Kidd destroyer class, as well as the Ticonderoga cruiser class.

Upon their launching, the first Spruance destroyers were heavily criticized by Congress and the media as being too lightly armed. Such criticism has proven to be way off the mark. In fact, the Spruance ships are quite heavily armed by the standards of their class.

Anti-air war (AAW) defensive armament consists of one eight-cell Mark 29 launcher for the short-range Sea Sparrow (RIM-7) missile and two 20 millimeter Phalanx multibarrel guns. For surface combat, the Spruance ships carry eight Harpoon (RGM-84A) missiles fired from the Mark 141 launcher. Spruance ships are also armed with two five-inch dual-purpose (antiaircraft and anti-surface) Mark 42 guns, and Tomahawk missiles. The Tomahawks are fired from two quadruple-mount Mark 143 missile launchers, or from the 61-cell Vertical Launch System

(VLS) Mark 41 launcher. In October 1982, the Merrill (DD 976) was fitted with Tomahawk missiles in an armored-box launcher (ABL). The Tomahawks in their ABLs are mounted in front of the bridge on either side of an ASROC Mark 16 launcher and behind the forward five-inch gun.

Spruance-class destroyers are also armed with ASROC (RUR-5A) antisubmarine torpedoes, which are fired from the Mark 16 launcher, or from the VLS in those ships that are equipped with it. The Mark 16 launcher and its reloader have a total capacity of 24 ASROC missiles. Additionally, six Mark 46 12.75-inch torpedoes can be fired from two Mark 32 triple tubes. The Mark 32 launchers are mounted on the enclosed main deck directly below the helicopter deck; to fire their

torpedoes, sliding hatches in the hull are opened.

To enhance their anti-submarine warfare (ASW) capability, all ships in this class are to be refitted with the SQS-53B sonar system. The SQS-53B will augment the SQR-19 tactical towed array sonar.

The Spruance ships were the first warships of this size (displacement: 8,040 tons) to be powered by gas turbine engines. The General Electric LM 2500 gas turbine engines produce a total of 80,000 horsepower, which enables these ships to run at 32.5 knots (37.4 miles per hour). They have an unrefueled range of 6,000 nautical miles (6,900 miles) at 20 knots (23 miles per hour), and 3,300 nautical miles (3,795 miles) at 30 knots (34.5 miles per hour)—a greater operating range than the earlier steam-

driven Farragut-class destroyers. The two gas turbine engines are paired to turn two controllable-pitch propellers. Even the electrical generators are run by small gas turbine engines. The use of gas turbines minimizes noise to an extent that makes the Spruance ships the world's quietest surface warships.

Spruance-class destroyers have received overhauls that will add many years to their active-duty careers. It is even conceivable that these ships will be in service into the second decade and possibly the third decade of the 21st century.

The John Young shells Iranian oil platforms in the Persian Gulf. Such incidents as these prove that guns are still a vital component of a destroyer's armament.

Operational (commissioned):

DD 963 USS *Spruance* (September 1975)
DD 964 USS *Paul F. Forester* (February 1976)
DD 965 USS *Kinkaid* (July 1976)
DD 966 USS *Hewitt* (September 1976)
DD 967 USS *Elliot* (January 1976)
DD 968 USS *Arthur W. Radford* (April 1977)
DD 969 USS *Peterson* (July 1977)
DD 970 USS *Caron* (October 1977)
DD 971 USS *David R. Ray* (November 1977)
DD 972 USS *Oldendorf* (March 1978)
DD 973 USS *John Young* (May 1978)
DD 974 USS *Comte De Grasse* (August 1978)
DD 975 USS *O'Brien* (December 1977)
DD 976 USS *Merrill* (March 1978)
DD 977 USS *Briscoe* (June 1978)
DD 978 USS *Stump* (August 1978)
DD 979 USS *Conolly* (October 1978)
DD 980 USS *Moosbrugger* (December 1978)
DD 981 USS *John Hancock* (March 1979)
DD 982 USS *Nicholson* (May 1979)
DD 983 USS *John Rodgers* (July 1979)
DD 984 USS *Leftwich* (August 1979)
DD 985 USS *Cushing* (October 1979)
DD 986 USS *Harry W. Hill* (November 1979)
DD 987 USS *O'Bannon* (December 1979)
DD 988 USS *Thorn* (February 1980)
DD 989 USS *Devo* (March 1980)
DD 990 USS *Ingersoll* (April 1980)
DD 991 USS *Fife* (May 1980)
DD 992 USS *Fletcher* (July 1980)
DD 997 USS *Hayler* (March 1983)

Displacement: 8,040 tons

Dimensions:
  Length: 529 ft.
  Width: 55 ft.
  Draft: 29 ft.
Propulsion: Four General Electric LM 2500 gas turbines, 80,000 hp
Speed: 32.5 knots (37.4 mph)
Armament:
  All: Sea Sparrow (RIM-7) SAMs fired from one Mk 29 octuple launcher
  Eight Harpoon (RGM-84A) SSM Mk 141 launchers (two quadruple mounts)
  Two 20mm Phalanx CIWS Mk 15 multibarrel guns
  Two Mk 42 5-inch dual-purpose guns
  Mark 46 torpedoes fired from two 12.75-inch Mk 32 triple tubes

  DD 963–973, 975, 977, 978, 980–982, 985–988, 991–992, 997: Mk 41 Vertical Launch System (VLS) firing Tomahawk and ASROC missiles

  DD 974, 976, 979, 983–984, 989–990: One ASROC (RUR-5A) Mk 16 octuple launcher
  Eight Tomahawk land-attack and antiship cruise missiles in two Mk 143 quadruple-mount armored-box launchers (ABL)

Fire control: SWG-2 Tomahawk weapon control system in ships fitted with ABL
  SWG-3 Tomahawk weapon control system in ships fitted with VLS
  Mk 91 missile fire control system with SPG-80 and SPQ-9A radars
  Mk 86 gun fire control system with SPG-60 and SPQ-9A radars
  Mk 116 ASW fire control system
Aircraft: Two SH-60B Seahawk LAMPS III helicopters
Surveillance radar: SPS-4OB/C/D surface search
  SPS-55 surface search
Sonar:
  All: SLQ-53A bow mount
  DD 980: SQR-19
Crew: Approximately 334

Kidd-Class (DDG) Guided-Missile Destroyers

KIDD-CLASS (DDG) GUIDED-MISSILE DESTROYERS

Operational (commissioned):	DDG 993 USS *Kidd* (July 1981) DDG 994 USS *Callaghan* (August 1981) DDG 995 USS *Scott* (October 1981) DDG 996 USS *Chandler* (March 1982)
Displacement:	9,574 tons

Dimensions:
  Length:
  Width:
  Draft:
	
	563.4 ft.
	55 ft.
	30 ft.

Propulsion:	Four General Electric LM 2500 gas turbines, 80,000 hp
Speed:	30+ knots (34.5+ mph)
Armament:	Standard-ER SAMs fired from two Mk 26 twin launchers Eight Harpoon (RGM-84A) SSM Mk 141 launchers (two quadruple mounts) One ASROC (RUR-5A) Mk 26 octuple launcher Two 20mm Phalanx CIWS Mk 15 multibarrel guns Two Mk 45 5-inch guns Mk 46 torpedoes fired from two 12.75-inch Mk 32 triple tubes
Fire control:	Two Mk 74 missiles fire control systems with SPG-51D radar Mk 86 gun fire control system with SPG 60 and SPQ-9A radars Mk 116 ASW fire control system
Aircraft:	SH-2F Seasprite LAMPS I helicopter
Surveillance radar:	SPS-53 surface search SPS-55 surface search SPS-48C 3D air search
Sonar:	SLQ-25 Nixie SLQ-32(V)2
Crew:	339

The *Kidd*-class destroyers were an outgrowth of this nation's relationship with Iran during the 1970s. At that time, the United States supported the government of the Shah of Iran and provided military assistance to the Iranian armed forces. A great deal of sophisticated military equipment was sold to Iran, and the sale of a great deal more was pending when the Shah was deposed by the 1979 Islamic Revolution. Among the military items that Iran was to have received were six extremely capable guided-missile destroyers that were based on an improved *Spruance*-class design. When the new Iranian government proved hostile to the United States, the sale of all six was suspended, and four—the *Karuroosh*, *Daryush*, *Ardeshir*, and *Nader*—were subsequently acquired by the U.S. Navy. Renamed, these destroyers now comprise the *Kidd* class.

The Iranian government wanted significant anti-air war (AAW) and antisubmarine warfare (ASW) capabilities in their new destroyers, which remain well armed for these roles. AAW missiles include the Standard-ER (RIM-67B) surface-to-air missile fired from two Mark 26 twin launchers. The forward missile launcher has a capacity of 24 missiles, while the after launcher has a 44-missile capacity. Eight Harpoon (RGM-84A) missiles in two Mark 141 quadruple-mount launchers are also carried. The Mark 26 missile launchers are located forward on the main deck ahead of the bridge and on the 01 level aft of the deckhouse. The Harpoon launchers are mounted on either side of the after deckhouse.

For antisubmarine warfare, the *Kidd* destroyers have the ASROC (RUR-5A) missile, which is also fired from the Mark 26 launcher. The ships of this class also have 12.75-inch Mark 46 torpedoes, which are fired from two Mark 32 triple tubes. These launchers are mounted inside the ship and fired through ports below the helicopter deck. Plans have been made to install the SQR-19 Tactical Towed Array Sonar.

Kidd ships are also armed with two five-inch Mark 45 guns, one on the main deck forward, and the other on the main deck aft. Two 20 millimeter Phalanx Close-In Weapons System Mark 15 multibarrel guns provide additional missile defense.

At present, *Kidd* ships carry a single SH-2F Seasprite LAMPS (Light Airborne Multi-Purpose System) I helicopter. However, the helicopter hangar (which is located aft of the stern deckhouse) is large enough to house two SH-60B Seahawks.

The *Kidd* ships have a top speed in excess of 30 knots (34.5 miles per hour). They are powered by four General Electric LM 2500 gas turbine engines that develop 80,000 horsepower, and have an unrefueled range of 6,000 nautical miles (6,900 miles) at 20 knots (23 miles per hour), and 3,300 nautical miles (3,795 miles) at full speed.

Opposite, top and bottom: Two views of the Chandler, *a* Kidd-*class guided-missile destroyer. The four ships in this class were originally built for the Iranian Navy in 1974. Following the revolution that deposed the Shah of Iran and his government, these ships were completed for the U.S. Navy at a cost of approximately $520 million each—a considerable bargain at the going rate for new ships!*

Arleigh Burke-Class (DDG) Guided-Missile Destroyers

The *Arleigh Burke*-class destroyers were designed in the late 1970s to provide anti-air warfare (AAW) support for aircraft carrier battle groups. The ships in this new class are far more capable than all other destroyer types.

The initial building program for this class called for a total of 49 ships. This figure was increased to 63 during the Reagan administration, then reduced to just 29 ships as a result of budgetary considerations during the mid-1980s. The ships are being built in two shipyards, Bath Iron Works in Maine and the Litton/Ingalls Shipyard in Mississippi. The first ship in this class, the *Arleigh Burke* (DDG 51), was laid down in December 1988, launched in September 1989, and is due to be commissioned in 1991.

Initially, the displacement of *Arleigh Burke*-class destroyers was not to exceed 6,000 tons, which would have made them smaller—and, it was hoped, less expensive to build—than the ships of the *Ticonderoga* class. The decision to build the superstructure of steel rather than aluminum increased the displacement to more than 8,000 tons. This decision was based in part on a study of a 1975 collision between the *Belknap* (CG 26) and the *John F. Kennedy* (CV 67). Compared to aluminum, steel provides far more protection against blast, fragmentation, fire damage, and the effects of electromagnetic pulse weapons. The ships of this class will also have additional Kevlar armor and nuclear-biological-chemical protection.

The *Arleigh Burke* ships will be powered by four gas turbine engines that will develop 100,000 horsepower at 30 knots (34.5 miles per hour). They will be equipped to land helicopters, although the helicopter type has not yet been specified. The Navy has determined that if the aft missile launcher facility were removed, two LAMPS III helicopters could be accommodated. But the loss of these 61 launching cells would greatly reduce the ship's effectiveness as an AAW ship and limit its antisubmarine warfare (ASW) capabilities.

Armament on the new destroyers will consist of two Mark 41 Vertical Launch System (VLS) launchers for the Standard (RIM-67) surface-to-air missile and Tomahawk (BGM-109) cruise missile. The forward launcher will have 29 launching cells, the after launcher 61. Vertical launch ASROC missiles will also be fired from the Mark 41 launchers. *Arleigh Burke* ships will also be armed with eight Harpoon (RGM-84A) missiles in two quadruple-mount Mark 141 launchers, and Mark 46

12.75-inch torpedoes fired from two Mark 32 triple tubes. Two 20 millimeter Phalanx multibarrel guns complete the armament of this class.

The *Arleigh Burke* ships will carry four SPY-1D

multifunction radars, the SQS-53C bow-mounted sonar, and the SQR-19 tactical towed array sonar. The electronic suite of these ships will thus be only slightly less capable than that of Aegis-equipped cruisers.

ARLEIGH BURKE-CLASS (DDG) GUIDED-MISSILE DESTROYERS

Operational (commissioned):	DDG 51 USS *Arleigh Burke* (scheduled 1991)
Under construction:	DDG 52 USS *John Barry*
Planned:	DDG 53 USS *John Paul Jones*
	DDG 54 USS *Curtis Wilbur*
	23 additional
Displacement:	8,300 tons
Dimensions:	
Length:	466 ft.
Width:	59 ft.
Draft:	37.58 ft.
Propulsion:	Four General Electric LM 2500-30 gas turbines, 100,000 hp
Speed:	30 knots (34.5 mph)
Armament:	Two Mk 41 Mod 2 Vertical Launch Systems (VLS) firing ASROC, Standard-MR SAMs, and Tomahawk missiles
	Eight Harpoon (RGM-84A) SSM Mk 141 launchers (two quadruple mounts)
	Two 20mm Phalanx CIWS Mk 15 multibarrel guns
	One Mk 75 5-inch dual-purpose gun
	Mark 46 torpedoes fired from two 12.75-inch Mk 32 triple tubes
Fire control:	SWG-3 Tomahawk fire control system
	Mk 99 Illuminators with SPG-62 radar
	Mk 56 gun fire control system
Aircraft:	Two SH-60B Seahawk LAMPS III (provisional)
Surveillance radar:	SPS-64 surface search
	SPS-67 surface search
	Four SPY-1D multifunction
Sonar:	SQS 53C
	SQR 19
Crew:	325

Four *Arleigh Burke* ships have been funded, one is under construction and at least 23 more are planned. If all are built, the *Arleigh Burke* ships will be the Navy's showpiece destroyers well into the 21st century.

Top and bottom: *Two artists' renderings of the* Arleigh Burke, *the first ship in the Navy's newest guided-missile destroyer class. Designed as an all-purpose destroyer that can function in a variety of high-threat environments, the* Arleigh Burke *ships will be armed with the most modern weaponry, and be fitted with nearly 130 tons of armor to protect their vital areas. They will also have the Aegis SPY-1D four-faced radar system, which is to be mounted on the forward superstructure.*

FRIGATES

Frigates were originally two-decked sailing ships that carried their armament on the top deck only. Among the more famous of the sail-powered frigates is the *Constitution* (otherwise known as "Old Ironsides"), which is still in commission and berthed in Boston Harbor.

The demise of sail-powered warships in the mid- to late-1800s resulted in the disappearance of frigates as well. With the coming of World War II, however, the frigate designation was revived in the U.S. Navy. A total of 100 *Ashville*-class and *Tacoma*-class frigates were built, and these ships were employed primarily as convoy escorts. All were retired immediately after the end of the war. In 1950 the *Dealy* class was designed and built, but these ships were termed "ocean escorts" rather than frigates. The *Dealy* ships have been turned over to friendly nations or stricken from the Navy list. Ten years later, at the urging of the Kennedy administration, the Navy revived the frigate class (FF) to serve as antisubmarine warfare (ASW) escorts. They were to be fast enough to accompany carrier task forces, and they would be armed with 12.75-inch torpedoes. For antiaircraft protection they would also carry one or more guns (either three-inch or five-inch). When the guns were replaced by guided missiles, these ships were termed guided-missile frigates (FFG).

Today, all Navy frigates are antisubmarine warfare escorts. The *Oliver Hazard Perry*-class frigates provide limited anti-air warfare (AAW) protection as well. The Navy currently has 98 frigates, with 19 more in the Naval Reserve fleet. The 19 Naval Reserve ships have combined active and reserve crews. No frigates are under construction, and none are planned. A plan to build an advanced-design frigate was canceled in 1986. The *Oliver Hazard Perry*-class of frigates contains 51 ships, making it

the largest single ship class in the U.S. Navy. There are an insufficient number of frigates to provide complete protection to NATO's Sea Lanes of Communication (SLOC) in case of an all-out war, but frigates are one of the few ship classes to have exceeded quotas in the Pentagon's proposed aim to establish a 600-ship navy.

The Lockwood, a Knox-class frigate, fires a Harpoon antiship missile.

Bronstein-Class (FF) Frigates

The *Bronstein*-class ships were developed in the mid-to-late 1950s, before any hard evidence that the Soviets were building nuclear-powered submarines. Since the *Bronstein* frigates were intended to serve as prototypes of subsequent escort classes, only two ships in this class were built. Both ships were laid down in 1961, launched the following year, and commissioned in 1963 as destroyer escorts (DE). In June 1975 they received the frigate (FF) classification as part of a Navy-wide reorganization of ship classes.

For antisubmarine warfare, the *Bronstein* frigates are armed with an eight-cell Mark 16 ASROC launcher. There is no room in this class of ships for the magazine. The two ships are also armed with Mark 46 torpedoes fired from two Mark 32 triple tubes, and three-inch guns. Two of the guns, designated Mark 33, are carried in a twin forward mount. A single three-inch gun was initially installed aft, but this weapon was later removed to make way for a towed array surveillance system (which was installed only on the *McLoy*). Both ships had the capability to carry the DASH (Drone Antisubmarine Helicopter). When the DASH project was cancelled, the area on the afterdeck was converted into a helicopter landing area. But neither ship has facilities for housing or maintaining a helicopter.

Among the features incorporated in the design of the *Bronstein*-class frigates were a raked "mack" and the huge SQS-23 active/passive sonar. Due to its size, the SQS-23 was mounted in the bow instead of the keel. The bow mount also allowed the SQS-23 to operate with minimal interference from the cavitation produced by the Drone Antisubmarine Helicopter's rotors, and to serve as a counterweight to the engines in the stern. The raked configuration is characteristic of the subsequent *Knox* class. The bow-mounted sonar was also used in later frigates until the *Oliver Hazard Perry* class, which uses keel-mounted SQS-56 passive sonar.

Instead of the diesel propulsion systems of World

BRONSTEIN-CLASS (FF) FRIGATES	
Operational (commissioned):	FF 1037 USS *Bronstein* (June 1963) FF 1038 USS *McCloy* (October 1963)
Displacement:	3,560 tons
Dimensions:	
Length:	371.5 ft.
Width:	40.5 ft.
Draft:	23 ft.
Propulsion:	One De Laval steam turbine, 20,000 hp
Speed:	24 knots (27.6 mph) Two Foster Wheeler 600-psi boilers
Armament:	One ASROC (RUR-5A) Mk 16 octuple launcher Two Mk 33 3-inch antiaircraft guns Mk 46 torpedoes fired from two 12.75-inch Mk 32 triple tubes
Fire control:	Mk 1 target designator Mk 114 ASW fire control system Mk 56 gun fire control system with Mk 35 radar
Aircraft:	None
Surveillance radar:	SPS-20 surface search SPS-40 air search
Sonar:	
All:	SQS-26AXR bow mounted
FF 1038:	SQR-15 TASS
Crew:	
FF 1037:	216
FF 1038:	218

War II destroyer escorts, the *Bronstein* frigates are equipped with a steam turbine that can produce 20,000 horsepower. Top

speed for these ships is 24 knots (27.6 miles per hour). At 15 knots (17.25 miles per hour), *Bronstein* ships have a range of 4,000 nautical miles (4,800 miles). *Bronstein* ships are lacking in armament and seakeeping capabilities, and for that reason no more ships of this class have been built.

The McCloy *displays the aging 76.2 millimeter twin guns on the bow that are a feature of the* Bonstein-*class frigates. This class has limited high-tech weaponry and radars.*

Knox-Class (FF) Frigates

Prior to the completion of the *Oliver Hazard Perry*-class of frigates, the 46 *Knox* frigates represented the Navy's largest post-World War II warship class. Built between 1965 and 1973, the *Knox* ships were originally classified as ocean escorts (DE) but were reclassified as frigates (FF) in 1975 in the Navy-wide reclassification program. Their primary task is to escort convoys, amphibious task forces, and replenishment ships. They are long, sleek ships, nearly as large as World War II destroyers, with a round "mack" (mast and stack combined) rising amidships.

Anti-submarine weapons in these ships consists of ASROCs (Anti-Submarine Rockets), and a Light Airborne Multipurpose System (LAMPS) I SH-2F Seasprite helicopter. The ASROCs are fired from a Mark 16 eight-cell launcher located in front of the bridge. The Seasprite is housed in a hangar with a telescopic extension. As with the *Brooke* ships, *Knox* frigates were originally fitted to carry the DASH (Drone Antisubmarine Helicopter), which is now defunct. All *Knox* frigates are equipped with bow-mounted sonars, and 32 ships in this class have the tactical towed array system sonar.

For anti-air defense, most *Knox* ships were initially equipped with a Sea Sparrow (RIM-7) point defense missile system. The Sea Sparrow's eight-cell Mark 25 launcher was mounted on the stern, and its missiles had a range

Like all Knox-*class frigates, the* Luzon *is designed primarily for antisubmarine warfare.*

of only ten nautical miles (11.5 miles). The Mark 25 launcher did not have a reload capability; once all eight missiles were fired, the launcher was useless until a replenishment ship supplied more missiles. The Sea

Sparrow missile system was therefore removed and replaced by the 20 millimeter Phalanx Close-In Weapons System multibarrel gun. Each *Knox*-class frigate also mounts a five-inch Mark 42 dual-purpose gun for use

against low-flying attack aircraft and surface threats. The Mark 42 is mounted in front of the ASROC launcher.

Surface warfare armament consists of Harpoon (RGM-84A) antiship missiles, which are fired from the ASROC

Operational (commissioned):

FF 1052 USS *Knox* (April 1969)
FF 1053 USS *Roark* (November 1969)
FF 1054 USS *Gray* (April 1970)
FF 1055 USS *Hepburn* (July 1969)
FF 1056 USS *Connole* (August 1969)
FF 1057 USS *Rathburne* (May 1970)
FF 1058 USS *Meyerkord* (November 1969)
FF 1059 USS *W.S. Sims* (January 1970)
FF 1060 USS *Lang* (March 1970)
FF 1061 USS *Patterson* (March 1970)

FF 1062 USS *Whipple* (August 1970)
FF 1063 USS *Reasoner* (July 1971)
FF 1064 USS *Lockwood* (December 1970)
FF 1065 USS *Stein* (January 1972)
FF 1066 USS *Marvin Shields* (April 1971)
FF 1067 USS *Francis Hammond* (July 1970)
FF 1068 USS *Vreeland* (June 1970)
FF 1069 USS *Bagley* (May 1972)
FF 1070 USS *Downes* (August 1971)
FF 1071 USS *Badger* (December 1970)
FF 1072 USS *Blakely* (July 1970)
FF 1073 USS *Robert E. Peary* (September 1972)

FF 1074 USS *Harold E. Holt* (March 1971)
FF 1075 USS *Trippe* (September 1970)
FF 1076 USS *Fanning* (July 1971)
FF 1077 USS *Ouellet* (December 1970)
FF 1078 USS *Joseph Hewes* (February 1971)
FF 1079 USS *Bowen* (May 1971)
FF 1080 USS *Paul* (August 1971)
FF 1081 USS *Aylwin* (September 1971)
FF 1082 USS *Elmer Montgomery* (October 1971)
FF 1083 USS *Cook* (December 1971)
FF 1084 USS *McCandless* (March 1972)
FF 1085 USS *Donald B.*

Beary (July 1972)
FF 1086 USS *Brewton* (July 1972)
FF 1087 USS *Kirk* (September 1972)
FF 1088 USS *Barbey* (November 1972)
FF 1089 USS *Jesse L. Brown* (February 1973)
FF 1090 USS *Ainsworth* (March 1973)
FF 1091 USS *Miller* (June 1973)
FF 1092 USS *Thomas C. Hart* (July 1973)
FF 1093 USS *Capodanno* (November 1973)
FF 1094 USS *Pharris* (January 1974)
FF 1095 USS *Truett* (June 1974)
FF 1096 USS *Valdez* (July 1974)
FF 1097 USS *Moinester* (November 1974)

Displacement:	4,250 tons
Dimensions:	
Length:	438 ft.
Width:	44.2 ft.
Draft:	24.75 ft.
Propulsion:	One Westinghouse steam turbine, 35,000 hp
	Two Combustion Engineering 1,200-psi boilers
Speed:	27 knots (31 mph)
Armament:	One ASROC (RUR-5A) Mk 16 octuple launcher for Harpoon (RGM-84A) missiles or Mk 46 torpedoes
	One Mk 42 5-inch dual-purpose gun
	One 20mm Phalanx CIWS Mk 15 multibarrel gun
	Mk 46 torpedoes fired from two Mk 32 twin tubes
Fire control:	Mk 1 target designator

Fire control cont'd:	Mk 114 ASW fire control system
	Mk 68 gun fire control system
Aircraft:	One LAMPS I SH-2F Seasprite helicopter
Surveillance radar:	SPS-10 surface search
	SPS-40B air search
	SPS-58 threat warning (in some ships)
Sonar:	
All:	
FF 1052, 1056, 1063–1071, 1073–1076, 1078–1097:	SQS-26CX bow mount/SQR-18V
	SQS-35 IVDS/SQR-18A TACTAS
Crew:	
FF 1052, 1054, 1056–1059, 1062–1071, 1073–1090, 1092–1095, 1097:	282
FF 1053, 1055, 1060, 1061, 1072, 1091, 1096:	175 active, 127–155 reserve

launcher. The Harpoon antiship missile can strike targets at distances of up to 85 nautical miles (98 miles). *Knox* frigates are also armed with Mark 46 torpedoes fired from two Mark 32 twin tubes.

Knox frigates have a top speed of more than 27 knots (31 miles per hour). Two non-pressure boilers built by Combustion Engineering drive a Westinghouse steam turbine that develops 35,000 horsepower. One ship of this

class was to have been built with a gas turbine powerplant for evaluation, but the order was cancelled.

All *Knox* frigates have been, or are being, fitted with raised bow extensions to prevent these ships from

taking on water in rough seas. The Pacific Fleet has 19 *Knox* frigates; 17 are assigned to the Atlantic Fleet, and seven are with the Naval Reserve Force. The latter are manned by combined active and reserve crews.

Oliver Hazard Perry-Class (FFG) Guided-Missile Frigates

The 51 *Oliver Hazard Perry* frigates comprise the Navy's largest ship class. A total of 75 *Oliver Hazard Perry* frigates were scheduled, but that number fluctuated considerably during the 1970s and 1980s before settling at the final number. All of the *Oliver Hazard Perry* frigates were completed between 1977 and 1987. Four additional ships in this class were built and sold to Australia, and two were built in Spain. Australia, Spain, and Taiwan are also building *Oliver Hazard Perry* frigates in their own shipyards.

In keeping with the contracting military budgets of the post-Vietnam War era, the construction program that produced the *Oliver Hazard Perry* frigates used the latest management and manufacturing procedures to hold down costs. This involved computerized planning, scheduling, design, and assembly techniques. Flat panels and uncomplicated bulkheads were used as much as possible in the construction of these ships, and the hulls were built in prefabricated sections.

The chief purpose of the *Oliver Hazard Perry* ships is to provide anti-submarine warfare (ASW) and anti-air warfare (AAW) defense for merchant ships, replenishment ships, and amphibious task forces. The principle AAW weapons on the *Oliver Hazard Perry* frigates are their two ASW Light Airborne Multipurpose System (LAMPS) helicopters. These aircraft, which may be either SH-2F Seasprites (LAMPS I), or SH-60B Seahawks (LAMPS III), are housed in twin adjacent hangars at the rear of the superstructure. A Recovery, Assistance, Securing, and Traversing system, which allows helicopters to hover above a ship in rough seas and be winched down to a safe landing, is also being installed.

Oliver Hazard Perry frigates are also armed with a single Mark 13 twin launcher capable of loading and firing the Standard-MR (RIM-67A) AAW missile or Harpoon (RGM-84) surface-to-surface missile. The launcher is mounted above a circular magazine (which holds 40 rounds) on the main deck, forward of the bridge. For defense against air and surface attack, the *Oliver Hazard Perry* ships are armed with the new single-barrel 76 millimeter Mark 75 rapid-firing gun. This weapon, which was developed by the Italian firm of Oto Melara, is housed in a

These Oliver Hazard Perry-*class frigates are (left to right) the* Oliver Hazard Perry, *the* Antrim, *and the* Jack Williams.

unmanned, aft-facing turret on top of the low, boxy superstructure. The *Oliver Hazard Perry* ships are also armed with 12.75-inch Mark 46 homing torpedoes, which are fired from two Mark 32 triple tubes, and a single 20 millimeter Phalanx multi-barrel gun, which is mounted atop the helicopter hangar, aft of the 76mm gun.

Like the destroyers of the *Spruance* class, the *Oliver Hazard Perry* ships are propelled by gas turbine engines. However, the *Oliver Hazard Perry* ships are driven by only one screw. Even so, some *Oliver Hazard Perry* frigates have reportedly attained speeds of up to 36 knots (41.4 miles per hour) during trials. The propulsion system produces a total of 40,000 horsepower at 28 knots (32.2 miles per hour).

OLIVER HAZARD PERRY-CLASS (FFG) GUIDED-MISSILE FRIGATES

Operational (commissioned):

FFG 7 USS *Oliver Hazard Perry* (December 1977)
FFG 8 USS *McInerney* (December 1979)
FFG 9 USS *Wadsworth* (April 1980)
FFG 10 USS *Duncan* (May 1980)
FFG 11 USS *Clark* (May 1980)
FFG 12 USS *George Philip* (November 1980)
FFG 13 USS *Samuel Eliot Morison* (October 1980)
FFG 14 USS *Sides* (May 1981)
FFG 15 USS *Estocin* (January 1981)
FFG 16 USS *Clifton Sprague* (March 1981)

FFG 19 USS *John A. Moore* (November 1981)
FFG 20 USS *Antrim* (September 1981)
FFG 21 USS *Flatley* (June 1981)
FFG 22 USS *Fahrion* (January 1982)
FFG 23 USS *Lewis B. Puller* (April 1982)
FFG 24 USS *Jack Williams* (September 1981)
FFG 25 USS *Copeland* (August 1982)
FFG 26 USS *Gallery* (December 1981)
FFG 27 USS *Mahlon S. Tisdale* (November 1982)
FFG 28 USS *Boone* (November 1982)
FFG 29 USS *Stephen W. Groves* (April 1982)
FFG 30 USS *Reid* (February 1983)
FFG 31 USS *Stark* (October 1982)

FFG 32 USS *John L. Hall* (June 1982)
FFG 33 USS *Jarrett* (July 1983)
FFG 34 USS *Aubrey Fitch* (October 1982)
FFG 36 USS *Underwood* (January 1983)
FFG 37 USS *Crommelin* (June 1983)
FFG 38 USS *Curts* (October 1983)
FFG 39 USS *Doyle* (May 1983)
FFG 40 USS *Halyburton* (January 1984)
FFG 41 USS *McClusky* (October 1983)
FFG 42 USS *Klakring* (August 1983)
FFG 43 USS *Thach* (March 1984)
FFG 45 USS *De Wert* (November 1983)
FFG 46 USS *Rentz* (June 1984)
FFG 47 USS *Nichols* (March 1984)

FFG 48 USS *Vandegrift* (November 1984)
FFG 49 USS *Robert G. Bradley* (August 1984)
FFG 50 USS *Taylor* (December 1984)
FFG 51 USS *Gary* (November 1984)
FFG 52 USS *Carr* (July 1985)
FFG 53 USS *Hawes* (September 1985)
FFG 54 USS *Ford* (June 1985)
FFG 55 USS *Elrod* (July 1985)
FFG 56 USS *Simpson* (November 1985)
FFG 57 USS *Reuben James* (March 1986)
FFG 58 USS *Samuel B. Roberts* (April 1986)
FFG 59 USS *Kauffman* (February 1987)
FFG 60 USS *Rodney M. Davis* (May 1987)
FFG 61 USS *Ingraham* (1988)

Displacement:	3,650 tons
Dimensions:	
Length:	
FFG 7, 9–35:	445 ft.
FFG 8, 36–61:	453 ft.
Width:	45 ft.
Draft:	24.5 ft.
Propulsion:	Four General Electric LM 2500 gas turbine engines, 40,000 hp
Speed:	28+ knots (32.2+ mph)
Armament:	Standard-MR (RIM-67A) AAW or Harpoon (RGM-84) SSMs fired from one Mk 13 twin launcher
	One Mk 75 76mm gun
	One 20mm Phalanx CIWS Mk 15 multibarrel gun

Armament cont'd:	Mk 46 torpedoes fired from two Mk 32 triple tubes
Fire control:	Mk 13 weapon director
	Mk 92 fire control system
	STIR radar
Aircraft:	
FFG 7, 9–35:	Two SH-2F Seasprite LAMPS I helicopters
FFG 8, 36–61:	Two SH-60B Seahawk LAMPS III helicopters
Surveillance radar:	SPS-49(V)214 surface search
	SPS-55 surface search
Sonar:	SLQ-56 keel mount
Crew:	
FFG 7, 9–20, 23:	114 active, 76 reserve
FFG 8, 21, 22, 24–61:	205

COMMAND SHIPS

The origins of command ships can be traced to World War II. The development of these ships answered a need by commanders of amphibious operations to exercise more effective control over the forces at their disposal. In the years since the end of World War II, Cold War tensions and the increasingly sophisticated nature of military operations have created a need for ships specially dedicated to the command ship role. Today, such ships provide the facilities that allow a unit commander to conduct a military operation at peak efficiency.

Usually, but not always, that operation is of an amphibious nature. The command staff of air, sea, and ground units have access to communications equipment and computers to keep track of the combat and support forces required to perform the operation. Information received from satellites, aircraft, other ships, and from ground units is relayed to the command ship to be analyzed. Satellite images, aerial reconnaissance photos obtained by manned and unmanned aircraft, and on-the-ground reports can all be received and collated to provide as complete a picture as possible of enemy force dispositions and the course of the actual battle. By having these facilities placed aboard a ship as close as possible to the operational site, communication delays are avoided. If necessary, command staff members can visit the combat area.

The Navy currently operates five command ships, although this number may be reduced in the next decade. The *La Salle, Coronado, Blue Ridge,* and *Mount Whitney* are profiled in this section; the guided-missile cruiser *Belknap,* which serves as flagship of the Sixth Fleet in the Mediterranean, is profiled in the section on cruisers.

The Blue Ridge *is the name-ship of the* Blue Ridge *class of amphibious command ships. Like its sister ship, the* Mount Whitney, *the* Blue Ridge *was specially designed and built for the command ship role.*

Blue Ridge- Class (LCC) Amphibious Command Ships

BLUE RIDGE-CLASS (LCC) AMPHIBIOUS COMMAND SHIP	
Operational (commissioned):	LCC 19 USS *Blue Ridge* (November 1970) LCC 20 USS *Mount Whitney* (January 1971)
Displacement:	19,200 tons
Dimensions:	
Length:	
LCC 19:	636.4 ft.
LCC 20:	620 ft.
Width:	82 ft.
Draft:	27 ft.
Propulsion:	One General Electric steam turbine, 22,000 hp Two Foster Wheeler 600 psi boilers
Speed:	23 knots (26.45 mph)
Armament:	Sea Sparrow SAMs fired from two Mk 25 octuple launchers Two 20mm Phalanx CIWS Mk 15 multibarrel guns Four Mk 33 3-inch twin-barrel antiaircraft guns
Fire Control:	Two Mk 115 missile fire control systems
Aircraft:	None
Surveillance radar:	SPS-10 surface search SPS-40 air search SPS-48 3D search SPS-65 threat detection
Sonar:	None
Crew:	
Regular crew:	
LCC 19:	799
LCC 20:	777
Fleet Staff:	
LCC 19:	170
LCC 20:	191

The *Blue Ridge* (LCC 19) and the *Mount Whitney* (LCC 20) are the only two ships in the *Blue Ridge* class. Both are large ships built specifically for the amphibious command ship role. The *Blue Ridge* is the flagship of the Seventh Fleet in the western Pacific, and has been stationed at Yoksuka, Japan, since October 1979; the *Mount Whitney* is the flagship of the Second Fleet in the Atlantic, and has been stationed at Norfolk, Virginia, since January 1981. A third ship in this class was planned but never constructed.

The *Blue Ridge* serves as an operations center for 40 officers and 130 enlisted men of the Seventh Fleet staff, which is responsible for the proper ordering, conduct, and disposition of the fleet. Additionally, *Blue Ridge* has aboard it the staffs of Amphibious Squadron 1 and the 3rd Marine Amphibious Group 2. *Mount Whitney* carries similar staff personnel for the Second Fleet.

The two *Blue Ridge*-class ships were built along the lines of the *Iwo Jima*-class amphibious assault ships. Both displace 19,200 tons when fully loaded, and both are equipped with two 600 psi Foster Wheeler boilers that provide steam to drive a single General Electric turbine developing 22,000 horsepower. Their ability to achieve a top speed of 23 knots makes them the first command ships able to keep pace with 20-knot amphibious task forces.

Although both ships have the same displacement, the *Blue Ridge* is the larger of the two, with a length of 636.4 feet compared to a length of 620 feet for the *Mount Whitney*. The *Blue*

Ridge carries a crew (not including fleet staff) of 799, while the *Mount Whitney* carries a crew of 777. Both ships have a helicopter landing area but no hangar. Provision has been made to carry five landing craft and a ship's launch in davits (cranes) under the upper deck. This deck, referred to

as the "antenna deck,"
provides space for the
various antennas needed by
the command staff to remain
in constant communication
with the fleet and with
various support units.

Both ships are armed with
two eight-cell Mark 25
launchers for the Sea
Sparrow antiaircraft missile

system. Each ship has two
Mark 115 missile fire control
systems. They also carry two
20 millimeter Phalanx Close-
In Weapons System (CIWS)
Mark 15 multibarrel guns,
and four three-inch Mark 33
twin-barrel guns.

Both ships are armed with
two eight-cell Mark 25
launchers for the Sea

Sparrow antiaircraft missile
system. Each ship has two
Mark 115 missile fire control
systems. They also carry two

As Cold War tensions ease
and the necessity for maintaining large naval fleets appears
to wane, it is altogether
unlikely that additional
purpose-built command ships
will be built or modified.

An overhead view of the Blue
Ridge, *showing to good effect
the helicopter deck, as well as
the radar and communications
antennas so vital to the tasks
these ships are required to
perform.*

Command Ships (AGF) *Coronado* and *La Salle*

The Navy maintains two other command ships, the *Coronado* (AGF 11) and the *La Salle* (AGF 3). The *Coronado* is a converted *Austin*-class ship that served as an amphibious ship until 1980, when it was modified to

COMMAND SHIPS (AGF) *CORONADO* AND *LA SALLE*	
Operational (commissioned):	AGF 3 USS *La Salle* (February 1964) AGF 11 USS *Coronado* (May 1970)
Displacement:	
AGF 3:	14,650 tons
AGF 11:	17,000 tons
Dimensions:	
Length:	
AGF 3:	521 ft.
AGF 11:	570 ft.
Width:	
AGF 3:	84 ft.
AGF 11:	84 ft.
Draft:	
AGF 3:	21 ft.
AGF 11:	23 ft.
Propulsion:	Two De Laval steam turbines, 24,000 hp Two Babcock & Wilcox 600 psi boilers
Speed:	
AGF 3:	20 knots (23 mph)
AGF 11:	21 knots (24 mph)
Armament:	Four Mk 33 3-inch antiaircraft guns Two 20mm Phalanx CIWS Mk 15 multibarrel guns
Fire Control:	None
Aircraft:	One SH-3 Sea King
Surveillance radar:	SPS-10 surface search SPS-40 air search
Sonar:	None
Crew:	
Regular crew:	
AGF 3:	487
AGF 11:	516
Fleet staff:	
AGF 3:	44
AGF 11:	50

Right: Formally an Austin-*class amphibious transport dock, the command ship* Coronado *still has the capability to perform in the amphibious assault ship role. Note the landing craft on the after deck in front of the helicopter landing area.* **Inset:** *This overhead view of command ship* La Salle *shows how its defensive armament is situated to provide defense toward all four angles of probable attack.*

a command ship and replaced the *La Salle* as flagship of the Middle East Force in the Persian Gulf and Indian Ocean. Between 1983 and 1984, *Coronado* underwent a major overhaul, then went to the Mediterranean as flagship of the Sixth Fleet until 1986. In that year, *Coronado* was shifted to the Pacific to become the flagship of the Third Fleet, based at Pearl Harbor, Hawaii.

The *La Salle* was one of three *Raleigh*-class amphibious transport docks. The *La Salle* was commissioned in 1964 and served as an amphibious ship until converted to a command ship in 1972. Additional air conditioning and a helicopter hangar were added, and command and communications equipment and facilities were expanded. From 1972 to 1980, *La Salle* served as the flagship of the Middle East Force in the Persian Gulf and Indian Ocean. Between 1980 and 1982, the ship underwent a major overhaul at the Philadelphia Naval Yard. *La Salle* returned to the Middle East Force to replace the *Coronado* as flagship of the Middle East Force.

The *Coronado* is a large ship of 17,000 tons displacement when fully loaded, and is 570 feet long. The ship is powered by two 600 psi boilers built by Babcock & Wilcox, which drive two De Laval steam turbines producing 24,000 horsepower. *Coronado* is capable of 20 knots (23 miles per hour) and can steam for more than 8,800 miles without refueling. The ship is armed with four three-inch Mark 33 antiaircraft guns and two 20 millimeter Phalanx Mark 15 multibarrel guns.

La Salle is a slightly smaller ship, displacing 14,650 tons when fully loaded and measuring 521 feet in length. The ship is also powered by two 600 psi boilers built by Babcock & Wilson which drive two De Laval steam turbines to produce 24,000 horsepower. *La Salle* has a cruising speed of 20 knots (23 miles per hour) and can steam nearly 19,000 miles without refueling. Armament is the same as *Coronado*'s but whereas the *Coronado*'s Phalanx guns are mounted fore and aft, the *La Salle*'s are mounted amidships.

Coronado carries a crew of 516 and has facilities for an additional 50 command staff members. *La Salle* carries a crew of 487 and has space for 44 command staff members.

AMPHIBIOUS SHIPS

The United States maintains military commitments to allies and friends around the world. It is understood by potential enemies that American forces will intervene if requested. To do so, U.S. military forces must be ready to move quickly to potential or actual trouble zones. The Marine Corps is the U.S. combat force that makes all initial landings on defended beachheads. To accomplish this task, the Marines have developed three tiers of organization. The smallest combat unit the Marines would use in an amphibious landing is the Marine Expeditionary Unit (MEU), which consists of about 2,350 Marines. The next tier up is the Marine Expeditionary Brigade (MEB), comprising about 14,800 troops. Finally, there is the Marine Expeditionary Force (MEF), which contains nearly 48,000 troops.

Only a small portion of any troop movement can be transported by military airlift. The majority of troops and equipment must be transported by sea. The complexity of such a task and the amount of shipping involved in moving one Marine division plus equipment requires 58 specialized ships.

Today's amphibious ships are not amphibious in the World War II sense of the term, when "amphibious" ships and landing craft could actually beach themselves to allow troops to come ashore. Amphibious ships now keep well offshore under the close air and antisubmarine protection of their escorts. Their cargo of troops and equipment are put ashore by a variety of smaller craft that load from the amphibious ship.

The United States Navy presently has 58 amphibious-class ships in commission. But it would be misleading to say the Navy has 58 ships available. First, the ships are divided between the Atlantic and Pacific oceans. Second, some are moving to or

from their fleet assignments or home ports, while others are being serviced or modernized. At best, the Navy currently has the capability to move half a division. The Navy's goal was to have 72 amphibious ships. This number would have provided enough

ships to move one Marine Expeditionary Force (comprising a Marine division and an air wing), plus a Marine Expeditionary Brigade (comprising a Marine regiment and an air group). The 72-ship goal is now being reconsidered in view of fleet reductions.

The Navy's amphibious ships
currently in service are divided into
seven classes. Class designations are
somewhat confusing even for
knowledgeable readers: LPH is a
helicopter amphibious assault ship;
LHA is a general-purpose amphibious
assault ship; LHD is a multipurpose
amphibious assault ship; LSD is a dock
landing ship; LPD is an amphibious
transport dock for loading and
unloading where there are no port
facilities; LST is a tank landing ship;
and LKA is an amphibious cargo ship.

The crew of the Wasp *"mans the rails" as
their ship heads out to sea. The* Wasp
*and its sister ships represent the Navy's
newest class of amphibious assault
ships.*

Iwo Jima- Class (LPH) Amphibious Assault Ships

IWO JIMA-CLASS (LPH) ASSAULT SHIPS

Operational (commissioned):	LPH 2 USS *Iwo Jima* (August 1961)
	LPH 3 USS *Okinawa* (April 1962)
	LPH 7 USS *Guadalcanal* (July 1963)
	LPH 9 USS *Guam* (January 1985)
	LPH 10 USS *Tripoli* (August 1966)
	LPH 11 USS *New Orleans* (November 1968)
	LPH 12 USS *Inchon* (June 1970)
Displacement:	18,300 tons
Dimensions:	
Length:	602.25 ft.
Width:	106 ft.
Draft:	26 ft.
Propulsion:	One steam turbine, 22,000 hp
	Two 600-psi boilers
Speed:	22 knots (25.3 mph)
Armament:	
All:	Two 20mm Phalanx CIWS Mk 15 multibarrel guns
	Two Mk 33 3-inch antiaircraft guns
LPH 2, 8–12:	Sea Sparrow SAMs fired from two Mk 25 octuple launchers
LPH 3, 7:	Sea Sparrow SAMs fired from one Mk 25 octuple launcher
Fire control:	Mk 115 fire control system
Aircraft:	25 helicopters
Surveillance radar:	SPS-10 surface search
	SPS-40 air search
Sonar:	None
Crew:	
Navy:	685
Marines:	2,000

The helicopter saw use only in the last stages of World War II, and then only in a search and rescue role. However, by the end of the 1940s the Marine Corps, impressed with the helicopter's possibilities, was already experimenting with the concept of "vertical envelopment"—airlifting lightly armed troops from widely dispersed amphibious ships to a single beachhead.

In the mid-1950s the World War II escort carrier *Thetis Bay* was converted to carry helicopters and troops. The concept was so successful that a second escort carrier was scheduled for conversion. Instead, a new class of amphibious assault ship—the *Iwo Jima* class—was developed. The *Iwo Jima* ships were the first ships in any of the world's navies to be designed specifically to carry and fly helicopters. They can carry a fully equipped battalion of Marines plus supporting elements; the helicopter complement can lift the battalion ashore.

An *Iwo Jima*-class ship carries seven CH-46 Sea Knights, 11 CH-53D Sea Stallions or CH-53E Super Stallions, and other utility and attack helicopters to support the landing parties ashore. The helicopters are housed in a large hangar deck and lifted to the flight deck by two elevators mounted at the deck edge. The starboard elevator is mounted aft of the island and the port side elevator forward of the island. The main deck has room for five helicopters on the port side and two on the starboard side. No provisions, such as catapults or arresting gear, have been made for fixed wing aircraft, although AV-8B Harriers regularly operate from these

ships. *Iwo Jima* ships do not carry surface landing craft.

Top speed for *Iwo Jima* ships is 22 knots (25.3 miles per hour), and the unrefueled cruising range is 16,600 nautical miles (18,975 miles) at 11.5 knots (13.2 miles per hour). Steam is furnished by

two boilers, which power a single steam turbine producing 22,000 horsepower and driving one propeller shaft.

The armament of the *Iwo Jima* ships consists of two eight-cell Mark 25 missile launchers for the Sea Sparrow missile (only one in the *Guadalcanal*), and two 20 millimeter Phalanx Close-In Weapons System (CIWS) Mark 15 multibarrel guns for missile defense. Originally, the *Iwo Jima*-class ships mounted four twin-mount three-inch antiaircraft guns. Two were removed to make way for the Mark 25 launchers.

The Inchon, *like all the ships in the* Iwo Jima *class, may operate AV-8B Harrier aircraft as well as the helicopters shown here. This photograph offers an excellent view of the Phalanx multibarrel gun system, located just below the flight deck at the stern of the ship.*

Tarawa-Class (LHA) Amphibious Assault Ships

TARAWA-CLASS (LHA) AMPHIBIOUS ASSAULT SHIPS

Operational (commissioned):	LHA 1 USS *Tarawa* (May 1976)
	LHA 2 USS *Saipan* (October 1977)
	LHA 3 USS *Belleau Wood* (September 1978)
	LHA 4 USS *Nassau* (July 1979)
	LHA 5 USS *Peleliu* (May 1980)
Displacement:	39,400 tons
Dimensions:	
Length:	820 ft.
Width:	107 ft.
Draft:	26 ft.
Propulsion:	One steam turbine driving two propeller shafts, 70,000 hp
	Two 600-psi boilers
Speed:	24 knots (27.8 mph)
Armament:	
All:	Six Mk 67 20mm antiaircraft guns
	Three Mk 45 5-inch dual-purpose guns
LHA 1:	Sea Sparrow SAMs fired from one Mk 25 octuple launcher
LHA 2–5:	Sea Sparrow SAMs fired from two Mk 25 octuple launchers
LHA 2, 4:	One 20mm Phalanx CIWS Mk 15 multibarrel gun
Fire control:	Mk 86 gun fire control system
	Mk 115 missile fire control system
Aircraft:	Approximately 30 helicopters and VSTOL aircraft
Surveillance radar:	SPS-10 F surface search
	SPS-52B 3-D search
	SPS-53 surface search
	SPS-40B air search
Sonar:	None
Crew:	
Navy:	940
Marines:	2,000

The ships of the *Tarawa*-class each combine in one ship the capabilities of an amphibious command ship, a general-purpose amphibious assault ship, an amphibious cargo ship, an amphibious transport dock, a helicopter amphibious assault ship, and a tank landing ship. They have been built with an aircraft carrier deck for landing fixed wing Vertical/Short Takeoff and Landing (VSTOL) aircraft and helicopters. They are fitted with a Tactical Amphibious Warfare Data System (TAWDS) and other command facilities, all of which enable an amphibious commander to make a *Tarawa*-class ship a command flagship. The TAWDS system keeps track of every element—troop units, vehicles, helicopters, landing craft, and supplies—in an amphibious force.

Nine ships were originally planned for this class, but four were canceled after the Vietnam War. The five *Tarawa* ships that were built entered Navy service between 1976 and 1980. Each ship is 820 feet long and 107 feet wide, and is fitted with both a hangar deck for aircraft and helicopters and a landing well for specialized landing craft. The hangar deck, which is 820 feet long, 78 feet wide, and 20 feet high, can accommodate every type of helicopter in the Marine Corps or Navy inventory. The usual aircraft deployment aboard a *Tarawa*-class ship varies according to the missions. A normal load might include 12 CH-46 Sea Knights, six CH-53D/E Sea Stallions or Super Stallions, four AH-1 SeaCobra assault helicopters, and two UH-1N Huey utility helicopters. Fixed wing aircraft such as the AV-8B Harrier and the OV-10 Bronco can also operate from the landing deck.

Up to eight AAV7A1 amphibious tractors can be launched at the same time from the stern docking well, which is 268 feet long and 78 feet wide. Up to four utility landing craft—which can carry three M60 tanks or two M1 Abrams tanks, or 150 tons of other cargo—can also be docked in the well. Two mechanized landing craft, each able to carry up to 80 fully equipped troops, can also be accommodated. The docking well can hold only one air cushion landing craft vehicle because of the interior arrangement. Up to 40 additional amphibious tractors can be carried on a third deck.

A central support structure divides the docking well into two parts, which are serviced by a conveyor belt. The conveyor belt runs to the vehicle decks, which can hold up to 200 tanks, artillery pieces, and trucks, and up to 40 AAV7A1 amphibious personnel carriers. The vehicle decks are all connected by ramps. The conveyor belt is served by five elevators—three at the forward, or vehicle deck, and two at the docking well. Up to 2,000 pounds of cargo can be stored on pallets in holds deeper in the ship. Cargo can be transferred to the landing craft in the docking well by a monorail system or lifted directly onto the hangar deck via the rear elevators. Cargo can also be moved onto the flight deck in transporters that drive up a sloping ramp and emerge at the forward base of the island.

Facilities for Marine and Navy personnel (2,000 troops, 940 Navy crew members) are equally impressive. Forward

in the hull is a 5,000 square foot acclimatization section, which also contains a gymnasium so troops can exercise. Temperature and humidity in this area can be controlled to ready the troops for the climate in which they will be fighting. Behind this area is a hospital.

Tarawa ships can attain a top speed of 24 knots (27.8 miles per hour); range at 20 knots (23 miles per hour) is 10,000 nautical miles (11,500 miles). Two steam boilers power a 70,000 horsepower steam turbine, as well as a 900 horsepower "through tunnel thruster." This device is a propeller that is encased in a tunnel in the forward part of the hull to assist in maneuvering.

Armament on *Tarawa* ships includes three five-inch Mark 45 dual-purpose guns and six 20 millimeter Mark 67 antiaircraft guns. Two eight-cell Mark 25 launchers for the Sea Sparrow missile (only one on the *Tarawa*) are also provided. The *Saipan* and the *Nassau* carry one 20mm Phalanx multibarrel gun for use against missiles.

A pair of AAV7A1s emerge from the massive stern docking well of the Tarawa.

Wasp-Class (LHD) Amphibious Assault Ships

Nearly the size of many World War II fleet aircraft carriers (and larger then some), the new Wasp-class amphibious assault ships, along with the Tarawa-class ships, are the world's largest and most capable amphibious ships. The Wasp-class ships are "aircraft carriers" that carry helicopters and the fixed wing AV-8B Harrier VSTOL (Vertical/Short Take-off and Landing) aircraft as well as the OV-10 Bronco. Five ships have been planned in this class; one is in service, and four are presently under construction.

In addition to a Navy crew of 940, Wasp ships can carry 2,000 Marine combat troops. Up to 40 Marine and Navy helicopters of any type can also be carried on Wasp ships. These aircraft may include CH-46 Sea Knights, CH-53D Sea Stallions, CH-53E Super Stallions, AH-1 SeaCobras, or UH-1N Hueys. Wasp-class ships can also carry the AV-8B Harrier.

Each ship of this class has 22,000 square feet of storage space for vehicles alone, and a total of 101,000 cubic feet has been devoted to cargo storage space. A large docking well inside the hull is spacious enough for three air cushion landing craft or three mechanized landing craft with conventional hulls. The Wasp ships displace 40,530 tons, and are 844 feet long and 140 feet wide. They are powered by two steam

turbines that produce 71,000 horsepower to turn two propeller shafts. Top speed for the Wasp ships is 22 knots (25.3 miles per hour). Unrefueled cruising range is 9,500 nautical miles (10,925 miles).

For protection against missile attack, the five ships of this class are being fitted with three 20 millimeter Phalanx multibarrel guns. Wasp ships are also armed with eight .50 caliber machine guns and two eight-cell Mark 29 launchers for the Sea Sparrow missile.

The Wasp, *shown here under construction in the Ingalls Shipbuilding yards prior to its commissioning in May 1989. A total of five ships are planned for this class.*

WASP-CLASS (LHD) AMPHIBIOUS ASSAULT SHIPS

Operational (commissioned):	LHD 1 USS *Wasp* (May 1989)
Building:	LHD 2 USS *Essex* (1992)
Planned:	LHD 3 USS *Kearsage* (1993)
	LHD 4 USS *Boxer* (1994)
	LHD 5 USS (unnamed) (1996)
Displacement:	40,530 tons
Dimensions:	
Length:	844 ft.
Width:	140 ft.
Draft:	26.6 ft.
Propulsion:	Two steam turbines driving two propeller shafts, 71,000 hp
	Two 600-psi boilers
Speed:	22 knots (25.3 mph)
Armament:	Sea Sparrow SAMs fired from two octuple launchers
	Three 20mm Phalanx CIWS Mk 15 multibarrel guns
	Eight .50 caliber machine guns
Fire control:	Mk 23 tactical air search
	Two Mk 91 missile fire control systems
Aircraft:	40 helicopters or VSTOL aircraft
Surveillance radar:	SPS-64 surface search
	SPS-52C 3-D search
	SPS-49(V)5 air search
Sonar:	None
Crew:	
Navy:	940
Marines:	2,000

Dock Landing (LSD/LPD) Ships

The ships of the *Thomaston* class were the first dock landing ships (LSD) to be built in the post-World War II era. Their development was spurred by lessons learned during World War II and the Korean War, when various amphibious operations revealed the inefficiency of using separate kinds of ships to function in these roles.

Thomaston ships had large docking wells in the after part of the ship and could carry up to 50 AAV-7 amphibious tractors, or three utility landing craft, or nine mechanized landing craft. For protection against air attack, they were heavily armed with 16 three-inch and twelve 20 millimeter antiaircraft guns. Today, they carry only six three-inch guns.

The ships of the *Anchorage* class, which were built in the early 1960s, were given larger docking wells that had a removable helicopter deck above them. *Anchorage* ships have 15,800 square feet of storage space.

As the *Thomaston*-class ships began to show their age, the Navy began lobbying for a new class of dock landing ships to replace them. After a long political battle, Congress agreed to fund the *Whidbey Island* class in the early 1980s. *Whidbey Island* ships have large docking wells that can accommodate four air cushion landing craft vehicles. The *Whidbey Island*-class ships are also able to land all helicopters and vertical/short takeoff and landing aircraft in the inventory of the Marine Corps or Navy.

Complementing the dock landing ships are ships known as amphibious transport docks (LPD).

THOMASTON-CLASS (LSD) DOCK LANDING SHIPS

Operational (commissioned):	LSD 28 USS *Thomaston* (September 1954)
	LSD 29 USS *Plymouth Rock* (November 1954)
	LSD 30 USS *Fort Snelling* (January 1955)
	LSD 31 USS *Point Defiance* (March 1955)
	LSD 32 USS *Spiegel Grove* (June 1956)
	LSD 33 USS *Alamo* (August 1956)
	LSD 34 USS *Hermitage* (December 1956)
	LSD 35 USS *Monticello* (March 1957)
Displacement:	11,270 tons
Dimensions:	
Length:	510 ft.
Width:	84 ft.
Draft:	19 ft.
Propulsion:	Two steam turbines, 24,000 hp Two 600-psi boilers
Speed:	22.5 knots (25.8 mph)
Armament:	Six Mk 33 3-inch antiaircraft guns
Fire control:	None
Aircraft:	None
Surveillance radar:	SPS-10B surface search SPS-6 air search
Sonar:	None
Crew:	
Navy:	348
Marines:	325

A UH-46 Sea Knight helicopter offloads supplies from the dock landing ship Thomaston. *The ships of the* Thomaston *class are being replaced by the* Whidbey Island-*class ships.*

Designed in the mid-1950s, these ships combine the carrying of troops, cargo, and equipment, and docking facilities for flat-bottomed landing craft and air cushion vehicles. The first such ships to enter service (in the early 1960s) were the two *Raleigh*-class LPDs. These ships have docking wells in the after part of the ship only; the forward part contains a large area for troops and vehicles. The docking well is large enough to contain two air cushion vehicles or a variety of smaller landing craft. Although a helicopter landing deck covers the docking well, these ships have no hangars or maintenance facilities.

The next LPDs to be built were the *Austin*-class ships. These ships are basically enlarged versions of the *Raleigh* ships. During construction, a 50-foot section was built forward of the docking well. This

provided sufficient space to build a telescoping helicopter hangar behind the super-structure. Troop and vehicle capacity, and even the size of the well deck, are the same as in the *Raleigh* class.

Whatever their class, the Navy's dock landing ships and amphibious transport docks are all pretty much the same size. They vary no more than 100 feet in length but range from 11,270 tons (*Thomaston* class) to 16,900 tons (*Austin* class) in displacement. All except the *Whidbey Island* class are equipped with two steam turbines that produce 24,000 horsepower; the turbines are powered by two boilers. The *Whidbey Island* class has four diesel engines that develop 41,600 horsepower through two propellers. All have helicopter landing areas, but except for the *Austin* class, no class has helicopter hangars or maintenance facilities.

The Anchorage, *like the other ships in its class, has a removable helicopter deck.*

ANCHORAGE-CLASS (LSD) DOCK LANDING SHIPS

Operational (commissioned):	LSD 36 USS *Anchorage* (March 1969)
	LSD 37 USS *Portland* (October 1970)
	LSD 38 USS *Pensacola* (March 1971)
	LSD 39 USS *Mount Vernon* (May 1972)
	LSD 40 USS *Fort Fisher* (December 1972)
Displacement:	14,000 tons
Dimensions:	
Length:	553 ft.
Width:	85 ft.
Draft:	19 ft.
Propulsion:	Two steam turbines, 24,000 hp
	Two 600-psi boilers
Speed:	22 knots (25.3 mph)
Armament:	Six Mk 33 3-inch antiaircraft guns
	Two 20mm Phalanx CIWS Mk 15 multibarrel guns
Fire control:	None
Aircraft:	None
Surveillance radar:	SPS-10 surface search
	SPS-40 air search
Sonar:	None
Crew:	
Navy:	358
Marines:	330

Above, left: *The* Whidbey Island *has a protection system that can shield its crew from the effects of nuclear fallout and chemical and biological agents.* **Right:** *The* Raleigh *has side ports for ro/ro vehicles, but no helicopter hangar facilities.*

WHIDBEY ISLAND-CLASS (LSD) DOCK LANDING SHIPS

Operational (commissioned):	LSD 41 USS *Whidbey Island* (February 1985)
	LSD 42 USS *Germantown* (February 1986)
	LSD 43 USS *Ft. McHenry* (August 1987)
Building:	LSD 44 USS *Gunston Hall*
Planned:	LSD 45 USS *Comstock*
	LSD 46 USS *Tortuga*
	LSD 47 USS *Rushmore*
	LSD 48 USS *Ashland*
	LSD 49 USS *Harpers Ferry*
Displacement:	15,704 tons
Dimensions:	
Length:	610 ft.
Width:	84 ft.
Draft:	20 ft.
Propulsion:	Four SEMT-Pielstick diesels, 41,600 hp
Speed:	22 knots (25.3 mph)
Armament:	Two 20mm Phalanx CIWS Mk 15 multibarrel guns
Fire control:	None
Aircraft:	None
Surveillance radar:	SPS-67 surface search SPS-49 air search
Sonar:	None
Crew:	
Navy:	342
Marines:	500

RALEIGH-CLASS (LPD) AMPHIBIOUS TRANSPORT DOCK SHIPS

Operational (commissioned):	LPD 1 USS *Raleigh* (September 1962)
	LPD 2 USS *Vancouver* (May 1963)
Displacement:	14,650 tons
Dimensions:	
Length:	521.5 ft.
Width:	84 ft.
Draft:	22 ft.
Propulsion:	Two steam turbines, 24,000 hp
	Two 600-psi boilers
Speed:	21 knots (24 mph)
Armament:	Four Mk 33 3-inch antiaircraft guns
	Two 20mm Phalanx CIWS Mk 15 multibarrel guns
Fire control:	None
Aircraft:	None
Surveillance radar:	SPS-10 surface search SPS-40 air search
Sonar:	None
Crew:	
LPD 1:	
Navy:	420
Marines:	930
LPD 2:	
Navy:	431
Marines:	930

AUSTIN-CLASS (LPD) AMPHIBIOUS TRANSPORT DOCK SHIPS

Operational (commissioned):	LPD 4 USS *Austin* (February 1965)	**Dimensions cont'd:**	
	LPD 5 USS *Ogden* (June 1965)	**Width:**	84 ft.
	LPD 6 USS *Duluth* (December 1985)	**Draft:**	23 ft.
	LPD 7 USS *Cleveland* (April 1967)	**Propulsion:**	Two steam turbines, 24,000 hp
	LPD 8 USS *Dubuque* (September 1967)		Two 600-psi boilers
	LPD 9 USS *Denver* (October 1968)	**Speed:**	21 knots (24 mph)
	LPD 10 USS *Juneau* (July 1969)	**Armament:**	Four Mk 33 3-inch antiaircraft guns
	LPD 12 USS *Shreveport* (December 1970)		Two 20mm Phalanx CIWS Mk 15 multibarrel guns
	LPD 13 USS *Nashville* (February 1970)	**Fire control:**	None
	LPD 14 USS *Trenton* (March 1971)	**Aircraft:**	None
	LPD 15 USS *Ponce* (July 1971)	**Surveillance radar:**	SPS-10F surface search
			SPS-40C air search
Displacement:	16,900 tons	**Sonar:**	None
Dimensions:		**Crew:**	
Length:	583 ft.	**LPD 4-6, 14, 15:**	
		Navy:	425
		Marines:	930
		LPD 7-10, 12, 13:	
		Navy:	425
		Marines:	840

In this photograph the Ogden, an Austin-*class amphibious transport dock, carries a cargo of new helicopters.*

Newport-Class (LST) Tank Landing Ships

In 1941 the Japanese made use of tank landing ships during their whirlwind conquest of the Western Pacific. The Allies were quick to develop ships for the same purpose. Long years of war-gaming a Pacific conflict had convinced the U.S. Navy that the only way to effectively assault the Japanese home islands was through the type of island-hopping campaign that they undertook between 1942 and 1945. Islands needed for air and naval bases in the final phase of the conflict had to be retrieved from Japanese military occupation forces. Troops, equipment, and particularly tanks and large artillery pieces had to be brought ashore during the attack to capture those islands.

The LST (Tank Landing Ship) was one of many amphibious designs that moved quickly from the drawing board to the shipyard at the start of the Pacific phase of World War II. LSTs served extensively throughout the Pacific as well as in the China-Burma-India theater. LSTs also proved decisive in putting Allied tanks, artillery, and other heavy equipment ashore during the invasions of North Africa, Sicily, Italy, Normandy, and southern France.

Unlike most ships, which seek to avoid running aground, the first LSTs were designed to deliberately beach themselves on a hostile shore—whereupon they would then lower a ramp, and unload their cargo directly onto dry land (or at least into shallow water). LSTs would then use their anchors to winch themselves off the beach. Although the modern *Newport* class can still do this, these ships are more likely to unload their cargo onto specially built pontoon causeways that are carried on the side of the hull. The pontoon causeways can support the weight of a 63-ton M1 Abrams tank. Each ship also carries four vehicle landing craft in davits (cranes).

Of the 20 ships in this class, 18 are in active service and two are in the Naval Reserve Force. Unlike the World War II LSTs, which had a boxy shape and flat bow ramps, the *Newport* ships have a more seaworthy configuration that includes pointed bow and stern ramps. The bow ramp is 12 feet long and set between two massive fixed booms that can lower the ramp to landing level or even with the landing pontoons. From the stern ramp, amphibious vehicles can debark directly into the water even while the ship is moving. The stern ramp can be attached to another amphibious ship or to a pier, if necessary. Vehicles can be driven the length of the deck via a tunnel through the superstructure.

Four three-inch Mark 32 guns in open mounts comprised the original armament of the *Newport* ships. These World War II-era antiaircraft guns have almost

all been exchanged for two 20 millimeter Phalanx Close-In Weapons System (CIWS) Mark 15 multibarrel guns.

A look into the interior of the tank landing ship Newport. *The device hanging to the right of the open door is the ship's anchor.*

173

NEWPORT-CLASS (LST) TANK LANDING SHIP

Operational (commissioned):

LST 1179 USS *Newport* (June 1969)
LST 1180 USS *Manitowoc* (January 1970)
LST 1181 USS *Sumter* (June 1970)
LST 1182 USS *Fresno* (February 1970)
LST 1183 USS *Peoria* (November 1969)
LST 1184 USS *Frederick* (February 1970)
LST 1185 USS *Schenectady* (April 1970)
LST 1186 USS *Cayuga* (August 1970)
LST 1187 USS *Tuscaloosa* (October 1970)
LST 1188 USS *Saginaw* (January 1971)
LST 1189 USS *San Bernadino* (March 1971)
LST 1190 USS *Boulder* (June 1971)
LST 1191 USS *Racine* (July 1971)
LST 1192 USS *Spartanburg County* (September 1971)
LST 1193 USS *Fairfax*

Commissioned cont'd:

County (October 1971)
LST 1194 USS *La Moure County* (December 1971)
LST 1195 USS *Barbour County* (February 1972)
LST 1196 USS *Harlan County* (April 1972)
LST 1197 USS *Barnstable County* (May 1972)
LST 1198 USS *Bristol County* (August 1972)

Displacement:	8,450 tons
Dimensions:	
Length:	522.2 ft.
Width:	69.5 ft.
Draft:	17.5 ft.
Propulsion:	Six Arco diesels, 16,500 hp
Speed:	21 knots (23 mph)
Armament:	Two 20mm Phalanx CIWS Mk 15 multibarrel guns
Fire control:	None
Aircraft:	None
Surveillance radar:	SPS-10F surface search
Sonar:	None
Crew:	
Navy:	253
Marines:	400

An excellent view of the twin derrick arms of the Schenectady, a Newport-*class tank landing ship. The derrick supports a ramp that is used for vehicle loading and offloading.*

Charleston-Class (LKA) Amphibious Cargo Ship

The ships of the *Charleston*-class were the first ships built specifically for the amphibious cargo ship role. Intended to serve as attack cargo ships (AKA), their designation was changed to amphibious cargo ships (LKA) in the Navy-wide reclassification of June 1975. All previous ships in the AKA or LKA classes had been converted from, or built according to, civilian merchant ship designs.

Charleston ships are designed to permit the rapid loading of equipment into landing craft and helicopters. Although they do not have helicopters, hangars, or maintenance facilities of their own, *Charleston* ships do have a helicopter landing area built over the stern. The original set of four three-inch Mark 33 twin antiaircraft guns has been replaced by two 20 millimeter Phalanx multibarrel guns.

A *Charleston* ship is easily identified by the two distinctive cargo booms before the bridge and the single boom aft. The forward booms have a capacity of 48 tons each, the aft boom, 78 tons. Each ship also has eight booms of 15-ton capacity, and an estimated 33,000 square feet of storage area for vehicles and 70,000 cubic feet of cargo space.

Charleston ships displace 18,600 tons, and are 578 feet long and 62 feet wide. Top speed for ships of this class is 20 knots (23 miles per hour). Two boilers built by Combustion Engineering power a single Westinghouse steam turbine producing 19,250 horsepower. Of the five ships in the *Charleston* class, four were placed in the Naval Reserve Force in 1979 and 1981. As tensions rose around the world in the mid-1980s, these ships were brought back into active service. All *Charleston* ships are currently in the active fleet; the *Charleston* and the *El Paso* serve with the Atlantic Fleet, the other three with the Pacific Fleet.

The Durham *lowers a landing craft into the water.*

CHARLESTON-CLASS (LKA) AMPHIBIOUS CARGO SHIP

Operational (commissioned):	LKA 113 USS *Charleston* (December 1968)
	LKA 114 USS *Durham* (May 1969)
	LKA 115 USS *Mobile* (September 1969)
	LKA 116 USS *St. Louis* (November 1969)
	LKA 117 USS *El Paso* (January 1970)
Displacement:	18,600 tons
Dimensions:	
Length:	578 ft.
Width:	62 ft.
Draft:	25.5 ft.
Propulsion:	One Westinghouse steam turbine, 19,250 hp
	Two Combustion Engineering 600-psi boilers
Speed:	20 knots (23 mph)
Armament:	Two 20mm Phalanx CIWS Mk 15 multibarrel guns
Fire control:	None
Aircraft:	None
Surveillance radar:	SPS-10 surface search
Sonar:	None
Crew:	
Navy:	360
Marines:	225

LANDING CRAFT

I n July 1898, 16,000 Army troops required four days to land on the beaches below Santiago, Cuba. On April 1, 1945, 16,000 troops from the Tenth Army went ashore on Okinawa in one hour. In the 47 years that separated these events, the Navy and the Marine Corps had obviously devoted considerable effort to the development of craft suitable for landing large bodies of men and equipment on hostile shores.

As the Okinawa landings might indicate, the U.S. armed forces became masters at the development and use of utility craft during World War II. In the Pacific theater, the role of landing craft proved crucial to dislodging Japanese forces from their many far-flung island strongholds. Since 1945, landing craft have found plenty of employment in Korea, Lebanon, South Vietnam, and Grenada.

The Navy now operates two types of landing craft: air cushion vehicles, and flat-bottomed boats classed as utility craft. Although manned by naval personnel, the primary function of both types is to put ashore combat Marines and their equipment.

Right: A Landing Craft Air Cushion (LCAC) vehicle literally flies over the water, thanks to the power supplied by its huge lift fans. Note the intake fans on the side of the craft. *Inset:* Marines hit the beach from an LCM 6 Type landing craft during a training exercise reminiscent of World War II in the Pacific. Nowadays, a landing on a "hot" enemy-held beach would probably be accomplished through the use of helicopters rather than landing craft.

U.S. NAVY

Landing Craft Air Cushion (LCAC)

The air cushion vehicle, which is somewhat better known as a "hovercraft," was invented after World War II by British designer Sir Christopher Cockerell. The air cushion vehicle is a flat-bottomed craft surrounded by a loose rubber or fabric skirt. Engines drive fans that blow air beneath the craft's bottom, where the air is trapped by the skirt. The craft is thus lifted off the water and can be propelled in any direction on a cushion of air with propellers or jets.

In the late 1960s the Navy used these British-built hovercrafts to patrol South Vietnam's Plain of Reeds. However, due to their noisy gas turbine engines and their extreme vulnerability to hostile fire, they were not entirely successful in these roles.

At present, the air cushion vehicle seems to have found its niche as a fast ship-to-shore means of transporting troops and equipment during amphibious operations. Traveling at speeds of up to 43 knots (50 mph), the Navy's Landing Craft Air Cushion (LCAC) can haul up to 75 tons of cargo from an assault ship lying as many as 100 miles offshore. They can literally fly over heavy surf and up onto a beach to unload above the tide line. Trucks or tanks can be driven on or off the craft at either end for the purposes of loading and off-loading cargo.

Since the LCAC rides on a cushion of air, it has zero draft. It is therefore not hampered by tidal action, shallow water depths, underwater obstacles, or marginal beach conditions. It can also surmount surface obstacles up to four feet in height. Furthermore, it is somewhat impervious to the underwater shock effects caused by exploding mines and torpedoes. All of this means that the LCAC can deliver troops and equipment across roughly 70 percent of the world's beaches, rather than the 20 percent that is available to conventional landing craft.

The LCAC is 87.9 feet long and 47 feet wide, and has 1,809 square feet of open deck space. It is propelled by two Avco-Lycoming TF40 gas turbine engines—the same engines used in the CH-53E Super Stallion and the M1 Abrams tank. These engines drive two four-bladed propellers, each with a diameter of 11.75 feet. Two additional Avco-Lycoming engines turn four centrifugal lift fans, each of them 63 inches in diameter.

The Navy plans to deploy the LCACs in amphibious squadrons of six craft each. A total of 90 LCACs have been requested; upon delivery, they will be divided between the Atlantic and Pacific fleets. The LCAC can be carried by a number of amphibious assault ships, particularly those of the *Wasp* and the *Tarawa* class.

A Landing Craft Air Cushion (LCAC) vehicle with a tank on board enters a tank landing ship.

LANDING CRAFT AIR CUSHION (LCAC)	
Operational (commissioned):	LCAC 1-42 (1982)
Weight:	87.2 tons
Dimensions:	
Length:	87.9 ft.
Width:	47 ft.
Draft:	0 ft.
Propulsion:	Two Avco-Lycoming TF40B gas turbines
Lift:	Two Avco-Lycoming TF40B gas turbines
Speed:	43 knots (50 mph)
Armament:	None
Fire control:	None
Aircraft:	None
Surveillance radar:	Navigation
Sonar:	None
Crew:	5

Additional Landing Craft Types

Utility landing craft are relatively large ships used to haul troops and vehicles ashore from transport ships. The 37 utility landing craft (LCU) of the 1610 class are the Navy's most recent type to enter service. Each steel-hulled 1610 craft is 134.9 long and 29.75 feet wide, displaces 390 tons fully loaded, and draws 6.9 feet of water. It can carry up to 170 tons of troops or equipment. It is powered by four 1,000 horsepower General Motors diesel engines and can travel at speeds of up to 12.5 knots (14.3 mph). It is manned by six enlisted personnel and is armed with two 20 millimeter antiaircraft weapons or two .50 caliber machine guns. It also carries a navigation radar system. Three 1610 craft have been converted into auxiliary swimmer delivery vehicles for use in Navy SEAL (Sea-Air-Land) operations.

The LCM (landing craft mechanized) classification contains two types: the LCM 6 Type and LCM 8 Type. Both were built in vast numbers for the Navy and for the Army during and after World War II. The older, smaller LCM 6 Type has a cargo capacity of 34 tons or 80 troops. Constructed of welded steel, it displaces 62.3 tons fully loaded, has a length of 56.2 feet and a width of 14.3 feet, and draws 3.8 feet of water. It is powered by two Gray Marine 64HN9 450 horsepower diesel engines at speeds of up to nine knots (10.3 mph). During the Vietnam War, many were converted to riverine warfare craft.

The LCM 8 craft can carry up to 60 tons of cargo or one M60 tank for a distance of 172 miles. Constructed of aluminum rather than welded steel, the LCM 8 craft displace 106.75 tons fully loaded, have a length of 73.7 feet and a width of 21.2 feet, and draw 4.6 feet of water. They are powered by two General Motors G-71 diesel engines at speeds of up to nine knots.

A pair of LCM 8 Type landing craft. The LCM 8 on the right carries an M48 Patton tank weighing 50 tons. It can also carry the M1 Abrams tank, which weighs over 63 tons.

Both the LCM 6 and LCM 8 are manned by five enlisted personnel. They are normally unarmed, although the LCM 8 can be outfitted with two .50 caliber machine guns.

The LCVP (landing craft vehicle and personnel) type is a wooden- or fiberglass-hulled craft that looks like a smaller version of an LCM. The LCVP displaces 13.5 tons fully loaded, and has a length of 35.8 feet and a width of 10.5 feet, and draws 3.5 feet of water. Powered by one 225 horsepower diesel engine at speeds of up to 8.6 knots (10 mph), it can carry four tons of cargo for a distance of 126 miles. It is manned by two or three enlisted personnel and carries no electronics or weapons.

The LCPL (landing craft personnel light) type is another small craft that resembles an LCM. The LCPL is used almost exclusively for personnel transport and for the command and control of other landing craft during operations. It displaces 13 tons fully loaded, has a length of 36 feet and a width of 13 feet, and draws 3.5 feet of water. It is propelled by a single 350 horsepower diesel engine at speeds of up to 19 knots (22 mph). It is manned by a crew of three enlisted personnel and is unarmed.

A platoon of Marines wades into shallow water off the lowered bow ramp of an LCU 1610 landing craft.

Operational (commissioned):

LCU 1610:	1959
LCM 8 Type:	1952
LCM 6 Type:	1944
LCVP:	1966
LCPL:	1981

Displacement:

LCU 1610:	390 tons
LCM 8 Type:	106.75 tons
LCM 6 Type:	62.3 tons
LCVP:	13.5 tons
LCPL:	13 tons

Dimensions:

Length:

LCU 1610:	134.9 ft.
LCM 8 Type:	73.7 ft.
LCM 6 Type:	56.2 ft.
LCVP:	35.8 ft.
LCPL:	36 ft.

Width:

LCU 1610:	29.75 ft.
LCM 8 Type:	21.2 ft.
LCM 6 Type:	14.3 ft.
LCVP:	10.5 ft.
LCPL:	13 ft.

Draft:

LCU 1610:	6.9 ft.
LCM 8 Type:	4.6 ft.
LCM 6 Type:	3.8 ft.
LCVP:	3.5 ft.
LCPL:	3.5 ft.

Propulsion:

LCU 1610:	Four General Motors diesels, 11,000 hp
LCM 8 Type:	Two General Motors diesels, 1,300 hp
LCM 6 Type:	Two Gray Marine diesels, 450 hp
LCVP:	One Gray Marine diesel, 225 hp
LCPL:	One General Motors diesel, 350 hp

Speed:

LCU 1610:	12.5 knots (14.3 mph)
LCM 8 Type:	9 knots (10.3 mph)
LCM 6 Type:	9 knots (10.3 mph)
LCVP:	8.6 knots (10 mph)
LCPL:	19 knots (22 mph)

Armament:

LCU 1610:	Two 20mm antiaircraft or two .50 caliber machine guns
LCM 8 Type:	None
LCM 6 Type:	None
LCVP:	None
LCPL:	None

Crew:

LCU 1610:	6
LCM 8 Type:	5
LCM 6 Type:	5
LCVP:	2–3
LCPL:	3

ASSAULT AMPHIBIAN VEHICLES (AAVP7)

ASSAULT AMPHIBIAN VEHICLES (AAV7A1)	
Operational:	984 (1983)
Displacement:	50,350 pounds loaded
Dimensions:	
Length:	26 ft.
Width:	10.75 ft.
Draft:	5.6 ft.
Propulsion:	Two Cummings VT400 diesels, 400 hp
Speed:	
Land:	40 mph
Sea:	7.2 knots (8.4 mph)
Armament:	One M2 .50 caliber machine gun
	One Mk 19 40mm grenade launcher
Fire control:	None
Surveillance:	None
Sonar:	None
Crew:	3
Date of Service Entry:	1980

Early in World War II, it became quickly evident to Navy and Marine Corps planners that the use in combat of open, unarmored landing craft would almost invariably result in excessively high casualties for the troops within. Here was a situation that called for an amphibious craft that was enclosed and armored to withstand small arms fire. Out of this need was born the amphibious tracked vehicle that came to be known as the "Amtrac." Countless American soldiers and Marines owe their lives to this durable craft. On more than one island assault, the Amtrac proved its worth as it clambered over offshore coral reefs and waddled up steep beaches with its cargo of well-protected troops huddled safely inside.

The original Amtrac model was designated LVT, or landing vehicle transport. More than 1,800 of these vehicles were built. Its successor was the LVT 5 Amtrac (landing vehicle tracked personnel), of which more than 1,300 were built between 1951 and 1957. In 1970, the designation of all such vehicles was changed to AAV, which stands for amphibious assault vehicle. The current AAV, design 7, entered service in 1970. Today, the Navy has more than 1,300 AAVP7s (amphibian assault vehicle personnel), and 106 AAVC7s (amphibian assault vehicle command). An additional 64 vehicles bearing the designation AAVR7 (assault amphibious vehicle repair) have been fitted to function in a repair and recovery role.

The AAV7 provides what the Navy terms an "over-the-beach" capability. That means that it has the capability for delivering troops and supplies onto a combat beachhead through heavy surfs up to ten feet high. Capacity is 21 fully equipped troops or 10,000 pounds of cargo. Troops are carried inside the vehicle and enter and leave through a rear, drop-down ramp or top hatches.

The AAV7 is powered by two turbocharged Cummings VT400 diesel engines, which drive its caterpillar tracks at a top speed of 40 mph on land. In the water, two waterjets enable it to achieve a maximum speed of 7.2 knots (8.4 mph). Armament consists of a turret-mounted .50 caliber M2 machine gun and one Mark 19 grenade launcher.

Due to budgetary constraints no new AAV types are planned. The Navy is therefore upgrading all AAVs currently in service. The upgrade program provides for a turret that will hold both a .50 caliber M2 machine gun and a 40 millimeter Mark 19 grenade launcher, an improved mine clearance unit that fires explosive charges (known as "snakes") in the vehicle's path, bolt-on applique armor that can withstand hits from the Soviet 14.7 mm heavy machine gun, a bow plane for improved stability in the water, and an automatic fire sensor and extinguisher system. The upgraded vehicles are designated AAV7A1. The first A1 model entered service in October 1983.

Left: Under the watchful eye of their comrades, the crew of a camouflaged AAVP7 cautiously maneuvers their vehicle up the ramp of a tank landing ship. **Below:** An AAV7 waddles up onto the beach. Upgrades of the AAV7, designated AAV7A1, will increase their offensive firepower with the addition of a turret armed with a .50 caliber machine gun and a 40 millimeter grenade launcher.

PATROL AND SPECIAL WARFARE CRAFT

The Navy has never shown much interest in small craft in peacetime; however, that attitude appears to be changing. Events in the Persian Gulf during the latter half of the 1980s, as well as the steady increase of drug smuggling activities in United States coastal waters, seems to have awakened the Navy to the need for more small, fast, and heavily armed boats. Today's patrol craft fulfill multiple roles: a high-speed, agile missile launching boat; a coastal interdiction boat; and a special warfare operations mission boat. In the first role, the boat would carry sea-skimming missiles for use against enemy warships and commercial shipping. The second role would involve assisting in patrolling the coastal waters of the United States to prevent drug smuggling. The third role would provide the Navy's Sea-Air-Land (SEAL) teams with a fast and stealthy means of infiltrating an enemy coast.

The most recent patrol boat class in regular Navy service is the *Pegasus* class. The Naval Reserve Force operates most of the Navy's patrol gunboats and fast gunboats. A new class of six patrol boats, currently referred to as Patrol Missile Craft: PXM Type, is planned for procurement beginning in fiscal year 1990. These boats are expected to be armed with Harpoon antiship missiles and a 30 millimeter or 57mm defensive gun system, but they are not expected to have offensive antisubmarine warfare capability.

The Pegasus a hydrofoil missile patrol boat, launches a Harpoon antiship missile while traveling at high speed.

Pegasus-Class Missile Patrol Boat

PEGASUS-CLASS MISSILE PATROL BOAT

Operational (commissioned):	PHM 1 USS *Pegasus* (July 1977) PHM 2 USS *Hercules* (March 1983) PHM 3 USS *Taurus* (October 1981) PHM 4 USS *Aquila* (October 1982) PHM 5 USS *Aries* (September 1982) PHM 6 USS *Gemini* (November 1982)
Displacement:	256 tons
Dimensions:	
Length:	
Overall:	118.08 ft.
Foils retracted:	147.16 ft.
Foils extended:	131.5 ft.
Width:	28.16 ft.
Draft:	
Foils retracted:	6.16 ft.
Foils extended:	23.16 ft.
Propulsion:	
Foil-borne:	One General Electric LM 2500 gas turbine driving one waterjet, 18,000 hp
Hull-borne:	Two MTU 8V331 diesel engines driving two waterjets
Speed:	
Foil-borne:	50 knots (57.5 mph)
Hull-borne:	12 knots (13.8 mph)
Armament:	Two Harpoon (RGM-84A) SSM Mk 141 launchers (quadruple mounts) One Mk 75 76mm antiaircraft gun
Fire control:	Mk 92 weapons fire control system
Aircraft:	None
Surveillance radar:	SPS-63 surface search
Sonar:	None
Crew:	23

The history of the *Pegasus* class is typical of small-boat development in the U.S. Navy. The class was championed by Admiral Elmo Zumwalt when he was Chief of Naval Operations (1970–1974). A total of 30 small craft were to be built to carry antiship missiles. But when Admiral Zumwalt retired, the program was downgraded.

Congress revived the program in 1976, and six craft were approved and designated PHM (Patrol Hydrofoil Missile). The first PHM, the *Pegasus,* was completed in 1977. In November 1982, PHM 6 *Gemini* was commissioned, and the construction program ended.

The *Pegasus*-class patrol boats are high-speed, heavily armed hydrofoil craft designed for antiship warfare in coastal or restricted waters. They are the first and thus far only class of Navy surface craft to use the hydrofoil hull in a non-experimental boat.

Pegasus-class boats ride on submerged, canard-shaped foils that lift the hull completely out of the water. The forward foil provides about 32 percent of lift and is mounted on a single strut. The rear foil provides the remaining lift and is mounted on a double strut, which is needed to carry the extra load. Both foils retract—the forward foil lifts even with and sticks out in front of the bow, the rear foil, up and beyond the stern. Step flaps fitted into the trailing edge of both foils serve as control surfaces.

Propulsion is provided by twin waterjet pumps that are powered by two diesel engines capable of developing 12 knots (13.8 miles per hour). When slow maneuvering is necessary, a bow thruster driven by the diesel engines is used. When riding on the hydrofoils, the craft is driven by a single waterjet powered by a General Electric LM 2500 gas turbine engine. This waterjet is mounted on the rear foil and can move the craft at speeds up to 50 knots (57.5

miles per hour). The waterjet pumps 141,000 gallons of water per minute. The *Pegasus*-class boats have a range of 1,400 miles at 11 knots (12.65 miles per hour) or, when using hydrofoils, 600 miles or more at 40 knots (46 miles per hour).

The PHMs are heavily armed. They carry eight Harpoon antiship missiles that are fired from two Mark 141 quadruple launchers. *Pegasus* boats also have one 76 millimeter Mark 75 antiaircraft gun mounted on the bow. They have no antisubmarine capability. All *Pegasus*-class patrol craft are assigned to PHMS Squadron 2.

The Pegasus *with a "bone in its teeth," the nautical term given to the bow wave a ship makes while underway. Note the Italian-made OTO Melara 76 millimeter cannon on the bow. This rapid-firing weapon can spew out shells at an astonishing 85-rounds-per-minute rate. The* Pegasus *is also armed with eight Harpoon antiship missiles, which are carried in the launching canisters in the stern.*

Patrol Boats (PB)

The U.S. Navy maintains several types of small craft, designated patrol boats (PB), which were developed for a variety of inshore missions.

The most numerous type of patrol boat in service is the PB Mark III Type, or *Sea Spectre*. The boats in this class are in use with both active and reserve units of the U.S. Navy, and in many foreign navies as well. The Mark III was developed from a commercial design for boats used to service offshore oil drilling platforms. It is powered by three General Motors 1,950 horsepower diesels, which are mufflered for quiet operation. It can reach a maximum speed of 26 knots (30 miles per hour). Its hull and deckhouse is constructed of aluminum, and its pilot house is located on the starboard (right) side to allow a maximum of deck space.

The Mark III is usually armed with either a 20 millimeter or a Bofors automatic 40mm antiaircraft gun, and four .50 caliber machine guns. It displaces 41.25 tons fully loaded and is slightly more than 18 feet wide. With its low profile and quiet engines, the Mark III is an ideal special warfare craft, and is often used in operations involving the Navy's Sea-Air-Land (SEAL) special forces.

A modification of the Mark III, termed PB Mark IV Type, was developed specifically for patrol duties in the Panama Canal Zone. Only three were built. The Mark IV is three feet longer than the PB Mark III; otherwise, all specifications are the same.

The predecessor of the Mark III was the PB Mark I Type. Although similar in design to the Mark III, the Mark I was smaller, more lightly armed, and had less powerful engines. It was developed to replace the earlier Mark 2 Type fast patrol craft (more popularly known as Swift boats after their builder, Swiftships of Morgan City, Louisiana). A few Mark I boats remain in service with the Naval Reserve Force. Swift boats were also used by Naval Reserve units until 1987, when they were all taken out of service.

Some 30 Mark 2 Type riverine patrol boats (PBR) also remain in service with the Naval Reserve Force. About 500 Mark 2 boats were built between 1965 and 1973, and were used for operations on the Mekong River and its tributaries in South Vietnam. The Mark 2 has a fiberglass hull and is protected against

PATROL BOATS (PB)

Operational		**Armament:**	
(commissioned):		**PB Mk III Type:**	One Mk 3 40mm or one
PB Mk III Type:	17 (1975)		Mk 68 20mm
PB Mk I Type:	2 (1972)		antiaircraft gun
PBR Mk 2 Type:	30 (1965)		Four .50 caliber machine
Displacement:			guns
PB Mk III Type:	41.25 tons	**PB Mk I Type:**	One Mk 2 81mm mortar
PB Mk I Type:	36.3 tons		One M2 .50 caliber
PBR Mk 2 Type:	8.9 tons		machine gun
Dimensions:			Two .50 caliber twin
Length:			machine guns
PB Mk III Type:	64.9 ft.	**PBR Mk 2 Type:**	One Mk 4 60mm mortar or
PB Mk I Type:	65 ft.		one Mk 19 40mm
PBR Mk 2 Type:	32 ft.		grenade launcher
Width:			One M2 .50 caliber
PB Mk III Type:	18.1 ft.		machine gun
PB Mk I Type:	16 ft.		One twin .50 caliber
PBR Mk 2 Type:	11.6 ft.		machine gun
Draft:		**Fire control:**	
PB Mk III Type:	5.8 ft.	**PB Mk III Type:**	None
PB Mk I Type:	4.8 ft.	**PB Mk I Type:**	None
PBR Mk 2 Type:	2.6 ft.	**PBR Mk 2 Type:**	None
Propulsion:		**Surveillance radar:**	
PB Mk III Type:	Three General Motors	**PB Mk III Type:**	Navigation
	8V71 diesels, 1,950 hp	**PB Mk I Type:**	Navigation
PB Mk I Type:	Three General Motors	**PBR Mk 2 Type:**	Navigation
	12V71 diesels, 1,200	**Sonar:**	
	hp	**PB Mk III Type:**	Usually none
PBR Mk 2 Type:	Two General Motors 6V53	**PB Mk I Type:**	None
	diesels, 430 hp	**PBR Mk 2 Type:**	None
Speed:		**Crew:**	
PB Mk III Type:	26 knots (30 mph)	**PB Mk III Type:**	5
PB Mk I Type:	20 knots (23 mph)	**PB Mk I Type:**	8
PBR Mk 2 Type:	23 knots (27 mph)	**PBR Mk 2 Type:**	4–5

small arms fire by ceramic armor. It is powered by two General Motors 6V53 diesel engines turning a pump jet propulsion unit that enables it to reach a maximum speed of 23 knots (27 miles per hour). During the Vietnam War it was typically armed with one 60mm Mark 4 mortar, one Mark 19 40mm grenade launcher, and one twin and one single .50 caliber machine gun.

Top: A PBR Mark II roars up the Mekong River during the Vietnam War. *Below:* A U.S. Navy PB Mark III patrol craft inspects a life raft in the Persian Gulf during the Iran-Iraq war.

Special Warfare Craft (SWC)

SPECIAL WARFARE CRAFT (SWC)	
Operational	
(commissioned):	
Seafox:	37 (1981)
Mini-ATC Type:	22 (1972)
Displacement:	
Seafox:	11.3 tons
Mini-ATC Type:	14.7 tons
Dimensions:	
Length:	
Seafox:	36 ft.
Mini-ATC Type:	36 ft.
Width:	
Seafox:	9.8 ft.
Mini-ATC Type:	12.75 ft.
Draft:	
Seafox:	2.75 ft.
Mini-ATC Type:	3.5 ft.
Propulsion:	
Seafox:	Two General Motors 6V92 diesels, 930 hp
Mini-ATC Type:	Two General Motors 8V53N diesels, 566 hp
Speed:	
Seafox:	32 knots (37 mph)
Mini-ATC Type:	24.3 knots (28 mph)
Armament:	
Seafox:	None
Mini-ATC Type:	None
Fire control:	
Seafox:	None
Mini-ATC Type:	None
Surveillance radar:	
Seafox:	Navigation
Mini-ATC Type:	Navigation
Sonar:	
Seafox:	None
Mini-ATC Type:	None
Crew:	
Seafox:	3
Mini-ATC Type:	2

The United States maintains two classes of special warfare craft, the medium *Sea Viking* and the light *Seafox* types. The *Sea Viking* was designed as a multimission special warfare patrol boat to replace earlier patrol boats used by Navy SEAL (Sea-Air-Land) teams. The *Seafox* is a small, high-speed boat that is also used to support SEAL operations.

The first *Sea Viking* boats were ordered as far back as 1984. However, the contract has not been fulfilled due to construction delays, cost overruns, and bankruptcy on the part of the builder. As planned, 18 *Sea Vikings* were to have been divided evenly between the Atlantic and Pacific fleets and operated by the Navy's Small Boat Squadrons. They were to have displaced 132 tons

*Right: A Mini-ATC Type armored troop carrier. **Opposite:** The* Seafox *special warfare craft were developed specifically for SEAL team operations.*

loaded, measure 95 feet in length and 35 feet in width, and draw 4.9 feet of water. Two 680 horsepower diesel engines were to have given them a top speed of 34.7 knots (40 miles per hour). The *Sea Vikings* were to have been operated by a crew of nine and be armed with a 25 millimeter multibarrel Sea Vulcan Close-in Weapon System (CIWS) and several .50 caliber machine guns. Air defense was to have been provided by shoulder-launched Stinger antiaircraft missiles. To date, the *Sea Viking* program is awaiting approval, but may be canceled.

The *Seafox* craft form the light end of the Navy's special warfare craft capability. Each *Seafox* is built of fiberglass and armored with Kevlar panels. It is 36 feet long, 9.8 feet wide, and draws 2.75 feet of water. Two 930 horsepower diesels enable it to travel at 32 knots (37 miles per hour). Its high speed and low draft make it ideal for the clandestine insertion of SEAL units. One boat can carry an entire SEAL platoon (12 swimmers) with a rubber boat lashed to the top of the after deckhouse.

The Mini-ATC Type armored troop carrier represents yet another special warfare craft variant. Really a miniature version of a utility landing craft, it is designed solely for riverine warfare operations as conducted by Navy SEAL and Army Special Forces teams. It is powered by two 566 horsepower diesel engines that drive waterjets, has a shallow 3.5-foot draft, and can carry 15 fully equipped troops.

MINE COUNTERMEASURES SHIPS

Mine countermeasures ships (MCM) are warships designed to counter a specific type of weapon: the underwater mine.

In the years following World War II, the development and procurement of mine countermeasures ships has not been a high priority for the Navy. Consequently, the U.S. has in service about 20 mine countermeasures craft, the majority of which are in the Naval Reserve Force.

This state of affairs was not significantly improved by construction

Above and right: Two views of the Avenger, shown while conducting mine-sweeping operations in the Persian Gulf during the Iran-Iraq War. This ship was the first in the new class of mine countermeasures ships. All ships of this class deploy the torpedo-shaped SLQ-48 Mine Neutralizing System shown here on the after deck.

programs begun in the late 1980s that were to produce two new classes of mine countermeasures ships. These classes were designated *Avenger* and *Cardinal*. Only two *Avenger*-class ships are now in service, although three additional ships are expected to enter service in 1993. The *Cardinal*-class vessels, which were actually to be air cushion vehicles, were cancelled in 1986 because of design problems.

To help fill the gap in MCM craft, the Navy has instituted a Craft of Opportunity Program (COOP) to obtain small craft as needed from civilian sources. To date, a few fishing boats and a few U.S. Naval Academy training craft have been converted for mine hunting duties.

Hunting mines involves the use of variable depth sonar systems. Once found, the mines are usually destroyed by the SLQ-48 Mine Neutralization System (MNS). Essentially, this consists of a sled containing a television camera and close range sonar. The sled may be towed by cable behind a ship or a helicopter. If the mines are moored by cables, the sled will cut them. The mine then floats to the surface and is detonated, usually by gunfire. If the mines are planted on the sea bottom, the MNS can plant a small explosive charge to destroy it.

Mine countermeasures ships are primarily operated by the Naval Reserve Force, which has nearly all of this nation's ocean-going minesweepers. These ships are manned by active duty/reserve crews.

Mine Countermeasures Ship Classes

The *Avenger* is the Navy's newest mine counter-measures class. The ships in this class are large vessels that have been designed to locate and destroy naval mines using conventional sweeping techniques. Improperly installed engines in the first two ships of this class, *Avenger* and *Defender*, led to a three-year delay in the building program. The *Avenger*-class ships are the first large minesweepers to be built since the late 1950s.

The hulls of these ships are constructed of oak framing and plywood planking, all reinforced with a fiberglass covering. The *Avenger* and *Defender* are powered by four Waukesha L-1616 2,600 horsepower diesel engines, while the remaining ships in the series will have four Isotta-Fraschini ID36 SS-6V AM 2,280 horsepower diesel engines. *Avenger* and *Defender* have a top speed of 13.5 knots (15.6 mph) and displace 1,312 tons. They are 224.3 feet long, 39 feet wide, and draw 11.5 feet of water. They are unarmed, except for the SLQ-48 Mine Neutralization System, described in the introduction to this section.

Avenger and *Defender* are fitted with the SQQ-30 mine detecting sonar; subsequent vessels will receive the upgraded SQQ-32 mine detecting sonar. All will have the SPS-55 surface search radar. The Navy has planned for the construction of 14 ships in the *Avenger* class, but it remains to be seen whether they will all actually be built.

The *Agile*- and *Aggressive*-class ocean minesweepers (MSO) were all built between September 1954 and April 1956. A total of 58 were built for the U.S. Navy, and 27 for various foreign navies. Only 19 remain in service, all of which are in the Naval Reserve Force.

The presence of magnetic metals on the *Agile* and *Avenger* ships has been kept to a minimum. Wherever possible, metal fittings are made of brass, bronze, or stainless steel. All carry the SQQ-14 Mine Detecting Variable Depth Sonar System, which is mounted on a rigid arm and lowered below the ship. Most of these ships are armed only with one or two .50 caliber machine guns.

The ships of the *Acme* class of minesweepers are improved *Agile* and *Aggressive* ships. They are one foot longer and wider and two knots slower than the *Agile* and *Aggressive* ships, but are otherwise similarly equipped. Of the four ships built in this class only two remain in service. Both are part of the Naval Reserve Force.

Top: *The MCM 3* Sentry, *commissioned in 1987.* **Right:** *The aging MSO 41* Exultant *is not equipped to sweep for modern sea mines.*

MINE COUNTERMEASURES SHIP CLASSES

Operational (commissioned):
Avenger: 2 (1987)
   Building: 3
Agile/Aggressive: 19 (1954-1956)
Acme: 2 (1957)

Displacement:
Avenger: 1,312 tons
Agile/Aggressive: 853 tons
Acme: 818 tons

Dimensions:
 Length:
   Avenger: 224.3 ft.
   Agile/Aggressive: 172 ft.
   Acme: 173 ft.
 Width:
   Avenger: 39 ft.
   Agile/Aggressive: 35 ft.
   Acme: 36 ft.
 Draft:
   Avenger: 11.5 ft.
   Agile/Aggressive: 14 ft.
   Acme: 14 ft.

Propulsion:
Avenger: Four Waukesha L-1616 diesels, 2,600 hp or four Isotta-Fraschini ID36 SS-6V AM diesels, 2,280 hp
Agile/Aggressive: Four Packard or four Waukesha diesels, 2,400 hp
Acme: Four Packard diesels 2,800 hp

Speed:
Avenger: 13.5 knots (15.6 mph)
Agile/Aggressive: 15.5 knots (17.8 mph)
Acme: 14 knots (16.1 mph)

Armament:
Avenger: None
Agile/Aggressive: One or two twin .50 caliber machine guns
Acme: Two twin .50 caliber machine guns

Fire control:
Avenger: None
Agile/Aggressive: None
Acme: None

Surveillance radar:
Avenger: SPS-55 surface search
Agile/Aggressive: SPS-53 surface search
Acme: SPS-53 surface search

Sonar:
Avenger: SQQ-30 or SQQ-32
Agile/Aggressive: UQS-1 or SQQ-14
Acme: SQQ-14

Crew:
Avenger: 72
Agile/Aggressive: 77
Acme: 57

AUXILIARY SHIPS

Above: The Holland *was designed specifically to support the nation's fleet ballistic missile submarines (SSBN). The* Holland *and its sister ships can resupply SSBNs with provisions, torpedoes and reloads of up to twenty ballistic missiles.* **Right:** *The* Emory S. Land *supports the* Los Angeles *class of attack submarines (SSN).*

A great number of ships which are not armed nor have assigned combat duties are needed to maintain the Navy's fighting ships. Many of these auxiliary ships are operated by active duty Navy crews; however, some have mixed active and reserve crews, and are part of the Naval Reserve Force (NRF). Many auxiliary ships are operated by civilian crews and are part of the Military

Sealift Command (MSC); a few Navy-owned research ships are operated by civilian academic institutions, which are under contract on specific research programs.

The Navy divides auxiliary ships into two broad categories: mobile logistic ships, which include those ships capable of supporting and replenishing fighting ships while underway or while based abroad; and support ships, which include a wide variety of ships from salvage ships to practice torpedo retrieval craft.

While few auxiliary ships are armed, most maintain some provision for carrying armament in a battle area—mostly antiaircraft guns or missiles. In general, all ships assigned to the Military Sealift Command are unarmed. Those auxiliary ships manned by Navy personnel rather than civilians are usually armed with at least .50 caliber or 20 millimeter antiaircraft weapons or 40mm grenade launchers. Those ships used in the replenishment role for the support of carrier battle groups are armed with the 20mm Phalanx Close-In Weapons System (CIWS) and/or the Sea Sparrow missile for antiaircraft defense. They usually have all-Navy crews.

Destroyer Tenders (AD)

The U.S. Navy has three classes of destroyer tenders in service. Despite their designation, they provide support to most fleet ships, and not just destroyers.

The six ships of the *Samuel Gompers* class are the Navy's most modern destroyer tenders. They were all built and commissioned between 1966 and 1983. The *Samuel Gompers* ships provide support for both nuclear- and conventionally powered ships, and have complete machine shops for fabricating parts, and storage facilities for transporting equipment and supplies.

The *Samuel Gompers* ships displace up to 20,500 tons when fully loaded. They are 643 feet long, 85 feet wide, and draw 22.5 feet of water. They normally carry a crew of 1,367 officers and enlisted personnel. Each ship in this class is powered by a single 20,000 horsepower steam

turbine that provides a maximum speed of 20 knots (23 miles per hour). Each also is fitted with helicopter landing facilities. Armament for ships of this class consists of two single-barrel 20 millimeter Mark 67 guns and two 40mm Mark 19 single-barrel grenade launchers.

Constructed near the end of World War II, the *Klondike*-class destroyer tenders were built to a merchant ship design. Only one, the *Everglades*, is still in commission. The *Everglades* displaces 14,700 tons fully loaded, and is 492 feet long, 69.5 feet wide, and has a draft of 27.2 feet. It is powered by a single 8,500 horsepower steam turbine and can make 17.3 knots (20 miles per hour). The *Everglades* is armed with two three-inch Mark 26 antiaircraft guns and carries a crew of 850.

The *Dixie* class of destroyer tenders contains the Navy's

oldest active-duty commissioned ship, the *Prairie*. The *Prairie* entered service in August 1940 and its two sister ships, *Sierra* and *Klondike*, were commissioned in 1944. All three ships have undergone modernization and can support all modern combat ships. When first built, all were armed with five-inch guns and eight 40 millimeter antiaircraft guns. These weapons have all been

replaced by four single-barrel 20mm Mark 68 antiaircraft guns. The *Dixie* ships displace 17,190 tons, are 530.5 feet long, 73.3 feet wide, and draw 25.5 feet of water. They are propelled by two 11,000 horsepower steam turbines and can reach a top speed of 19.5 knots (22.5 miles per hour). The crew consists of 872 officers and enlisted personnel. They have no helicopter facilities.

SAMUEL GOMPERS-CLASS DESTROYER TENDERS (AD)

Operational (commissioned):	AD 37 USS *Samuel Gompers* (July 1967) AD 38 USS *Puget Sound* (April 1968) AD 41 USS *Yellowstone* (June 1980) AD 42 USS *Acadia* (June 1981) AD 43 USS *Cape Cod* (April 1982) AD 44 USS *Shenandoah* (December 1983)
Displacement:	
AD 37, 38:	20,500 tons
AD 41, 42, 43, 44:	20,225 tons
Dimensions:	
Length:	643 ft.
Width:	85 ft.
Draft:	22.5 ft.
Propulsion:	One steam turbine, 20,000 hp
Speed:	20 knots (23 mph)
Crew:	1,367

DIXIE-CLASS DESTROYER TENDERS (AD)

Operational (commissioned):	AD 15 USS *Prairie* (August 1940) AD 18 USS *Sierra* (March 1944) AD 19 USS *Yosemite* (May 1944)
Displacement:	17,190 tons
Dimensions:	
Length:	530.5 ft
Width:	73.3 ft
Draft:	25.5 ft
Propulsion:	Two steam turbines, 11,000 hp
Speed:	19.5 knots (22.5 mph)
Crew:	872

KLONDIKE-CLASS DESTROYER TENDERS (AD)

Operational (commissioned):	AD 24 *Everglades* (May 1951)
Displacement:	14,700 tons
Dimensions:	
Length:	492 ft
Width:	69.5 ft
Draft:	27.2 ft
Propulsion:	One steam turbine, 8,500 hp
Speed:	17.3 knots (20 mph)
Crew:	850

Submarine Tenders (AS)

Most submarine tenders can service both ballistic missile submarines and attack submarines. Designed to repair and replenish such vessels, the modern submarine tender has machine shops and storage facilities for missiles, munitions, and a wide assortment of supplies. All submarine tenders have landing areas for helicopters, but no helicopter maintenance facilities.

The oldest submarine tenders in service today are the three ships of the *Fulton* class. Built during World War II, all *Fulton* ships have been modernized to support modern nuclear submarines. Displacing 9,734 tons, these ships have an onboard foundry capable of casting needed submarine parts up to 550 pounds. Defensive armament consists of four 20 millimeter Mark 67 guns.

The *Proteus* is a rebuilt *Fulton*-class ship. In 1960 it became the Navy's first Fleet Ballistic Missile (FBM) submarine tender through the addition of a 44-foot section amidships that provided space for onboard workshops as well as vertical storage for 20 Polaris nuclear missiles. This addition measured six decks in height and weighed over 500 tons. The *Proteus* displaces 14,195 tons and is armed with four 20mm Mark 67 guns. Placed in the National Defense Reserve Fleet from 1947 to 1951 and then reactivated during the Korean War, the *Proteus* is currently based in Guam.

The two ships of the *Hunley* class were designed and built from the outset as ballistic missile submarine tenders. Both ships were commissioned in the early 1960s, and were upgraded in the mid-1970s to carry 20 Poseidon submarine-launched ballistic missiles. Both ships are fitted with two 30-ton cranes amid-

Top: *The* Fulton *at State Pier in New London, Connecticut.* ***Above:*** *The* Proteus *services a pair of submarines.*

FULTON-CLASS SUBMARINE TENDERS (AS)

Operational (commissioned):	AS 11 *Fulton* (September 1941)
	AS 12 *Sperry* (October 1942)
	AS 18 *Orion* (September 1943)
Displacement:	9,734 tons
Dimensions:	
Length:	529 ft.
Width:	73 ft.
Draft:	25 ft.
Propulsion:	Eight General Electric diesels, 11,200 hp
Speed:	15 knots (17 mph)
Crew:	
AS 11:	575
AS 18:	746

PROTEUS-CLASS SUBMARINE TENDERS (AS)

Operational (commissioned):	AS 19 *Proteus* (January 1944)
Displacement:	14,195 tons
Dimensions:	
Length:	574 ft.
Width:	73 ft.
Draft:	25 ft.
Propulsion:	Eight General Electric diesels, 11,200 hp
Speed:	18 knots (20.7 mph)
Crew:	677

ships, and can service three ballistic missiles submarines simultaneously. The *Hunley* ships displace 11,000 tons and are armed with four 20mm Mark 67 guns.

The two ships of the *Simon Lake* class also mount two 30-ton capacity cranes, and can service three ballistic missile submarines at the same time. Originally designed to carry the Polaris missile, they were modified in the early 1970s to support the Poseidon missile. The *Simon Lake* ships have subsequently been modified to carry the Trident C-4 missile. It is believed that the *Simon Lake* ships can carry 16 Trident missiles in vertical storage. The *Simon Lake* ships displace 12,000 tons and are armed with four three-inch Mark 33 guns.

Commissioned in the early 1970s, the two ships of the *L.Y. Spear* class of submarine tenders were the first ships designed to service the *Los Angeles*-class attack submarines. Displacing 12,770 tons, they carry enough supplies and equipment to service a dozen attack boats, and can support up to four submarines simultaneously. The ships have 53 specialized repair workshops, and onboard medical facilities that include two operating rooms, a 23-bed hospital ward, and a dental clinic. Defensive armament consists of four 20mm Mark 67 guns.

The three ships of the *Emory S. Land* class are the Navy's most up-to-date submarine tenders, carrying the very latest repair and replacement facilities. Defensive armament is also slightly heavier than other submarine tenders, and consists of four 20mm Mark 67 guns and two 40mm Mark 19 grenade launchers. These 13,842-ton ships are the last of the submarine tenders planned by the Navy at this time. As the new generation of Seawolf (SSN-21) attack submarines nears completion, however, there is talk that a new generation of submarine tenders may also be required.

SIMON LAKE-CLASS SUBMARINE TENDERS (AS)

Operational (commissioned):	AS 33 *Simon Lake* (November 1964) AS 34 *Canopus* (November 1965)
Displacement:	12,000 tons
Dimensions:	
Length:	643 ft.
Width:	85 ft.
Draft:	24 ft.
Propulsion:	One De Laval steam turbine, 20,000 hp
Speed:	18 knots (20.7 mph)
Crew:	
AS 33:	915
AS 34:	660

L.Y. SPEAR-CLASS SUBMARINE TENDERS (AS)

Operational (commissioned):	AS 36 *L.Y. Spear* (February 1970) AS 37 *Dixon* (August 1971)
Displacement:	12,770 tons
Dimensions:	
Length:	645 ft.
Width:	85 ft.
Draft:	24 ft., 8 in.
Propulsion:	One General Electric steam turbine, 20,000 hp
Speed:	18 knots (20.7 mph)
Crew:	532

HUNLEY-CLASS SUBMARINE TENDERS (AS)

Operational (commissioned):	AS 31 *Hunley* (June 1962) AS 32 *Holland* (September 1963)
Displacement:	11,000 tons
Dimensions:	
Length:	599 ft.
Width:	83 ft.
Draft:	24 ft.
Propulsion:	Ten Fairbanks-Morse diesel engines, 15,000 hp
Speed:	19 knots (21.8 mph)
Crew:	
AS 31:	612
AS 32:	659

EMORY S. LAND-CLASS SUBMARINE TENDERS (AS)

Operational (commissioned):	AS 39 *Emory S. Land* (July 1979) AS 40 *Frank Cable* (February 1980) AS 41 *McKee* (August 1981)
Displacement:	13,842 tons
Dimensions:	
Length:	645 ft.
Width:	85 ft.
Draft:	25 ft.
Propulsion:	One De Laval steam turbine, 20,000 hp
Speed:	20 knots (23 mph)
Crew:	620

Ammunition Ships (AE)

Ammunition ships transport and store munitions of all types, ranging from .38 caliber revolver rounds to nuclear-tipped guided missiles. There are two classes of specialized ammunition ships in commission today, and a third class is planned.

The eight ammunition ships of the *Kilauea* class were built in the late 1960s and early 1970s. They were constructed after the design of high-speed replenishment ships but with special provisions for handling and storing munitions. They can carry 6,500 tons of cargo, and were built with most of the storage areas and holds forward of the superstructure. Aft of the superstructure is a helicopter landing area with a helicopter hangar built into the superstructure. Two UH-46 Sea Knight helicopters are carried by each ship for transport of stores and munitions at sea. The ships are armed with four three-inch Mark 33 twin antiaircraft guns, and a few of the ships have the 20mm Phalanx Close-In Weapons System (CIWS) installed. They are powered by a General Electric steam turbine and can reach a top speed of 21.7 knots (25 miles per hour). All *Kilauea* ships are on active duty with the Navy except for the *Kilauea* itself, which is operated by the Navy's Military Sealift Command.

The five ships of the *Suribachi* class have been in service since the mid-to-late 1950s. Like the *Kilauea* ships, they were designed specifically as munitions ships and have a cargo capacity of 7,500 tons. In the late 1960s the *Suribachi* ships were completely modernized and fitted with improved fire fighting equipment, and storage facilities to handle guided missiles. As built, all *Suribachi* ships were armed with eight three-inch guns in twin mounts. After the modernization, the aft three-inch guns were removed to provide for a helicopter landing platform.

The Nitro *is a* Suribachi-*class ammunition ship, stationed with the Atlantic Fleet.*

KILAUEA-CLASS AMMUNITION SHIPS (AE)

Operational (commissioned):	T-AE 26 USS *Kilauea* (August 1968)
	AE 27 USS *Butte* (November 1968)
	AE 28 USS *Santa Barbara* (July 1970)
	AE 29 USS *Mount Hood* (May 1971)
	AE 32 USS *Flint* (November 1971)
	AE 33 USS *Shasta* (February 1972)
	AE 34 USS *Mount Baker* (July 1972)
	AE 35 USS *Kiska* (December 1972)
Displacement:	19,937 tons
Dimensions:	
Length:	564 ft.
Width:	81 ft.
Draft:	25.75 ft.
Propulsion:	One General Electric steam turbine, 22,000 hp
Speed:	21.7 knots (25 mph)
Crew:	385

SURIBACHI-CLASS AMMUNITION SHIPS (AE)

Operational (commissioned):	AE 21 USS *Suribachi* (November 1956)
	AE 22 USS *Mauna Kea* (March 1957)
	AE 23 USS *Nitro* (May 1959)
	AE 24 USS *Pyro* (July 1959)
	AE 25 USS *Haleakala* (November 1959)
Displacement:	17,500 tons
Dimensions:	
Length:	512 ft.
Width:	72 ft.
Draft:	29 ft.
Propulsion:	One steam turbine, 16,000 hp
Speed:	20.5 knots (23.7 mph)
Crew:	348

MODIFIED *KILAUEA*-CLASS AMMUNITION SHIPS (AE)

Operational (commissioned):	None yet named
Displacement:	22,970 tons
Dimensions:	
Length:	577 ft.
Width:	87.9 ft.
Draft:	27.9 ft.
Propulsion:	One General Electric LM 2500 gas turbine, 25,000 hp
Speed:	20+ knots (23+ mph)
Crew:	Unknown

Below: The Mauna Kea *is an ammunition ship that can replenish warships while underway.* **Bottom:** *Racked shells for the battleship* Iowa's *16-inch guns are about to be transferred from the* Nitro.

Suribachi ships can land helicopters but have no hangar or major maintenance facilities. Two of these ships, the *Mauna Kea* and the *Pyro*, were placed in the Naval Reserve Force in 1979 and 1980, then returned to active duty in 1984 when Iran and Iraq began to interfere with commercial shipping in the Persian Gulf.

The third and latest class of ammunition ship will be a modification of the *Kilauea* class. Five ships are planned for this new class, which is as yet unnamed. Construction is expected to begin during fiscal year 1991. The new ships will be fitted with a General Electric LM 2500 gas turbine engine developing nearly 25,000 horsepower, which will propel them at speeds in excess of 20 knots (23 miles per hour). They will be slightly longer and broader than the *Kilauea* ships and will be armed with two 20mm MK 88 single-barrel antiaircraft guns and two 20mm Phalanx multibarrel guns.

Stores Ships (AFS)

The United States Navy maintains three classes of stores ships, the *Mars* (AFS) and *Sirius* (T-AFS) classes of combat stores ships, and the *Rigel* (T-AF) class of refrigerated stores ship. The *T* prefix indicates that the ships so designated are operated by the Military Sealift Command.

The seven ships of the *Mars*-class combat stores ships were built in the 1960s, with the last entering service in 1970. They combine in one class the functions of three previous ship classes: stores (AF), stores issue (AKS), and aviation stores (AVS) ships. They were further designed for replenishing warships while underway. The *Mars* ships do not carry aviation or ship fuel for transfers. The ships each have five cargo holds, one of which is refrigerated, and can carry a total of 7,000 tons of supplies. Each of the ships has three boilers, although they usually steam with only two in operation. A single steam turbine produces 22,000 horsepower. Each *Mars* ship carries two UH-46 Sea Knight

MARS-CLASS STORES SHIPS (AFS)	
Operational (commissioned):	AFS 1 USS *Mars* (December 1963)
	AFS 2 USS *Sylvania* (July 1964)
	AFS 3 USS *Niagara Falls* (April 1967)
	AFS 4 USS *White Plains* (November 1968)
	AFS 5 USS *Concord* (November 1968)
	AFS 6 USS *San Diego* (May 1969)
	AFS 7 USS *San Jose* (October 1970)
Displacement:	16,070 tons
Dimensions:	
Length:	581.4 ft.
Width:	79 ft.
Draft:	24 ft.
Propulsion:	One steam turbine, 22,000 hp
Speed:	21 knots (24 mph)
Crew:	435

The White Plains *is a large stores ship built in the early 1960s to replenish warships while underway with all the essentials except petroleum products.*

transport helicopters, which are housed in a helicopter hangar on the stern. Armament consists of four twin three-inch Mark 33 guns. The two guns located midships are being replaced by the Phalanx Close-In Weapons System (CIWS). The *Mars* ships form an integral part of the replenishment system that allows the U.S. Navy to maintain its fleet at sea over extended periods of time.

The acquisition of a second class of stores ships came about as a result of the Iranian hostage crisis of 1979 and the start of the Iran-Iraq war in 1980. When in response to these events two carrier battle groups were sent to the Indian Ocean, the Navy found that it did not have enough stores ships to adequately maintain them. To solve the shortfall problem, three replenishment ships were leased, then purchased, from Britain. Originally named the *Lyness*, *Tarbatness*, and *Stromness*, the ships underwent a complete modernization and "Americanization" and were renamed *Sirius*, *Spica*, and *Saturn*. They are operated by the Military

Sealift Command. Their commissioning meets the Navy's requirements for stores ships to supply a 600-ship fleet. The *Sirius*-class ships are powered by a single turbocharged diesel engine that generates 11,520 horsepower and enables them to make nearly 19 knots (22 miles per hour). All have a helicopter landing area, but only the *Sirius* has hangar and maintenance facilities for two UH-46 Sea Knight helicopters.

The *Rigel* class originally consisted of the *Rigel* and the *Vega*, both built in the early 1950s. Only the *Rigel* remains in service, now with the Military Sealift Command. (The *Vega* was decommissioned in 1977.) *Rigel* is the last refrigerated stores ship still in Navy service. Its main assignment is to provide fresh food to ships of the Atlantic Fleet. It is powered by a single steam turbine providing 16,000 horsepower and can reach a maximum speed of 21 knots (24 miles per hour). Its original stern-mounted three-inch antiaircraft guns have been removed to make way for a helicopter landing platform.

Top: The Vanguard's huge telemetry antennas are used for tracking space craft. **Above:** The Mercury is a converted Mission-class oiler that was used as a tracking ship to support project Apollo.

SIRIUS-CLASS STORES SHIPS (AFS)

Operational (commissioned):	T-AFS 8 *Sirius* (January 1981) T-AFS 9 *Spica* (November 1981) T-AFS 10 *Saturn* (September 1984)
Displacement:	16,792 tons
Dimensions:	
Length:	524 ft.
Width:	72 ft.
Draft:	22 ft.
Propulsion:	One turbocharged diesel engine, 11,520 hp
Speed:	19 knots (22 mph)
Crew:	169

RIGEL-CLASS STORES SHIPS (AF)

Operational (commissioned):	T-AF 58 *Rigel* (September 1955)
Displacement:	15,540 tons
Dimensions:	
Length:	502 ft.
Width:	72 ft.
Draft:	29 ft.
Propulsion:	One steam turbine, 16,000 hp
Speed:	21 knots (24 mph)
Crew:	116

Missile Range Instrumentation Ships

Only four of these ships remain in Navy service. They are used in conjunction with the development of submarine-launched ballistic missiles (SLBM) and serve as sea-going tracking stations. They can also be used to track missile launches by the Soviet Union and other foreign nations.

The most sophisticated missile range instrumentation ship is the *Observation Island* (T-AGM 23), which was formerly the *Mariner*-class commercial cargo ship *Empire State Mariner*. It was acquired by the Navy in February 1954, but was laid up the following autumn in the National Defense Reserve Fleet. In September 1956 it was once again transferred to the Navy, which converted it to a missile test ship. In that capacity it served as a test launch platform for the Polaris SLBM, then was modified again to serve the same purpose for the Poseidon SLBM. Upon completion of the Poseidon test program in 1972 it was returned to the National Defense Reserve Fleet.

In 1977 the *Observation Island* was converted to serve in its present function as a missile range instrumentation ship. A phased array radar system was mounted on its after deck and twin radar drones were installed on its superstructure. The *Observation Island* is operated in the Pacific by the Military Sealift Command for the Air Force and NASA.

The *Range Sentinel* (T-AGM) is a missile range instrumentation ship that operates in the Atlantic. The *Range Sentinel* supports test firings of all SLBM launches in the Atlantic.

The *Vanguard* (T-AG 94) and the *Redstone* (T-AGM 20) are former *Mission*-class oilers that were converted to missile range instrumentation ships in 1964. They were first used to support Project Apollo and subsequent lunar landings. In 1978 the *Vanguard* was converted to a navigation research ship and used to support the Trident SLBM missile test program. The *Redstone* supports NASA and Air Force missile activities in the Atlantic. The *Vanguard* is now laid up in the National Defense Reserve Fleet.

T-AGM 23 *OBSERVATION ISLAND* MISSILE RANGE INSTRUMENTATION SHIP

Operational (commissioned):	December 1953
Displacement:	17,015 tons
Dimensions:	
Length:	563 ft.
Width:	76 ft.
Draft:	29 ft.
Propulsion:	One steam turbine, 22,500 hp
Speed:	20 knots (23 mph)
Crew:	141

T-AG *VANGUARD* NAVIGATION RESEARCH SHIP AND T-AGM *REDSTONE* MISSILE RANGE RESEARCH SHIP

Operational (commissioned):	T-AG 94 *Vanguard* (October 1947)
	T-AGM 20 *Redstone* (October 1947)
Displacement:	16,800 tons
Dimensions:	
Length:	595 ft.
Width:	75 ft.
Draft:	25 ft.
Propulsion:	One steam turbine and turbo-electric drive engine, 10,000 hp
Speed:	16 knots (18.4 mph)
Crew:	
Vanguard:	200
Redstone:	192

T-AGM 22 *RANGE SENTINEL* MISSILE RANGE INSTRUMENTATION SHIP

Operational (commissioned):	September 1944
Displacement:	11,860 tons
Dimensions:	
Length:	455 ft.
Width:	62 ft.
Draft:	23 ft.
Propulsion:	One steam turbine, 8,500 hp
Speed:	17.3 knots (20 mph)
Crew:	96

Oceanographic Research Ships (AGOR)

MELVILLE-CLASS OCEANOGRAPHIC RESEARCH SHIPS (AGOR)

Operational	
(commissioned):	AGOR 14 *Melville* (August 1969)
	AGOR 15 *Knorr* (January 1970)
Displacement:	2,080 tons
Dimensions:	
Length:	244.8 ft.
Width:	46.3 ft.
Draft:	15 ft.
Propulsion:	Two Enterprise diesel engines, 2,500 hp
Speed:	12.4 knots (14.3 mph)
Crew:	
AGOR 14:	61
AGOR 15:	49

CONRAD-CLASS OCEANOGRAPHIC RESEARCH SHIPS (AGOR)

Operational	
(commissioned):	AGOR 3 *Robert D. Conrad* (November 1962)
	T-AGOR 7 *Lynch* (October 1965)
	AGOR 9 *Thomas G. Thompson* (September 1965)
	AGOR 10 *Thomas Washington* (September 1965)
	T-AGOR 12 *De Steiguer* (February 1969)
	T-AGOR 13 *Bartlett* (April 1969)
Displacement:	1,380 tons
Dimensions:	
Length:	208.8 ft.
Width:	37.3 ft.
Draft:	14.5 ft.
Propulsion:	One Caterpillar diesel engine, 10,000 hp
Speed:	13.4 knots (15.5 mph)
Crew:	Varies from 43-50

The Navy has long conducted oceanographic research to increase knowledge of ocean dynamics. To that end it maintains four classes of oceanographic research ships with a total of 12 ships. Seven ships are operated by various academic institutions, four are operated by the Military Sealift Command, and one is laid up in the National Defense Reserve Fleet.

The *Gyre* class contains two ships. The *Gyre* (AGOR 21) is operated by Texas A&M University, and the *Moana Wave* (AGOR 22) is operated by the Hawaii Institute of Geophysics. The design of these ships is similar to offshore oil drilling rig resupply ships. Like the latter ships they have a large open deck aft of the deckhouse that provides room for equipment. They have a small 50 horsepower motor for low-speed maneuvers.

The *Melville* class contains two ships, the *Melville* (AGOR 14) and the *Knorr* (AGOR 15). These are large research ships with unique "cycloidal" propellers fore and aft. The propellers are actually long, curved vanes mounted on a wheel fitted flush with the hull. The vaned wheels turn perpendicular to the ship's hull and enable the ship to move in any direction. The pilot steers with a joystick.

The *Conrad* class contains six ships, making it the largest class in this category. The Military Sealift Command operates three *Conrad* ships, while one ship each is operated by Columbia University, the University of Washington, and the Scripps Institute of Oceanography. Three additional ships in this class are now operated by the navies of Brazil, Mexico, and New Zealand. The *Conrad* ships were the Navy's first purpose-built oceanographic research ships.

The two ships of the *Eltanin* class started their careers as arctic cargo ships. They were converted to oceanographic research ships in 1962 and 1964, respectively. The *Eltanin* (T-AGOR 8) is currently laid up in the National Defense Reserve Fleet. The *Mizar* (T-AGOR 11) participated in the search for the U.S. attack submarine *Thresher* (which sank in the Atlantic in 1963), and also in the search for the submarine *Scorpion* (which sank in the Atlantic in 1968). It was also involved in the search for a hydrogen bomb lost at sea off the coast of Spain in 1966, and in the hunt for the French submarine *Eurydice*, which sank in the Atlantic Ocean in 1970. The *Mizar* is still in Navy service.

GRYE-CLASS OCEANOGRAPHIC RESEARCH SHIPS (AGOR)

Operational (commissioned):	AGOR 21 *Gyre* (November 1973) AGOR 22 *Moana Wave* (January 1974)
Displacement:	1,190 tons
Dimensions:	
Length:	
AGOR 21:	176 ft.
AGOR 22:	204 ft.
Width:	36 ft.
Draft:	14.5 ft.
Propulsion:	Two Caterpillar diesel engines, 1,700 hp
Speed:	12.4 knots (14.3 mph)
Crew:	
AGOR 21:	30
AGOR 22:	28

ELTANIN-CLASS OCEANOGRAPHIC RESEARCH SHIPS (AGOR)

Operational (commissioned):	T-AGOR 8 *Eltanin* (January 1957) T-AGOR 11 *Mizar* (March 1958)
Displacement:	4,942 tons
Dimensions:	
Length:	262.2 ft.
Width:	51.5 ft.
Draft:	22.75 ft.
Propulsion:	One diesel-electric engine, 3,200 hp
Speed:	12 knots (14 mph)
Crew:	60

Opposite: The *Lynch,* a Conrad-*class ship, stands by as a submersible craft prepares to dive.* **Below:** *The Melville is an oceanographic research ship that uses a unique cycloidal propeller for station keeping.*

Ocean Surveillance Ships (AGOS)

STALWART-CLASS OCEAN SURVEILLANCE SHIPS (AGOS)	
Operational (commissioned):	T-AGOS 1 Stalwart (April 1984)
	T-AGOS 2 Contender (July 1984)
	T-AGOS 3 Vindicator (November 1984)
	T-AGOS 4 Triumph (February 1985)
	T-AGOS 5 Assurance (May 1985)
	T-AGOS 6 Persistent (August 1985)
	T-AGOS 7 Indomitable (December 1985)
	T-AGOS 8 Prevail (February 1986)
	T-AGOS 9 Assertive (September 1986)
	T-AGOS 10 Invincible (January 1987)
Displacement:	2,285 tons
Dimensions:	
Length:	224 ft.
Width:	43 ft.
Draft:	15 ft.
Propulsion:	Four diesel-electric engines, 3,200 hp
Speed:	11 knots (12.5 mph)
Crew:	26

SWATH-CLASS OCEAN SURVEILLANCE SHIPS (AGOS)	
Operational (commissioned):	
Building:	T-AGOS 17 Intrepid
Planned:	T-AGOS 21-28
Displacement:	4,200 tons
Dimensions:	
Length:	231 ft.
Width:	93 ft.
Draft:	25 ft.
Propulsion:	Two diesel-electric engines, hp data unavailable
Speed:	10.6 knots (12.3 mph)
Crew:	Data unavailable

Ocean surveillance ships are designed to deploy surveillance towed array sensor systems (SURTASS) to detect submarines. These systems are similar to the sensor systems that are distributed on the ocean floor in areas of heavy submarine traffic. The towed systems supplement the fixed systems, or replace those that have been damaged. Like the fixed systems, the towed systems are exceptionally sensitive and precise.

The arrays are made up of hydrophones that listen for sounds of enemy submarines. The data they acquire are first processed on board the towing vessel, then transmitted by satellite to shore-based installations for analysis by powerful computers. Objectives are to develop acoustic identification patterns that identify new submarines, and establish the traffic patterns and operational procedures of known submarines.

The Navy plans to build a total of 28 AGOS ships by the turn of the century. All these ships are operated by the Military Sealift Command.

Currently in Navy service are the ten ships of the Stalwart class, which are operated by the Military Sealift Command. Eventually, this class will include 19 ships. Stalwart ships have a single hull and are 224 feet long and 43 feet wide. They are powered by four Caterpillar D-348B diesel engines, which turn General Electric motors. These ships also have a bow-thruster—a 550 horsepower electric motor that is used for station keeping. While towing their arrays, they travel at three knots (3.5 miles per hour); otherwise, they are capable of an 11-knot (12.5 miles per hour) cruising speed.

Stalwart ships carry a small crew of 19 civilian sailors and seven technicians (who operate the towed array). The size of these ships provides plenty of space for crew accommodations. A typical tour of duty on a Stalwart ship requires between 60 and 74 days on station, and eight days in transit. The ships are divided between the Atlantic and Pacific fleets.

To complement the Stalwart class, the Navy has begun building a new class of ocean surveillance ships that will feature the technology called Small Waterplane Area Twin Hull (SWATH) design. As their name suggests, SWATH ships will have twin hulls that will support a main deck that rides above the water. Unlike catamaran hulls, which they will somewhat resemble, SWATH hulls will be fully submerged. Compared to conventional hulls, SWATH will have a smaller surface area, which will result in lower power and fuel requirements, and a smoother, more stable ride. The SWATH design also provides for more usable deck space than conventional hulls or catamaran hulls.

The Navy intends to build a total of nine SWATH ships by the mid-1990s. Each ship will be 231 feet long and 93 feet wide, and will carry a 2,600-feet tube containing the sensor arrays. To reduce the effects of hull noise, this tube will be attached to a 6,000-foot cable and towed at depths reaching 1,500 feet.

Opposite: The Contender (**top**) and Stalwart (**bottom**) are specially built to tow submarine surveillance sonar arrays, which are designated the UQQ-2 SURTASS.

Submersibles

ALVIN SUBMERSIBLE (DSV)

Operational (commissioned):	DSV 2 Alvin (May 1965)
Displacement:	16 tons
Dimensions:	
Length:	22 ft.
Width:	8 ft.
Diving depth:	13,124 ft.
Propulsion:	Three electric motors (one prop, two thrusters)
Speed:	2 knots (2.3 mph)
Crew:	One crew, two scientists

TURTLE-CLASS SUBMERSIBLES (DSV)

Operational (commissioned):	DSV 3 Turtle (December 1968)
	DSV 4 Sea Cliff (March 1969)
Displacement:	
DSV 3:	21 tons
DSV 4:	29 tons
Dimensions:	
Length:	
DSV 3:	23 ft., 7 in.
DSV 4:	28 ft., 3 in.
Width:	8 ft
Diving depth:	
DSV 3:	10,000+ ft.
DSV 4:	20,000+ ft.
Propulsion:	Three electric motors (one prop, two thrusters)
Speed:	2.5 knots (2.8 mph)
Crew:	Two crew, one scientist

MYSTIC-CLASS SUBMERSIBLES (DSRV)

Operational (commissioned):	DSRV 1 Mystic (August 1971)
	DSRV 2 Avalon (July 1972)
Displacement:	37 tons
Dimensions:	
Length:	49 ft., 9 in.
Width:	8 ft.
Diving depth:	5,000 ft.
Propulsion:	One electric motor
Speed:	5 knots (5.7 mph)
Crew:	Three crew, 24 rescuees

Submersibles differ from submarines in that these smaller craft are used primarily for search, rescue, research, deep-ocean recovery, and covert deep-diving operations. It is generally believed that in addition to the manned submersibles profiled here, the Navy maintains another, secret fleet of deep-ocean research vessels—some of which are designed to be launched and later retrieved by submerged submarines. Needless to say, information about these submersibles is virtually nonexistent and classified with the highest ratings.

The oldest research submersible in the Navy's inventory is the Alvin, which has been in service since the mid-1960s. This craft is operated by the Woods Hole Oceanographic Institution for the Office of Naval Research, which sponsored its construction. In 1968, the Alvin sank in over 5,000 feet of water, but was recovered. It was then fitted with a titanium sphere that has increased its diving depth from 6,000 feet to 13,000 feet. It was also fitted with a remote-controlled manipulator, or grasping arm. In 1966 the Alvin was used to recover a hydrogen bomb that fell from a U.S. B-52 bomber into the Atlantic off the coast of Spain; in 1986, it located the sunken luxury liner Titanic in the waters off Nova Scotia.

The two submersibles of the Turtle class are modified Alvin-class submersibles. The Turtle can dive to depths exceeding 10,000 feet, and the Sea Cliff can dive to a depth exceeding 20,000 feet. The ability to reach such depths gives the Turtle submersibles an access coverage range in excess of 98 percent of the ocean floor. Operated by the Submarine Development Group 1 at Point Loma in San Diego, California, these submersibles carry a crew of two and one scientist. They are built with a fiberglass outershell that is fitted to its high strength spheres, and they are equipped with a closed-circuit television, external lights, recording cameras, high technology sonars, and hydraulic remote-controlled manipulator arms.

The two Mystic-class Deep Submerged Rescue Vehicles, or DSRVs, are the Navy's most sophisticated submersibles. Designed and built as rescue craft for trapped submarine crews, these submersibles can operate at depths reaching 5,000 feet, rise at 100 feet per minute, remain submerged for 30 hours, maintain 5 knots while under water, and bring back to the surface up to 24 men at once. Operated by a crew of three, the DSRVs are outfitted with an elaborate search-and-rescue system of navigational equipment that includes high technology sonars, closed circuit television, cameras, remote control, a manipulating arm, and several monitoring devices. They are launched and recovered by either submerged attack submarines, or a Pigeon-class submarine rescue ship. Twelve such submersibles were originally planned and called for, but cost considerations and redesign to double the rescue capacity resulted in the funding of only two submersibles.

Opposite, top: The Turtle is a modified Alvin-class research submersible used for deep-ocean research. Bottom: The Alvin was the first of this design.

Surveying Ships (AGS)

MAURY-CLASS SURVEYING SHIPS (AGS)

Operational (commissioned):	T-AGS 39 *Maury* (March 1989)
Building:	T-AGS 40 *Tanner*
Displacement:	15,281 tons
Dimensions:	
Length:	449.8 ft.
Width:	72 ft.
Draft:	30.5 ft.
Propulsion:	Two diesels, 25,000 hp
Speed:	20.8 (24 mph)
Crew:	108

SILAS BENT-CLASS SURVEYING SHIPS (AGS)

Operational (commissioned):	T-AGS 26 *Silas Bent* (July 1965)
	T-AGS 27 *Kane* (May 1967)
	T-AGS 33 *Wilkes* (June 1971)
	T-AGS 34 *Wyman* (November 1971)
Displacement:	2,558 tons
Dimensions:	
Length:	285.3 ft.
Width:	48 ft.
Draft:	15 ft.
Propulsion:	One diesel-electric, 3,600 hp
Speed:	14 knots (16 mph)
Crew:	69

H.H. HESS SURVEYING SHIP (AGS)

Operational (commissioned):	T-AGS 38 *H.H. Hess* (January 1976)
Displacement:	21,250 tons
Dimensions:	
Length:	563.5 ft.
Width:	76 ft.
Draft:	32.5 ft.
Propulsion:	One steam turbine, 19,250 hp
Speed:	20.8 (24 mph)
Crew:	122

Currently in Navy service are nine ocean survey ships in four classes. Survey ships conduct oceanographic research and map the ocean floors. In addition to making possible the safe and efficient navigation of nuclear submarines, this work also produces a more profound knowledge of ocean dynamics. All survey ships are operated by the Military Sealift Command.

The *Chauvenet* class of survey ships includes the *Chauvenet* (T-AGS 29) and the *Harkness* (T-AGS 32), both of which were designed and built specifically as surveying ships for the U.S. Navy in Great Britain in the late 1960s. Both have hangars and full support equipment for helicopters, the only class of surveying ship to be so outfitted. Both are propelled by diesel-electric motors and are capable of 14.7 knots (17 miles per hour).

The *Silas Bent* class of surveying ships includes four ships, also designed specifically for this role, and all built in the mid- to late 1960s. Three operate with the Atlantic Fleet and one with the Pacific Fleet. All are over 285 feet long and are propelled by a diesel-electric engine capable of propelling at 14 knots (16 miles per hour). They have a cruising range of nearly 14,000 miles.

The *H.H. Hess* is a former merchant ship purchased by the U.S. Navy in 1975 and converted to an ocean survey ship. It is the largest of all survey ships with a displacement of 21,250 tons and a length of 563.5 feet. One 19,250 horsepower steam turbine enables it to reach a top speed of 20.8 knots (24 miles per hour).

The two new *Maury*-class survey ships are the *Maury* (T-AGS 39) and the *Tanner* (T-AGS 40). They were designed specifically as ocean surveying ships to conduct hydrographic, magnetic, and gravity surveys. Both will be fitted with the SQN-12 Sonar Array Sounding System, which permits continuous mapping of a broad strip of ocean bottom. The two new ships will displace 15,821 tons and be nearly 450 feet long. They will be powered by two 25,000 horsepower diesel engines and will have a speed of 20.8 knots (24 miles per hour).

CHAUVENET-CLASS SURVEYING SHIPS (AGS)

Operational (commissioned):	T-AGS 29 *Chauvenet* (November 1970)
	T-AGS 32 *Harkness* (January 1971)
Displacement:	4,330 tons
Dimensions:	
Length:	393.2 ft.
Width:	54 ft.
Draft:	16 ft.
Propulsion:	Two diesel-electrics, 3,600 hp
Speed:	14.7 (17 mph)
Crew:	146

Hospital Ships (AH)

The Navy has three hospital ships, two in service and one in the National Defense Reserve Fleet. All three ships have been converted, two from oil tankers and one from a cargo ship. All three are fully equipped hospitals that support U.S. military operations and personnel, and they have also been used as goodwill ships while sailing to and from duty stations.

The *Sanctuary* (AH-17) is the single ship in the *Haven* class of hospital ships. Designed originally as the merchant vessel *Merchant Owl*, it is a relatively small ship that displaces 15,400 tons, and is 529 feet long and 71.5 feet wide. One steam turbine propels it at a top speed of 17.3 knots (20 miles per hour). It was launched in August 1944 and commissioned in June 1945 as a hospital ship. In 1946 the *Sanctuary* was decommissioned; in 1961 it was transferred to the Maritime Administration. In 1966 the *Sanctuary* was reacquired by the Navy and served during the Vietnam War. In 1972 the ship was converted to a dependent support ship and sent to Greece with the Navy's first mixed male/female crew. The ship was again decommissioned in 1974.

The two hospital ships of the *Mercy* class are former tankers that were converted to hospital ships in 1986 and 1987. Both ships, *Mercy* (T-AH 19) and *Comfort* (T-AH 20), are operated by the Military Sealift Command and are part of the Ready Reserve Force (RRF). *Mercy* is stationed in the Pacific Fleet and *Comfort* in the Atlantic Fleet. Both ships are 894 feet long and displace 69,320 tons. They are powered by 24,500 horsepower General Electric steam turbines and are capable of making 17.3 knots (20 miles per hour). The *Mercy* ships have 12 operating rooms, four X-ray rooms, an 80-bed intensive care ward, and additional beds for 1,000 patients.

The *Mercy* ships are based at U.S. ports. When needed, they are assigned staff from military hospitals and can deploy within five days. The *Mercy* was sent to the Philippines in 1986 to serve U.S. military installations and Philippine civilian organizations. In 1987, it made several stops at remote Pacific islands to provide medical services to the islanders.

The *Comfort* *began life as an oil tanker before being converted to a hospital ship.*

MERCY-CLASS HOSPITAL SHIPS (AH)

Operational (commissioned):	T-AH 19 *Mercy* (November 1986) T-AH 20 *Comfort* (September 1987)
Displacement:	69,320 tons
Dimensions:	
Length:	894 ft.
Width:	105.75 ft.
Draft:	32.8 ft.
Propulsion:	Two General Electric steam turbines, 24,500 hp
Speed:	17.3 knots (20 mph)
Crew:	76 plus 1083 medical staff

HAVEN-CLASS HOSPITAL SHIP (AH)

Operational (commissioned):	AH 17 *Sanctuary* (June 1945)
Displacement:	15,400 tons
Dimensions:	
Length:	529 ft.
Width:	71.5 ft.
Draft:	24 ft.
Propulsion:	One General Electric steam turbine, 9,000 hp
Speed:	17.3 knots (20 mph)
Crew:	530 (including medical staff)

Maritime Prepositioning Ships (AK)

The United States military is often called upon to send military forces to remote areas of the globe. Such was the case, for example, when Navy ships were dispatched to the Persian Gulf in 1986 to provide security for nonbelligerent vessels during the Iran-Iraq war.

The Military Airlift Command of the U.S. Air Force is charged with moving troops and supplies quickly to trouble spots. The Navy is charged with moving reinforcements and additional supplies to support the first echelons of combat troops. To do so, it warehouses, or prepositions, supplies and equipment at U.S. Naval bases worldwide. To accomplish this task, the Navy has obtained 13 large cargo vessels that have been assigned to three squadrons. Each squadron carries sufficient supplies to support a Marine Expeditionary Brigade (MEB) for 30 days.

In 1981 a number of cargo vessels were leased and loaded with combat supplies and sent to the U.S. Naval Base at Diego Garcia in the Indian Ocean. These vessels were designated near-term prepositioning ships (NTPS). When the 13 new ships became available, 12 of the NTPS ships were kept in service.

All maritime prepositioning ships (MPS) are leased to the Navy long-term, and are operated by private commercial firms. Strictly speaking they are not U.S. Navy ships. Nevertheless, they have been assigned Navy hull numbers for accounting and data base purposes. All have helicopter landing areas but no helicopter hangars or maintenance facilities. None have facilities for berthing troops, other than the "surge" force that will arrive in advance of the main body to coordinate distribution of supplies and equipment.

CPL. LOUIS J. HAUGE, JR.-CLASS MARITIME PREPOSITIONING SHIPS (AK)

Operational (commissioned):	T-AK 3000 *Cpl. L.J. Hauge* (September 1984) T-AK 3001 *Pfc. W.B. Baugh, Jr.* (September 1985) T-AK 3002 *Pfc. James Anderson, Jr.* (March 1985) T-AK 3003 *1st Lt. A. Bonnyman, Jr.* (October 1984) T-AK 3004 *Pvt. Harry Fisher* (September 1985)
Displacement:	46,484 tons
Dimensions:	
Length:	755.5 ft.
Width:	90 ft.
Draft:	32.5 ft.
Propulsion:	One Sulzer diesel, 16,800 hp
Speed:	18.2 knots (21 mph)
Crew:	49

SGT. MATEJ KOCAK-CLASS MARITIME PREPOSITIONING SHIPS (AK)

Operational (commissioned):	T-AK 3005 *Sgt. Matej Kocak* (October 1984) T-AK 3006 *Pvt. E.A. Obregon* (January 1985) T-AK 3007 *Maj. S.W. Pless* (October 1984)
Displacement:	48,754 tons
Dimensions:	
Length:	821 ft.
Width:	105.5 ft.
Draft:	32.2 ft.
Propulsion:	Two steam turbines, 30,000 hp
Speed:	20 knots (23 mph)
Crew:	51

2ND LT. JOHN P. BOBO-CLASS MARITIME PREPOSITIONING SHIPS (AK)

Operational (commissioned):	T-AK 3008 *2nd Lt. John P. Bobo* (February 1985) T-AK 3009 *Pfc. D.T. Williams* (June 1985) T-AK 3010 *1st Lt. Baldomero Lopez* (November 1985) T-AK 3011 *1st Lt. Jack Lummus* (March 1986) T-AK 3012 *Sgt. W.R. Burton* (May 1986)
Displacement:	40,846 tons
Dimensions:	
Length:	673 ft.
Width:	105.5 ft.
Draft:	29.5 ft.
Propulsion:	Two Stork Werkspoor diesels, 26,040 hp
Speed:	18.2 (21 mph)
Crew:	55

All MPS ships are named after Marine Corps heroes. The *2nd Lt. John P. Bobo* class carry sufficient equipment and supplies to support one quarter of a MEB for thirty days. They displace 40,846 tons, have 162,500 square feet of storage space for vehicles, and can carry 1,605,000 gallons of petroleum products and 81,770 gallons of fresh water. A massive stern ramp is provided for use in unloading vehicles directly onto landing craft or onto docks and quays. The ships also have a 1,000 horsepower bow thruster to enable them to maneuver in port without the aid of tugs, as well as a helicopter landing area that extends from the top deck of the after deckhouse.

The *Sgt. Matej Kocak* class contains three ships displacing 48,754 tons each. These vessels were built as container ships and were purchased for conversion to the MPS role. They each have 152,500 square feet of vehicle storage space and can carry 1,544,000 gallons of petroleum products and 94,780 gallons of fresh water. They also have a massive stern ramp and a helicopter landing area located aft of the deckhouse.

The *Cpl. Louis J. Hauge, Jr.* class contains five ships displacing 46,484 tons each. These vessels were built originally as roll-on/roll-off (ro/ro) cargo ships. They each have 120,000 square feet of vehicle storage space and can carry 1,283 gallons of petroleum products and 65,000 gallons of fresh water. Their helicopter landing platform is raised on girders above the after deckhouse.

The prepositioning ship concept helped to supply the 7th Marine Expeditionary Brigade in the Persian Gulf during Operation Desert Shield. Shown here are the Cpl. Louis J. Hauge (**top**) and the Sgt. Matej Kocak (**bottom**).

Cargo Ships (AK)

The United States Navy maintains 26 cargo ships in 12 classes. All are used for transporting a wide variety of military cargoes, and all are operated by the Military Sealift Command. Eight ships are kept in American ports where they can be loaded and manned at short notice to carry additional military equipment to Europe. Eight additional cargo ships are used as near-term prepositioning ships (NTPS) and are kept in readiness to move military cargoes quickly to areas of the world to supply American troops as they are flown in. Such ships were put in service after it became clear that the Navy had no way to support a military operation in the Persian Gulf to free American diplomats taken hostage by Iran in 1979. The Military Sealift Command maintains a NTPS in the Indian Ocean at Diego Garcia.

In addition to NTPS and various maritime prepositioning ships, the Military Sealift Command also maintains the ships of the Ready Reserve Force, which are laid up in the National Defense Reserve Fleet. These vessels can be placed into service rapidly in the event of a national crisis. The National Defense Reserve Fleet also contains more than 100 merchant ships for national crisis situations. All cargo ships are operated by the Military Sealift Command and are manned by contract civilian crews. As matters now stand, the number of trained merchant seamen in the United States are insufficient to man even a small number of these reserve ships.

Perhaps the most unusual cargo ship in naval service is the *American Cormorant*, (T-AK 2062). Built in 1975 as the oil tanker *Kollbris* by Eriksbergs of Gothenburg, Sweden, it was laid up almost immediately because of a glut of shipping at that time. In 1981–82 it underwent modifications at the Gothaverken Cityvaret shipyard in Sweden that lengthened it by 180 feet. It was bought by an American firm in 1985 and leased to the Navy, which now uses it as an ultra-heavy lift ship. This ship is also referred to as a flo/flo, or float on/float off cargo ship. Its main deck can be submerged to a depth of 26 feet by ballasting the ship. Once submerged, barges, landing craft, and other heavy equipment can be floated over the deck. When all are in place, the ballast is pumped out, bringing the deck up under the cargo, which is then fastened in place. Barges or other vessels up to 45,000 tons can be loaded aboard the *American Cormorant* in this manner.

The Navy has six classes of vehicle cargo ships. The most advanced ships in this category are the eight ships of the SL-7 class. They were built originally as fast merchant ships capable of attaining speeds of 33 knots (38 miles per hour), the fastest cargo ships ever built for the Navy. These ships

Opposite: *The* Comet *is a ro/ro ship that carries vehicles.* **Inset:** *The* American Cormorant *is a flo/flo ship that carries loaded barges.*

COMET VEHICLE CARGO SHIP (AKR)

Operational (commissioned):	T-AKR 7 *Comet* (January 1958)
Displacement:	18,286 tons
Dimensions:	
Length:	499 ft.
Width:	78 ft.
Draft:	28.75 ft.
Propulsion:	Two steam turbines, 13,200 hp
Speed:	18.2 knots (21 mph)
Crew:	40

ULTRA-HEAVY LIFT CARGO SHIPS (AK)

Operational (commissioned):	T-AK 2062 *American Cormorant* (October 1985)
Displacement:	47,500 tons
Dimensions:	
Length:	738.2 ft.
Width:	135 ft.
Draft:	33 ft.
Propulsion:	One diesel engine, 25,000 hp
Speed:	16 knots (18.4 mph)
Crew:	19

CONVERTED SL-7 VEHICLE CARGO SHIPS (AKR)

Operational (commissioned):	T-AKR 287 *Agol* (June 1984)
	T-AKR 288 *Bellatrix* (September 1984)
	T-AKR 289 *Denebola* (Unavailable)
	T-AKR 290 *Pollux* (March 1986)
	T-AKR 291 *Altair* (November 1985)
	T-AKR 292 *Regulus* (August 1985)
	T-AKR 293 *Capella* (July 1984)
	T-AKR 294 *Antares* (July 1984)
Displacement:	31,000 tons
Dimensions:	
Length:	946.2 ft.
Width:	105.5 ft.
Draft:	36.7 ft.
Propulsion:	Two steam turbines, 120,000 hp
Speed:	33 knots (38 mph)
Crew:	45

METEOR VEHICLE CARGO SHIP (AKR)

Operational (commissioned):	T-AKR 9 *Meteor* (May 1967)
Displacement:	22,150 tons
Dimensions:	
Length:	540 ft.
Width:	83 ft.
Draft:	29 ft.
Propulsion:	Two steam turbines, 19,400 hp
Speed:	20 knots (23 mph)
Crew:	40

VEHICLE CARGO SHIPS (AKR)

Operational (commissioned):	T-AKR 10 *Mercury* (June 1980)
	T-AKR 11 *Jupiter* (May 1980)
Displacement:	33,765 tons
Dimensions:	
Length:	684.5 ft.
Width:	102 ft.
Draft:	32 ft.
Propulsion:	Two steam turbines, 37,000 hp
Speed:	23 knots (26.5 mph)
Crew:	40

THE SURFACE FLEET: AUXILIARY SHIPS

have roll on/roll off (ro/ro) capability through large loading ports on the ships' sides. They each have 185,000 square feet of parking space for vehicles as well as space for 46 cargo containers (20 feet long) and 78 trailer flatbeds (35 feet long) on which the containers are loaded for hauling. The ships also carry twin cranes forward that can each lift 35 tons of cargo and two more cranes aft that have lifting capacities of 50 tons.

Each of the SL-7 ships has a large helicopter platform on the main deck. These ships are not used as prepositioning

ships but are berthed at Atlantic and Gulf ports, fully loaded and ready to sail. They are on long-term lease to the Navy.

The *Mercury* (T-AKR 10) and the *Jupiter* (T-AKR 11) represent a second class of fast vehicle cargo ships. They were leased by the Navy in 1980 from the States Steamship Company for use as maritime prepositioning ships. They can carry 19,172 tons of cargo each, which can be loaded through stern ramps and side ports.

Three vehicle cargo ship classes only contain one ship each. The *Meteor* (T-AK 9) is

a ro/ro cargo ship launched in 1965. During the middle 1980s it was used as a maritime prepositioning ship at Diego Garcia, carrying equipment for a Marine Corps Expeditionary Brigade. The *Comet* (T-AKR 7) and the *Admiral William M. Callaghan* (T-AKR 1001) were both built as Navy ships. The former was a general cargo vessel that was converted to its present role in 1969, and the latter was an early ro/ro cargo ship that entered service in 1967. The *Callaghan* was the first Navy ship to be powered by an all-gas turbine power plant.

Originally fitted with two Pratt & Whitney FT-4 engines, these were replaced in 1977 with two General Electric LM2500 gas turbines.

Two *Lykes*-class merchant ships, *Elizabeth Lykes* (T-AK 2040) and *Letitia Lykes* (T-AK 2043), are vehicle cargo ships that were chartered by the Military Sealift Command to serve as near-term prepositioning ships. Both ships can carry 14,662 tons of cargo.

The Military Sealift Command retains in service four LASH (Lighter Aboard Ship) cargo ships. The acronym LASH refers to the

MIRFAK ARCTIC CARGO SHIP (AK)

Operational (commissioned):	T-AK 271 *Mirfak* (December 1957)
Displacement:	4,800 tons
Dimensions:	
Length:	266 ft.
Width:	51.5 ft.
Draft:	23 ft.
Propulsion:	One diesel-electric, 3,200 hp
Speed:	13 knots (15 mph)
Crew:	48

NORTHERN LIGHT-CLASS CARGO SHIP (AK)

Operational (commissioned):	T-AK 284 *Northern Light* (May 1980) T-AK 286 *Southern Cross* (March 1983)
Displacement:	18,365 tons
Dimensions:	
Length:	483.25 ft.
Width:	68 ft.
Draft:	32.8 ft.
Propulsion:	One steam turbine, 11,000 hp
Speed:	19 knots (22 mph)
Crew:	
T-AK 284:	50
T-AK 285:	39

ADM. WM. CALLAGHAN VEHICLE CARGO SHIP (AKR)

Operational (commissioned):	T-AKR 1001 *Adm. Wm. Callaghan* (December 1967)
Displacement:	26,573 tons
Dimensions:	
Length:	694 ft.
Width:	92 ft.
Draft:	29 ft.
Propulsion:	Two General Electric LM2500 gas turbines, 40,000 hp
Speed:	26 knots (30 mph)
Crew:	33

ELIZABETH LYKES-CLASS VEHICLE CARGO SHIP (AK)

Operational (commissioned):	T-AK 2040 *Elizabeth Lykes* (1983) T-AK 2043 *Letitia Lykes* (1983)
Displacement:	21,840 tons
Dimensions:	
Length:	539.8 ft.
Width:	76 ft.
Draft:	32.7 ft.
Propulsion:	Two steam turbines, 15,000 hp
Speed:	20 knots (23 mph)
Crew:	38

fact that these are combination barge/container ships. The cargo is packed in containers placed aboard barges (or lighters), which are then sailed out to the ship and loaded aboard. The *Austral Rainbow* (T-AK 2046) and *Green Harbour* (T-AK 2064) are LASH ships that were built in the early 1970s. They currently serve as near-term prepositioning ships. The *Green Island* (T-AK 1015) and the *Green Valley* (T-AK 2049) are former Central Lines cargo ships leased by the Military Sealift Command. They can carry 89 barges as well as a small tug to move the barges into position for loading.

The *Santa Victoria* (T-AK 1010) is a self-loading container ship that has been leased from the United States Lines by the Military Sealift Command. It can carry 13,074 tons of cargo at speeds reaching 23 knots (26.5 miles per hour).

The *Eltanin*-class cargo ship, *Mirfak* (T-AK 271), was originally built to deliver cargo to radar stations in the Arctic. The *Mirfak* is now in the National Defense Reserve Fleet.

Three converted *Mormac*-class cargo ships, *Northern Light* (T-AK-284), *Southern Cross* (T-AK-285) and *Vega* (T-AK-286), were acquired by the Navy to be used as maritime prepositioning ships at Diego Garcia. The *Vega* was also used as a fleet ballistic missile (FBM) replenishment ship. It is now fitted out to transport up to 16 Trident submarine-launched ballistic missiles to submarine tenders. Of these ships, only the *Vega* remains in active service; the others are in reserve.

The *Marshfield* (T-AK 282) is a former *Victory*-class cargo ship built in 1944 that is now used as a fleet ballistic missile replenishment ship. In addition to carrying 16 Trident missiles in upright storage in its number three hold, the *Marshfield* can carry a general cargo that may include 355,000 gallons of diesel fuel oil as well as 430,000 gallons of various other petroleum products.

SANTA VICTORIA CARGO SHIP (AK)

Operational (commissioned):	T-AK 1010 *Santa Victoria* (January 1981)
Displacement:	21,617 tons
Dimensions:	
Length:	575.8 ft.
Width:	82 ft.
Draft:	32.5 ft.
Propulsion:	Two steam turbines, 15,000 hp
Speed:	23 knots (26.5 mph)
Crew:	29

FLEET BALLISTIC MISSILE SUPPLY CARGO SHIPS (AK)

Operational (commissioned):	T-AK 282 *Marshfield* (May 1970)
	T-AK 286 *Vega* (March 1980)
Displacement:	
T-AK 282:	11,150 tons
T-AK 286:	16,363 tons
Dimensions:	
Length:	
T-AK 282:	455.25 ft.
T-AK 286:	483.25 ft.
Width:	
T-AK 282:	62 ft.
T-AK 286:	68 ft.
Draft:	
T-AK 282:	24 ft.
T-AK 286:	32.8 ft.
Propulsion:	
T-AK 282:	One steam turbine, 8,500 hp
T-AK 286:	One steam turbine, 11,000 hp
Speed:	
T-AK 282:	17.3 knots (20 mph)
T-AK 286:	19 knots (22 mph)
Crew:	
T-AK 282:	65 civilian and 7 Navy
T-AK 286:	63 civilian and 7 Navy

LASH CARGO SHIPS (AK)

Operational (commissioned):	T-AK 1015 *Green Island* (September 1982)
	T-AK 2046 *Austral Rainbow* (April 1984)
	T-AK 2049 *Green Valley* (February 1984)
	T-AK 2064 *Green Harbour* (October 1981)
Displacement:	
T-AK 1015, 2049:	62,314 tons
T-AK 2046, 2064:	44,606 tons
Dimensions:	
Length:	
T-AK 1015, 2049:	893.2 ft.
T-AK 2046, 2064:	819.8 ft.
Width:	100 ft.
Draft:	
T-AK 1015, 2049:	40.8 ft.
T-AK 2046, 2064:	35 ft.
Propulsion:	
T-AK 1015, 2049:	Two steam turbines, 32,000 hp
T-AK 2046, 2064:	One steam turbine, 32,000 hp
Speed:	
T-AK 1015, 2049:	21.7 knots (25 mph)
T-AK 2046, 2064:	22.5 knots (26 mph)
Crew:	
T-AK 1015, 2049, 2064:	27
T-AK 2046:	32

Oilers and Tankers (AO)

The Navy, through the Military Sealift Command, maintains 60 oilers and tankers on active duty, six in the National Defense Reserve Fleet, eight in the Ready Reserve fleet, and four in the Near-Term Prepositioning Squadron. Whereas oilers are designed to replenish other ships while underway, tankers are designed as point-to-point ships that can only offload oil while docked.

The four ships of the *Sacramento* class are fast combat support ships. These ships have an underway replenishment capability that enables them to provide a carrier battle group with everything it needs in terms of fuel, munitions, food, and other supplies. They can carry 194,000 barrels of oil, 2,100 tons of munitions, 250 tons of frozen food, and 250 tons of other food and supplies. All are highly automated to assist in moving stores, and all have a three-bay helicopter hangar on the after deck. Each *Sacramento* ship carries two CH-46 Sea Knight helicopters.

The Navy originally wanted to build 15 ships in this class—one for each carrier task force in the 600-ship Navy. But now that the Navy has been scaled back to a planned 545 ships by 1991, and may face even more cutbacks, the number of fast combat support ships is likely to be diminished.

Six ship classes are represented by the fleet oilers currently in service. These ships generally travel with a naval task force and carry additional fuel oil to replenish warships at sea. The newest class is the *Henry J. Kaiser*, named after the World War II-era industrialist who designed and built the *Victory*-class cargo ships. The *Henry J. Kaiser* ships carry 180,000 barrels of fuel oil and a limited amount of other cargo. They have a large helicopter landing deck aft and a massive underway replenishment area forward. They are powered by two diesel engines and can attain 20 knots (23 miles per hour). Provision has been made to mount the 20 millimeter Phalanx Close-In Weapons System Mark 15 multibarrel gun. Five ships in this class have been built and the Navy is hoping to obtain at least ten additional units.

The five fleet oilers of the *Cimarron* class were completed in the mid-1980s. Each carry enough oil to accomplish two refuelings of a non-nuclear fleet aircraft carrier and its aircraft, and up to eight escort ships as well. At least two ships of this class, *Merrimack* (AO 179) and *Willamette* (AO 180), are undergoing modifications to increase their cargo capacity from 120,000 to 160,000 barrels of ship fuel.

The six *Neosho*-class fleet oilers were all built in the early to mid-1950s. Each ship carries 180,000 barrels of petroleum and all were armed with two five-inch guns in single mounts as well as 12 .50 caliber antiaircraft machine guns. They lost their armament when taken over by the Military Sealift Command.

KAISER-CLASS FLEET OILER SHIPS (AO)	
Operational (commissioned):	T-AO 187 *Henry J. Kaiser* (December 1986)
	T-AO 188 *Joshua Humphreys* (April 1987)
	T-AO 189 *John Lenthall* (May 1988)
	T-AO 190 *Andrew Higgins* (October 1987)
	T-AO 193 *W. Diehl* (October 1989)
Displacement:	40,700 tons
Dimensions:	
Length:	677.5 ft.
Width:	97.5 ft.
Draft:	35 ft.
Propulsion:	Two diesels, 32,000 hp
Speed:	20 knots (23 mph)
Crew:	98 civilian and 21 Navy

CIMARRON-CLASS FLEET OILER SHIPS (AO)

Operational (commissioned):	AO 177 *Cimarron* (January 1981)
	AO 178 *Monongahela* (September 1981)
	AO 179 *Merrimack* (November 1981)
	AO 180 *Willamette* (December 1982)
	AO 181 *Platte* (April 1983)
Displacement:	27,500 tons
Dimensions:	
Length:	591.3 ft.
Width:	88 ft.
Draft:	33.5 ft.
Propulsion:	One steam turbine, 24,000 hp
Speed:	20 knots (23 mph)
Crew:	212 Navy

NEOSHO-CLASS FLEET OILER SHIPS (AO)

Operational (commissioned):	T-AO 143 *Neosho* (September 1954)
	T-AO 144 *Misissinewa* (January 1955)
	T-AO 145 *Hassayampa* (April 1955)
	T-AO 146 *Kawishiwi* (July 1955)
	T-AO 147 *Truckee* (November 1955)
	T-AO 148 *Ponchatoula* (January 1956)
Displacement:	36,840 tons
Dimensions:	
Length:	655.7 ft.
Width:	86 ft.
Draft:	35 ft.
Propulsion:	Two steam turbines, 28,000 hp
Speed:	20 knots (23 mph)
Crew:	108 civilian and 21 Navy

MISPILLION-CLASS FLEET OILER SHIPS (AO)

Operational (commissioned):	T-AO 105 *Mispillion* (December 1945)
	T-AO 106 *Navasota* (February 1946)
	T-AO 107 *Passumpsic* (April 1946)
	T-AO 108 *Pawcatuck* (May 1946)
	T-AO 109 *Waccamaw* (June 1946)
Displacement:	35,000 tons
Dimensions:	
Length:	646 ft.
Width:	75 ft.
Draft:	35.5 ft.
Propulsion:	Two steam turbines, 13,500 hp
Speed:	16 knots (18.5 mph)
Crew:	111 civilian and 21 Navy

The Monongahela *is a* Cimmaron-*class oiler. It can carry enough fuel to completely refuel two aircraft carriers.*

The five *Mispillion*-class fleet oilers were building or launched in the waning days of World War II. They have since been modernized, with a 93-foot section inserted amidships to increase their capacity to 150,000 barrels of fuel oil.

The three fleet oilers of the *Ashtabula* class were all built during World War II. The *Ashtabula*, built and commissioned in 1943, was placed in the National Defense Reserve Fleet in 1982. All three of the *Ashtabula*-class ships have been modified to include a 91-foot area amidships that gives them a cargo capacity of 143,000 barrels of fuel oil.

A second *Cimarron* class of fleet oilers contains two ships, the *Marias* and the *Taluga*. (This class is not to be confused with the five-ship *Cimmaron* class that contains the *Merrimack* and the *Willamette*.) Both ships have cargo capacities of 115,000 barrels and both are now laid up in the National Defense Reserve Fleet.

The Navy also maintains seven replenishment oiler ships of the *Wichita* class. These ships are both oilers and underway replenishment cargo ships that can carry 160,000 barrels of fuel oil, 600 tons of munitions, 100 tons of frozen food, and 200 tons of non-frozen stores. All but one

ship in this class were built with twin helicopter bays to carry two CH-46 Sea Knight helicopters. Armament consists of Sea Sparrow antiaircraft missiles and two 20mm Phalanx multibarrel guns.

The Military Sealift Command operates two classes of gasoline tankers, the *Alatna* and the *Tonti* classes. The two ships of the *Alatna* class were built to operate in the Arctic. These are point-to-point cargo vessels and have no underway replenishment capability. The *Nodaway* is the only *Tonti*-class ship still in operation, and it is in the Ready Reserve fleet.

The Military Sealift Command operates transport oilers from 12 additional ship classes. Four entire classes and one ship from another class remain in active service; the ships of all other classes are either in the Ready Reserve fleet or the National Defense Reserve Fleet. The 12 classes include: the *T-5 Type*, *Modified Falcon* class, *Overseas* class, *Zapata* class, *Bravado* class, *Potomac* class, *Sealift* class, *Maumee* class, *Suamico* class, and two single-ship classes, the *Mission* and *American Explorer* classes. All are operated by civilian crews under contract to the Military Sealift Command.

The Roanoke, *a* Wichita-*class replenishment oiler, is seen here refueling the frigate* Francis Hammond *and the destroyer* Waddell *while underway.*

ASHTABULA-CLASS FLEET OILER SHIPS (AO)

Operational (commissioned):	AO 51 *Ashtabula* (August 1943) AO 98 *Caloosahatchee* (October 1945) AO 99 *Canisteo* (December 1945)
Displacement:	36,500 tons
Dimensions:	
Length:	644 ft.
Width:	75 ft.
Draft:	31.5 ft.
Propulsion:	One steam turbine, 13,500 hp
Speed:	18.2 knots (21 mph)
Crew:	317 Navy

SACRAMENTO-CLASS FAST COMBAT SUPPORT SHIPS (AOE)

Operational (commissioned):	AOE 1 *Sacramento* (March 1964) AOE 2 *Camden* (April 1967) AOE 3 *Seattle* (April 1969) AOE 4 *Detroit* (March 1970)
Displacement:	53,600 tons
Dimensions:	
Length:	794.75 ft.
Width:	107 ft.
Draft:	39.3 ft.
Propulsion:	Two steam turbines, 100,000 hp
Speed:	27 knots (32 mph)
Crew:	611 Navy

CIMARRON-CLASS FLEET OILER SHIPS (AO)

Operational (commissioned):	T-AO 57 *Marias* (February 1944) T-AO 62 *Taluga* (August 1944)
Displacement:	24,450 tons
Dimensions:	
Length:	553 ft.
Width:	75 ft.
Draft:	31.5 ft.
Propulsion:	Two steam turbines, 13,500 hp
Speed:	18.2 knots (21 mph)
Crew:	105 civilian

WICHITA-CLASS REPLENISHMENT OILER (AOR)

Operational (commissioned):	AOR 1 *Wichita* (June 1969) AOR 2 *Milwaukee* (November 1969) AOR 3 *Kansas City* (June 1970) AOR 4 *Savannah* (December 1970) AOR 5 *Wabash* (November 1971) AOR 6 *Kalamazoo* (August 1973) AOR 7 *Roanoke* (October 1976)
Displacement:	41,350 tons
Dimensions:	
Length:	659 ft.
Width:	96 ft.
Draft:	33.3 ft.
Propulsion:	Two steam turbines, 32,000 hp
Speed:	20 knots (23 mph)
Crew:	450 Navy

ALATNA-CLASS GASOLINE TANKER (AOG)

Operational (commissioned):	T-AOG 81 *Alatna* (July 1957) T-AOG 82 *Chattahoochee* (October 1957)
Displacement:	5,720 tons
Dimensions:	
Length:	302 ft.
Width:	61 ft.
Draft:	19 ft.
Propulsion:	One diesel electric, 4,000 hp
Speed:	13 knots (15 mph)
Crew:	24 civilian

TONTI-CLASS GASOLINE TANKER (AOG)

Operational (commissioned):	T-AOG 78 *Nodaway* (September 1950)
Displacement:	5,984 tons
Dimensions:	
Length:	325 ft.
Width:	28.2 ft.
Draft:	19 ft.
Propulsion:	Two diesels, 1,400 hp
Speed:	10 knots (11.5 mph)
Crew:	24 civilian

Repair Ships (AR)

VULCAN-CLASS REPAIR SHIPS (AR)

Operational (commissioned):	AR-5 *Vulcan* (June 1941)
	AR-6 *Ajax* (October 1943)
	AR-7 *Hector* (February 1944)
	AR-8 *Jason* (June 1944)
Displacement:	16,245 tons
Dimensions:	
Length:	529.4 ft.
Width:	73.3 ft.
Draft:	23.3 ft.
Propulsion:	Two steam turbines, 11,000 hp
Speed:	19 knots (22 mph)
Crew:	
AR-5:	842
AR-8:	840

ZEUS REPAIR SHIP (ARC)

Operational (commissioned):	T-ARC 7 *Zeus* (March 1984)
Displacement:	14,255 tons
Dimensions:	
Length:	502.5 ft.
Width:	73.2 ft.
Draft:	23.8 ft.
Propulsion:	One diesel-electric, 12,500 hp
Speed:	15.6 knots (18 mph)
Crew:	80 civilian and 40 Navy

NEPTUNE-CLASS REPAIR SHIPS (ARC)

Operational (commissioned):	T-ARC 2 *Neptune* (June 1953)
	T-ARC 6 *Albert J. Meyer* (May 1963)
Displacement:	5,818 tons
Dimensions:	
Length:	370 ft.
Width:	47 ft.
Draft:	24.9 ft.
Propulsion:	Four diesel-electrics, 4,000 hp
Speed:	13 knots (15 mph)
Crew:	74 civilian and 24 Navy

The Navy operates two types of repair ships, one to conduct general repairs at sea or in ports, and the other for laying, maintaining, and repairing undersea cables.

Only one general repair class is in operation today, the *Vulcan* class. Of the four ships in this class, two are in active service—one with the Atlantic Fleet (*Vulcan*) and one with the Pacific Fleet (*Jason*)—and two are in the Naval Reserve fleet (*Ajax* and *Hector*). These ships are quite large, displacing 16,245 tons and measuring 529.4 feet in length. They are equipped to effect all major repairs on all but the most sophisticated weapons and electronics equipment. They have a small vertical replenishment (VERTREP) helicopter landing pad in the bow. Their original four five-inch guns and eight 40 millimeter antiaircraft guns were removed and have been replaced by four 20mm Mark 67 single antiaircraft guns. It is anticipated that the *Vulcan* and the *Jason* will be placed in the Naval Reserve fleet in the early 1990s.

The Military Sealift Command operates two cable repair ship classes, the *Zeus* and the *Neptune*. The *Zeus* (T-ARC 7) was built specifically to repair and maintain the Sound Surveillance System (SOSUS) and other underwater cables used by the Navy. This ship has the capability of laying up to 1,000 miles of cable ten miles deep. The *Zeus* is also equipped to conduct oceanographic research.

The *Neptune* class includes two ships, *Neptune* and *Albert J. Meyer*, which were also built for cable laying, maintenance, and repair. The ships have been modernized and fitted with new diesel-electric engines and updated electronics and navigation equipment.

The *Jason* is equipped to carry out most repairs needed by naval vessels at sea. The *Jason* is assigned to the Pacific Fleet.

Salvage/Rescue Ships (ASR)

The ships in this category are variously configured, depending on the specific mission they have been designed to carry out. The four ships of the *Chanticleer* class date back to World War II, which makes them the Navy's oldest submarine rescue ships. Displacing 1,670 tons, these large tug-type ships have a limited submarine rescue capability when outfitted with a McCann rescue chamber. All four ships are equipped for helium/oxygen diving missions, and carry updated sonar and underwater communications equipment. The *Chanticleer* ships are likely to remain in service until the late 1990s.

The two *Pigeon*-class submarine rescue ships were built specifically to carry Deep Submergence Rescue Vehicles (DSRV). They can also carry the McCann rescue chamber, and are capable of supporting up to eight divers operating at depths exceeding 1,000 feet. *Pigeon* ships have the largest catamaran hull on any Navy ship, a feature that aids in the lowering and raising of diving chambers and DSRVs. Each hull has "through-bow" thrusters that enable the ship to maneuver and continually reposition itself during salvage operations. *Pigeon* ships displace 3,411 tons and have a helicopter landing deck, and precision three-dimensional sonar tracking systems.

The three *Edenton*-class ships may be used for a variety of salvage and rescue operations, particularly those involving the towing of disabled ships. They displace 2,650 tons and feature a powerful crane located on

CHANTICLEER-CLASS SALVAGE/RESCUE SHIPS (ASR)

Operational (commissioned):	ASR 3 *Florikan* (April 1943)
	ASR 13 *Kittiwake* (July 1946)
	ASR 14 *Petrel* (September 1946)
	ASR 15 *Sunbird* (January 1947)
Displacement:	1,670 tons
Dimensions:	
Length:	251 ft.
Width:	42 ft.
Draft:	14 ft., 10 in.
Propulsion:	Four diesel electrics, 3,000 hp
Speed:	15 knots (17.2 mph)
Crew:	103

BOLSTER-CLASS SALVAGE/RESCUE SHIPS (ARS)

Operational (commissioned):	ARS 8 *Preserver* (January 1944)
	ARS 38 *Bolster* (May 1945)
	ARS 39 *Conserver* (June 1945)
	ARS 40 *Hoist* (July 1945)
	ARS 41 *Opportune* (October 1945)
	ARS 42 *Reclaimer* (December 1945)
	ARS 43 *Recovery* (May 1946)
Displacement:	
ARS 8:	1,530 tons
ARS 38–43:	2,045 tons
Dimensions:	
Length:	213 ft., 6 in.
Width:	
ARS 8:	39 ft.
ARS 38–43:	43 ft.
Draft:	13 ft.
Propulsion:	Four diesels, 3,060 hp
Speed:	
ARS 8:	14.8 knots (17 mph)
ARS 38–43:	16 knots (18.4)
Crew:	83

SAFEGUARD-CLASS SALVAGE/RESCUE SHIPS (ARS)

Operational (commissioned):	ARS 50 *Safeguard* (August 1985)
	ARS 51 *Grasp* (December 1985)
	ARS 52 *Salvor* (June 1986)
	ARS 53 *Grapple* (November 1986)
Displacement:	2,300 tons
Dimensions:	
Length:	255 ft.
Width:	51 ft.
Draft:	15 ft., 5 in.
Propulsion:	Four diesels, 4,200 hp
Speed:	13.5 knots (15.5 mph)
Crew:	90

the forward deck that is capable of dead-lifting objects weighing up to 272 tons over the bow. The *Edenton* ships can also support diving operations to a depth of 800 feet, and have all the requisite gear to fight fires on other ships.

The seven ships of the *Bolster* class are World War II-era ships designed for uncomplicated salvage and towing operations. The *Bolster* ships displace 1,530 tons (ARS 8) or 2,045 tons (ARS 38–43), and can support relatively shallow diving operations requiring compressed air only.

Originally this class contained 22 ships, but age has reduced its number to the present level.

The four ships of the *Safeguard* class were designed to replace the *Bolster* class. The *Safeguard* ships displace 2,300 tons and have a limited diving support capability. In open water, these ships can exert up to 54 tons of pulling power; using beach extraction gear, they can pull up to 360 tons. In addition to the four operational ships in this class, a fifth ship is planned, and will likely enter service in the mid-1990s.

Ocean-Going Tugs (ATF)

The Navy's group of "fleet" or "ocean-going" tugs is at present limited to but one class. Known as the *Powhatan* class, these vessels are variants of a design applied to ships that are used to support oil derrick drilling operations. Relatively modern by current standards, they have replaced all of the World War II-era tugs in the *Abnaki* and *Achomawi* classes.

Slightly larger and more powerful than the older vessels, the *Powhatan* tugs differ from their predecessors in that they lack salvage and diving equipment. In addition, the new craft have a more limited towing capacity than the earlier vessels.

Powhatan vessels are easily recognizable due to their unusual low, open stern design, and large side-by-side funnels. Displacing just over 2,000 tons, they carry a ten-ton crane and a 300-horse-power bow thruster system up front. A ship in this class can carry the Mark 1, Model 1 deep diving support module. Tipping the scales at 90 tons, this diving module works with a 20-man support crew used for salvage operations. The *Powhatan* ships have a 60-ton towing capacity on open water, and a complete foam fire-fighting system.

PIGEON-CLASS SALVAGE/RESCUE SHIPS (ASR)

Operational (commissioned):	ASR 21 *Pigeon* (April 1973) ASR 22 *Ortolan* (July 1973)
Displacement:	3,411 tons
Dimensions:	
Length:	251 ft.
Width:	86 ft.
Draft:	21 ft.
Propulsion:	Four diesels, 6,000 hp
Speed:	15 knots (17.2 mph)
Crew:	195

EDENTON-CLASS SALVAGE/RESCUE SHIPS (ATS)

Operational (commissioned):	ATS 1 *Edenton* (January 1971) ATS 2 *Beaufort* (January 1972) ATS 3 *Brunswick* (December 1972)
Displacement:	2,650 tons
Dimensions:	
Length:	264 ft.
Width:	45 ft., 9 in.
Draft:	13 ft., 8 in.
Propulsion:	Four diesels, 6,000 hp
Speed:	16 knots (18.4 mph)
Crew:	113

POWHATAN-CLASS OCEAN-GOING TUGS (ATF)

Operational (commissioned):	T-ATF 166 *Powhatan* (June 1979) T-ATF 167 *Narragansett* (January 1979) T-ATF 168 *Catawba* (May 1980) T-ATF-169 *Navajo* (June 1980) T-ATF-170 *Mohawk* (October 1980) T-ATF-171 *Sioux* (May 1981) T-ATF-172 *Apache* (July 1981)
Displacement:	2,000 tons
Dimensions:	
Length:	240 ft., 6 in.
Width:	42 ft.
Draft:	15 ft.
Propulsion:	Two diesels, 4,500 hp
Speed:	15 knots (19.5 mph)
Crew:	17 civilians and 4 Navy

Miscellaneous Auxiliary Ships

Four of the most interesting ships in the Navy fall into this category of one-of-kind ships that do not fit comfortably into any other description or class.

The sound trials ship *Hayes* (T-AG 195) is a catamaran-hull vessel built specifically to conduct oceanographic research. The *Hayes* carries a wide inventory of acoustic buoys and hydrophone arrays, which are used to measure the noise produced by nuclear submarines. The data it gathers are used in studies undertaken to further refine nuclear submarine design.

The *Hayes* was converted to its role as an oceano-graphic research ship between 1987 and early 1990, and has replaced the older *Monob One* (YAG 61), a self-propelled barge. The catamaran hull was chosen for its stability. It also provides an area of calmer water into which research equipment can be lowered during heavy weather.

Each of the *Hayes'* hulls are 24 feet wide and spaced 27 feet apart. Crew quarters are located in the forward superstructure; laboratories are in the after superstructure. In addition to its two main 5,400 horsepower General Motors diesel engines, each *Hayes* has its own 165 horsepower auxiliary diesel engine in each hull. These

The Hayes *is a catamaran-hulled vessel used for oceanographic research.*

HAYES SOUND TRIALS SHIP (AF)	
Operational (commissioned):	T-AF 195 *Hayes* (July 1971)
Displacement:	3,952 tons
Dimensions:	
Length:	265 ft.
Width:	75 ft.
Individual hull width:	24 ft.
Draft:	22.3 ft.
Propulsion:	Two diesel-electrics, 5,400 hp
Speed:	15 knots (17.2 mph)
Crew:	60

GLOMAR EXPLORER HEAVY-LIFT SHIP (AG)	
Operational (commissioned):	AG 193 *Glomar Explorer* (July 1973)
Displacement:	63,300 tons
Dimensions:	
Length:	618.75 ft.
Width:	115.6 ft.
Draft:	46.6 ft.
Propulsion:	Two diesel-electrics, 13,200 hp
Speed:	10.8 knots (12.5 mph)
Crew:	189

smaller engines can move the ship forward at a maximum speed of 3.9 knots (4.6 miles per hour) when the main engines are shut down. The *Hayes* is operated for the Navy by the Military Sealift Command.

Built in 1944, the hydrographic research ship *Kingsport* (T-AG 164) was a "Liberty Ship" named *Kingsport Victory*. In 1950 it was assigned to the Military Sea Transport Service, the forerunner of the Military Sealift Command. Converted in 1961 from a cargo carrier to a research ship, it was assigned the role of supporting the Project Advent communications satellite as well as other space-related programs. At that time, its name was shortened to *Kingsport*. In 1964 it was converted to a hydrographic research ship and used to support the development of underwater surveillance systems. The *Kingsport* is now assigned to the National Defense Reserve Fleet.

In the early 1970s the heavy-lift ship *Glomar Explorer* (AG-193) was designed and built by the Central Intelligence Agency for a specific purpose: to retrieve a Soviet *Golf I*-class submarine that sank with all hands in the Pacific in 1968.

With a length of 618 feet, a width of 115 feet, and a displacement weight of 63,300 tons, the *Glomar Explorer* is a very large ship that was well suited to its original task. Two Nordberg diesel engines provide power to turbines that turn two General Electric 13,200 horsepower electric motors. Top speed is 10.8 knots (12.5 miles per hour).

A heavy-lift system including a grappling claw (which also could be attached to a submersible barge for clandestine operations) was built to raise the 2,700-ton Soviet submarine from a depth of nearly 16,000 feet. The *Glomar Explorer* began operations on July 4, 1974. During the next 30 days it only managed to raise the forward section of the

submarine. No report of what was found has ever been released, but it is suspected that none of the Soviet SS-N-5 "Serb" submarine-launched ballistic missiles were recovered, as they are carried in a special compartment amidships of the submarine. It is believed that at least one nuclear-tipped torpedo was recovered.

The *Glomar Explorer* was turned over to the Navy in 1976. Transferred to the Maritime Administration the following year, all attempts to sell the ship or use it as a deep-sea drilling ship failed. The ship was mothballed as part of the National Defense Reserve Fleet at Suisan Bay, California.

The deep submergence support ship *Point Loma* (T-AGDS 1) was built in the late 1950s as the *Point Barrow*. In its original role it functioned as a "wet well deck" cargo ship that carried equipment and supplies to American Distant Early Warning (DEW) line radar installations in the Arctic Ocean. Between 1965 and 1970, the ship carried the Saturn rocket and other rockets from their manufacturer in California to Cape Kennedy. The *Point Loma* also hauled landing craft to Vietnam during the Vietnam War.

The ship was mothballed in 1971 but was returned to active duty in 1973 as part of the Military Sealift Command. The following year operations were begun to convert the ship to a deep submergence support ship, to be used in support of the deep diving bathyscaphe *Trieste II*. When the *Trieste II* was retired in 1986, the *Point Loma* was operated as support ship for tests involving the Trident submarine-launched missile.

KINGSPORT HYDROGRAPHIC RESEARCH SHIP (AG)

Operational (commissioned):	T-AG 164 *Kingsport* (June 1944)
Displacement:	10,680 tons
Dimensions:	
Length:	455 ft.
Width:	62 ft.
Draft:	22 ft.
Propulsion:	One steam turbine, 8,500 hp
Speed:	15 knots (17.5 mph)
Crew:	69

USS POINT LOMA DEEP SUBMERGENCE SHIP (AGDS)

Operational (commissioned):	T-AGDS 1 *Point Loma* (February 1976)
Displacement:	9,478 tons
Dimensions:	
Length:	465.5 ft.
Width:	74 ft.
Draft:	22.5 ft.
Propulsion:	Two Westinghouse steam turbines, 6,000 hp
Speed:	14.7 (17 mph)
Crew:	44

The Kingsport, *a hydrographic research ship, was originally built to carry military cargoes.*

Service Craft and Small Craft

Publicly and before those that control the purse strings in Congress, the U.S. Navy has repeatedly claimed that its long-term goal is to build a 600-ship Navy. The argument could be made, however, that this goal has not only been achieved, it has been far surpassed. At least 450 vessels are found in the category known as "service craft"; at least 3,000 vessels are classified as "small craft."

Service craft and small craft encompass a host of varying job responsibilities, operations, and missions. For the most part, these vessels of World War II-vintage were produced in such limited numbers that the Navy isn't sure where to place them in the fleet hierarchy. Despite the Navy's uncertainty in this regard, it should be noted

that these vessels serve a worthwhile and often vital role. It should also be noted that they are operated by crews as competent and dedicated as those found on high-profile warships. In a figurative sense, service craft and small craft are the grease that keeps the big wheels of the Navy turning. Without the support of ships and vessels that do everything from removing garbage and driving underwater piles, to ·fueling warships and shuttling fleet commanders between ship and shore, the Navy would lack the vital infrastructure needed to keep it afloat and running.

Support vessels and related equipment include the following: AFDB floating dry docks; AFDL small auxiliary floating dry docks; AFDM medium auxiliary floating dry

docks; APL barracks craft; ARD auxiliary repair dry docks; ARDM submarine support docks; YAG miscellaneous auxiliary yard craft; YC open lighters; YCF car float; YCV aircraft transportation lighters; YD floating cranes; YDT diving tenders; YF covered lighters; YFB ferryboats; YFNB large covered lighters; YFND dry dock companion craft; YFNX special-purpose lighters; YFP floating power barges; YFRN refrigerated cargo lighters; YFRT covered lighter range tenders; YFU harbor utility craft; YGN garbage lighters; YHLC salvage lift craft heavy; YM dredges; YNG gate craft; YO fuel-oil lighters; YOG gasoline lighters; YOGN gasoline barges; YON fuel-oil barges; YOS oil-storage barges; YP patrol craft/ training tenders; YPD floating pile drivers; YRB repair and

berthing barges; YRBM repair, berthing and messing barges; YRDH floating dry dock/ workshop hull; YRDM floating dry dock/workshop machinery; YRR radiological repair barges; YRST salvage craft tender; YSD seaplane wrecking derricks; YSR sludge-removal barge; YTB large harbor tugs; YTL small harbor tug; YTT torpedo trial ships; YW water barges.

Those vessels that are considered part of the Navy's 3,000 pieces of floating equipment and are not assigned an official name or hull number include everything from the Naval Academy's rowing shells up through significantly larger vessels. They include the following: TWR torpedo retrievers; TR torpedo retrievers; DR drone retrievers; and the 50WB work boats.

Yard patrol craft (YP) like the one shown here are assigned to the Naval Academy to train midshipmen in the fundamentals of seamanship.

SUBMARINES

The submarine is as old as the United States itself. In America's Revolutionary War, a crude, human-powered submersible craft named the *Turtle* unsuccessfully attacked a British warship in New York Harbor; in the Civil War, the Confederate submarine *Hunley* sank the Federal sloop *Housatonic*. During World War II, American submarines established a devastatingly effective blockade around the Japanese home islands that all but destroyed Japan's merchant fleet and inflicted considerable losses on its Navy.

The Navy's fleet of ballistic missile submarines constitutes one leg of America's nuclear triad (land-based missiles and bombers carrying nuclear-tipped weapons constitute the triad's other two legs). These submarines are nicknamed "boomers," and are designated SSBN. To protect their own boomers, and to hunt down enemy missile-carrying submarines, the U.S. Navy has developed a special class of attack submarines, which are designated SSN and nicknamed "hunter/killers."

The numbers of active-duty boomers and hunter/killers vary from year to year as new submarines are commissioned, while older submarines are either retired, laid up for modifications, or deactivated to comply with arms control accords. In 1990 the submarine fleet constituted approximately 34 boomers, and approximately 90 hunter/killers. By the year 2,000, those numbers will have declined to around 20 ballistic missile submarines (all of the *Ohio* class), and perhaps 65 to 70 attack submarines.

Modern boomers and hunter/killers can operate at speeds comparable to those attained by surface ships, and dive to depths that would have crushed the hulls of earlier submarines. Moreover, today's submarines are so silent as to be virtually undetectable. In a sense, they are stealth systems that can make themselves, if not totally invisible, than at least extremely difficult to find. The advanced technology that has been fitted on the U.S. Navy's submarines reflect the increasingly important role these vessels play in the nation's defense.

1. Bridge
2. Captain's quarters
3. Officers' wardroom
4. Officer's quarters
5. Free flooding area
6. Forward torpedo room
7. Crew mess
8. Batteries
9. Crew quarters
10. Control room
11. Gyroscopic room
12. Missile tubes
13. Workshops
14. Engine
15. Aft hydroplane
16. Rudders
17. Multiblade propeller
18. Steering gear
19. Aft crew quarters
20. Generators
21. Heat exchanger
22. Reactor
23. Free flooding area
24. Missile control room
25. Navigation room
26. Radar
27. Radio antennas
28. Periscopes

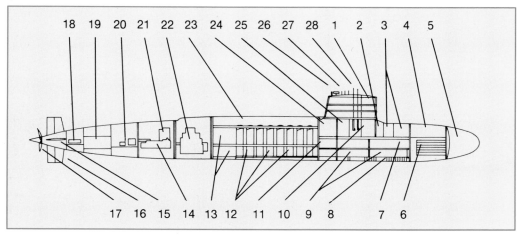

Left: *Schematic of a typical U.S. submarine, showing the location of major systems and weaponry.* **Main image, above:** *The L. Mendel Rivers, a* Sturgeon-*class attack submarine, cruises on the surface.* **Insets, clockwise from top:** *The* Sturgeon-*class* Whale *surfaces through the ice pack at the North Pole; artist's rendering of the Continental Navy submarine* Turtle *attacking a British warship during the Revolutionary war; draped with a lei, the* Los Angeles-*class* Honolulu *arrives in Pearl Harbor, Hawaii, after a tour of duty.*

BALLISTIC MISSILE SUBMARINES

Armed with 16 or 24 nuclear-tipped missiles (with ranges varying between 4,000 and 5,000 miles), *each one* of the Navy's ballistic missile submarines has more firepower in its nuclear arsenal than all the armies and navies of World War I and World War II combined.

Ballistic missile submarines can trace their roots to the waning days of World War II. At that time, Nazi German naval leaders were planning to bombard American cities with V-2 ballistic missiles housed in canisters that were to be towed across the Atlantic by U-boats. Fortunately for the Allies, this scheme was never put into practice. But it did lead, eventually, to the development of the U.S. Navy's first ballistic missile-carrying submarines, the submarines of the *George Washington* class.

The five submarines of the *George Washington* class, which were developed in the late 1950s and early 1960s, were lengthened versions of the *Skipjack*-class hunter/killer submarines. They were followed in 1961 by the five submarines of the *Ethan Allen* class, which were the U.S. Navy's first purpose-built SSBNs. Like the *George Washington* submarines, the *Ethan Allen* boomers carried the Polaris ballistic missile. The *George Washington* and *Ethan Allen* submarines are no longer in service.

The Navy currently deploys two boomer classes, the *Lafayette/ Benjamin Franklin* and *Ohio* classes. Although the *Benjamin Franklin* submarines are upgraded versions of the *Lafayette* submarines, both submarine types share the same essential design; they are therefore regarded as being in the same class. The submarines of the *Ohio* class are the Navy's newest, most powerful, and most technologically advanced

boomers. The submarines of both classes are products of the Cold War, answering a need to establish a balance of power—and terror—to prevent the outbreak of a war far more horrifying than World War II. As one

leg of the U.S. military's triad of nuclear weapons systems, boomers are really nothing more than mobile launching pads that can roam—or hide—almost at will in the depths of the world's oceans.

Above: The Alabama, an Ohio-class ballistic missile submarine, goes out on partol. **Inset:** A look at the open missile tubes of the Ohio.

Lafayette-Class (SSBN) and Benjamin Franklin-Class (SSBN) Ballistic Missile Submarines

LAFAYETTE-CLASS AND BENJAMIN FRANKLIN-CLASS (ISSN) BALLISTIC MISSILE SUBMARINES

Operational (commissioned):

SSBN 616 USS *Lafayette* (April 1963)
SSBN 617 USS *Alexander Hamilton* (June 1963)
SSBN 619 USS *Andrew Jackson* (July 1963)
SSBN 620 USS *John Adams* (May 1964)
SSBN 622 USS *James Monroe* (December 1963)
SSBN 623 USS *Nathan Hale* (November 1963)
SSBN 624 USS *Woodrow Wilson* (December 1963)
SSBN 625 USS *Henry Clay* (February 1964)
SSBN 626 USS *Daniel Webster* (April 1964)
SSBN 627 USS *James Madison* (July 1964)
SSBN 628 USS *Tecumseh* (May 1964)
SSBN 629 USS *Daniel Boone* (April 1964)
SSBN 630 USS *John C. Calhoun* (September 1964)
SSBN 631 USS *Ulysses S. Grant* (July 1964)
SSBN 632 USS *Von Steuben* (September 1964)
SSBN 633 USS *Casimir Pulaski* (August 1964)
SSBN 634 USS *Stonewall Jackson* (August 1964)

Commissioned cont'd:

SSBN 635 USS *Sam Rayburn* (December 1964)
SSBN 636 USS *Nathaniel Greene* (December 1964)
SSBN 640 USS *Benjamin Franklin* (October 1965)
SSBN 641 USS *Simon Bolivar* (October 1965)
SSBN 642 USS *Kamehameha* (December 1965)
SSBN 643 USS *George Bancroft* (January 1966)
SSBN 644 USS *Lewis and Clark* (December 1965)
SSBN 645 USS *James K. Polk* (April 1966)
SSBN 654 USS *George C. Marshall* (April 1966)
SSBN 655 USS *Henry L. Stimson* (August 1966)
SSBN 656 USS *George Washington Carver* (June 1966)
SSBN 657 USS *Francis Scott Key* (December 1966)
SSBN 658 USS *Mariano G. Vallejo* (December 1966)
SSBN 659 USS *Will Rogers* (April 1967)

Displacement:	
Surfaced:	7,350 tons
Submerged:	8,250 tons
Dimensions:	
Length:	425 ft.
Width:	33 ft.
Draft:	29 ft.
Propulsion:	One S5W water-cooled, pressurized nuclear reactor, 15,000 hp
Speed:	20+ knots (23+ mph)
Diving depth:	984 ft.
Armament:	
All:	Four tubes for Mk 48 torpedoes
SSBN 616–636:	Sixteen Poseidon C-3 ballistic missiles
SSBN 640–659:	Sixteen Trident I C-4 ballistic missiles
Fire control:	Mk 88 fire control system Mk 113 fire control system
Surveillance radar:	Either BPS-11 or BPS-15
Sonar:	Either BQR-7, BQR-15, BQR-19, BQR-21, or BQS-4; exact information is classified
Crew:	142–147

Opposite, left: Lookouts stand watch on the diving planes of the John C. Calhoun, a Lafayette/Benjamin Franklin-class submarine. *Opposite, right:* Cutaway diagram showing the arrangement of missile tubes on a Lafayette/Benjamin Franklin-class submarine. The missile on the left is a Polaris A-3, no longer in use; on the right is a Poseidon C-3. In reality, a ballistic missile submarine would only be armed with one type of missile.

With a length of 425 feet and a displacement of just over 8,250 tons submerged, the *Lafayette* submarines are rather small when compared to other boomers. In terms of general layout and weapon/sensor packages, they are similar to the earlier *Ethan Allen*-class submarines. The *Lafayette* submarines differ from their predecessors in having larger missile tubes, and hulls that are 15 feet longer than the hulls of the *Ethan Allen* submarines. Otherwise, the two submarine types have the same dimensions.

When the first eight *Lafayette* submarines entered service, each submarine was armed with 16 Polaris A-2 missiles. These weapons carried a single nuclear warhead and had a range of only 1,500 nautical miles (1,700 miles). The next 23 submarines in the *Lafayette* class were armed with the Polaris A-3 missile, which had three warheads and a range of nearly 2,500 nautical miles (2,800 miles). In 1970, *Lafayette* submarines were retrofitted with the more potent Poseidon missile. The Poseidon has a range similar to the older Polaris A-3, but carries up to ten 150-kiloton warheads.

Not the most technologically advanced boomers in Navy service, *Lafayette* submarines can nevertheless dive to depths nearly equal to those that can be reached by the newer submarines of the *Ohio* class. They are powered by one S5W water-cooled, pressurized nuclear reactor producing 15,000 horsepower, and can move at submerged speeds of 20 knots (23 miles per hour) or faster.

Beginning in 1979, the Navy began extensive modifications on 12 *Lafayette* submarines. When work was completed in 1982, these submarines received the *Benjamin Franklin*-class designation. As part of their modification program, the *Benjamin Franklin* submarines received the Trident C-4 missile, which is far more capable than the Poseidon; two Mark 2 Ship's Inertial Navigation Systems; and upgraded commercial navigation systems/radars.

The *Lafayette* and *Benjamin Franklin* class were built at four different shipyards between 1963 and 1967. A total of 31 submarines were completed. To comply with the provisions of the unratified SALT II treaty limits, some of these submarines were decommissioned and removed from active inventory. Many others, still on active service, are slated for decommissioning and retirement as the United States plans further force reductions in the 1990s.

Ohio-Class (SSBN) Ballistic Missile Submarines

Since they first began entering service in 1981, the *Ohio*-class submarines have been on the cutting edge of technology in areas ranging from weapons and propulsion systems to sensors and sonars. Originally designed to replace the older *George Washington* and *Ethan Allen* boomer classes—which could not be converted to carry the Poseidon or Trident I—the *Ohio* submarines are the Navy's largest and most heavily armed submarines.

Such power derives from an armament consisting of 24 Trident I C-4 missiles. Each C-4 missile is 34 feet long, 6 feet 2 inches in diameter, and can carry up to eight 100-kiloton nuclear missiles over a distance of approximately 4,000 nautical miles (4,600 miles). The Trident II D-5 missile, which is scheduled to replace the C-4 in the late 1990s, will make the *Ohio* submarines even mightier than they already are. Each Trident D-5 missile carries eight Mark 5 Reentry Vehicles, and each Mark 5 carries a warhead with a 150-kiloton yield. The D-5 is 45.5 feet long, seven feet in diameter, and can strike within 390 feet of the center of its target after traveling 6,000 nautical miles (6,900 miles).

For defense, *Ohio* submarines have Mark 48 torpedoes, as well as an array of decoy, deception, and masking devices. Augmenting these devices is the ability to remain submerged for more than two months at a time. Once underwater, *Ohio*-class submarines are capable of attaining submerged speeds of 30 knots (35 miles per hour) or faster.

The *Ohio*-class submarines are 560 feet long, 42 feet wide, and displace 18,750 tons when submerged. They are powered by a General Electric S8G pressurized

OHIO-CLASS (SSBN) BALLISTIC MISSILE SUBMARINES

Operational (commissioned):	SSBN 726 USS *Ohio* (November 1981) SSBN 727 USS *Michigan* (September 1982) SSBN 728 USS *Florida* (June 1983) SSBN 729 USS *Georgia* (February 1984) SSBN 730 USS *Henry M. Jackson* (October 1984) SSBN 731 USS *Alabama* (May 1985) SSBN 732 USS *Alaska* (January 1986) SSBN 733 USS *Nevada* (August 1986) SSBN 734 USS *Tennessee* (December 1988) SSBN 735 USS *Pennsylvania* (September 1989)	**Commissioned cont'd:**	SSBN 743 (unnamed) (mid-1997) SSBN 744 (unnamed) (mid-1998) SSBN 745 (unnamed) (mid-1999)
		Displacement:	
		Surfaced:	16,765 tons
		Submerged:	18,750 tons
		Dimensions:	
		Length:	560 ft.
		Width:	42 ft.
		Draft:	36.5 ft.
Building:	SSBN 736 *West Virginia* (mid-1990) SSBN 737 *Kentucky* (early 1991) SSBN 738 *Maryland* (early 1992) SSBN 739 *Nebraska* (mid-1993) SSBN 740 (unnamed) (mid-1994)	**Propulsion:**	One General Electric S8G natural circulation nuclear reactor, 45,000 hp
		Speed:	30+ knots (35+ mph)
		Diving depth:	1,180+ ft.
		Armament:	Twenty-four Trident I C-4 or Trident II D-5 ballistic missiles Four tubes for Mk 48 torpedoes
		Fire control:	Mk 98 fire control system Mk 118 fire control system
Planned:	SSBN 741 (unnamed) (mid-1995) SSBN 742 (unnamed) (mid-1996)	**Surveillance radar:**	BPS-15
		Sonar:	BQQ-6, BQQ-9, BQS-13, BQS-15, BQR-15, or BQR-19; exact information is classified
		Crew:	157–160

nuclear reactor that produces up to 45,000 horsepower. The reactor drives two sets of turbines—one for high-speed operations, another for slow and silent maneuvering.

For fire control of its deadly missiles, *Ohio* submarines are equipped with two Mark 2 Ship's Inertial Navigation Systems, which receive targeting data via satellite relays to insure the missiles are accurately targeted. The *Ohio* submarines also carry

sophisticated listening devices, a towed array sonar system, hydrophone arrays for fire control, side-looking sonars for mapping the ocean floor, and a special sonar that allows the submarines to operate under the polar ice cap.

Before the end of the century, some 20 submarines of the *Ohio* class are expected to be in service. These submarines will form what is perhaps the key element of America's nuclear

triad. In the event of a sneak attack against land-based bomber aircraft or land-based long-range nuclear missiles, the *Ohio* submarines would be able to retaliate against enemy targets anywhere in the world with a total of 3,840 nuclear warheads. It is this awesome retaliatory capability that has made the *Ohio* submarines such an effective deterrent to war. Potential enemies of the United States will not attack this nation for the simple

reason that they do not want to be attacked—and destroyed—by the missiles of the *Ohio* submarines.

Below, left: A Trident submarine-launched ballistic missile emerges from the sea. Tridents arm the Ohio-*class and* Benjamin Franklin-*class submarines.* ***Below, right:*** *This front view of the* Ohio-*class* Georgia *shows the massive beam of these submarines.*

ATTACK SUBMARINES

In the event of war the foremost job of the Navy's attack, or "hunter/killer," submarines is to hunt down and destroy enemy ballistic missile submarines before the latter can launch their deadly cargo of nuclear-tipped missiles. Hunter/killer submarines may also be used to attack surface warships and merchant vessels, and to conduct clandestine operations involving the use of Sea-Air-Land (SEAL) teams. The submarines of the *Sturgeon* and *Los Angeles* classes are armed with land-attack Tomahawk long-range cruise missiles, which can be fired from the 21-inch torpedo tubes

Following the end of World War II, three classes of conventional diesel/electric-powered hunter/killer submarines were built. There were six *Tang*-class submarines, three *Barbel*-class submarines, and one submarine of the *Darter* class. None of these submarines remain in service.

The *Nautilus* was the world's first nuclear-powered submarine. Upon its completion in 1954, the *Nautilus* functioned primarily as a research submarine, although it was a fully active and capable hunter/killer submarine. The *Nautilus* was decommissioned in March 1980 and is now moored at Groton, Connecticut, as a memorial.

Similar in design to the *Nautilus*, the *Seawolf* was the U.S. Navy's second nuclear-powered submarine. It was launched in 1955 with a troublesome liquid metal-cooled nuclear reactor that was replaced in 1960 by a pressurized water reactor. The *Seawolf* is no longer in service.

The *Skate* class was the U.S. Navy's first class of nuclear-powered hunter/killers to have more than one submarine. Four submarines of this class were built between December 1957 and December 1959. All have been decommissioned.

The *Skipjack*-class submarines were built between April 1959 and October 1961. They were the first nuclear-powered submarines in U.S. Navy service that had a streamlined hull for high-speed operations. The *Skipjack* submarines could travel at a submerged speed of more than 30 knots. All have been taken out of active service.

Three classes of attack submarines are currently in service with the U.S.

Navy—the *Permit*, the *Sturgeon*, and the *Los Angeles* classes. The new *Seawolf* class has received funding for one submarine, which is currently building and due to be completed in the early-to-mid 1990s.

Above: *The* Los Angeles*-class attack submarine* Cincinnati *shows the flag.* **Inset:** *The* Skate, *no longer in service, was the name ship of the U.S. Navy's first class of nuclear attack submarines. It is shown here in a "polynya," or open space, in the Polar ice pack.*

Permit-Class (SSN) Attack Submarines

PERMIT-CLASS (SSN) ATTACK SUBMARINES

Operational (commissioned):	SSN 593 USS *Thresher* (Lost April 1963)
	SSN 594 USS *Permit* (May 1962)
	SSN 595 USS *Plunger* (November 1962)
	SSN 596 USS *Barb* (August 1963)
	SSN 603 USS *Pollack* (May 1964)
	SSN 604 USS *Haddo* (December 1964)
	SSN 605 USS *Jack* (March 1967)
	SSN 606 USS *Tinoba* (October 1964)
	SSN 607 USS *Dace* (April 1964)
	SSN 612 USS *Guardfish* (December 1966)
	SSN 613 USS *Flasher* (July 1966)
	SSN 614 USS *Greenling* (November 1967)
	SSN 615 USS *Gato* (January 1968)
	SSN 621 USS *Haddock* (December 1967)
Displacement:	
Surfaced:	3,750 tons
Submerged:	4,300 tons
Dimensions:	
Length:	278 ft.
Width:	31.6 ft.
Draft:	29 ft.
Propulsion:	Two steam turbines, 15,000 hp
	One S5W water-cooled, pressurized nuclear reactor
Speed:	27 knots (31 mph)
Diving depth:	1,300 ft.
Armament:	Four tubes for Mk 48 torpedoes, Harpoon antiship missiles, and mines
Fire control:	Mk 113 fire control system
Surveillance radar:	Either BPS-5, BPS-9, or BPS-15
Sonar:	Either BQQ-2 or BQQ-5
Crew:	127

It is practically a given in hunter/killer submarine design that slow submarines are fairly silent, while fast submarines are fairly noisy. Whether one hunter/killer type is preferable to another is an issue that has divided submarine ranks since the advent of undersea warfare.

Shortly after the Korean War, the Navy attempted to resolve the controversy by deploying two types of attack submarines. The first was to be a high-performance, high-speed (but relatively noisy) submarine (SSK) designed to work in conjunction with fleet operations. The second would be a silent but relatively slow stalker (SSKN) that would either sneak up on, or lie in wait for, an enemy's submarine force. After building the slow nuclear-powered *Tullibee* (SSKN), however, it became apparent to Navy planners that Congress would never provide the funds for two distinct hunter/killer classes. The Navy therefore attempted to combine the attributes of both speed and silence in the new *Thresher* submarine class. Now called the *Permit* class, this category of submarines was designed with an emphasis on antisubmarine warfare.

The nuclear-powered *Permit*-class submarines entered service in the early 1960s. They measure only 278 feet in length, and displace slightly less than 4,300 tons when submerged. Main propulsion is derived from a S5W water-cooled pressurized nuclear reactor that enables these

submarines to travel at speeds up to 27 knots (31 miles per hour). The hull design features a large spherical bow sonar system that necessitated the positioning of the torpedo tubes in the amidships area. Another design innovation involved the use of new steels in building the single pressure hull used on these submarines. The extra strength gained from such steels enabled *Permit* submarines to reach diving

The Permit-*class* Haddo, *with periscopes and radio antennas in the raised position.*

depths of more than 1,300 feet.

Instead of developing a new powerplant for the *Permit* class, the Navy decided to use an existing nuclear reactor in these submarines. The design phase was thus accelerated and, since the reactor was a known commodity, the risk of diving deep was minimized. However, the Navy was also forced to address concerns that the older reactor would result in lower-than-desired speeds for the *Permit* submarines. The sail was therefore redesigned to minimize drag, and thus increase speed. But this created new problems in the fitting of various mast-mounted sensors that came into use when the submarines were functioning in the attack role.

Permit submarines originally carried a mixed armament of conventional and nuclear torpedoes. The torpedoes could be fired from four 21-inch torpedo tubes that were angled outward at about ten degrees. Although built to launch torpedoes, the tubes were designed to fire the Navy's nuclear-tipped SUBROC antisubmarine missile as well. All SUBROC missiles have been removed from *Permit* submarines. They were to have been replaced by Sea Lance missiles, but budgetary constraints forced the cancellation of the Sea Lance program. Since 1976, all *Permit*-class submarines have been fitted to carry the Mark 48 torpedo. These same modifications also enable the submarines to carry Harpoon antiship missiles.

Five different shipbuilding yards were involved in the *Permit*-class building program, which lasted from 1961 through 1968. Including the *Thresher*, a total of 14 *Permit*-class submarines were constructed. As of 1990, ten remain in service.

Sturgeon-Class (SSN) Attack Submarines

STURGEON-CLASS (SSN) ATTACK SUBMARINES

Operational (commissioned):

SSN 637 USS *Sturgeon* (March 1967)
SSN 638 USS *Whale* (October 1968)
SSN 639 USS *Tautog* (August 1968)
SSN 646 USS *Grayling* (October 1969)
SSN 647 USS *Pogy* (May 1971)
SSN 648 USS *Aspro* (February 1969)
SSN 649 USS *Sunfish* (March 1969)
SSN 650 USS *Fargo* (January 1968)
SSN 651 USS *Queenfish* (December 1968)
SSN 652 USS *Puffer* (August 1969)
SSN 653 USS *Ray* (April 1967)
SSN 660 USS *Sand Lance* (September 1971)
SSN 661 USS *Lapon* (December 1967)
SSN 662 USS *Gurnard* (December 1968)
SSN 663 USS *Hammerhead* (June 1968)
SSN 664 USS *Sea Devil* (January 1969)
SSN 665 USS *Guitarro* (September 1972)
SSN 666 USS *Hawkbill* (February 1971)
SSN 667 USS *Begall* (June 1969)
SSN 668 USS *Spacefish* (August 1969)
SSN 669 USS *Seahorse* (September 1969)
SSN 670 USS *Finback* (February 1970)
SSN 672 USS *Pintado* (April 1971)
SSN 673 USS *Flying Fish* (April 1970)
SSN 674 USS *Trefang* (August 1970)
SSN 675 USS *Bluefish* (January 1971)

Commissioned cont'd:

SSN 676 USS *Billfish* (March 1971)
SSN 677 USS *Drum* (April 1972)
SSN 678 USS *Archerfish* (December 1971)
SSN 679 USS *Silversides* (May 1972)
SSN 680 USS *William H. Bates* (May 1973)
SSN 681 USS *Batfish* (September 1972)
SSN 682 USS *Tunny* (January 1974)
SSN 683 USS *Parche* (August 1974)
SSN 684 USS *Cavalla* (February 1973)
SSN 686 USS *L. Mendel Rivers* (February 1975)
SSN 687 USS *Richard B. Russell* (August 1975)

Displacement:	
Surfaced:	4,250 tons
Submerged:	4,780 tons
Dimensions:	
Length:	292 ft.
Width:	31.6 ft.
Draft:	29 ft.
Propulsion:	Two steam turbines, 15,000 hp One S5W water-cooled, pressurized nuclear reactor
Speed:	26 knots (30 mph)
Diving depth:	1,300 ft.
Armament:	Tomahawk cruise missiles (land-attack and antiship) Four tubes for Mk 48 torpedoes, Harpoon antiship missiles, and mines
Fire control:	Mk 117 fire control system
Surveillance radar:	Either BPS-14, BPS-15, or WLQ-4; exact information is classified
Sonar:	BQR-15 towed array Either BQQ-2 or BQQ-5
Crew:	107

The *Sturgeon*-class submarines represented an improvement over the *Permit* design. From the late 1960s until the introduction of the highly sophisticated *Los Angeles*-class hunter/killers, the *Sturgeon* submarines set the design standard by which all other attack submarines were compared.

Although these submarines had the same basic hull design as *Permit* submarines, they were given more internal space for the addition of new electronics. This extra space has come at the expense of performance. The *Sturgeon* submarines use the same S5W nuclear reactor found on the *Permit* class, yet displace 4,780 tons compared to *Permit*'s 4,300 tons. Accordingly, the *Sturgeon* submarines can attain a maximum submerged speed of 26 knots (30 miles per hour), which makes them slightly slower than the 27-knot (31 miles per hour) *Permit* submarines.

Sturgeon submarines have the BQQ-2 or BQQ-5 active/passive sonar. The sonar is mounted in the bow in a sphere some 15 feet in diameter. Compared to the *Permit* submarines, *Sturgeon* submarines have a larger attack center and control room, which are crowded with computer consoles and targeting equipment that enable the simultaneous engagement of multiple targets. The *Sturgeon* submarines also have a larger sail, which can accommodate more mast-mounted sensors. The sail-mounted diving planes can be rotated downward, thus enabling *Permit* submarines to surface and submerge through the ice in arctic regions.

The main armament of *Sturgeon* submarines consists of Mark 48 torpedoes, Harpoon antiship missiles, Tomahawk antiship and land-attack cruise missiles, and mines. The weapons are fired out of four bow tubes located amidships and angled ten degrees outward.

To minimize detection by enemy ships and submarines, several *Sturgeon* submarines are being fitted with noise-reducing anechoic hull coatings. All *Sturgeon* submarines are scheduled to be retired by the year 2,000.

The Sturgeon, *name ship of the* Sturgeon-*class of attack submarines.*

Los Angeles-Class (SSN) Attack Submarines

The nuclear-powered *Los Angeles* attack submarines are the world's deadliest hunter/killer submarines. Some Soviet hunter/killer types may be able to dive deeper, while others may run more quietly, but no single Soviet submarine can match the overall quieting and detection capabilities of the *Los Angeles* submarines.

Developed in the late 1960s, the *Los Angeles* submarines are large submarines with a hull length of 360 feet and a submerged displacement of 6,927 tons. They were designed to run quietly at speeds exceeding 31 knots (35.6 miles per hour). Such speeds are attained through the use of a water-cooled nuclear reactor, which drives two geared steam turbines producing 35,000 horsepower. An efficient reactor core design enables *Los Angeles* submarines to cruise without refueling for up to 13 years, as opposed to the seven- to ten-year refueling spans common to most attack submarines.

While on patrol, the *Los Angeles* submarines seek out Soviet submarines in order to chart their movements and identify their sonar characteristics. Should war break out between the United States and the Soviet Union, the *Los Angeles* submarines would use this information to attack the Soviet submarines. While stalking its prey, the submarine's sophisticated electronics, sonars, and sensors would serve as its eyes and ears. The entire bow section is taken up by the large active/passive BQQ-5 spherical sonar system that enables the *Los Angeles* submarine to detect and identify enemy targets. That information is then sent to the submarine's fire control system, which can simultaneously engage multiple targets with a variety of weapons.

Los Angeles submarines have a heavy armament to match their high performance capabilities. One of the most potent weapons in their arsenal is the long-range Tomahawk missile. Armed with either conventional or nuclear warheads, the Tomahawk Land-Attack Missile (TLAM) can be fired from the submarine's torpedo tubes at ground-based targets as far away as 1,400 miles. The Tomahawk Antiship Missile (TASM) can be fired at targets as far away as 250 nautical miles (287 miles). All *Los Angeles* submarines are armed with Mark 48 torpedoes, and some are armed with Harpoon antiship missiles.

It is expected that 62 *Los Angeles* submarines will be built. Of these, the second group of 31 (from SSN 719 *Providence* onwards) have been extensively redesigned. These submarines operate more quietly, and have under-ice and minelaying capabilities. They also have 12 vertical launch tubes for Tomahawk missiles installed between the pressure hull and the outer hull. Although the class is far from complete in terms of construction, it is already the most numerous class of nuclear submarine ever built.

LOS ANGELES-CLASS (SSN) ATTACK SUBMARINE

Operational (commissioned):

SSN 688 USS *Los Angeles* (November 1976)
SSN 689 USS *Baton Rouge* (June 1977)
SSN 690 USS *Philadelphia* (June 1977)
SSN 691 USS *Memphis* (December 1977)
SSN 692 USS *Omaha* (March 1978)
SSN 693 USS *Cincinnati* (June 1978)
SSN 694 USS *Groton* (July 1978)
SSN 695 USS *Birmingham* (December 1978)
SSN 696 USS *New York City* (March 1978)
SSN 697 USS *Indianapolis* (January 1980)
SSN 698 USS *Bremerton* (March 1981)
SSN 699 USS *Jacksonville* (May 1981)
SSN 700 USS *Dallas* (July 1981)
SSN 701 USS *La Jolla* (October 1981)
SSN 702 USS *Phoenix* (December 1981)
SSN 703 USS *Boston* (January 1982)
SSN 704 USS *Baltimore* (July 1982)
SSN 705 USS *City of Corpus Christi* (January 1983)
SSN 706 USS *Albuquerque* (May 1983)
SSN 707 USS *Portsmouth* (October 1983)
SSN 708 USS *Minneapolis-Saint Paul* (March 1984)
SSN 709 USS *Hyman G. Rickover* (September 1984)
SSN 710 USS *Augusta* (January 1985)
SSN 711 USS *San Francisco* (April 1981)
SSN 712 USS *Atlanta* (March 1982)

Commissioned cont'd:

SSN 713 USS *Houston* (September 1982)
SSN 714 USS *Norfolk* (May 1983)
SSN 715 USS *Buffalo* (November 1983)
SSN 716 USS *Salt Lake City* (May 1984)
SSN 717 USS *Olympia* (November 1984)
SSN 718 USS *Honolulu* (July 1985)
SSN 719 USS *Providence* (July 1985)
SSN 720 USS *Pittsburgh* (November 1985)
SSN 721 USS *Chicago* (September 1986)
SSN 722 USS *Key West* (September 1987)
SSN 723 USS *Oklahoma City* (June 1988)
SSN 724 USS *Louisville* (November 1986)
SSN 725 USS *Helena* (July 1987)
SSN 750 USS *Newport News* (June 1989)
SSN 751 USS *San Juan* (August 1988)
SSN 752 USS *Pasadena* (February 1989)
SSN 753 USS *Albany* (March 1989)
SSN 754 USS *Topeka* (October 1988)
SSN 755 USS *Miami* (1990)

Building:

SSN 756 USS *Scranton* (1991)
SSN 757 USS *Alexandria* (1991)
SSN 758 USS *Asheville* (1991)
SSN 759 USS *Jefferson City* (1992)
SSN 760 USS *Annapolis* (1992)
SSN 761 USS *Springfield* (1992)
SSN 762 USS *Columbus* (1993)

Commissioned cont'd:

SSN 763 USS *Santa Fe* (1994)
SSN 764 USS *Boise* (1992)
SSN 765 USS *Montpelier* (1993)
SSN 766 USS *Charlotte* (1993)
SSN 767 USS *Hampton* (1993)
SSN 768 USS *Hartford* (1994)
SSN 769 USS *Toledo* (1994)
SSN 770 USS *Tucson* (1994)
SSN 771 USS *Columbia* (1995)
SSN 772 USS *Greeneville* (1995)
SSN 773 USS *Cheyenne* (1997)

Displacement:	
Surfaced:	6,080 tons
Submerged:	6,927 tons
Dimensions:	
Length:	360 ft.
Width:	33 ft.
Draft:	32.3 ft.
Propulsion:	Two geared steam turbines, 35,000 hp
	One S6G water-cooled pressurized nuclear reactor
Speed:	31+ knots (35.6+ mph)
Diving depth:	1,475 ft.
Armament:	Tomahawk cruise missiles (land-attack and antiship)
	Four tubes for Mk 48 torpedoes, Harpoon antiship missiles, and mines
Fire control:	Either one Mk 113 or one Mk 117 fire control system; exact information is classified
Surveillance radar:	BPS-15A
Sonar:	Either BQQ-5A, BQQ-5D, BQS-5, BQR-15, or BSY-1
Crew:	127

Los Angeles-*class submarines like the* Providence, *pictured here, are the world's largest attack submarines. Designed to hunt down enemy submarines and surface warships, they can travel at submerged speeds in excess of 35 miles per hour.*

NAVAL AIRCRAFT

The Navy's aviation arm dates to 1911, when Congress approved the purchase of the first naval aircraft. Since then, naval aviation has grown in importance through two world wars, two large-scale conventional wars, and numerous smaller conflicts around the world. As it has grown in importance it has grown in size. At present the combined aviation arm of the United States Navy and Marine Corps (which is part of the Navy) is today the fourth largest air force in the world, with some 5,500 fixed wing aircraft and helicopters in its inventory.

These aircraft include the most modern fighters and attack aircraft flying anywhere in the world, supported by electronic warfare and countermeasures aircraft. Most of these aircraft are based on aircraft carriers, enabling them to strike at targets virtually anywhere in the world.

Specialized aircraft have been developed to search the seas for submerged enemy submarines, as well as surface fleets. These aircraft can range for thousands of miles or fly tight orbits around a cruising Navy task force.

The Navy and Marine Corp's helicopter force is one of the largest in the world. It includes every type of helicopter, from gunships to antisubmarine warfare aircraft.

The Naval aviation effort is supported by a wide range of utility aircraft, many of them capable of landing and taking off from aircraft carriers. These aircraft are used to carry troops and supplies, and to provision the fleets at sea. The Navy and Marine Corps also employ several aircraft types for basic undergraduate flight training, and for specialized post-graduate training.

Below: Schematic of a modern jet warplane, showing typical weaponry, equipment, and design.
Right: A tight formation of F-14 Tomcat fighters. Based on aircraft carriers, the F-14 is charged with protecting carrier task forces.

1. Cockpit 2. Radome 3. Tactical navigation electronics 4. Ordnance pylon 5. Sidewinder missile 6. Sparrow missile 7. Arrester hook 8. Elevator 9. Exhaust nozzle 10. Electronic countermeasures equipment 11. Vertical stabilizer 12. UHF/VHF antennas 13. Engine air intake

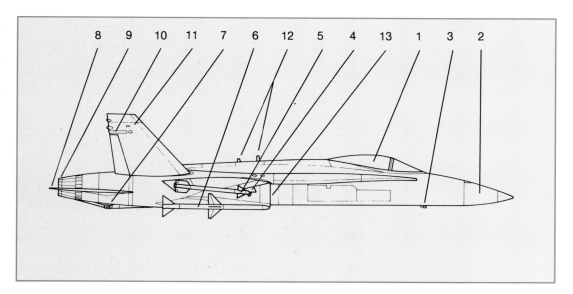

FIGHTERS

The task of fighter aircraft today is no different now than it has been in the past—intercept and destroy enemy aircraft. As was proven over and over in the early days of World War II, surface battle groups are vulnerable to air attack. But carrier-borne aircraft can stave off that threat and allow attack, reconnaissance, antisubmarine warfare, and electronic warfare aircraft to operate safely.

The F-14 Tomcat and the F/A-18 Hornet are the Navy's first-line fighter aircraft, and have replaced the venerable F-4 Phantom in the fighter role. Both the Tomcat and the Hornet can achieve supersonic speed and are very agile and can, if necessary, function in the attack bomber or reconnaissance roles.

Training fighter pilots is a high priority exercise within the Navy and Marine Corps. The F-16N Fighting Falcon and the F-5E Tiger are used by Navy and Marine Corps Adversary Squadrons to simulate Soviet fighter aircraft in training exercises.

An F-14 Tomcat fighter climbs for altitude after taking off from the aircraft carrier below. F-14s have proved their combat effectiveness by twice shooting down Libyan fighter aircraft over the Gulf of Sidra in the Mediterranean Sea.

F/A-18 Hornet

McDONNELL DOUGLAS F/A-18 HORNET	
Dimensions:	
Wingspan:	37 ft., 6 in.
Length:	56 ft.
Height:	15 ft, 3.5 in.
Weight (maximum take-off):	36,710 lbs.
Engines:	Two General Electric F404-GE-400 turbofans
Engine thrust:	16,000 lbs.
Operating altitude:	50,000+ ft.
Top speed:	1,190 mph
Maximum range:	2,303 miles
Date of service:	1982

The Hornet is a small, relatively low-cost, and highly maneuverable jet aircraft. This single-seat fighter can trace its beginnings to the Northrop YF-17, which was rejected by the Air Force in favor of the YF-16. It was designed to replace three aircraft: the A-6 Intruder, the A-7 Corsair, and the A-4 Skyhawk. A dual-role aircraft, the Hornet performs both as a close-in air-superiority fighter and as a strike fighter for the Navy and the Marine Corps. It thus may be used to provide air defense for aircraft carrier task forces, or ground support for Marine infantry units. In either case it is the same plane; the "F" and "A" designations simply describe its double role as fighter and attack jet.

Every piece of equipment in the Hornet has been designed and installed with the ease of repair and maintenance in mind. Each of the F/A-18's two General Electric turbofan engines can be replaced in less than 20 minutes, and avionics problems can be diagnosed through the use of hand-held computers that plug into special sockets throughout the aircraft. As a result of these design features, the Hornet is a low-maintenance aircraft that can significantly ease the burden on fleet and ground-based logistics systems.

The Hornet can fly at speeds in excess of 1,100 miles per hour at 40,000 feet and its service ceiling is over 50,000 feet. The two General Electric F404-GE-400 turbofans each provide 16,000 pounds of thrust.

In addition to the single-seat variant, the Navy has procured a large number of two-seat Hornets (F/A-18C/D). These aircraft have been developed to provide all-weather/night attack capabilities.

The F/A-18 Hornet entered Navy service in 1982 after making its first carrier flight in 1981. Several foreign countries such as Australia and Canada also selected the Hornet for their air forces due to its low cost and versatility. Another important factor in Canada's choice of the Hornet (designated CF-18) was that Canada—like the U.S. Navy—uses the "hose & drogue" method of aerial refueling, rather than the "flying boom" method used by the U.S. Air Force. The Hornet had the equipment for this option installed in the factory.

The Hornet's armament includes a 20 millimeter M61 Vulcan multibarrel cannon mounted on the top center of the nose. This mounting differs from the F-14, F-15, and F-16, which mount the cannon on the side of the fuselage. For attack/fighter-bomber missions, the F/A-18 Hornet can be armed with conventional or nuclear

bombs and AGM-88 HARM antiradar missiles or AGM-65 Maverick air-to-ground missiles. For its naval attack mission, the Hornet can also carry the AGM-109 Harpoon, a sea-skimming, antiship missile that is the Navy equivalent of the French-built Exocet. In its fighter configuration, the Hornet carries AIM-9 Sidewinder air-to-air missiles on wingtip racks.

When projecting the future role of the Hornet, the Marine Corps motto "First to Fight" comes to mind. The Navy and the Marine Corps are the leading edge of American military power worldwide. If the United States must "send in the Marines," the F/A-18 will be leading the way.

The F/A-18 is a dual mission aircraft. By changing its armament it can fly either air-superiority or ground-attack missions. In the ground-attack role, it provides close air support for the Marines; in the air superiority role, it establishes a close-in air defense for a carrier task force.

F-14 Tomcat

GRUMMAN F-14A/D TOMCAT	
Dimensions:	
Wingspan (unswept):	64 ft., 0.5 in.
Wingspan (swept):	38 ft., 2.5 in.
Length:	62 ft., 8 in.
Height:	16 ft.
Weight (maximum take-off):	74,349 lbs.
Engines:	Two General Electric F110-GE-400 turbofans
Engine thrust:	28,500 lbs.
Operating altitude:	50,000+ ft.
Top speed:	1,544 mph
Maximum range:	2,000 miles
Date of service:	
F-14A:	1972
F-14D:	1990

The F-14 Tomcat was designed as a fleet air-defense interceptor capable of serving into the 21st century. As the Navy's premier fighter aircraft, it is the latest in a long line of Grumman "carrier cats," which date back to before World War II. Tomcats are always present at Top Gun training sessions, and are often seen in the aggressor role in Red Flag exercises over the Nevada desert. Two Navy F-14 aircrews shot down two Libyan Su-22 fighters over the Gulf of Sidra in the Mediterranean Sea on August 19, 1981, when the latter attempted to attack the aircraft carrier *Nimitz*. On January 4, 1989, two F-14 crews from the carrier *John F. Kennedy* shot down a pair of Libyan MiG-23s in the same area. The American crews had all undergone Top Gun training at the Naval Fighter Weapons School, Miramar Naval Air Station, California.

The F-14 evolved in the late 1960s, when the Navy dropped out of the multi-service, multipurpose TFX (tactical fighter, experimental) program and began work on an aircraft dedicated solely to fleet air defense. Since the F-14 was being developed by Grumman, it would be a "Cat," and since the man behind the project was Vice Admiral Tom Connolly, then Deputy Chief of Naval Operations for Air, the new airplane was instantly called "Tom's Cat."

The Tomcat first flew in 1970. Four years later the first two F-14 carrier squadrons—VF-1 Wolfpack and VF-2 Bounty Hunters— became operational aboard the carrier *Enterprise*. Nearly 400 Tomcats are operational today on Navy carriers.

Like the TFX, which became the Air Force F-111, the F-14 Tomcat has variable-geometry wings that can change angle in flight to match altitude conditions and speed. The wings may be swept forward to a nearly straight position for slow-speed operations like aircraft carrier landings, or swept back for such high-speed operations as supersonic dashes to catch enemy aircraft.

The Tomcat is a *big* but agile aircraft that is capable of out-turning and out-maneuvering the smaller and older F-4 Phantom. Most of its pilots agree that it is a joy to fly. Like the Phantom, the Tomcat carries a crew of two. Like the F-4's weapons system operator, the Tomcat backseater operates the complex offensive radar and weapons systems. The Tomcat is armed with a 20 millimeter cannon, as well as an assortment of guided missiles. The latter includes AIM-9 Sidewinders and the new AIM-120 AMRAAM air-to-air missile.

The centerpiece of the Tomcat arsenal is its array of

six AIM-54 Phoenix air-to-air missiles. The Phoenix was designed for the F-14 and is unique to it. Developed by Hughes Aircraft at the same time that Grumman was developing the Tomcat, the Phoenix has the longest range—over 100 miles—of any air-to-air missile in U.S. service. The combined range capability of the Tomcat and Phoenix means that enemy aircraft armed with antiship missiles could, theoretically, be intercepted and shot

down before they could get close enough to endanger the American fleet.

The F-14A was the earliest version of the Tomcat. It was powered by two Pratt & Whitney TF-30-P-412A turbofan engines with afterburners, each delivering 20,900 pounds of thrust. Plans to build a more powerful B and C model were canceled. In 1984, the decision was made to upgrade the F-14A with two General Electric F110-GE-

400s, which provide 28,500 pounds of thrust. The new engines provide more power and extend the Tomcat's combat range as well. The F110 engines are also installed on the F-14D, which has had some 60 percent of is avionics updated as well.

The F-14 Tomcat is such a powerful, agile bird that few enemies have tried to knock the chip off the Tomcat's shoulder. And when they have, they were invariably shot down.

The F-14 Tomcat is the U.S. Navy's premier air-superiority fighter. It carries a wide range of weapons, including up to six Phoenix air-to-air missiles (seen here), two Sidewinder air-to-air missiles, and a 20 millimeter multibarrel cannon.

F-16 Fighting Falcon

GENERAL DYNAMICS F-16N FIGHTING FALCON	
Dimensions:	
Wingspan:	31 ft.
Length:	49 ft., 3 in.
Height:	16 ft., 8.5 in.
Weight (maximum take-off):	37,500 lbs.
Engine:	One General Electric F110-GE-100 turbofan
Engine thrust:	29,000 lbs.
Operating altitude:	50,000 ft.
Top speed:	1,350 mph
Maximum range:	2,415 miles
Date of service:	1984

While the F-16 Fighting Falcon is widely used by the Air Force as a fighter, the Navy has purchased 26 specially configured F-16Cs for use as adversary aircraft in Dissimilar Aerial Combat Training (DACT) exercises. Four of these aircraft are two-seat trainers. All are designated F-16N (Navy), and simulate late-model Soviet fighters. The F-16Ns carry wingtip launchers for practice AIM-9 missiles, but have removed their M61A1 20mm cannons for cameras. They are fitted with the APG-66 radar used in the Air Force's F-16A/B fighters. The F-16Ns also have the more powerful General Electric F110-GE-100 turbofan delivering 29,000 pounds of thrust. These Navy fighters are not equipped for aircraft carrier landings. But as Soviet fighter simulators, they are just what the Navy needs for Top Gun training in DACT exercises.

The F-16 was originally developed to replace the Air Force F-4 Phantom. Advanced computer-controlled "fly-by-wire" controls have made the F-16 the most maneuverable fighter yet built. Additional advanced technology has been used throughout this aircraft, including carbon fiber composites to replace metal skin panels to reduce drag and weight. The F-16 is equipped with automatic variable-wing leading-edge flaps and the powerful Pratt & Whitney F100-PE-220 or General Electric F110-GE-100 turbofans.

The idea behind the F-16 was to build a large number of lightweight, low-cost fighters to augment the squadrons of larger, more expensive (albeit more capable) F-15s. The F-16 was also designed to meet the needs of several NATO countries that were about to replace their aging Lockheed F-104 Starfighters. The new aircraft was to be coproduced by American and European factories as a NATO fighter. In 1974, the Air Force conducted a fly-off between the General Dynamics YF-16 and the Northrop YF-17 aircraft and picked the former.

The Fighting Falcon is a jack-of-all-trades. Like its namesake, the mascot of the U.S. Air Force Academy at Colorado Springs, it is a swift, agile aircraft. Yet since it is also capable of carrying heavy bomb loads to a maximum of 33,000 pounds, it is suitable for the fighter-bomber as well as the interceptor role. Pilots accustomed to the hydraulic control system on aircraft like the F-4 are usually pleasantly surprised by their F-16 flight. The Fighting Falcon's control surfaces are entirely fly-by-wire, meaning that the work once done by hydraulics is now done in the F-16 by a computerized network of

electric motors. This makes the F-16 much more responsive and has led to its nickname: "The Electric Jet."

Like the larger F-15, the F-16 Fighting Falcon is a one-seat aircraft. However, a number of combat-capable two-seaters have been built that function as training aircraft. In its interceptor mode, the Air Force Fighting Falcon can carry the AIM-9 Sidewinder and AIM-120 AMRAAM air-to-air missiles. Equipped as a strike fighter, the Fighting Falcon carries a variety of air-to-ground ordnance including conventional and nuclear bombs, the AGM-65 Maverick rocket, and the AGM-45 Shrike and AGM-88 HARM antiradar missiles. Like all post-Vietnam American fighters, the F-16 is also equipped with an M61A1 20 millimeter multibarrel cannon.

If the contoured lines and advanced digital technology of the F-16 make it seem like something out of a science fiction movie, its selection for the Advanced Fighter Technology Integration program represents a merger of science fiction and reality. The F-16 provides a window on future fighter technology.

The F-16N is the Navy's newest fighter, and is flown by Top Gun instructors in the aggressor role. Here, a pair of Navy F-16Ns with "foreign" markings are shown engaging an F-14 Tomcat fighter.

F-5 Tiger

NORTHROP F-5E TIGER	
Dimensions:	
Wingspan:	26 ft., 8 in.
Length:	47 ft., 3.75 in.
Height:	13 ft., 4.25 in.
Weight (maximum take-off):	24,722 lbs.
Engines:	Two General Electric J85-GE-21 turbojets
Engine thrust:	5,000 lbs.
Operating altitude:	51,800 ft.
Top speed:	1,077 mph
Maximum range:	1,543 miles
Date of service:	1973

The F-5 was developed in the late 1950s as an inexpensive, single-seat supersonic fighter that the U.S. government could buy at low cost and transfer to allied nations under the Military Assistance Program (MAP). It was never intended to serve with American Forces. Today, however, in addition to serving with nations around the world, the F-5 also serves in the Navy and U.S. Air Force Aggressor squadrons for post-graduate training programs.

The first F-5 was based on Northrop's Model N-156, which was in turn based on the Northrop T-38 supersonic trainer. The first N-156 prototype was ready in 1957, but intragovernmental disagreements over the parameters of the program kept the F-5, which was nicknamed the "Freedom Fighter," out of production until 1961. Nevertheless, the F-5 Freedom Fighter concept was a success; the F-5 sold for less than one-third the price of the contemporary F-4 Phantom, and it could

perform on equal terms with the Soviet MiG aircraft.

In 1964 Iran and South Korea became the first nations to purchase the F-5. They were soon followed by the Philippines and Taiwan. Pakistan and Libya received F-5s under MAP, as did such NATO countries as Norway, the Netherlands, Greece, and Turkey. The Freedom Fighter received its baptism of fire in 1965, when American pilots flew them in combat in Vietnam before turning them over to the South Vietnamese Air Force.

It was in the Far East that the F-5 acquired its "Tiger" name. There they became known as "Skoshi Tiger," or "Little Tiger," because of their size and tenacity. Little Tiger was also their code name for deployment to South Vietnam. Tiger became an official name for the aircraft in 1973, after the F-5E (and dual-control F-5F) was introduced. More than 1,200 F-5As and dual control F-5Bs were built, and more than 1,400 F-5E and F-5F Tigers were built through 1987.

The Navy's F-5s are unarmed, since they function solely in a training role. The Air Force F-5s have a main armament that consists of a pair of 20 millimeter cannons, each with 280 rounds of ammunition. Sidewinder air-to-air missiles can be carried in wingtip racks, and underwing pylons can heft an impressive 3.5 tons of

bombs, electronic countermeasure pods, and AGM-65 Maverick missiles.

The Air Force has not shown a great deal of enthusiasm for the F-5. Most of the original F-5s the Air Force bought were for export. There were no operational F-5 units in the Air Force until 1975. In that year the Air Force found itself with more

than 100 F-5s that could not be delivered to the South Vietnamese Air Force because South Vietnam had ceased to exist.

At about the same time, both the Air Force and the Navy post-graduate training courses for fighter pilots needed an aircraft that could simulate the Soviet MiG-21— a small, fast, and agile fighter for Dissimilar Aerial Combat Training (DACT) exercises. The F-5E Tiger was the answer. Since there were no F-5 squadrons in American service, the F-5E and its flight characteristics were unfamiliar to Navy and Air Force pilots. The F-5E quickly became a favorite aggressor aircraft for Red Flag and Top Gun exercises.

The Northrop F-5E Tiger was built as a follow-on to the F-5A Freedom Fighter. The F-5E flies with Air Force Aggressor squadrons and the Navy's Top Gun School. The aircraft is used for Dissimilar Aerial Combat Training (DACT).

ATTACK AIRCRAFT

T he principal mission of Navy attack aircraft is to kill enemy ships. Attack aircraft, both Navy and Marine, also provide close support for ground troops and fly bombing missions against a variety of enemy positions. These might include troop concentrations, transportation and communication facilities, and manufacturing and production concerns deep inside enemy territory. The attack pilot is often called upon to fly at tree-top level where he is vulnerable to small arms fire.

All Navy and Marine Corps attack aircraft and crews are qualified for carrier takeoffs and landings. All can also operate from fixed ground bases, and the AV-8B Harrier can operate from hastily prepared forward bases that are little more than cleared areas protected from enemy ground fire.

By 1992, it is expected that Navy attack squadrons will have replaced their A-7 Corsairs with F/A-18 Hornets. The primary Navy attack plane is the A-6E Intruder, which is expected to remain in service beyond the turn of the century. The Department of Defense is planning to replace the A-6E with the A-12 Advanced Tactical Aircraft, which is scheduled to enter service in the late 1990s.

In the Marine Corps, attack squadrons flying the A-4 Skyhawk are replacing these aircraft with either the F/A-18 Hornet or the AV-8B Harrier, while those squadrons flying the A-6E Intruder are switching to the F/A-18 Hornet.

An A-7 Corsair from the 23rd Tactical Air Wing drops a load of bombs that use fin-like devices to slow their rate of descent. Note the artwork on the jet intake.

AV-8B Harrier

McDONNELL DOUGLAS AV-8B HARRIER	
Dimensions:	
Wingspan:	30 ft., 3.5 in.
Length:	42 ft., 10 in.
Height:	11 ft., 3.5 in.
Weight (maximum take-off):	29,750 lbs.
Engine:	One Rolls-Royce F402-RR-406 turbofan
Engine thrust:	21,500 lbs.
Operating altitude:	51,000 ft.
Top speed:	662 mph
Maximum range:	1,550 miles
Date of service:	1983

Soon after World War II, a number of nations began to develop a Vertical/Short Take-off and Landing (VSTOL) combat aircraft that could combine the flight characteristics of helicopters and fixed wing aircraft. In 1960 Hawker Aircraft in England successfully test flew their Model P.1127. Called the Kestrel, its production version performance did not live up to expectations. But it was the first operational VSTOL aircraft in the world.

By 1968 the Kestrel had evolved into the Harrier, a more practical and versatile VSTOL aircraft. The following year, Royal Air Force Harriers took part in the *Daily Mail* London-to-New York air race. Although their six-hour flight time did not set any speed records, it was presentable. More importantly, the Harriers were the only planes in the race to land *in* Manhattan.

The U.S. Marine Corps was very interested in using VSTOL aircraft that could be based on assault ships as well as aircraft carriers for close air support of amphibious operations. The Marine Corps subsequently ordered 102 single-seat Harriers and eight two-seat trainer variants. Designated the AV-8A and TAV-8A Harrier, in 1971 they became the first fixed wing VSTOL aircraft in regular U.S. service.

In 1975 McDonnell Douglas developed an improved Harrier, originally designated AV-8B and named Harrier II, that had a larger wing that nearly doubled the aircraft's range and payload. New and larger trailing-edge wing flaps were added along with stronger landing gear, redesigned engine air intakes, and a more powerful Rolls Royce F402-RR-406 Pegasus 11 Mark 103 turbofan engine. This new engine, which delivers 21,500 pounds of thrust, is twice as powerful as the earlier engine and enables the Harrier to carry twice the payload. A training version, dubbed the TAV-8B, has an enlarged fuselage for a second cockpit occupied by the instructor.

The AV-8B is armed with a 25 millimeter GAU-12/U multibarrel cannon in an external pack. A second external pack carries 150 rounds of ammunition. The Harrier can also carry up to sixteen 500 pound bombs or four AIM-9L Sidewinder air-to-air missiles or four Maverick AGM-65 air-to-surface missiles and two Sidewinders. By 1982, a joint manufacturing agreement had been worked out between British Aerospace (which had absorbed Hawker) and McDonnell

Douglas whereby the American company would produce the upgraded VSTOL aircraft.

The Harrier received its baptism of fire, and more than proved its worth, in the Falkland Islands war of 1982. When the Falklands were invaded by Argentina in April of that year, the British task force sent to retake the islands used carrier-borne Harriers. These so-called "jump jets" flew more than 2,000 attack missions and shot down at least 20 enemy aircraft without a single loss.

Today's U.S. Marine Corps AV-8B Harriers would fly and fight in much the same way the British Harriers did in the Falklands: in support of a joint Navy/Marine Corps amphibious assault landing or in the context of Marine operations ashore.

An AV-8B Harrier executes a vertical landing aboard an aircraft carrier. In the background are F-14 Tomcats and A-6E Intruders.

A-7 Corsair

LTV (LING-TEMCO-VOUGHT) A-7E CORSAIR	
Dimensions:	
Wingspan:	38 ft., 9 in.
Length:	46 ft., 1.5 in.
Height:	16 ft., 0.75 in.
Weight (maximum take-off):	42,000 lbs.
Engine:	One Allison TF41-A-2 turbofan
Engine thrust:	15,000 lbs.
Operating altitude:	42,600 ft.
Top speed:	691 mph
Maximum range:	2,861 miles
Date of service:	1969

The A-7 Corsair was developed from the Vought F8U Crusader, which served as one of the Navy's top carrier fighters before and during the Vietnam War. The Corsair was designed and built as a subsonic light-attack plane to replace the Navy's A-4 Skyhawk by carrying twice the weight of ordnance. Vought, which merged with Ling-Temco in 1961, won the contract by suggesting a compact aircraft based on the F-8. The contractor was allowed four years to design, develop, flight test, and qualify the new aircraft, which LTV did in 1967. The A-7 flew for the first time on December 27, 1965 and the first deliveries were made to the Navy on September 13, 1966. The first A-7A Corsair, belonging to VA-147 Squadron on the carrier *Ranger*, went into action off the coast of Vietnam on December 3, 1967, almost two years to the day after the aircraft's first flight.

An improved version, the A-7B Corsair, entered service in early 1968. This version was equipped with the Pratt & Whitney TF30-P-8 turbojet engine delivering 12,200 pounds of thrust.

Even as A-7 deliveries to the Navy were getting under way, Secretary of Defense Robert S. McNamara directed

the Air Force to procure these aircraft. This was done, despite Air Force opposition to the A-7. Designated the A-7D, the Air Force version had a more powerful Allison/ Rolls Royce TF41-A-1 turbofan engine, which delivered 14,250 pounds of thrust.

The Navy soon decided that their A-7 also needed a more powerful engine—an engine that would enable the Corsair to increase its range and payload on close air support and air interdiction missions. The aircraft that answered this need were based on the Air Force A-7D version. The first 67 aircraft used the Pratt & Whitney TF30 engine and were designated the A-7C. Beginning with aircraft number 68, the designation changed to A-7D. These aircraft used the same Allison engine that was installed in the Air Force's A-7D. They entered service in July 1967. All earlier aircraft in service were upgraded to the E configuration.

The final American combat mission in Southeast Asia was flown by Air Force A-7Ds against targets in Cambodia on August 15, 1973. The A-7 proved to be a very reliable, stable performer. The Air Force, for example, flew 2,928 Corsair missions in Southeast Asia—including many against targets in heavily defended North Vietnam—with only four losses.

The Corsair is a single-seat aircraft, although 60 models have been converted to two-seat combat-capable trainers that can be used in the attack role. The aircraft can carry nearly eight tons of bombs and two AIM-9L Sidewinder air-to-air missiles. The Corsair also has the M61A1 Vulcan 20 millimeter cannon and 1,000 rounds of ammunition. The A-7E is also equipped with the APQ-126(V) multimode radar for search, tracking, and fire control.

A total of 1,551 Corsairs were built when production ended in 1983. Of that number, 997 went to the Navy and 490 went to the Air Force. The rest were purchased by Greece. The A-7 was not flown by the Marine Corps, which flew the A-4 Skyhawk in the attack role.

A few carrier air wings have two squadrons of A-7 Corsairs. The A-7s replaced the A-4 Skyhawk in the light-attack role, and they in turn are being replaced by the F/A-18 Hornet strike fighter.

Below: A heavily bomb-laden A-7 Corsair takes off. ***Below, left:*** A crewman on the Nimitz inspects the massive intake of an A-7 Corsair.

A-6 Intruder

GRUMMAN A-6E INTRUDER	
Dimensions:	
Wingspan:	53 ft.
Length:	54 ft., 9 in.
Height:	16 ft., 2 in.
Weight (maximum take-off):	60,400 lbs.
Engines:	Two Pratt & Whitney J-52-P-8B turbojet engines
Engine thrust:	9,300 lbs.
Operating altitude:	42,400 ft.
Top speed:	644 mph
Maximum range:	2,740 miles
Date of service:	1963

Below: A bird's-eye view of an A-6E Intruder, showing the side-by-side seating arrangement. *Right, top:* Wings still folded, an A-6E taxis into position for takeoff. *Right, bottom:* An A-6E displays another facet of its offensive capabilities by launching a Tomahawk cruise missile.

The A-6 Intruder is a versatile medium-attack aircraft with all-weather, day-night attack capabilities. At least one A-6 squadron is attached to each carrier wing now in operation.

The A-6 is a two-seat aircraft that carries a side-by-side seating arrangement. The pilot occupies the left seat, while the weapons system operator/navigator occupies the seat on the right. The aircraft was developed to answer the Navy's need for an all-weather attack plane with an eight-ton bomb load that could support both Navy and Marine Corps operations. Built by Grumman, one of the leading builders of American carrier-based aircraft for the last half century, the Intruder was first flown in April 1960. Today, new Intruder acquisitions are still part of the Navy's budget.

The basic Intruder version was the A-6A, of which 484 were built. Many of these were in turn converted or adapted for roles other than ground attack, including 58 that were converted to KA-6D aerial tankers.

The Intruder (A-6E configuration) is powered by two Pratt & Whitney J52-P-8B turbojets delivering 9,300 pounds of thrust each. It has a 1,012 mile range with full combat load of 30 500-pound bombs, or ten 1,000-pound bombs, or three 2,000-pound bombs. In all, the aircraft can carry up to 18,000 pounds of bombs on exterior hardpoints.

The most numerous version of the Intruder is the A-6E, which was born in 1970 as a converted A-6A. More than 300 A-6Es were eventually ordered. All A-6Es have since been converted into A-6E/TRAMs (Target Recognition and Attack Multisensor). TRAM's electronics, which are carried in a turret located under the nose, include infrared- and laser-targeting sensors and multimode radar. The lasers are used in conjunction with laser-guided weapons. The TRAM system in an A-6E can illuminate a target with a laser while a second A-6E launches weapons against it, using the first A-6E's laser reflection to guide the projectile. In addition to laser-guided munitions, the A-6E can carry "iron" bombs and AGM-84 Harpoon antiship missiles. The A-6E can also carry AIM-9 Sidewinders to defend itself from hostile aircraft. A bomb load may consist of up to 30 500-pound bombs, and the maximum combined load of ordnance and drop tanks is 18,000 pounds.

The newest Intruder variant is the A-6F, which is powered by two General Electric T04-GE engines that deliver 10,800 pounds of thrust (12,000 pounds in upgraded versions).

Another A-6 variant in Navy service is the EA-6B, or "Prowler." This is an electronic warfare aircraft with a crew of four. In order to accommodate the additional two crew members (who operate electronic-countermeasures hardware), the Prowler is five feet longer than the Intruder.

Attack missions flown by Intruders against targets protected by radar-directed missiles would include a Prowler to confuse the enemy and give the A-6Es a chance to slip in and do their work. The Intruder/Prowler team, because they use the same basic aircraft, are an ideal carrier-borne combination from the standpoint of maintenance, as well as operations.

Yet another Intruder variant, the KA-6D, serves as a carrier-based refueling plane. All KA-6D tankers were converted from earlier A-6 attack aircraft. Some of their avionics systems were removed, and a hose-and-drogue refueling system was installed along with two more 500 gallon wing-mounted drop tanks. Altogether, a KA-6D tanker could transfer up to 21,000 pounds of fuel immediately upon takeoff, or 15,000 pounds of fuel at any distance up to 288 nautical miles from the carrier. Some 60 KA-6D tankers are currently in service with the Navy and Marine Corps. The ability of A-6Es to carry large quantities of fuel in wing-mounted drop tanks has rendered the KA-6Ds obsolete, and all are scheduled to be phased out of service.

The A-6E will remain in Navy service into the next century. Its planned replacement is the A-12 Advanced Tactical Aircraft (ATA), which is named "Avenger" after the World War II torpedo bomber flown by President George Bush. The first A-12s are scheduled to enter service in the late 1990s, and will incorporate stealth technologies. Two top aerospace contractors are working on this new aircraft (McDonnell Douglas and General Dynamics), and the Navy has stated publicly that it will purchase at least 650 A-12s. However, the final number may be lowered due to cost overruns. Needless to say, this has made the A-12 a rather controversial topic on Capitol Hill. The whole project remains shrouded in secrecy, and little hard information about the aircraft is currently available.

A-4 Skyhawk

McDONNELL DOUGLAS A-4F SKYHAWK	
Dimensions:	
Wingspan:	27 ft., 6 in.
Length:	41 ft., 4 in.
Height:	15 ft.
Weight (maximum take-off):	24,500 lbs.
Engine:	Two Pratt & Whitney J52-P8A turbojets
Engine thrust:	9,300 lbs.
Operating altitude:	58,600 ft.
Top speed:	646 mph (loaded)
Maximum range:	2,000 miles
Date of service:	1956

Since it was to be based on aircraft carriers, the A-4 Skyhawk was designed to carry the maximum weapons load for the minimum weight and size. Designed by the Douglas Aircraft Company's famed Ed Heinemann, the "Hot Rod," as the A-4 was quickly nicknamed, first flew under the A4D designation in 1954. In 1962, the A-4D was redesignated the A-4. The single-seat aircraft weighed four tons empty, but it could *carry* three tons of weapons, including a nuclear bomb. Incredibly, the Skyhawk was in production for over a quarter of a century. In that time a total of 2,960 Skyhawks rolled off the Douglas assembly line.

In August 1964, when U.S. destroyers were attacked by North Vietnamese patrol boats, A-4s were among the first American aircraft to participate in the counter-strike against North Vietnam. Skyhawks continued to play an important role as part of the Navy's strike force throughout the duration of the war against North Vietnam.

Equipped with a 20 millimeter cannon and AIM-9 Sidewinders for air defense, the A-4 can also carry a variety of air-to-ground munitions as part of its three-ton load. These include "iron" bombs, radar-guided "smart" bombs, AGM-62 Walleye television-guided air-to-ground missiles, and the AGM-65 Maverick. It also carries launchers for unguided 2.75-inch rockets. A-4s can refuel one another in-flight.

The A-4 is flown today as the A-4M in the light-attack role by the Marine Corps. This version is equipped with the angle rate bombing system, which makes use of a computer-controlled television camera and laser tracker to achieve near-pinpoint bombing accuracy.

The A-4 is gradually being withdrawn from active service; the Marine Corps is replacing it with the AV-8B Harrier, while the Navy is using it as a utility and trainer aircraft. It is also flown by aggressor pilots at the Navy Fighter Weapons School, where is it used (under the designation TA-4J Mongoose) in Dissimilar Aerial Combat Training (DACT) exercises on a postgraduate level.

Above: An A-4F Skyhawk launches a missile. **Right:** An A-4 simulator, used for training prospective Skyhawk pilots.

ANTISUBMARINE WARFARE AIRCRAFT

Today's submarines, whether nuclear or diesel-electric powered, pose a great threat to surface vessels, even when the latter are organized into carrier- or battleship-led task forces. When submerged, nuclear submarines are fast enough to catch a surface task force, and may even outrun many of the task force's component vessels.

To reduce this threat and assist surface antisubmarine warfare vessels in detecting and destroying enemy submarines, the Navy has developed two highly specialized aircraft equipped for this role. They are the P-3 Orion and the S-3 Viking.

The P-3 Orion is a long-range aircraft equipped with sensitive detection equipment and a variety of weaponry. It can stay aloft over a task force for up to 12 hours. The S-3 Viking is a shorter-range carrier- and land-based aircraft. One Viking squadron serves aboard every carrier except for the *Midway*. Vikings patrol the middle distance between the areas covered by the fixed wing P-3 Orion and the LAMPS (Light Airborne Multi-Purpose System) helicopters. Like the P-3, the Viking carries sensitive detection equipment and a mixed armament of torpedoes, bombs, missiles, and depth charges.

Left: A radar operator learns the nuances of antisubmarine detection in a P-3 Orion trainer. *Above:* The U.S. Navy's premier antisubmarine warfare aircraft, an S-3A Viking (top) and a P-3C Orion. *Right:* The P-3C Orion is a versatile long-range antisubmarine warfare patrol plane that can carry a variety of sensors and weapons. Here, it is armed with a Harpoon antiship missile for surface warfare.

P-3 Orion

LOCKHEED P-3C ORION	
Dimensions:	
Wingspan:	99 ft., 8 in.
Length:	116 ft., 10 in.
Height:	33 ft., 8.5 in.
Weight (maximum take-off):	142,000 lbs.
Engines:	Four Allison T56-A-14 turboprops
Engine horsepower:	4,910
Operating altitude:	28,300 ft.
Top speed:	473 mph
Maximum range:	3,100 miles
Date of service:	1962

Top: A P-3C Orion on patrol. **Above:** *The cockpit of a P-3C Orion from VP-68 squadron operating out of Barbar's Point Naval Air Station in Hawaii.*

The Lockheed P-3 Orion was developed from the Lockheed Electra airliner. It first entered Navy service in 1962, and functions as a shore-based long-range reconnaissance and antisubmarine warfare aircraft.

The P-3 Orion has been upgraded several times to the P-3C model that is currently in service. The P-3C variant has undergone three major upgrades itself. Digital computers replaced earlier analog computers, which tended to overwhelm the sensor operators with too much useless data from the sonobouys. IBM provided the new Proteus UYS-1 acoustic signal processor, which enables sensor operators to handle up to 16 sonobouys at a time. Previously, the operators were hard pressed to handle eight sonobouys.

The P-3C Orion can carry eight Mark 46 homing torpedoes in the bomb bay, or up to 4,000 pounds of depth charges (including nuclear depth charges) and bombs in the bomb bay as well as four Mark 46 torpedoes on wing pylons. Sixteen five-inch air-to-surface missiles can be substituted on the wing mounts. The P-3C is also being equipped to carry the Harpoon antiship missile. It usually carries a crew of ten.

Antisubmarine warfare sensors include the ASQ-81 magnetic anomaly detector and 48 sonobouys carried in chutes built into the bottom surface of the fuselage. The P-3 is powered by four Allison T56-A-14 turboprops, which provide 4,190 horsepower each. The aircraft has a range of 3,100 miles and can remain on station for 13 hours.

An electronics warfare surveillance variant, the EP-3E Orion, was developed in the late 1960s. Some 28 EP-3Es are currently in service; each has an electronics suite that is believed to comprise a communications, interception, and analysis system, instantaneous frequency measuring equipment, infrared jammers and detectors, noise jamming equipment, and agile frequency search radar. The Kawasaki Aircraft Company is the prime contractor for another electronic surveillance variant, the EP-3C, which has been built under license for Japan's armed forces.

Other P-3 variants have been used by the National Oceans and Atmospheric Administration as weather aircraft and several have been used by the Customs Service for anti-drug surveillance. More than 500 P-3 Orion aircraft have been built for the Navy in all variations. They are also flown by eight other nations. The P-3 Orion is the most capable long-range antisubmarine warfare aircraft flying today.

S-3A/B Viking

LOCKHEED S-3A/B VIKING

Dimensions:	
Wingspan:	68 ft., 8 in.
Length:	57 ft., 4 in.
Height:	22 ft., 9 in.
Weight (maximum take-off):	52,539 lbs.
Engines:	Two General Electric TF33-GE-400 turbofans
Engine thrust:	9,275 lbs.
Operating altitude:	40,800 ft.
Top speed:	506 mph
Maximum range:	2,600 miles
Date of service:	1974

The S-3 Viking is a turbofan-powered, carrier-based antisubmarine warfare aircraft that replaced the earlier, piston-engined S-2 Tracker. It carries a variety of antisubmarine warfare weapons. These weapons, combined with its ability to fly for nine hours over 2,600 miles, makes it a formidable threat to enemy submarine craft.

The S-3s are equipped with the APS-116 high resolution radar, the ASQ-81 magnetic anomaly detector, forward-looking infrared (FLIR) sensors, and 60 sonobouys that can be dropped by parachute to pinpoint a submarine. In the bomb bay it can carry four Mark 46 homing torpedoes or up to four depth bombs. An additional 3,000 pounds of bombs or depth charges can be carried on wing pylons: on the new S-3B version, wing pylons have been added to carry the Harpoon antiship missile. The S-3B will also carry an improved APS-137

high resolution radar and an improved acoustic processor.

The ES-3A is an S-3 variant that has been developed to replace the EA-3B Skywarrior in the electronic surveillance role. Sixteen of these aircraft are expected to enter service in the early 1990s; they will be operated by Navy squadrons VQ-5 (Pacific Fleet) and VQ-6 (Atlantic Fleet). These carrier-based aircraft have a crew of four, and electronics that provide them with over-the-horizon surveillance capabilities.

The S-3 is powered by two General Electric TF33-GE-400 turbofans that produce 9,275 pounds of thrust each. The aircraft's wings and tail assembly fold for carrier storage. The Viking carries a crew of four: pilot, copilot, tactical coordinator, and sensor operator. The Viking can provide a data link to other Vikings, or to surface ships. The first S-3 Vikings entered Navy service in 1974, and a total of 187 were built by 1978. Most have now been upgraded to the S-3B

Top: An S-3B Viking in flight. *Above:* An air-to-air view of an S-3A Viking from VS-38 squadron being refueled over the Sierra Nevada mountains. Note the "hose and droque" refueling device to the right of the aircraft's canopy.

configuration. One squadron of ten S-3 Vikings is currently assigned aboard each aircraft carrier in the Navy (with the exception of the *Midway*,

which doesn't have the space to accommodate Vikings and the extensive antisubmarine warfare control center they require).

ELECTRONIC WARFARE AND RECONNAISSANCE AIRCRAFT

W hile circling a battle fleet or shore position, electronic warfare and observation aircraft blanket enemy communications with interference and detect the movement of enemy ground, sea, and air assets. The Navy operates several electronic warfare aircraft and observation aircraft, five of which are profiled on

Although not the most glamorous of aircraft, these E-2C Hawkeyes perform the vital airborne early warning (AEW) role for surface task forces.

the following pages. (Two other electronic warfare aircraft—the EP-3 Orion and the ES-3A Viking—are discussed in the antisubmarine warfare chapter in the profiles for the P-3 Orion and the S-3 Viking, respectively.) All electronic warfare aircraft are unarmed so as to make room for the sensors and receiving and transmitting equipment they need to accomplish their task.

It should be noted that modern technology is swiftly changing how much information is gathered. Satellites are replacing large manned aircraft in the role of gathering data on enemy movements, while unmanned aerial vehicles are being developed to investigate conditions on an actual battlefield. These unmanned aerial vehicles, which are not yet in regular service, are small and agile and largely invisible to enemy radar. However, neither satellites nor unmanned aircraft have thus far managed to replace manned aircraft in the electronic warfare role.

E-6A Hermes

BOEING E-6A HERMES	
Dimensions:	
Wingspan:	148 ft., 2 in.
Length:	152 ft., 11 in.
Height:	42 ft., 5 in.
Weight (maximum take-off):	342,000 lbs.
Engines:	Four General Electric/SNECMA CFM-56-2A2 turbofans
Engine thrust:	21,000 lbs.
Operating altitude:	40,000+ ft.
Top speed:	610 mph
Maximum range:	7,845 miles
Date of service:	1989

The E-6A Hermes is a Navy-modified Boeing 707-320B aircraft. In time of war—particularly nuclear war—it will be used to provide a communications link between the National Command Authority of the United States and the nuclear submarine fleet. Since only the President of the United States can give the order to use nuclear weapons of any kind, a means of passing these orders to the commanders of strategic submarines equipped with submarine-launched missiles and attack submarines carrying cruise missiles had to be developed. Just as importantly, updated land-attack information, including orders to halt preparations for an attack, must also be passed. The command, control, and communications system for doing so is known as Take Charge and Move Out (TACAMO). The E-6As are known as TACAMO aircraft.

Communication with submerged submarines is accomplished through extremely long radio waves (ELF). Only radio waves that have cycle lengths in terms of meters can penetrate water. ELF requires large antenna arrays; transmission times are very slow. It is presumed that ELF will alert submerged submarines to move to predetermined locations and approach the surface with a special antenna to receive messages. The E-6A Hermes carries communications equipment that can transmit directly to these submarines. It can thus pass on instructions and receive information and, if necessary, act as an interface between the submarine commander and the National Command Authority if nuclear weapons should be used.

The E-6A has two trailing wire antennas that can be unreeled in flight. The first antenna is nearly 5,000 feet long and the second is 30,000 feet—nearly six miles in length! Most additional details regarding the equipment of the TACAMO aircraft are highly classified; however, it is known that the wingtips carry pods that contain satellite-receiving antennas.

The E-6A Hermes is powered by four General Electric/SNECMA CFM-56-2A2 turbofans that allow the aircraft to cruise at 523 miles per hour for up to 15 hours. Flight time can be extended to 72 hours with inflight refueling. The aircraft has a mission capability of 7,845 miles on internal fuel.

The Navy intends to purchase a total of 16 Hermes aircraft. Some entered service in 1989; all are scheduled for delivery before the end of 1991.

E-2 Hawkeye

GRUMMAN E-2 HAWKEYE	
Dimensions:	
Wingspan:	80 ft., 7 in.
Length:	57 ft., 6.75 in.
Height:	18 ft., 3.75 in.
Weight (maximum	
take-off):	51,933 lbs.
Engines:	Two Allison T56-A-425
	turboprops
Engine horsepower:	4,910
Operating altitude:	30,800 ft.
Top speed:	372 mph
Maximum range:	460 miles
Date of service:	1964

Operating from a vantage point high in the sky, the E-2 Hawkeye carries electronic equipment and technicians to manage an entire field of action for a carrier battle group. The idea of battlefield management from an airborne command post was explored in both world wars, but the technology was lacking. It was not until the mid-1950s that communications and radar technology developed to the point where airborne battlefield management became feasible.

Beginning in 1945, the first aircraft to function in this role were the PB-1W, the TBM-3W, and the AD-3W. The AD series aircraft were used in large numbers, and were assigned to all Navy aircraft carriers. Next in line were the land-based Lockheed WV-2 (EC-121 after 1962) Warning Star and the carrier-based Grumman WF-2 (E-1 after 1962) Tracer. Both Navy and Air Force EC-121s served in Vietnam.

Based on the S-2 Tracker, the E-1 Tracer demonstrated the concept of a carrier-based airborne early warning (AEW) and flying command post. However, the Tracer's effectiveness was limited by the state of contemporary radar technology as well as its cramped quarters (which did not provide enough space for the high-speed digital computer needed to sort out the haze of blips on a radar screen). In 1957 the Navy selected Grumman to develop a larger and more capable aircraft. The result was a fixed wing aircraft powered by two Allison T56-A-422 turboprop engines. The Hawkeye, as this aircraft came to be known, made its first flight in 1960. The Hawkeye has a 460-mile range, a top speed of 372 miles per hour, and a loiter time of six hours.

Originally designated the W2F, the Hawkeye was redesignated E-2 in 1962. The current standard Hawkeye is the E-2C, which entered service aboard Navy carriers in 1974. More than 100 E-2C variants have been built, and more are on the way. The Hawkeye's most distinguishing feature is its huge, saucerlike radome perched above its fuselage. To compensate for the airflow from this unusual appendage, Grumman engineers gave the plane a tail with four vertical tail surfaces. The 24-foot radome revolves in the airstream once every ten seconds.

A crew of three operates the radar equipment while a crew of two flies the Hawkeye. The crew can see nearly 300 miles in any direction with the radar, which has a surveillance

envelope of three million cubic miles. The system can handle more than 600 airborne targets and track ships and aerial targets at the same time, while the radar crew can control 40 intercept operations simultaneously.

Each carrier air wing has an airborne early warning squadron of four Hawkeyes. Hawkeyes also serve in civilian functions. For instance, Coast Guard Hawkeyes have been assigned to detect drug smugglers in Florida.

The E-2C Hawkeye carries a sophisticated radar and computer system to detect and track hostile aircraft approaching a surface task force. It can then vector Navy fighters to intercept them. The Hawkeye is usually operated from aircraft carriers.

EA-6B Prowler

GRUMMAN EA-6B PROWLER

Dimensions:	
Wingspan:	53 ft.
Length:	59 ft., 10 in.
Height:	16 ft., 3 in.
Weight (maximum	
take-off):	65,000 lbs.
Engines:	Two Pratt & Whitney
	J52-P-408 turbojets
Engine thrust:	11,200 lbs.
Operating altitude:	41,000 ft.
Top speed:	613 mph
Maximum range:	805 miles
Date of service:	1971

EA-6B Prowlers provide electronic shields against enemy air-defense radars and jam enemy communications, and generally accompany A-6Es on bombing missions. Here, a formation of EA-6Bs flies over the aircraft carrier Eisenhower.

The EA-6B Prowler is based on the A-6A Intruder, and was developed as an electronic countermeasures aircraft by Grumman for the Navy and the Marine Corps. The EA-6B Prowler is distinguished from the A-6A Intruder by a capped vertical stabilizer that contains jamming equipment and antenna, and by a fuselage that is nearly five feet longer and contains an enlarged cockpit. Besides the pilot and the copilot, the Prowler's cockpit holds two technicians to operate the sophisticated jamming system. The Prowler also carries a total of five jammer pods on the fuselage and wing pylons.

The Prowler is powered by two Pratt & Whitney J52-P-408 turbojets that deliver 11,200 pounds of thrust each. The aircraft has gone through a series of electronic upgrades that have provided it with an improved computer (AN/AYK-14) and software, and an improved communications system with additional frequencies for the jamming system. Another series of upgrades, planned for the early 1990s, would extend the jamming frequency range from 4,000 megahertz to 18,000 megahertz. A Prowler can carry two AGM-88A HARM antiradiation missiles that home in on enemy radar transmitters.

The Prowler first entered service with the Navy and Marine Corps in January 1971. More than 95 aircraft have now been built. The Prowler is currently flown by 15 Navy carrier-based tactical electronic warfare squadrons (VAQ) and one Marine Corps electronic warfare squadron (VMAQ). One Prowler squadron serves aboard each of the 14 aircraft carriers now in service.

EA-3B Skywarrior

DOUGLAS EA-3B SKYWARRIOR

Dimensions:	
Wingspan:	72 ft., 6 in.
Length:	74 ft., 4 in.
Height:	22 ft., 8 in.
Weight (maximum take-off):	78,000 lbs.
Engines:	Two Pratt & Whitney J57- P-10 turbojets
Engine thrust:	12,400 lbs.
Operating altitude:	41,300 ft.
Top speed:	640 mph
Maximum range:	2,400 miles
Date of service:	1958

The oldest combat aircraft in the Navy, the Skywarrior made its maiden flight on October 22, 1952 and entered service with the Navy in March 1956. At the time it was the Navy's heaviest carrier-based aircraft. Originally designed as a bomber, the Skywarrior was built with a roomy internal weapons bay that could carry nearly 13,000 pounds of conventional bombs or one nuclear bomb. Defensive armament consisted of a twin 20 millimeter radar-controlled tail gun. The A-3B Skywarrior was also modified to the RA-3B reconnaissance version; 30 of these aircraft were built. As a strike plane, the Skywarrior compiled a limited combat service record in Vietnam.

In December 1958 the first electronic warfare version of the Skywarrior, the A3D-2Q, began a series of test flights. In 1962 the A3D-2Q became

the EA-3B as a result of a service-wide reorganization of aircraft designations. Eventually, 282 EA-3Bs were built. Today, the EA-3B is flown by a number of squadrons in the electronic countermeasures role with all armament removed. The weapons bay has been rebuilt to hold electronic intelligence gathering equipment and four sensor technicians. A second version, the KA-3B, was modified as a refueling aircraft. In this variant, the weapons bay has been modified to hold 5,026 gallons of aviation fuel in an internal tank.

The Skywarrior was designed and built by the Douglas company prior to its merger with the McDonnell company. It has a crew of six, high-mounted wings swept back at a 36-degree angle, and two turbojet engines mounted on pods

suspended under the wings by pylons. Although designed to be powered by the Wright J40 turbojet engines, Pratt & Whitney J57 turbojets were substituted early in production.

The EA-3B is being replaced by the ES-3A Viking, a variant of the S-3 Viking

antisubmarine warfare aircraft. Twelve ES-3As are scheduled to enter service in the early 1990s. Performance specifications for the ES-3A are nearly identical to the S-3A/B Viking, which is profiled in the chapter on antisubmarine warfare aircraft.

Shown here on the ground, this EA-3B Skywarrior represents one of the largest aircraft types to operate from carriers. It is currently used exclusively in a reconnaissance role.

OV-10 Bronco

ROCKWELL INTERNATIONAL OV-10A BRONCO

Dimensions:	
Wingspan:	40 ft.
Length:	41.7 ft.
Height:	15 ft., 2 in.
Weight (maximum take-off):	14,444 lbs.
Engines:	Two Garrett T76-G-416/417 turboprops
Engine horsepower:	715
Operating altitude:	24,000 ft.
Top speed:	280 mph
Maximum range:	1,140 miles
Date of service:	1967

During the Vietnam War the OV-10 Bronco was flown by a special Navy squadron, VAL 4 ("Black Ponies"), which was assigned the task of protecting convoys on the Mekong River and to seek out and destroy enemy forces in the area. The Bronco was also used by U.S. Air Force forward air control (FAC) units, and by Marine Corps observation squadrons. Its use by the three service branches was due to the fact that it was light, easy to handle, heavily armed, relatively quiet, and possessed good endurance.

The OV-10A Bronco was designed to be a counterinsurgency aircraft that would patrol a specific area and attack enemy units from the air. As originally built, the Bronco even had provisions for carrying a small number of paratroops.

By the time the Bronco reached Vietnam, however, its mission had changed. It was used and became famous for its role as a FAC aircraft. The same attributes that made it ideal for the counterinsurgency role (which it never filled) made it a perfect FAC aircraft. The Bronco's maximum speed of 280 miles per hour and range of 1,140 miles enabled its pilots to watch a specific patch of ground on a daily basis and note any unusual occurrences. If the aircraft was on the receiving end of enemy fire, it could fight back with rockets, four 7.62 millimeter machine guns, or up to 3,600 pounds of other weapons or bombs. The Bronco's crew of two could also mark targets with smoke grenades, rockets, or bombs for attack aircraft or for ground-based artillery. They could also serve as the airborne eyes and ears of ground-based infantry units. Today, the Bronco is also equipped to carry two Sidewinder air-to-air missiles.

Designed and built by Rockwell International, the Bronco has a central cockpit and cargo compartment slung from a high wing with a 40-foot span. The wing connects two separate engine pylons that sweep back into two vertical stabilizers connected by a high horizontal stabilizer. The aircraft is powered by two Garrett T76-G-416/417 turboprop engines that provide 715 horsepower each. The aircraft is a little over 41 feet in length and weighs 6,893 pounds empty. A total of 157 OV-10A Broncos were built before

production ended in April 1969.

The Bronco is in service today with the Marine Corps, which uses it in the scout/reconnaissance and artillery spotter role. The Marines periodically operate the OV-10 from helicopter assault ships. The Air Force also uses the Bronco as a FAC aircraft and to provide quick ground support in advance of fighter aircraft.

The OV-10 Bronco was originally designed for counterinsurgency warfare, but proved to be a superior aircraft in the night observation role.

CARGO AIRCRAFT

While the Military Airlift Command is responsible for hauling cargoes and personnel for all military service branches, the Navy retains its own fleet of transport aircraft to move specialized cargo and to supply carrier task forces. The Navy's most frequently used aircraft is the C-2 Greyhound, which is small enough to make carrier landings, yet large enough to carry a worthwhile payload.

For larger cargo, the Navy and Marine Corps both fly the C-130 Hercules. The C-130 does not make carrier landings.

For short hauls of light payloads and for transporting personnel, the Navy flies the C-12 Huron, a variant of the commercial Beech Aircraft Corporation's Super King Air 200. The Navy also owns a few smaller aircraft that are flown in the cargo and utility roles.

A trio of C-130 transport aircraft. The C-130 comprises the mainstay of the Navy's cargo hauling capability.

C-130 Hercules

The C-130 has played a role in virtually every American military operation since its introduction in the late 1950s. The Hercules has delivered supplies under withering ground fire in Vietnam and in near-blizzard weather conditions at the South Pole.

The turboprop-powered Hercules made its first flight in 1954. The Navy, Marines, Coast Guard, and Air Force all purchased the C-130, as did more than 50 foreign air forces from Abu Dhabi to Zaire. Lockheed has also developed a nearly identical commercial freighter called the L-100, which has been sold to customers in more than a dozen countries.

The Navy, Marines, and Coast Guard operate about 100 of the versatile Hercules in various roles, ranging from the Coast Guard's HC-130H

rescue aircraft to the Navy's ski-equipped LC-130s, which are used in Antarctica by squadron VXE-6. The C-130 usually carries a crew of five, although this figure may vary depending on the role it is performing. The Marines fly the KC-130 for aerial refueling of fixed and rotary winged aircraft. The Navy uses the Hercules as a transport to move supplies over short to medium distances, and as a strategic communications aircraft (EC-130G/Q) to communicate with nuclear submarines in the TACAMO (Take Charge and Move Out) role. The LC-130G/Q is now being superceded in this role by the E-6A Hermes.

The Marine Corps' fleet of KC-130F/R/T carry removable aluminum tanks holding 3,600 gallons of fuel in the cargo bay and can stream two refueling hoses,

or drogues, at the same time to refuel fixed wing aircraft or helicopters. When not used as refueling aircraft, the KC-130s can haul cargo.

A variation of the Hercules is the Spectre gunship, flown by the Air Force to support ground operations of the Army and Marines. First introduced in Vietnam with an armament of 20 millimeter, 40mm, and even 75mm cannons, the Spectre remains in service to this day with the

Air Force. Current variants include one 105mm howitzer as well as 20mm multibarrel guns. In the early 1990s, the new AC-130U will be on line with a deadly combination of 25mm, 40mm, and 105mm cannons directed by sophisticated low-light TV and infrared target locators.

The Navy has used the C-130A to launch pilotless reconnaissance aircraft.

LOCKHEED C-130H HERCULES	
Dimensions:	
Wingspan:	132 ft., 7 in.
Length:	97 ft., 9 in.
Height:	38 ft., 3 in.
Weight (maximum take-off):	155,000 lbs.
Engines:	Four Allison T56-A-15 turboprops
Engine horsepower:	4,508
Operating altitude:	3,000 ft.
Top speed:	375 mph
Maximum range:	4,894 miles
Date of service:	1956

UC-12B Huron

The UC-12B Huron is based on the Beech Aircraft Corporation's Super King Air 200, and is used for personnel and cargo transport and as a utility aircraft. It also provides support to attaché and military assistance advisory missions around the world, and is used to supplement the Navy's airlift capability, and to serve as an air ambulance.

The Huron has a complete cabin pressurization and heating system, and can be equipped with a variety of electronics for particular roles. The Huron can carry up to eight passengers or 2,000 pounds of cargo. The usual Navy variant provides space for eight passengers, with the remaining space dedicated to cargo. The crew consists of a pilot and a copilot. Because of the aircraft's inertial navigation system, no navigator is required.

The UC-12B Huron is powered by two Pratt & Whitney PT6A-41 turboprop engines delivering 850 horsepower each. The engines are quite long and although the wings are located well aft of the compartment, the propellers are ahead of the cockpit near the nose. The Huron has a T-tail configuration that distinguishes it from other, similar models. The aircraft are not armed.

The Navy purchased 49 UC-12B Hurons; 29 have been purchased by the Marine Corps.

BEECH AIRCRAFT CORPORATION UC-12B HURON	
Dimensions:	
Wingspan:	54 ft., 6 in.
Length:	43 ft., 9 in.
Height:	14 ft., 6 in.
Weight (maximum take-off):	12,500 lbs.
Engines:	Two Pratt & Whitney PT6A-41 turboprops
Engine horsepower:	850
Operating altitude:	31,000 ft.
Top speed:	310 mph
Maximum range:	2,024 miles
Date of service:	1979

The T-44A is the Navy's trainer version of the Beechcraft King Air commercial aircraft.

C-2A Greyhound

In the past, one of the major problems experienced by the Navy involved the speedy transfer of supplies and personnel to the fleets at sea. With the advent of the aircraft carrier, this problem was eased somewhat. To ease it still further, the Navy developed a series of cargo aircraft small enough to be landed on board carriers, but large enough to carry sufficient cargo to make them useful. They are termed Carrier Onboard Delivery, or COD, aircraft. The latest in this line of aircraft is the C-2A Greyhound, which is a variant of the E-2 Hawkeye Airborne Early Warning (AEW) aircraft. The Greyhound has a boxy, lengthened fuselage and a rear-loading ramp; many subsystems are the same as those found on the Hawkeye.

The C-2A has a flight crew of three—pilot, copilot, and flight engineer—and can carry 39 passengers, or 20 litter patients, or 10,000 pounds of cargo in 674 cubic feet of cargo space. The aircraft is powered by two Allison T56-A-8A turboprop engines that deliver 4,050 horsepower each. The Greyhound is unarmed, has a range of 1,656 miles and a maximum speed of 352 miles per hour, and has a navigational radar.

The Navy procured a total of 58 C-2A Greyhounds, 51 of which are still in service. The C-2A Greyhound first flew on November 18, 1964 and entered Navy service on December 1966.

Main image: The C-2 Greyhound is known as a Carrier On-board Delivery Aircraft. It can land on an aircraft carrier with up to 10,000 pounds of cargo. Its cargo capacity is 675 cubic feet. *Inset:* A C-2A Greyhound lands on the carrier Independence.

GRUMMAN C-2A GREYHOUND	
Dimensions:	
Wingspan:	80 ft., 7 in.
Length:	56 ft., 8 in.
Height:	15 ft., 11 in.
Weight (maximum take-off):	54,382 lbs.
Engines:	Two Allison T56-A-8A turboprops
Engine horsepower:	4,050
Operating altitude:	28,800 ft.
Top speed:	352 mph
Maximum range:	1,656 miles
Date of service:	1966

TRAINERS

In terms of public awareness, training aircraft are perhaps the most neglected aspect of Naval and Marine Corps aviation. This, despite the fact that they play a vital role in turning out the pilots and flight crews needed to operate the more familiar aircraft employed by both service branches.

The Navy and the Marine Corps use several different training aircraft, the design of which are the product of a great deal of thought and planning. A training aircraft must mimic the operational aircraft the pilot will fly in the fleet, yet it must be sufficiently easy to fly and forgiving of mistakes to assure that the new pilot will get past the training stage unharmed.

Of course, a pilot's training never really ends. Post-graduate training in the more esoteric aspects of his craft continues throughout his career. All aircrew members are subject to rigorous and frequent refresher training, some of which takes place in simulators, but the majority of which must be carried out in real aircraft.

The T-2 Buckeye is the Navy's "undergraduate" jet trainer. It is the first jet aircraft that aspiring Navy and Marine Corps pilots learn to fly.

T-47A Citation

The T-47A is based on the Cessna Model 550 aircraft, which made its first flight in 1976. The Model 550 was in turn based on the Model 500 and Model 501. Cessna's stated objective in building the Citation was to produce a twin-jet aircraft that could take off and land on the same airfields used by light aircraft such as those operated by civilians.

The Navy's version is used to train Naval flight officers in the use of radar equipment. It has slightly shorter wings than the civilian version but both are powered by Pratt & Whitney Aircraft JT15D-5 turbofan engines which produce 2,500 pounds of thrust each. The Navy has taken delivery of 15 T-47As, which are assigned to training squadron VT-86.

CESSNA T-47A CITATION	
Dimensions:	
Wingspan:	51 ft., 8 in.
Length:	47 ft., 2 in.
Height:	14 ft., 9 in.
Weight (maximum take-off):	13,300 lbs.
Engines:	Two Pratt & Whitney JT15D-5 turbofans
Engine thrust:	2,500 lbs.
Operating altitude:	43,000 ft.
Top speed:	483 mph
Maximum range:	1,900 miles
Date of service:	1984
Crew:	One student, one instructor

The T-47A Citation is used to train Navy and Marine Corps flight officers. Naval flight officers are the "backseaters" who handle the weapons and navigation in aircraft like the F-14 Tomcat.

T-45 Goshawk

The T-45 Goshawk is a variant of the British Aerospace Hawk. The Hawk was originally designed as a jet trainer for the Royal Air Force (RAF). Produced in the United States by McDonnell Douglas, it entered Navy service as a trainer in 1990.

The Hawk was originally designed by the Hawker Siddeley Company and entered RAF service in 1976. The aircraft is powered by the Rolls Royce-Turbomecca Adour turbofan engine delivering 5,200 pounds of thrust.

The Red Arrows RAF demonstration team has flown the Hawk since 1980. Highly maneuverable and easy to fly, the Hawk is entirely suited to the light ground-attack role in which the RAF employs it.

The U.S. Navy selected this aircraft as an off-the-shelf procurement item in 1982 to replace the T-2C Buckeye and the TA-4J Skyhawk. The new trainer aircraft has been designated the T-45 Goshawk. Planned procurement is quoted at 253 aircraft, of which all will be fitted for aircraft carrier landings and takeoffs. The aircraft will not be armed, although it will have wing pylons for practice bomb racks (and fuel tanks). Modifications include folding wings, tail hook, ventral fin, and strengthened landing gear for carrier landings.

BRITISH AEROSPACE/McDONNELL DOUGLAS T-45 GOSHAWK

Dimensions:	
Wingspan:	30 ft., 9.75 in.
Length:	35 ft., 9 in.
Height:	13 ft., 6 in.
Weight (maximum take-off):	12,700 lbs.
Engine:	One Rolls Royce-Turbomecca Adour Mk 861 turbofan
Engine thrust:	5,200 lbs.
Operating altitude:	42,500 ft.
Top speed:	609 mph
Maximum range:	1,600 miles
Date of service:	1990
Crew:	One student, one instructor

The T-45 Goshawk is the Navy's newest undergraduate training aircraft, replacing the T-2 Buckeye and the TA-4J Skyhawk. It is based on the British Hawk trainer and ground-attack aircraft.

T-44A King Air

BEECH AIRCRAFT CORPORATION T-44A KING AIR

The Beech Aircraft Corporation T-44A is based on the Beech King Air Model 90, which entered the commercial market in September 1970. The Model 90 is a twin-turboprop business aircraft with seating for up to ten passengers and a cruising range of nearly 1,500 miles. Its cabin is pressurized and heated, and it is powered by two Pratt & Whitney (Canada) PT6A-21 turboprops that deliver up to 550 horsepower each.

The Navy's T-44A Beech King Air was acquired to replace the TS-2 Tracker aircraft as a multi-engine trainer. It can also be configured as a transport to carry three passengers in addition to the pilot and copilot. The T-44A military version is powered by two Pratt & Whitney (Canada) PT6A-34B turboprops, the militarized version of the engines used in the commercial aircraft. The Navy has purchased a total of 76 T-44As.

Dimensions:	
Wingspan:	50 ft., 3 in.
Length:	35 ft., 6 in.
Height:	14 ft., 3 in.
Weight (maximum take-off):	9,650 lbs.
Engines:	Two Pratt & Whitney (Canada) PT6A-34B turboprops
Engine horsepower:	550
Operating altitude:	29,500 ft.
Top speed:	276 mph
Maximum range:	1,474 miles
Date of service:	1977
Crew:	Two students, one/two instructor(s) or two pilots, three passengers

The UC-12B Huron, the Navy's version of the Beechcraft Super King Air 200, is a turboprop-powered transport and utility aircraft.

T-38 Talon

In the late 1950s the Northrop company designed and built the F-5 Tiger in response to a post-Korean War study by the Pentagon that called for the building in great quantities of a small, very agile, and relatively inexpensive fighter. The T-38 is an outgrowth of that design effort. The first three prototypes of what was to become the T-38 Talon were ordered and flight testing was conducted at Edwards Air Force Base (AFB) in California.

The prototype flight testing showed that more powerful engines were needed. A new J85-GE-5 turbojet engine fitted with an afterburner replaced the original J58-GE-1 engine. Whereas the original engines had produced only 2,680 pounds of thrust each, the new engines could each produce 3,850 pounds of thrust, or 3,600 pounds when the afterburner was lit. The improvement in performance was dramatic. Designated T-38, the new aircraft joined the Air Force on March 17, 1961, when the USAF's 3510th Flying Training Wing, Randolph AFB, Texas, received their first aircraft.

The Navy uses the T-38 Talon in Top Gun training for Dissimilar Aerial Combat Training (DACT). These variants have cameras, but no armament. The Navy also employs a T-38 variant as a test-pilot proficiency aircraft. Navy and Air Force pilots alike give the T-38 high marks as an aircraft that is both beautiful to look at and to fly. It is a little over 46 feet long and has sharp-edged, triangular wings only slightly more than 25 feet across. The powerful twin engines enable the Talon to achieve Mach 1.3, or allow it to cruise at 627 miles per hour at 36,000 feet for 1,140 miles. The T-38 has a high wing loading for its size, yet stall speed remains exceptionally low at 146 miles per hour. This combination of high performance and inherent safety make it an ideal training aircraft.

All controls are duplicated in the T-38 for the instructor, who is seated behind and some ten inches higher than the student in front. This not only provides the instructor with a better view outside the cockpit but enables him to watch the student more closely.

A total of 1,187 T-38 Talon's were built by the time production ended in 1972. In addition to the Navy, T-38s are used as trainers by the U.S. Air Force, the West German Air Force, and NASA.

NORTHROP T-38A TALON	
Dimensions:	
Wingspan:	25 ft., 3 in.
Length:	46 ft., 4.5 in.
Height:	12 ft., 10.5 in.
Weight (maximum take-off):	11,820 lbs.
Engines:	Two General Electric J85-GE-5 turbojets
Engine thrust:	3,850 lbs.
Operating altitude:	55,000 ft.
Top speed:	858 mph
Maximum range:	1,140 miles
Date of service:	1961
Crew:	One student, one instructor

The T-38 Talon is probably the most popular aircraft in the Navy. Highly enjoyable to fly, it is used by test pilots to maintain proficiency and by the Navy's aggressor squadrons to simulate Soviet aerial tactics.

T-34 Mentor

BEECH AIRCRAFT CORPORATION T-34C MENTOR

Dimensions:
  Wingspan: 33 ft., 8 in.
  Length: 28 ft., 8.5 in.
  Height: 9 ft., 7 in.
Weight (maximum take-off): 4,300 lbs.
Engine: One Pratt & Whitney (Canada) PT6A-25 turboprop
Engine horsepower: 400
Operating altitude: 30,000 ft.
Top speed: 257 mph
Maximum range: 850 miles
Date of service: 1976
Crew: One student, one instructor

The T-34 Mentor is the first aircraft fledgling Navy and Marine Corps pilots learn to fly. All are powered by turboprop engines.

The venerable V-tailed Beech Bonanza provided the design basis for the original piston-engined version of the Mentor, designated Beech Model 45. Flown for the first time in December 1948, the Beech Model 45 subsequently won a runoff competition with two other trainer aircraft. In 1953 it was purchased by the Air Force as the T-34A Mentor. In 1954 the Navy also selected the T-34A. A total of 450 T-34As were built.

In 1973 the Navy asked Beech Aircraft Corporation to investigate the possibility of fitting the T-34As then in service with turboprop engines. This was done, and the resulting aircraft was designated T-34B. New production Mentors with turboprops were designated the T-34C, and they entered service with the Navy between 1976–1990. A total of 353 T-34Cs have been built

for the Navy All T-34Bs have now been removed from service.

To date, Mentors have flown well over one million hours and have established a record for safety and reliability unequaled by any other aircraft in the Navy.

The T-34C is powered by a Pratt & Whitney (Canada) PT6A-25 turboprop engine that delivers 400 horsepower. The aircraft seats the student pilot in front and the instructor in the back. The cockpit is air conditioned—a blessing for students and instructors stationed at Pensacola Naval Air Station in Florida, where most of the Navy's T-34s are based.

The T-34C has been sold widely to other governments, both as a trainer and as a tactical aircraft. Designated T-34C-1, such aircraft have four wing pylons for the mounting of up to 1,200 pounds of weapons.

T-2 Buckeye

ROCKWELL INTERNATIONAL T-2C BUCKEYE

Dimensions:	
Wingspan:	38 ft., 4 in.
Length:	38 ft., 2 in.
Height:	14 ft., 10 in.
Weight (maximum take-off):	13,179 lbs.
Engines:	Two General Electric J85-GE-4 turbojets
Engine thrust:	2,950 lbs.
Operating altitude:	40,400 ft.
Top speed:	522 mph
Maximum range:	1,045 miles
Date of service:	1968
Crew:	One student, one instructor

Navy pilots learn the techniques of aircraft carrier landings in the T-2 Buckeye. Designed and built in the late 1950s by North American Aviation (now Rockwell International), the T-2 is a small aircraft powered by two turbojet engines. It has a high tail assembly and straight wings set in the middle of the fuselage. The pilot and flight instructor sit in tandem with the instructor behind. The engines are mounted in the bottom of the fuselage below the wings. Because the aircraft has an amazing ability to recover from spin-induced stalls, it is also used for spin-recovery training. A number of T-2s have also been assigned to the Naval Test Pilots School at Patuxent Naval Air Station in Maryland, where it is used for proficiency training.

Five different versions of the Buckeye were built. A total of 217 T-2As were built; these aircraft were powered by a single Westinghouse J34-WE-36 turbojet with 3,400 pounds of thrust. Two Pratt & Whitney J60-P-6 turbojets were installed in the T-2B, which entered service in 1966. The Pratt & Whitney engines delivered 3,000 pounds of thrust each and greatly improved the aircraft's performance. The current T-2C model, which entered service in 1968, is powered by two General Electric J85-GE-4 turbojets that deliver 2,950 pounds of thrust each.

The T-2C is equipped with a single hard-point mounting beneath each wing and can carry an armament weighing up to 640 pounds. Weapons may include practice as well as real bombs and rockets, and a gun pack. The T-2C may also have target towing gear. More than 230 of this model were built.

A T-2C Buckeye. All Buckeyes now in Navy service are undergoing a Service Life Extension Program (SLEP) that will extend their life from 7,500 to 12,000 hours of flying time.

TC-4 Academe

A derivation of Grumman's popular Gulfstream commercial executive jet transport, the TC-4 Academe is used by the Navy and Marine Corps as a trainer for A-6 Intruder bombardier/navigators.

One Gulfstream is also used as an executive jet transport by the Coast Guard, which has given it the designation VC-4A. The Coast Guard retains the commercial name, Gulfstream I.

The TC-4 is powered by two Rolls Royce Dart Mark 529-8X turboprop engines that deliver 2,210 horsepower each. The aircraft has a range of nearly 2,000 miles on its own fuel tanks. It is not equipped for inflight refueling. The TC-4 has a service ceiling of 30,000 feet and a maximum speed of 365 miles per hour. It cruises at 250 miles per hour, and is not armed.

The TC-4 has a basic cockpit crew of two, and a simulated A-6 Intruder cockpit aft of the flight deck. The simulated cockpit has both pilot and bombardier/navigator positions. Additional bombardier/navigator control panels are located further forward.

GRUMMAN TC-4 ACADEME

Dimensions:	
Wingspan:	78 ft., 4 in.
Length:	67 ft., 11 in.
Height:	23 ft., 4 in.
Weight (maximum take-off):	36,000 lbs.
Engines:	Two Rolls Royce Dart Mk 529-8X turboprops
Engine horsepower:	2,210
Operating altitude:	30,000 ft.
Top speed:	365 mph
Maximum range:	1,979 miles
Date of service:	1967
Crew:	Two, plus one pilot, one bombardier/navigator in simulated cockpit

HELICOPTERS

The naval helicopter received its baptism of fire during World War II, when the German Navy first used such aircraft for reconnaissance and antisubmarine warfare. The United States also innovated the use of helicopters when it sent several of the new Sikorsky R-4 helicopters to the China-Burma-India theater in 1945 to be used as search-and-rescue craft.

Today, the Navy uses the helicopter in four principle roles: antisubmarine warfare, search-and-rescue, supply, and mine hunting and clearing operations. The SH-60 Seahawk is the newest Navy helicopter, and is fitted with a full range of submarine detection gear and weapons. The SH-60B is based aboard antisubmarine warfare surface ships, whereas the SH-60F is based aboard aircraft carriers.

The Marine Corps has made extensive use of the helicopter in the troop transport, cargo, and gunship roles. The Marine Corps also provides the helicopters that ferry the President on official duties.

1. Pilot's seat
2. Copilot/gunner's seat
3. Target acquisition system/night vision sensor
4. 30mm multibarrel gun
5. Main landing gear
6. Air-to-ground missiles
7. Stores rack
8. Stabilator
9. 4-blade tail rotor
10. Infrared heat suppressor
11. Engine pods
12. 4-blade main rotor

Below: Diagram of a helicopter gunship, showing weapons systems, avionics, and other elements common to most helicopters. **Right:** An MH-53E Super Stallion, used for mine hunting activities.

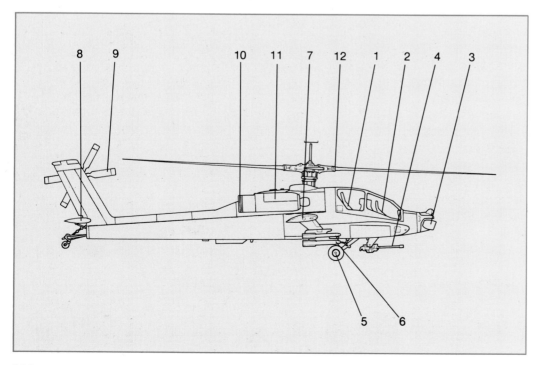

H-60 Seahawk

The Sikorsky SH-60B/F Seahawk is the Navy's ASW (antisubmarine warfare) version of the Army's UH-60 Black Hawk utility helicopter. The SH-60B fills the Light Airborne Multipurpose System (LAMPS) III role as an antisubmarine warfare helicopter and an over-the-horizon targeting aircraft for surface-to-surface missiles on cruisers, destroyers, and frigates. The SH-60F is used in the same role aboard aircraft carriers. The Navy also uses the HH-60H Seahawk for combat search and rescue.

The Black Hawk, from which the Seahawk derived, was developed in the early 1970s to answer the Army's need for a helicopter to replace the UH-1 Huey. As part of this program two companies—Sikorsky and Boeing Vertol—were selected to develop prototypes. In late December 1976, the Army selected the Sikorsky helicopter, and the first deliveries of the new UH-60A Black Hawk were made in 1978. The Navy settled on the Sikorsky helicopter shortly afterward.

The Seahawk has the same fuselage as the Black Hawk. And, like the Black Hawk, it is typically operated by a crew of three. It is also powered by two General Electric T700-GE-401 turboshaft engines providing 1,713 horsepower each and driving a single transmission. The Seahawk has a single main rotor and a boom-mounted tail rotor. The main rotor can survive hits from .50 caliber or 23 millimeter armor-piercing shells. The fuselage is sufficiently armored to withstand hits from .30 caliber weapons, and the fuel system was designed to be crashworthy—that is, in most crashes the fuel is not expected to catch fire or explode. The rotor hub uses elastomeric bearings that do not need lubrication and require far less maintenance than traditional metal bearings. The blade tips are swept back 20 degrees, and the trailing edges have tabs to improve airflow. The blades are made of hollow titanium spars, Nomex honeycomb cores, graphite trailing edges, and glass fiber leading edges, all covered with glass fiber and epoxy skins. The leading edges are sheathed in titanium.

The Navy's Seahawk differs from the Army's Black Hawk in having the following: sonobuoys and other antisubmarine warfare sensors and radars; gas turbine engines specially constructed for operation in humid and salty environments; chin pods; pylon mounts to hold two Mark 46 homing torpedoes or extra fuel tanks; magnetic anomaly equipment; a fourth crew space for the sensor operator; greater fuel capacity; a rescue hoist; automatic blade-folding devices for the main and tail rotors; and a haul-down device for landing the helicopter on small ships in rough seas. The Seahawk is to be deployed on all *Oliver Hazard Perry*-class frigates, *Spruance*-class and *Kidd*-class destroyers, and *Ticonderoga*-class cruisers.

Patrolling the inner zone of an aircraft carrier battle group is the responsibility of another Seahawk variant, the SH-60F. Specialized ASW instrumentation, including dipping sonar and Mark 46 homing torpedoes, is a primary feature of this aircraft. The Navy's combat search-and-rescue Seahawk variant, the HH-60H, can support Navy SEAL (Sea-Air-Land) special forces.

The HH-60H Seahawk is armed with 7.62mm M60D machine guns when functioning in its search-and-rescue role. As an ASW helicopter, the SH-60B carries 2,000 pounds of avionics, including a dispenser holding 25 sonobuoys, the APS-124 radar, forward looking infrared sensors, and the ASQ-81 magnetic anomaly detector. The SH-60F variant also carries AQS-13F dipping sonar, but does not have any radar. Both variants carry two Mk 46 homing torpedoes.

The Marine Corps has purchased nine VH-60A Black Hawks to replace its VH-1N Hueys in the Executive Flight Detachment of Marine Helicopter Squadron 1, the unit that provides transport for the President and other top administration officials.

Right: An SH-60B armed with a Mark 46 torpedo. Below: Cockpit view of an SH-60B. Opposite, below: An SH-60B overflies a U.S. attack submarine.

SIKORSKY SH-60B/F SEAHAWK

Dimensions:

Main rotor diameter:	53 ft., 8 in.
Tail rotor diameter:	11 ft.
Length:	50 ft., 0.75 in.
Width:	7 ft., 9 in.
Height:	16 ft., 10 in.
Weight (maximum take-off):	16,260 lbs.
Maximum altitude:	19,000 ft.
Top speed:	184 mph
Maximum range:	373 miles
Date of service:	
SH-60B:	1983
SH-60F:	1987

H-53 Sea Stallion

SIKORSKY CH-53D SEA STALLION

Dimensions:

Main rotor diameter:	72 ft., 3 in.
Tail rotor diameter:	16 ft.
Length:	67 ft., 2 in.
Width:	15 ft., 5 in.
Height:	24 ft., 11 in.
Weight (maximum take-off):	36,400 lbs.
Maximum altitude:	6,500 ft.
Top speed:	196 mph
Maximum range:	257 miles
Date of service:	1969

As the Marines gained experience with vertical assault tactics, the need to move larger troop units imposed even greater replenishment and support needs on its aviation branch. At the same time, the Navy was developing requirements for larger helicopters in the antisubmarine and mine countermeasures warfare areas. A new helicopter capable of lifting twice the payload of the CH-46 Sea Knight was required. Sikorsky proposed a version of their CH-54 Tarhe Flying Crane with more powerful engines and an enclosed fuselage. The result was the CH-53A Sea Stallion, which first flew in October 1964. To improve performance and payload capability, Sikorsky installed more powerful engines and nearly doubled the lifting capacity of the CH-53A.

The CH-53's cargo compartment, which is equipped with reversible skid-roller strips set into a titanium floor, is 30 feet long, seven feet six inches wide, and six feet six inches high. Light vehicles and artillery pieces can be winched into the hold through a rear-opening ramp. A total of 37 fully equipped troops, or 24 stretchers loaded on special racks, or up to 8,000 pounds of cargo can be carried. With its rotors turning, the CH-53 Sea Stallion can operate directly on the water, thanks to a watertight hull. Its rear cargo ramp can be lowered after an inflatable waterproof dam is erected.

The CH-53's cockpit seats three crew members: pilot, copilot, and crew chief. The blades are pressurized to warn of cracks. Since the CH-53 operates from amphibious ships, the main rotor blades and the tail rotor (which carries the vertical/ horizontal stabilizer), fold hydraulically.

Normally unarmed, the CH-53 can be configured to carry a fairly wide variety of weapons. In a combat zone the minimum armament would be a door-mounted 50 caliber gun or 7.62mm machine gun.

The CH-53A entered service with the Marine Corps in September 1966 and was sent to Vietnam in January of the following year. It moved troops and equipment around the country and hauled Marines into hot landing zones until the U.S. withdrawal from Vietnam. Since then, CH-53s have formed the backbone of the Marine Corps' heavy-lift capability.

The CH-53 has been extensively uprated since the introduction of the initial A model, which was powered by two 2,850 horsepower General Electric T64-6 turboshaft engines. In 1966, the United States Air Force ordered a more powerful version of the CH-53A, powered by twin 3,080 horsepower T64-GE-3 turboshaft engines, to

supplement its HH-3 Jolly Green Giants.

The current version of the CH-53 used by the Marine Corps is the CH-53D, which entered service in March 1969. The CH-53D has a unique cargo handling system that permits one man to load the aircraft. The CH-53D's more powerful (and more easily maintained) T64-GE-413 turboshaft engines deliver 3,925 horsepower each and give the helicopter a maximum speed of 196 miles per hour. The CH-53D can carry 55 fully equipped troops.

The CH-53 is also operated by the United States Navy as a minesweeping helicopter. Designated the MH-53D, it possesses a variety of mineclearing equipment and electronics. Four MH-53Ds aboard the USS *Shreveport* took part in the 1984 Red Sea operation to clear mines placed by Libya in an attempt to shut down that international waterway.

Sikorsky's CH-53 series has a long and honorable history of service with the Marine Corps, Navy, and Air Force. It has compiled one of the best safety records of all military aircraft flying today.

A CH-53D (foreground) on flight operations at Halifax, Nova Scotia.

H-53E Super Stallion/Sea Dragon

SIKORSKY CH-53E SUPER STALLION/ MH-53E SEA DRAGON	
Dimensions:	
Main rotor diameter:	79 ft.
Tail rotor diameter:	20 ft.
Length:	73 ft., 4 in.
Width:	13 ft.
Height:	18 ft., 7 in.
Weight (maximum take-off):	73,500 lbs.
Maximum altitude:	9,500 ft.
Top speed:	193 mph
Maximum range:	1,290 miles
Date of service:	1981

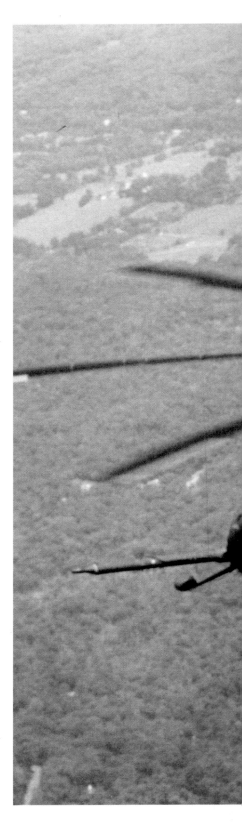

Needing a helicopter with more lifting capacity than contemporary rotary wing aircraft could provide, the Marine Corps teamed with Sikorsky in the early 1970s to evolve the CH-53E Super Stallion version of the CH-53 Sea Stallion. This aircraft flew for the first time in March 1974.

Although similar in appearance to its predecessor, the Super Stallion has a third General Electric T64-GE-416 turboshaft engine mounted above and slightly behind the starboard engine. It is thus able to achieve a top speed of 193 miles per hour, which is fast enough to permit in-flight refueling from a KC-130 Hercules tanker.

The CH-53E and the CH-53A/D both carry a crew of three in similarly configured cockpits. However, the CH-53E's instrumentation and flight controls have been up-rated. The Super Stallion uses two computers and a new autopilot in addition to the latest in automated navigation equipment.

The Super Stallion also has wider, thicker sponsons located on either side of the fuselage. In addition to adding stability for emergency operations, the sponsons are used as fuel tanks that give the CH-53E an internal fuel capacity of 1,017 gallons. Additional external drop tanks can be mounted on the sponsons.

The Super Stallion is also different in that it has a vertical stabilizer and a larger tail rotor, both of which are angled to the right. The horizontal stabilizer forms a gull-like wing and is supported by a strut. The Super Stallion also has a. seven-bladed main rotor, whereas the earlier CH-53A/D models had a six-bladed main motor. The CH-53E's blades are made of titanium and glass fiber, and are attached to the main hub by extension straps that make it appear as if the main rotor is greater in diameter than that of the A/D models.

The CH-53E's blades are pressurized to warn of cracks. The presence of a seventh blade required modifications to the main rotor assembly, particularly the main hub, which nearly doubled in size. The main hub is manufactured of steel and titanium and uses elastomeric rather than mechanical bearings.

The Super Stallion is one of the most powerful heavy-lift helicopters outside the Soviet Union, with nearly double the lifting capability of the CH-53A/D. Such prowess is due to its seventh blade as well as its three General Electric T64-416 turboshaft engines.

The CH-53E and the CH-53A/D differ in cargo-carrying ability as well— despite the fact that the cargo holds on both aircraft are about the same size. Because it has such powerful engines, the CH-53E can carry a maximum payload in excess of 36,000 pounds compared with the 8,000-pound payload of the CH-53A/D Sea Stallion. Instead of 37 fully equipped troops, the Super Stallion can carry 55 troops, although it functions mainly as an equipment, vehicle, and weapons lift helicopter. The CH-53E can also carry up to seven standard cargo pallets. Using its winch and cargo hook, the Super Stallion can carry one LAV-25 (a light armored vehicle that weighs 24,400 pounds), plus add-on fuel tanks.

The Navy version of the CH-53E is designated MH-53E Sea Dragon. This aircraft has larger side sponsons for added fuel capacity. The MH-53E is used in the mine counter-measures role, and to tow mechanical, acoustical, or magnetic hydrofoil devices to detect and detonate various types of mines.

For combat the Navy and Marine Corps variants may

be armed with either a .50 caliber or a 7.62 millimeter machine gun. Provision can be made for additional weapons such as depth charges. Under normal circumstances, however, both the CH-53E and the MH-53E are unarmed.

Main image; above: A CH-53E Super Stallion. Note the seven rotors and the strut supporting the gull-like horizontal stabilizer on the tail—both distinctive features of the Super Stallion. *Left:* An MH-53E on a mine hunting exercise.

H-46 Sea Knight

BOEING CH-46E SEA KNIGHT

Dimensions:

Main rotor diameter:	51 ft.
Tail rotor diameter:	51 ft.
Length:	44 ft., 7 in.
Width:	12 ft., 8 in.
Height:	16 ft., 9 in.
Weight (maximum take-off):	21,400 lbs.
Maximum altitude:	10,000 ft.
Top speed:	166 mph
Maximum range:	222 miles
Date of service:	1965

The Marine Corps began to develop helicopter assault tactics in 1946. The 1946 atomic bomb tests on Bikini atoll in the Pacific demonstrated that amphibious ships bunched up near a beach to launch landing craft could be very vulnerable to nuclear attack. Helicopters, the Marines discovered, could let ships stand farther offshore and be more dispersed.

The Marines continued to experiment with helicopter assault during the Korean War. In the period between 1953 and the start of American involvement in the Vietnam War in 1964, the Marines studied French and British experiences using helicopters to carry troops into battle zones and to keep them resupplied. During the 1950s the Marines used the Piasecki HRP-1 "Flying Banana" as their medium-lift capability helicopter. But the HRP-1 had a small payload and was quite slow. Seeking a more powerful helicopter, the Marines turned to Vertol Helicopters, which was then developing a more powerful

tandem rotor helicopter for the Army.

Ten prototypes of this craft were ordered by the Army, which subsequently found them too small for its needs. But when the Marine Corps and the Navy tested a more powerful version of the Model 107, they found it perfectly acceptable as a medium-lift assault and transport helicopter. It entered Navy and Marine Corps service in February 1961 as the HRB-1 Sea Knight.

The following year, in a reordering of all United States military aircraft designations, the Sea Knight was given the Navy-Marine designation H-46. The Navy designation is UH-46 when used for supply and ship replenishment; these comprise the majority of H-46s in Navy service. The HH-46 is the Navy's designation for the search-and-rescue role. CH-46 is the Marine designation. The latter reached Marine Corps squadrons in early 1965 and were promptly sent to South Vietnam.

The two three-bladed rotors on the Sea Knight are

driven by two engines in opposite directions. The need for a tail rotor is thereby eliminated. The twin General Electric T58-GE-16 turboshaft engines deliver 1,870 horsepower each in the current E model but only 1,400 horsepower in the earlier D and F models. The engines are mounted on either side of the after pylon.

The forward rotor, which is mounted on the front pylon, is linked to the engines by a high-speed drive shaft running through a tunnel atop the stressed-skin fuselage. Either engine can drive either rotor, or one engine can drive both in an emergency.

The CH-46 is flown by a crew of three and can carry

25 fully equipped troops. The cockpit seats the pilot and copilot side by side in front of a cargo hold that measures 24 feet long, six feet wide, and six feet high. A large side door and a rear ramp offer two entrances for loading. Light vehicles can be driven into the cargo hold. When used as a medevac helicopter, as many as 15 stretchers can be accommodated.

The Navy's Sea Knights do not carry antisubmarine warfare (ASW) weapons. Marine Corps Sea Knights can be equipped with a door-mounted 7.62 millimeter machine gun or a .50 caliber machine gun. In general, however, the Sea Knight is unarmed.

Although production of the Sea Knight ceased in the early 1970s, a series of upgrades has been instituted to extend its service life for at least another decade. The Navy and the Marine Corps purchased 624 Sea Knights; of these, the earlier D and F models are slated to be upgraded to the more powerful E model.

A CH-46D, whimsically dubbed "Air Savannah" by its crew. The two rotors turn in opposite directions to eliminate torque, as well as the need for a tail rotor.

SH-3 SEA KING

SIKORSKY SH-3D SEA KING	
Dimensions:	
Main rotor diameter:	62 ft.
Tail rotor diameter:	10 ft., 7 in.
Length:	54 ft., 9 in.
Width:	16 ft., 4 in.
Height:	16 ft., 10 in.
Weight (maximum take-off):	18,626 lbs.
Maximum altitude:	4,900 ft.
Top speed:	166 mph
Maximum range:	625 miles
Date of service:	1961

The SH-3 Sea King, like the SH-60F Seahawk, is based aboard aircraft carriers and is charged specifically with protecting the carrier battle group from enemy submarines. When necessary, Sea Kings can also carry out air-sea rescue operations as well.

The origin of the Sea King goes back to 1957, when the Navy asked Sikorsky for a new antisubmarine warfare (ASW) helicopter that could carry out both the "hunter" and "killer" roles. Previously this function had been carried out by two SH-34 Seabats, one serving as the hunter, the other as the killer.

Sikorsky's response was an amphibious, all-weather helicopter that could perform antisubmarine duties, and serve as a transport or a search-and-rescue aircraft as well. Designated Model S-61, the new helicopter was powered by two General Electric T58-GE-8 engines, and carried a full complement of antisubmarine electronics, including a Bendix AQS-13 or AQS-18 dipping sonar; doppler radar and radar altimeter; smoke markers and smoke floats; and Texas Instruments' AQS-81(V) Magnetic Anomaly Detector.

First deliveries of this aircraft, designated SH-3 Sea King, were made to the Navy in September 1961. As the first dedicated ASW helicopter to enter service anywhere in the world, the Sea King was armed with the Mark 44 or Mark 46 homing torpedoes.

The Sea King can land on water and remain stable even during heavy seas so long as its rotors are turning. Two pontoonlike floats carried in pods extending from either side of the SH-3's watertight fuselage provide stability during water landings. The SH-3 has both a fully functional autopilot and autostabilization system, which are linked to the doppler radar and the radar altimeter. This allows the pilot to program a set course and altitude for the helicopter to fly while hunting a submarine.

Performance in current Sea King variants has been significantly enhanced by the installation of two T58-GE-8R turboshaft engines that deliver 1,500 horsepower each. The engines are mounted above the cockpit and drive the five-bladed rotors. Since the SH-3 was designed primarily for shipboard use, the rotor blades fold automatically. The tail rotor also folds for storage.

The Sea King typically carries a crew of four and an armament that normally includes Mark 46 torpedoes,

depth bombs, or mines. The UH-3 Sea Kings are part of the fleet of helicopters belonging to Marine Helicopter Squadron 1, which is responsible for transporting the President of the United States.

A formation of SH-3 Sea Kings. The SH-3 has a watertight fuselage that enables it to land on the water.

SH-2 LAMPS I (Seasprite)

KAMAN SH-2F SEASPRITE	
Dimensions:	
Main rotor diameter:	44 ft.
Tail rotor diameter:	8 ft.
Length:	40 ft., 6 in.
Width:	12 ft., 3 in.
Height:	13 ft., 7 in.
Weight (maximum take-off):	13,500 lbs.
Maximum altitude:	22,500 ft.
Top speed:	165 mph
Maximum range:	431 miles
Date of service:	1973

The Light Airborne Multi-Purpose System (LAMPS) is the program designation applied to all antisubmarine warfare helicopters serving aboard Navy ships. The LAMPS helicopters pinpoint and attack enemy submarines after they have been detected by ship or airborne detection systems. The Kaman SH-2F Seasprite is designated LAMPS I, and is flown off a number of cruisers, destroyers, and frigates. LAMPS I is also what these helicopters are called; their given name—Seasprite—has fallen into disuse since the conversion of all SH-2s to the antisubmarine warfare role.

The Kaman SH-2 Seasprite is the brainchild of Charles H. Kaman, one of the foremost pioneers in the field of helicopter design. One of Kaman's most outstanding design features was a helicopter flight control system that did not angle the blade to change pitch.

Instead, the outer portion of each blade had hinged trailing-edge flaps, or "servo tabs," that moved to change the blade's angle of attack. When Kaman won a mid-1950s Navy competition to devise a high-speed, all-weather utility helicopter, he incorporated this unique blade-control mechanism into a design that included the more traditional single main and tail rotor.

This design eventually evolved into the UH-2 Seasprite. Additional features of this aircraft included a retractable landing gear, a watertight hull, and a small fuselage that could carry 11 passengers. Its nose could be folded back to reduce the aircraft's length, and it was also fitted with folding rotor blades and a cable haul-and-tie down system (an innovation of the German Navy during World War II).

The Seasprite entered Navy service in 1962 with the UH-2A designation. This variant was powered by a single 1,250 horsepower General Electric T58-GE-8B turboshaft engine. This single engine arrangement soon proved inadequate, and in 1965 two GE T58 engines in outboard mountings were substituted. These engines provided much improved performance plus the safety of an additional engine for operations over water. All single engine UH-2A/Bs were later converted to the twin-engine model UH-2C.

When employed in the search-and-rescue role, the UH-2C was designated HH-2C. This Seasprite variant was protected by armor plating and armed with a 7.62 millimeter NATO minigun in a chin turret as well as door-mounted .50 caliber or .30 caliber machine guns. A subsequent HH-2 variant, the HH-2D, was unarmed and unarmored.

In the early 1970s all UH-2s that were then in service were converted from the utility role to the

antisubmarine warfare role and redesignated SH-2 LAMPS I. Initially, 20 of these aircraft became SH-2D models, and another 85 became SH-2F models. All D models have since been converted to F standards, and subsequent F models were purpose-built as LAMPS aircraft. In 1990 an SH-2G model was test-flown, but the Navy has yet to commit to procuring this variant.

The SH-2F has tricycle landing gear with two wheels on each side that retract by folding forward. The rear landing gear is a steerable, fixed, single tire. The main rotor hub is made of titanium, and the blades, which can be folded, are made of aluminum and glass fiber. Two General Electric 1,350 horsepower T58-GE-8F turboshaft engines provide the power. The SH-2F can carry 476 U.S. gallons of fuel. It can also be fitted with two external tanks and can be refueled ship-to-helicopter, while the aircraft is hovering.

In the LAMPS role, the electronics of the SH-2F include surveillance radar; tactical navigation systems; UHF radios; magnetic anomaly detector; sonobuoy receiver, recorder, and data link; sonobuoys; eight Mark 25 smoke markers; up to two Mark 46 torpedoes; cargo hook; and rescue hoist. The SH-2F carries a crew of three: pilot, copilot/tactical coordinator (also known as a Taco), and sensor operator. Armament consists of two Mark 46 torpedoes.

This SH-2F LAMPS I Seasprite comes equipped with sonobouys and is armed with Mark 46 torpedoes.

AH-1 SeaCobra/ SuperCobra

The AH-1 SeaCobra was based on the Army's HueyCobra, which derived from the UH-1 Iroquois (Huey). This twin-engined, heavily armed helicopter was the Marine Corp's first dedicated helicopter gunship, and is used primarily in the ground support role.

Bell Helicopter began development of the AH-1 in 1965 to answer a need for an armed helicopter to provide combat escort for slow, unarmed, or lightly armed transports and medevac helicopters. The first HueyCobra was flown in September of that year. The new helicopter retained the engine, transmission, and other major parts of the Huey; in appearance, however, it was a far more slender aircraft than its parent. The narrow fuselage dictated a tandem cockpit seating arrangement,

with the pilot sitting behind and above the copilot/ weapons operator. Stub wings were added to ease the load on the main rotor and serve as attaching points for additional weapons.

The SeaCobra is flown by a crew of two. Both the copilot/weapons operator and the pilot can fly the helicopter. The copilot/ weapons operator also controls the turret mounted under the nose. The turret comes armed with miniguns, rapid-firing cannon, or the M19 grenade launcher. When the copilot/ weapons operator releases the weapon controls, the turret resumes a locked fore and aft position and the pilot can fire the weapons while flying the helicopter. The weapons are then aimed by turning the helicopter.

The United States Army acquired the majority of

HueyCobras, which were initially designated AH-1G. The AH-1G was powered by a Lycoming T53-L-13 turboshaft engine producing 1,100 horsepower. The United States Marine Corps ordered a twin engine version of the AH-1G, the AH-1J SeaCobra. The AH-1J was powered by two Pratt & Whitney Canada T400-CP-400 twin turboshaft engines coupled to a single transmission and providing 1,100 horsepower.

The growing threat of Soviet tanks soon led to another HueyCobra variation, one that was armed with BGM-71 TOW (Tube-launched, Optically-tracked, Wire-guided) antitank missiles. The first HueyCobra model to be fitted with the TOW was the AH-1Q, which served as an interim solution until the modernized HueyCobra, the AH-1S, could be developed.

The first AH-1S variant entered Army service in March 1977. It had a flat plate canopy, new and more extensive electronics, and the uprated Lycoming T53-L-703 1,800 horsepower turboshaft engine. A second variant had a new turret mounting either a 20 millimeter or 30mm gun. A third AH-1S variant had new composite rotor blades, a new fire control system that included a laser range finder, an improved navigation system, and an infrared jammer. All versions of the AH-1S are capable of firing the TOW missile.

Like the Army, the Marine Corps also instituted extensive modifications on its SeaCobra variant. The resulting aircraft were designated the AH-1T SeaCobra and AH-1W SuperCobra. The AH-1T is an uprated version of the twin-engine AH-1J, and is

powered by Pratt & Whitney Canada T400-WV-402 engines. The AH-1W SuperCobra was originally designated the AH-1T+; it is powered by twin General Electric T700-GE-401 turboshaft engines producing 3,250 horsepower. All AH-1T SeaCobras in the Marine Corps inventory have now been uprated to the AH-1W configuration.

The AH-1T was armed with one 20mm M197 multibarrel cannon and eight TOW antitank missiles. The AH-1W carries either eight TOW or Hellfire missiles, or 38 2.75-inch Zuni rockets, or two Sidewinder AIM-9L air-to-air missiles.

Below: Front view of an AH-1W, showing the narrow fuselage width. Right: An AH-1T flies a low-level mission. Opposite, below: The 20 millimeter cannon on an AH-1T.

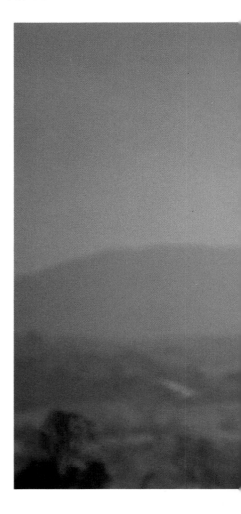

BELL AH-1T/W SEACOBRA/SUPERCOBRA

Dimensions:	
Main rotor diameter:	48 ft.
Tail rotor diameter:	8 ft., 6 in.
Length:	48 ft., 2 in.
Width:	3 ft., 3 in.
Height:	13 ft., 5 in.
Weight (maximum take-off):	14,000 lbs.
Maximum altitude:	12,450 ft.
Top speed:	
AH-1T:	150 mph
AH-1W:	175 mph
Maximum range:	
AH-1T:	320 miles
AH-1W:	365 miles
Date of service:	
AH-1T:	1977
AH-1W:	1986

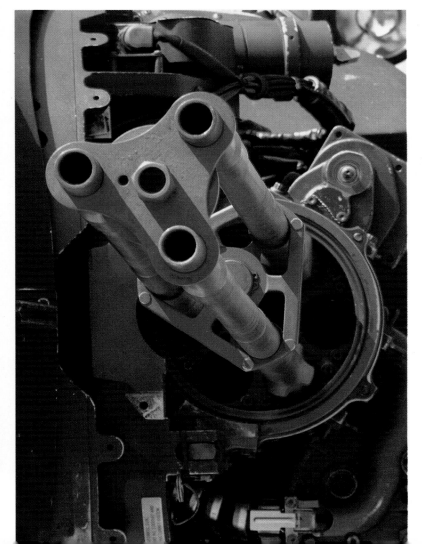

TH-57 SeaRanger

BELL TH-57C SEARANGER	
Dimensions:	
Main rotor diameter:	35 ft., 4 in.
Tail rotor diameter:	5 ft., 4 in.
Length:	41 ft.
Width:	6 ft., 4 in.
Height:	9 ft., 7 in.
Weight (maximum take-off):	3,000 lbs.
Maximum altitude:	18,900 ft.
Top speed:	127 mph
Maximum range:	318 miles
Date of service:	1968

The Navy's basic helicopter trainer is the Bell SeaRanger, a developmental branch of the Bell commercial Model 206 JetRanger. The other U.S. military variant is the Army's OH-58 Kiowa.

The Model 206 design was developed in response to an Army-sponsored competition for a new light observation helicopter. The Army proved to be uninterested in the JetRanger, but not so the Navy, which was impressed by the easy-to-fly aircraft's potential as a primary trainer. In 1968 the Navy purchased 40 JetRangers with dual-control systems for the training role. Designated the TH-57A SeaRanger, these aircraft were powered by an Allison 250-C-18 turboshaft engine.

The up-rated JetRanger III (Model 206B) series provided the basis for the subsequent TH-57B. The 51 TH-57Bs ordered by the Navy were powered by an Allison T63-A-700 turboshaft engine, and featured additional safety and avionics improvements.

Next in line was the TH-57C. To fulfill its purpose as an advanced instrument training helicopter, this variant is equipped with a completely new avionics system. It also features doors that can be jettisoned in flight, a rotor brake, and mountings for an external cargo hook. The Navy ordered 55 TH-57Cs, all of which are in service with Helicopter Training Squadron 18 at Whiting Field, Florida.

The TH-57 series carries an instructor and four student pilots. As helicopters go, the SeaRanger is a stable craft that is very forgiving of a trainee pilot's mistakes. Small wonder, then, that virtually every helicopter pilot in the Navy and Marine Corps since 1968 has learned to fly in this aircraft.

Since it is a training aircraft, the Navy's SeaRanger does not carry weapons. However the OH-58 Kiowa, a SeaRanger variant used by the Army as an observation helicopter, can carry the M134 7.62 millimeter minigun and two Stinger antiaircraft missiles.

Student pilots cautiously put these TH-57C SeaRangers through their paces.

UH-1 Iroquois (Huey)

BELL UH-1N IROQUOIS (HUEY)

Dimensions:

Main rotor diameter:	48 ft., 2 in.
Tail rotor diameter:	8 ft., 6 in.
Length:	57 ft., 3 in.
Width:	9 ft., 6.5 in.
Height:	11 ft., 9.75 in.
Weight (maximum take-off):	10,500 lbs.
Maximum altitude:	15,000 ft.
Top speed:	126 mph
Maximum range:	288 miles
Date of service:	1964

The UH-1N Iroquois, known as the Huey from its original designation HU-1, is the Navy and Marine Corp's twin-engined version of the Bell helicopter that was used extensively in the Vietnam War. The original single engine version of the Huey first flew in 1956 as the Bell Helicopter Model 204. The Model 204 was originally designed as a light utility helicopter to meet the specifications of the United States Army's XH-40 program. The Huey entered military service as the HU-1A and first went to Vietnam as an air ambulance in 1962.

The Huey is still widely used by both the Marine Corps and the Navy as a utility helicopter—meaning that it can perform virtually any job that comes along, from ferrying combat troops to search and rescue to carrying cargo. The Marines also use the Huey as an assault helicopter; and the Navy as a combat rescue helicopter, designated HH-1K. In these latter two roles it is always armed. The UH-1N carries the 7.62 millimeter minigun, .50 caliber machine guns, 2.75 inch rockets, and 40mm grenade launchers. The UH-1N is also flown as a training helicopter, designated TH-L.

The Huey was the first U.S. production helicopter equipped with a gas turbine engine. The original engine model was a Lycoming T33 capable of producing 770 horsepower. Lycoming engineers improved the T33 engine until it was capable of producing 1,100 horsepower. With the more powerful engine, Bell engineers were able to build an even larger airframe, the UH-1H.

In addition to a crew of three, the UH-1H could carry up to 14 fully equipped troops or six stretcher casualties, compared with the eight soldiers or three stretchers of the earlier UH-1. The UH-1H (Bell civilian designation: Model 205) is powered by a T53-L-13 gas turbine engine.

In the early 1960s, the Navy settled on the versatile Huey as its basic utility helicopter. The Navy variant was powered by the Pratt &

Whitney Canada T400-CP-400 Turbo "Twin Pac," which is comprised of two engines producing 900 horsepower each. The second engine provides an extra margin of safety for flights over the water.

The Huey was the first U.S. military helicopter to have an engine mounted on top of and behind the cabin roof. This type of mounting eased the problems of gearing the main shaft and tail rotor and left the cargo and cockpit space clear of drive shafts and engine bulkheads. Five separate fuel tanks hold a total of 223 gallons of fuel.

The rotor blades originally were extruded aluminum spars laminated together but are now being replaced by stronger blades of glass fiber composite over a Nomex honeycomb core construction. The trailing blade edge is also glass fiber. The leading edge has a polyurethane covering over a stainless steel sheath, which enables the blade to cut through unexpected obstructions (such as small tree branches) when the aircraft is flying at low altitudes.

Armament for the Huey varies. The 7,000 UH-1s that have been purchased by more than a dozen nations have carried just about every type of weapon that helicopters of the Huey's weight and payload capacity can carry. But if there is a standard weapon load for the Huey, it is three 7.62 millimeter M60 machine guns, one mounted on each skid and one in a door mount operated by the crew chief.

Although the Huey has been in U.S. military service since 1962, it has by no means outlived its usefulness. Today's Huey is far more capable than the first UH-1s that saved so

many lives in Vietnam; and the Hueys of tomorrow will become even more capable as they are fitted with new composite blades, radar altimeters, infrared jammers and suppressor, new chaff and flare dispensers, and improved avionics and communications gear. That's why the Huey will continue to remain in service through the 1990s, performing as needed in a variety of important roles.

A Navy UH-1 on a combat mission during the Vietnam War. Although some 25 years have elapsed since this photo was taken, UH-1s remain in Navy service.

315

GLOSSARY

Active sonar: Sonar that transmits a sound wave, which is intercepted by the sender when its echo bounces off a solid object.

Aegis: From the Latin word for the war shield of Jupiter. Aegis is an integrated shipboard system of computers, radars, and air defense missiles that provides an umbrella for surface fleets. Aegis systems can detect, identify, track, launch, and guide missiles and fire guns to destroy airborne, surface, or land-launched weapons.

Aerial combat maneuvering: A series of maneuvers and tactics carried out by fighter aircraft to shoot down or defend themselves against attack by other fighter aircraft.

Afterburner: A tube attached at the exhaust end of a turbojet or turbofan engine into which additional fuel is injected and ignited by hot exhaust gases. Use of the afterburner can dramatically increase the speed of a jet aircraft.

After deck: Generally refers to the area of deck in the rear portion of a ship. May include deck structures such as helicopter hangars.

Ailerons: Moveable control surfaces on an aircraft that permit lateral control in flight.

Air cushion vehicle: A surface vehicle that floats on an air bubble or cushion created by large fans blowing straight down. To increase lift, the air is usually contained within a large rubber skirt as it emerges from the fans.

Air-to-air missile (AAM): An antiaircraft missile fired from an aircraft.

Air-to-ground missile (AGM): A missile fired from an aircraft at a ground target.

Air-to-surface missile (ASM): Similar to an air-to-ground missile except that it is usually fired at ships and other surface vessels.

All big-gun battleship: Type of battleship introduced in the early years of the twentieth century that had an armament consisting solely of big guns.

Anechoic tiles: Rubbery pieces of material affixed to the hulls of submarines to absorb sonar signals and reduce the sound of a submarine moving through the water.

Angle of attack: The direction and altitude at which an aircraft or missile approaches its target. Also refers to the angle at which a wing surface meets the airstream in flight.

Angle rate bombing system: A computerized bomb aiming system that computes aircraft speed, wind speed, temperature, bomb aerodynamics, and size of target to automatically release the bomb at the optimum time to strike the target accurately.

Antisubmarine warfare (ASW): The techniques, tactics, weapons, and equipment associated with the detection and destruction of hostile submarines.

ASDIC: The British term for sonar, introduced during World War I and derived from the initials for Anti-Submarine Detection Committee.

Attack submarine: A type of submarine designed to hunt and destroy enemy submarines and naval and merchant shipping.

Autorotate: The process by which air flowing up through a helicopter's blades as it descends without power will cause lift, thus slowing the helicopter and allowing it to land safely.

Autostabilization system: A system in which electronic sensors coupled with mechanical control and pumping systems enable a ship to remain as level as possible even when moving at high speeds in rough seas.

Auxiliary ships: Noncombatant vessels that support the combat fleet. They are usually operated by the Military Sealift Command and may have civilian crew.

Avionics: Electronic instrumentation and controls used in air and spacecraft.

Ballistic missile: A rocket-propelled missile that follows an arcing trajectory toward its target. The trajectory, or flight path, is dependent on the thrust and the length of time the rocket engine burns.

Battle group: A mix of aircraft carriers or battleships accompanied by cruisers, destroyers, frigates, submarines, and logistics ships. A battle group is charged with patrolling a specific area of the ocean, and usually has sufficient naval ships, aircraft, and land forces to both mount an offensive operation and defend itself. Actual composition varies with missions assigned.

Beachhead: A secure area established ashore by an amphibious assault force through which additional troops and supplies can be moved up to support the fighting forces.

Boomer: A nuclear-powered submarine that carries long-range, ballistic missiles.

Buddy packs: Spare fuel tanks carried by KA-6 Intruders to refuel A-6 Intruder aircraft during long duration missions.

Caliber: Diameter, or a gun's bore. In naval usage, the size of a gun is expressed in calibers that are a multiple of the gun's bore.

Carrier air wing: The grouping of fighter, attack, electronic countermeasures and other aircraft squadrons into one tactical unit based aboard an aircraft carrier.

Catamaran hull: Two boat hulls connected by a deck. The use of two hulls instead of one larger one decreases water and air resistance.

Choke point: An area of an ocean where natural features restrict the movement of surface ships and submarines. For example, the area between Greenland and Newfoundland, or the Straits of Malacca.

Close air support: Gunfire, rocket, and bombing missions flown by military aircraft in support of ground troops.

Commissioned ship: Vessel listed officially as a naval vessel and charged with carrying out specific types of military missions.

Conventional power: Usually taken to mean non-nuclear sources of propulsive power.

Craft of Opportunity Program (COOP): U.S. Navy project in which suitable civilian or non-military vessels are converted at low cost for naval missions. A good example is the COOP minesweepers program in which training and fishing vessels have been converted to minesweepers.

Cruise missile: Jet or rocket powered missile carrying an explosive warhead that is guided by an internal computer and navigation system to a distant target.

Degaussing: The process of demagnetizing a ship to prevent its destruction by sea mines, which are triggered by fuses that react to the presence of strong magnetic fields.

Delta wings: A triangular aircraft wing in which both wing and horizontal stabilizer are combined in a single wing surface.

Dipping sonar: Active or passive sonar transmitter and receiver that is suspended from a long cable beneath the surface of the sea.

Displacement: Generally refers to the amount of water (in tons) that a ship's hull replaces in any body of ocean.

Dissimilar Aerial Combat Training (DACT): The process by which fighter pilots practice combat maneuvers against aircraft that simulate the capabilities and flight characteristics of potential enemy aircraft.

Dogfighting: A slang term for aerial combat maneuvering.

Doppler radar: The radar systems that measure the distance to an object as it approaches the radar transmitter. Characteristic signals are emitted at timed intervals and the rate of return is measured and compared to previous signals.

Double hull: On a ship, a second hull built within a hull for added strength and protection.

Draft: The distance a ship's hull resides below the water line.

East Bloc: Generally used to refer to the Warsaw Pact nations.

Electronic countermeasures: A variety of radio and radar signals transmitted to confuse enemy communications and detection devices.

ELF: Extremely long frequency radio waves that have the ability to penetrate water. ELF systems are used to communicate with submerged submarines.

Fire-and-forget missile: A missile that has an onboard guidance system that can direct it to the target. Once fired, no further external guidance is needed and the missile-firing computer can "forget" about it and seek out another target.

Fire control system: A system of computers and sensors that can aim and fire a gun or missile at an enemy ship or aircraft.

Fixed wing aircraft: Not a helicopter.

Flagship: Any naval vessel that has the fleet commander onboard.

Flight deck: The main deck of an aircraft carrier or amphibious landing ship from which aircraft operations are conducted.

Flo/flo ships: Cargo vessels that can increase their draft by pumping water into tanks, thus lowering their cargo deck so that heavy cargoes can be floated into place.

Flush decked: A ship whose main deck reaches from stem to stern (front to back) without a step up or down.

Fly-by-wire aircraft: An aircraft in which the control surfaces are activated by computers transmitting signals through electrical wires to small motors.

Flying boom: A U.S. Air Force device involving the use of a long, semirigid refueling boom that is equipped with an aerodynamic lifting surface and can be "flown" by the operator in the refueling aircraft to mate with the aircraft to be refueled.

Forward air control: The process by which tactical aircraft are directed to targets in support of ground troops by specially trained airmen or soldiers traveling with ground troops.

Hardpoints: Attachment positions for ordnance mounted on the wings and fuselage of an aircraft.

Heavy-lift capacity: The ability of a fixed wing aircraft or helicopter to carry very heavy payloads.

Hose and drogue: The system of aerial refueling used by the U.S. Navy and Marine Corps in which a flexible hose is streamed behind the refueling aircraft and the aircraft to be refueled maneuvers up to it.

Hunter/killer submarine: An attack submarine whose mission is to find and destroy enemy submarines.

Hydrofoil: A winglike surface that travels through the water much as an aircraft wing travels through the air to produce lift.

Hydrophone: A microphone placed underwater.

Inertial navigation system: A self-contained computer that measures changes in acceleration, angle of movement, and altitude

for any vehicle in which it is installed, and predicts course and time of arrival compared to an ideal.

Intercontinental ballistic missile: Any rocket-propelled vehicle that carries a nuclear warhead and has a range in excess of 2,500 miles.

Iron bomb: Slang term for any non-guided aerial bomb that contains high explosives.

Kiloton: A measure of the destructive power of a nuclear weapon as compared to the explosion of one ton of trinitrotoluene (TNT).

Knot: Abbreviation for nautical mile (1.15 statute miles).

Laid up: Term used when a ship is taken out of service.

LAMPS: Light Airborne Multi-Purpose System. Refers to a type of helicopter and its mission when stationed aboard naval vessels.

LASH: Lighter-Aboard-Ship. A specially constructed cargo vessel that carries cargo barges.

Leading edge: Generally refers to the front surface of an aircraft or hydrofoil wing that strikes the approaching airstream first.

Mack: A combination of mast and smokestack found on some modern naval vessels.

Magnetic Anomaly Detector: A device that can sense a change in the magnetic field of a large metal object, such as a submarine.

Medevac: Medical Evacuation. Techniques used to remove wounded men from a battlefield for medical treatment. Usually accomplished by helicopter.

Minigun: A motor-driven, multibarrel gun capable of firing at a very high rate.

MIRV: Multiple Independent Reentry Vehicle. Two or more nuclear weapons carried in separate vehicles designed to withstand the rigors of reentering the atmosphere from space. They can be programmed to strike separate targets.

Monopropellant fuel: A mixture that contains both fuel and oxidizer and requires only a catalyst or a spark to ignite.

Mothball fleet: Slang term which refers to ships removed from active service but preserved in serviceable condition for reactivation in time of war. More correctly referred to as the National Defense Reserve Fleet.

Multibarrel gun: A gun with more than one barrel that operates on the Gatling principle whereby the barrels revolve past a fixed breech. See *Minigun*.

National Command Authority: Beginning with the President of the United States, those officials

empowered by law to order the use of nuclear weapons in time of war.

National Defense Reserve Fleet (NDRF): Ships no longer in active service but retained in good condition for later reactivation. See *Mothball fleet*.

NATO: North Atlantic Treaty Organization. Alliance of European and North American Nations formed in 1949 to present a united front against Soviet expansionism in Europe.

Naval Reserve Force: The reserve component of the United States Navy.

Nuclear Triad: Separate fleets of bombers, nuclear-powered strategic submarines, and land-based ballistic missiles, all equipped with nuclear weapons and intended to deter aggression with the threat of instant and massive nuclear retaliation.

Ordnance: All military weaponry.

Over-the-beach-capability: The ability to land an assault force from the sea, then maintain it with men and equipment.

Over-the-horizon capability: The ability to land an assault force from far out to sea, out of visual sight of land, then maintain it with men and equipment.

Passive sonar: Sonar that only "listens" for underwater activity, rather than sending out a signal.

Payload: The weapons, munitions, and/or cargo that an aircraft may carry.

Pod: Generally refers to an aerodynamically-designed enclosure for weapons or electronic equipment intended to be mounted on an aircraft.

Point defense weapon: A shipboard missile or gun system with the capability to identify a threat and defend against it within a 3,000-yard diameter area.

Port: Nautical term for "left."

Prepositioned ship: A cargo ship loaded with sufficient supplies and ammunition to sustain a combat force for a set period of time. They are usually stationed in proximity to a geographic area in which combat operations may occur.

PSI: Pounds per square inch. A measure of the ability of a vessel to hold internal pressure.

Purpose-built: Specially designed to fulfil a mission.

Pylons: Structures attached to aircraft hardpoints on which weapons are mounted.

Radome: The aerodynamic covering for a radar antenna.

Radar: Stands for "radio detection and ranging." A system for detecting a distant object by transmitting high-frequency radio waves at the object.

Ready Reserve Force: Ships held in readiness for active duty with the Navy in times of war. Although they are administered by the Military Sealift Command, they are often owned or leased by private companies, which pay or share the cost of maintenance.

Realtime: As it is happening now.

Retrofit: To install a new piece of equipment in an existing aircraft, ship, tank, or other piece of military hardware.

Rifled cannon: Artillery guns with curving lands and grooves machined into the bore to cause the shell to spin in flight, thus increasing its accuracy.

Ro/ro ship: A specially constructed cargo ship that allows vehicles to be driven, or "rolled," on and off.

Rotor torque: Inertia generated by a spinning helicopter rotor that tends to move the helicopter in the direction of the spin. It is countered usually by mounting a smaller rotor to force air in the direction opposite to the torque, or by using two main rotors that spin in opposite directions.

Rotary-wing aircraft: A helicopter.

SEAL: Sea-Air-Land. Refers to U.S. Navy personnel trained in underwater operations and special forces military tactics.

Sea Lines of Communication (SLOC): Shipping routes.

Search-and-rescue squadrons: Naval and Air Force aviation squadrons that fly specially designed fixed wing aircraft and helicopters to find and rescue downed aircrews.

Side-by-side: Cockpit arrangement in which the pilot and copilot/navigator sit beside one another.

Smart bomb: An aerial bomb that can be guided to its target by radio control or a laser targeting system.

Smoothbore cannon: An artillery piece lacking lands and grooves to cause the projectile to spin. Large guns were not rifled before the invention of breechloading mechanisms because of the difficulty in loading shells. Today, many guns are smoothbored to reduce friction as the shell moves up the bore, thus increasing range.

Snorkel: Essentially a breathing tube that extends to the surface to allow a non-nuclear submarine to operate while traveling submerged.

Sonar: Sound navigation and ranging. A process by which sound waves are used to detect solid objects underwater. See *Active sonar* and *Passive sonar.*

Sonar array: Strings of sonar antennas that are towed behind submarines on cables up to one mile long. The length of the array increases sensitivity, while the length of the cable reduces or eliminates the disturbances caused by the towing submarine.

Sonobuoy: A robot sonar transmitter/receiver that can be dropped in the water to detect hostile submarine movements.

Sound Surveillance System (SOSUS): Arrays of passive sonar receivers deployed in the "choke" points of the oceans to detect hostile submarine movements.

Standoff: Generally taken to mean the distance at which a surface ship can remain while it fires surface-to-surface missiles or torpedoes at hostile surface vessels or submarines.

Starboard: Right side of a ship

Stealth technology: The combination of design parameters and radar absorbing coatings that reduce the visibility of an aircraft or ship to radar detection.

Submarine-launched ballistic missile (SLBM): Nuclear-tipped, rocket-propelled missiles with ranges in excess of 1,500 miles that can be launched underwater from submarines.

Supersonic speed: Any speed beyond the speed of sound, which is 760 miles per hour at sea level. The speed of sound is referred to as Mach 1.

Surface-to-air missile (SAM): Any rocket or jet-propelled missile fired from a ship- or ground-based launcher at hostile aircraft.

SURTASS: Surface Towed Array Surveillance System. An array of passive sonar receivers towed behind antisubmarine warfare ships.

Surveillance envelope: The area within which a ship's or aircraft's sensors can watch for hostile aircraft, surface ships, or submarines.

SWATH: Small Waterplane Area Twin Hull. Ship design that uses twin hulls connected by a main deck. The underwater portion of the hulls are torpedo-shaped for greater hydrodynamic efficiency.

TACAMO: Take Charge And Move Out. Specially equipped aircraft capable of maintaining communications with submerged submarines.

Tail rotor: A small, vertically spinning propeller on the tail end of a helicopter that offsets the torque of the main rotor.

Tandem seating: Cockpit arrangement in which the pilot and copilot or tactical officer are seated one behind the other.

Third world: Generally taken to mean those nations not as advanced technologically or economically as those of North America and Western and Northern Europe.

Thrust: The force developed by hot gases leaving a jet or rocket engine.

Tonnage: The capacity of a ship to carry cargo, usually given in metric or English tons.

Top Gun: Slang term originally used in reference to graduates of the Navy's Fighter Weapons School at Miramar Naval Air Station, California and which is now used to denote any well-trained American military pilot.

Torque: The angular force exerted by a spinning object.

Trailing edge: The back end of an aircraft wing.

Turbofan: A turbojet engine that also turns a large ducted fan ahead of the compressor to produce additional thrust.

Turbojet: An engine that burns fuel in a combustion chamber and allows the fuel to escape through a constricted nozzle. The velocity of the hot gases imparts thrust to the vehicle and moves it forward.

Turboprop: A gas turbine engine in which the escaping exhaust gases are harnessed to turn a propeller.

Underway replenishment: The process by which a ship is refueled and reprovisioned from another ship while both are in motion.

Variable-geometry wings: Aircraft wings that can be extended or retracted to change their shape to achieve optimum efficiency for varying flight conditions.

Vertical and Short Takeoff and Landing (VSTOL): Refers to aircraft designed to take off and land vertically or after a short approach.

Vertical envelopment: Tactical insertion into combat of airborne troops by parachute or helicopter.

Vertical replenishment (VERTREP): The process by which ships can refuel and reprovision helicopters, or vice-versa.

Warsaw Pact: The central and east European nations allied with the Soviet Union to oppose the North Atlantic Treaty Organization. The Warsaw Pact nations are Poland, Czechoslovakia, the former East Germany, Rumania, Hungary, and Bulgaria.

Wire-guided torpedo: A torpedo like the U.S. Navy's Mark 48, which can be guided toward its target by transmitting signals through thin wires unreeling behind the torpedo to the submarine that launched it. As the torpedo nears its target, its own built-in sonar capability takes over and guides it during the terminal phases.

INDEX

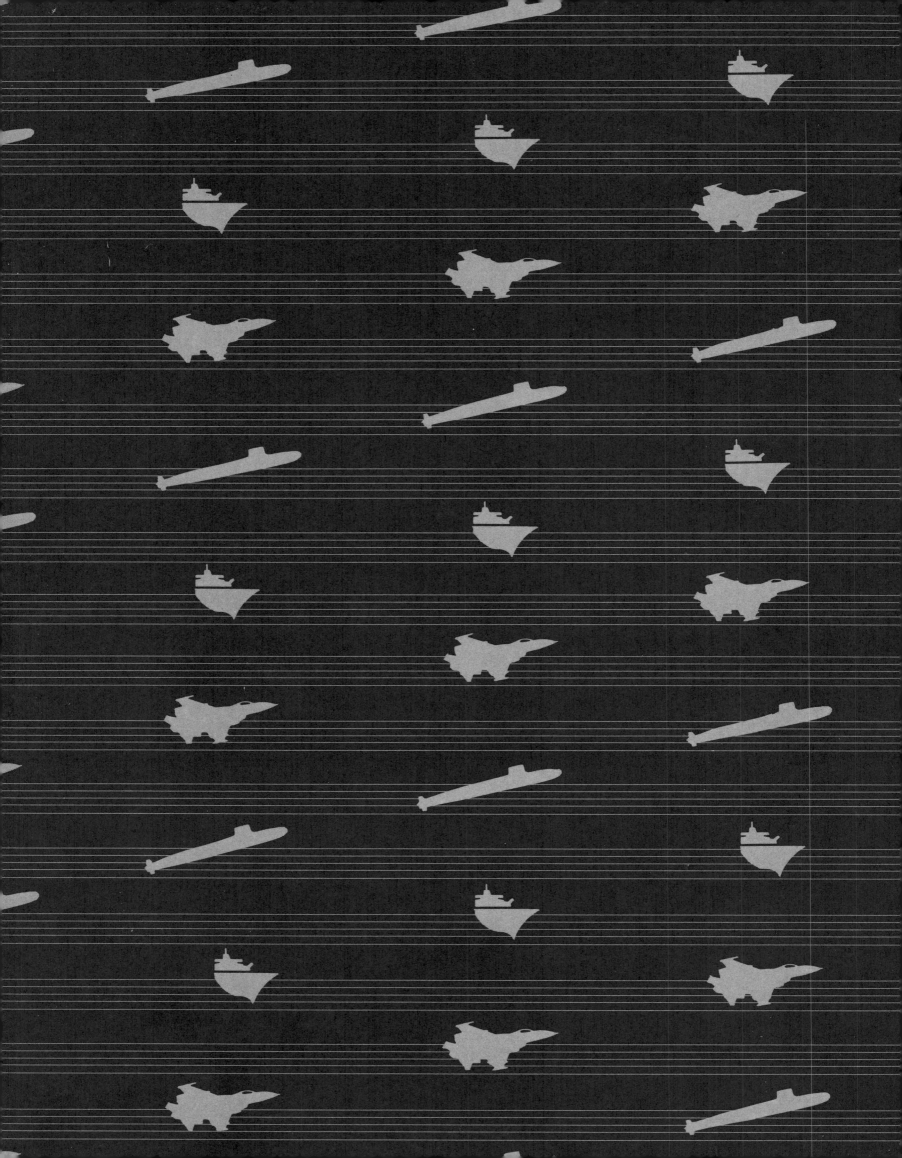